Patterns of Religious Narrative in the Canterbury Tales

ROGER ELLIS

CROOM HELM
London & Sydney

© Roger Ellis 1986
Croom Helm Ltd, Provident House, Burrell Row
Beckenham, Kent BR3 1AT

Croom Helm Australia Pty Ltd, Suite 4, 6th Floor,
64-76 Kippax Street, Surry Hills, NSW 2010, Australia

British Library Cataloguing in Publication Data

Ellis, Roger
    Patterns of religious narrative in the
    Canterbury tales.
    1. Chaucer, Geoffrey. Canterbury Tales
    I. Title
    821'.1   PR1874
    ISBN 0-7099-0914-4

For Kate

Typeset by Leaper & Gard Ltd, Bristol, England
Printed and bound in Great Britain
by Billing & Sons Limited, Worcester.

CONTENTS

PREFACE

Acknowledgements

Several people have helped at different stages in the production of this work. Richard Stoneman, like his royal namesake, commissioned the work; Mrs Sheila Morgan typed an early draft; Sabina Thompson and Kate McMahon helped with the final draft (Adam Scriveyn would have been glad of their electric typewriters and word-processors). Dr Anne Hudson saw an early draft of material and was very encouraging; Drs Vincent Gillespie and Helen Spencer kindly answered questions about sermons and related writing. But my greatest thanks go to Professor Stanley Hussey, who, in his capacity of 'moral Gower' (or perhaps 'philosophical Strode') saw the work in draft and undertook 'ther nede [was] to correcte'. (For the errors that remain, of course, I must beg the readers 'my werk amende'.) Another debt, to former teachers and present students, is harder to quantify: but I could not have told this story without them.

Notes

The notes, which are given at the end of each chapter, aim to provide readings which sometimes support, and sometimes challenge, my own, so as to suggest a range of possible readings and to isolate those places which cause greatest divergence of opinion. They do not claim to be comprehensive; nor can I be sure that I have always acknowledged debts to previous writers. I have consistently abbreviated titles of medieval works, such as *The Canterbury Tales* (*CT*) even when they appear as part of the title of a modern book or article (e.g. *The Idea of CT*). Works cited more than once are given in abbreviated form (see Abbreviations, pp. 301-2, and Bibliography, pp. 303-7, for fuller reference); in particular, individual contributions to scholarly or critical anthologies are cited in the notes under authors' and editors' names (the Bibliography does not itemise the contents of such anthologies). Except where otherwise indicated, translations are my own.

1 INTRODUCTION

A study of religious narratives in *The Canterbury Tales* needs to address a number of questions at the outset so as to explain the terms within which it was conceived and the limits within which it had to operate. Three suggest themselves immediately. Why this particular selection of religious narratives? What is the status of the individual narrative in relation to the framing narrative of the Canterbury pilgrimage? And, as a practical expression of this latter, how are we to describe the voice, or voices, we hear telling the individual tales?

A good place to begin is provided by the title of the work ('here bygynneth the Book of the tales of Caunterbury').[1] We are beginning a single work, made up of a collection of tales formally connected with Canterbury. The precise nature of that connection, and hence the kind of reading the work appears to demand, is explained in the prologue to the book, the so-called General Prologue. It tells how Chaucer went on pilgrimage to Canterbury in the company of a group 'of sondry folk, by aventure yfalle/ In felaweship' (I, 25-6) at the start of their journey from the Tabard Inn in Southwark; and how the innkeeper, the Host, decided to accompany the pilgrims, and proposed, as an agreeable pastime, that they should tell stories to one another. 'The Book of the tales of Caunterbury' is therefore the record of a journey, and a collection of the stories told during that journey.

This simple device of framing the collection of stories by means of another story does what the collection itself could not: it authorises a reading of the stories as a continuous sequence. The logic of an unframed collection is that of an anthology;[2] the reader may — but need not — follow the author's arrangement of the individual tales. The logic of the framed collection is that of a novel or a play; or, to use a metaphor beloved of critics of *The Canterbury Tales*, a drama or a debate, in which the story told by one person directly or indirectly acknowledges one or more of the stories already told, and marks a point of departure for stories yet to come.[3] And there is more. The completed collection is in intention coextensive with the completed journey of the framing narrative.[4] Narratives structured about the idea of journey

1

regularly work on a symbolic as well as a literal level: the hero's journey is thus metaphorically a quest for self-fulfilment. Therefore, we seem entitled to approach the individual tales of *The Canterbury Tales* as elements in a larger metaphoric structure.[5]

Strongest evidence for such a reading comes at the end of the work. Day is drawing to a close, and the pilgrims are entering 'at a thropes ende', when the Host, reckoning only one tale remains to be told, that of the Parson, asks the Parson, as he believes he can, to 'knytte up wel a greet mateere' (X, 1-28). After the Parson's tale, no voice is heard but that of the 'makere of this book', who reviews his total literary output to that point in an epilogue commonly called the 'retracciouns', and 'taketh ... his leve' of the reader (X, 1081-92). The completion of the storytelling also suggests the end of the pilgrimage with which, for so long as it lasted, it was coextensive. Though clearest at beginning and end of *The Canterbury Tales*, links are forged elsewhere too between the two narrative events of pilgrimage and storytelling.[6] One set of links has to do with the literal dimension of the pilgrimage as a continuous process in time and space. Shortly after the beginning, for example, when the Reeve prepares to tell his tale, the company have been on the road some three hours, and covered some 2 miles: it is now 'half-wey pryme', that is, 7.30 a.m., and they are within sight or sound of Deptford and Greenwich (I, 3905-7). Another considers less the literal dimension than the idea or image of journey, and provides a symbolic expression of the overarching narrative form. Thus the Man of Law begins at 10 in the morning, and ends only as night approaches (II, 1-14, 1117). Three tales begin even earlier: the Squire's at 'pryme' (V, 73); the Manciple's 'by the morwe' (IX, 16); the Second Nun's, 'in the morwe-tyde' — at all events, that is when the group have been seen leaving the inn by a canon who wants to ride with them. He does not catch up with them until the pilgrims have travelled nearly 5 miles; and by then the Second Nun has finished her story (VIII, 554-5, 588-9). Likewise, story's end is marked, at the end of the Man of Law's tale, by the drawing of day to a close (II, 1117), and, of the Summoner's Tale, by the company's approach to a township (III, 2294).[7]

In the light of this symbolic reading of the temporal and geographical coordinates of the pilgrimage, readers have felt justified in looking for a symbolic ordering of the narratives themselves: the Parson's tale will thus 'knytte up wel a greet mateere' both literally and metaphorically. The 'greet mateere' is initiated by a group of tales (those of the Knight, Miller, Reeve and Cook) directly dependent on the unfolding pilgrimage narrative in the General Prologue. Shortly after the pilgrims have set out, the Host initiates the storytelling by inviting the pilgrims to draw lots. The short straw, and with it the first story, falls to the social superior of the group. A story of princely rivalry in love, ending with a death and a marriage, and with earthly and heavenly rulers to dispense justice, the Knight's offering sets a tone for the whole work.[8] But the principles of order which the narrator appears to embody, and expresses so movingly in his tale in the concluding words of Theseus the earthly ruler, are not allowed to pass without question. When, at the end of the Knight's tale, the Host turns to the ecclesiastical superior of the group, the Monk, for the next story, the drunken Miller interrupts with a tale of his own. This features a cuckolded carpenter, and therefore leads to a row with the Reeve (in his youth 'a wel good wrighte, a carpenter': I, 614). At the end of the tale the Reeve gets his own back with a story at the Miller's expense. And even when the Reeve has finished his story, the Host is unable to resume his lost authority, for another *cherl*, the Cook, has been so taken with the story that he immediately proposes a story of his own. His interruption earns him a witty put-down by the Host, and leads him to propose a tale 'of an hostileer' at the latter's expense. The story he then tells comes to an abrupt end after only 56 lines. By then we have heard of 'thefte and riot', sojourns in the Newgate prison, and the wife of a friend who 'heeld for contenance/ A shoppe, and swyved for hir sustenance' (I, 4421-2).

So far, the unfolding pattern is most easily described as one of order disturbed, and decline from noble beginnings.[9] The single story which follows the unfinished Cook's tale can be read in much the same way as the Knight's. This time, the Host does not leave the choice of the speaker to chance, but requests a story from one of the intellectual superiors of the group, the Man of Law. The latter agrees, and tells the story of a Christian missionary martyr, daughter to the Emperor of Rome and mother of a future emperor by her marriage to an English king. His agreement, and the story he tells, clearly reassert the principles of order and return us to our noble beginnings — even if, as we shall see, it is difficult to decide what precise principles narrator and narrative claim to embody.[10] Order does not, however, pass unchallenged. At the end of the tale the Host proposes another learned man, the Parson, for the next offering. Like his earlier proposal for the Monk to follow the Knight, this plan is immediately rejected by an uneducated pilgrim, who insists on having his say and telling not a learned but a 'mery' tale (II, 1166-90).

At the end of the work this pattern appears in reverse. Now the order — social, ecclesiastical, moral, intellectual — which the self-assertion of the *cherles* seemed so likely to overthrow is restored. At the beginning of the penultimate tale, that of the Manciple, the Cook reappears with the Host, so drunk that he cannot tell the story demanded by the Host. The Manciple intervenes, ostensibly as an act of kindness to all parties, but in reality to make fun of a fuddled opponent. He overrules the Host's demand for a story from the Cook, and tells a story himself. In different ways this moment returns us to the beginning of the work, and operates as a mirror-image for the opening session of storytelling. The Cook's drunkenness re-enacts the Miller's, and effectively reverses his own role in the earlier session.[11] The Manciple, likewise, negates the image projected by the Man of Law, since, as the rascally steward of a London Inn of Court, and servant of the future lawyers of the country, he represents the dark underside of law. Moreover, his story realises the theme of disorder and decline concretely in mythological terms: it explains how the crow, once white all over and a beautiful singer, acquired his black feathers and raucous voice. Finally order is restored. The Parson points us towards the heavenly Jerusalem with the 'predicacioun' which the Host had ironically reckoned to hear from him (II, 1176).[12] With his tale, it seems, the 'greet mateere' is well and truly 'knytte up'. Not a Rake's Progress after all, but the Pilgrims' Progress which its beginning seemed to authorise.

Unfortunately, the form in which *The Canterbury Tales* has come down to us authorises this approach only to a limited extent. Every tale, it is true, carries some reference to the frame, but most of them only in a brief narrative prelude or postlude. In these so-called head-links and end-links pilgrims talk about the tales they are to hear or tell, or have just heard or told. Three of the tales — those of the Physician, Shipman and Second Nun — are attached to the frame only after their own event, when each generates a story (or, in the case of the Shipman's tale, stories) which explicitly or implicitly challenges its assumptions, and relativises them. Before the event they have only their own titles (for example, 'heere folweth the Phisiciens tale') to connect them to the containing narrative.[13] A similar difficulty attends stories like those of the Man of Law, Clerk, Manciple and Parson. These are clearly linked at their outset to the frame, but have only a notional connection with the preceding story, either because it is unfinished or because it ends without clear reference to the frame. By virtue of their narrative head-links, we can read such stories without difficulty as episodes in the Canterbury book: yet the absence of end-links for the preceding stories makes for a sense of fragmentariness, or a grinding of narrative gears, as we jerk out of one story into another by way of an unspecified moment in the pilgrimage narrative.[14]

We ought not to exaggerate this sense of fragmentariness. Well over half the tales are securely anchored to their fellows by head-links and end-links; others were joined together even when their respective end- and head-links did not clearly run on in a single narrative moment;[15] scribes regularly concealed the gaps between tales by running one straight into another.[16] Even so, the work as we now have it is not a whole but a series of fragments or groups of tales. Only the first group (I: Knight, Miller, Reeve and Cook) has a secure place in the temporal and geographical context of the pilgrimage narrative, by virtue of its already noted dependence on the General Prologue. The tale normally found in copies of the work immediately after this group (II: Man of Law), and the two normally found in sequence at the very end of the work (IX: Manciple, X: Parson) have only a symbolic connection with that temporal and geographical context.[17] The remaining groups, linked equally loosely to the framing narrative, have no secure place relative to one another or to the outermost groups (I–II, and IX–X).[18] In the Ellesmere order the groups are: III: Wife of Bath, Friar and Summoner; IV: Clerk and Merchant; V: Squire and Franklin; VI: Physician and Pardoner; VII: Shipman, Prioress, Chaucer (twice), Monk and Nun's Priest; and VIII: Second Nun and Canon's Yeoman. But this order is not found in all the manuscripts, and cannot certainly be traced to Chaucer himself.[19] Moreover, it is far from certain that these groups generate the same idea as the controlling outer units of the work seem to authorise.

To take only two examples, those of the largest groups (III and VII): the tales of group III normally follow the Man of Law's tale and might, thus, be expected to repeat or develop patterns set up in the earlier groups. To a degree they do: the Wife of Bath's tale stands in much the same relation to the following pair of tales (Friar and Summoner) as the Knight's to the pair following it (Miller and Reeve).[20] The authority accorded to the Knight has an ironic equivalent in the authority claimed by the Wife of Bath for herself, and playfully conceded to her by some of the men in the audience (III, 187, 1271-6). In both cases the disturbance to that order is then given concrete expression in the tales subsequently told by pilgrims at one another's expense. And where the tales of group I had realised disorder directly only in the linking passages, the tales of group III represent it directly in interruptions to the speaker. The Pardoner interrupts the Wife's prologue, and the Friar and Summoner break in upon one another's tales near their respective beginnings. For all that, the patterns of group III seem to me to connect only formally with those of group I. In the tales of group I, as other writers have noted, each story redefines the common concern of the group — love — and consciously questions the positions taken up by its predecessors. By contrast, the narratives of the Friar and Summoner do not so much challenge or redefine the Wife of Bath's position as ignore it. We note, for instance, how the Friar seems to have been scowling at the Summoner all through her story — at all events, he is unable to comment on her story except in the most general terms (III, 1265-9).

The tales of group VII are equally difficult to accommodate to any overall pattern.[21] Here disorder seems to have set in at the outset, with the Shipman's story of an immoral monk and the venal wife of his merchant friend. The following tales — four of them included in this study — reveal no clear pattern but that of contrast, embodied visibly in the Host's desire for another story completely different from the one just heard. The Nun's Priest's tale, it is commonly argued, draws the threads of this group together.[22] Yet it knits up its own 'greet mateere', as we shall see, in a very different way from the Parson's tale (which, ironically enough, it precedes in a number of manuscripts), and in a way that works against the proposed symbolic design of the whole.

These observations lead to the conclusion that the tales of the great middle, as it is sometimes called, do not so much contribute to the development of an idea as individually enact or dramatise that idea.[23] Consequently, tales could be, and were, removed from their narrative context and presented as virtually independent items. A most striking instance of this occurs in one of the earliest, and most important, copies of the work, the Hengwrt manu-script.[24] Hengwrt's copyist originally presented four tales — those of the Squire, Merchant, Franklin and Nun — as a sequence of stories linked only by their titles to the framing narrative. This sequence combines with the Man of Law's tale at one end and the Clerk's tale at the other to make a noteworthy shape, something of a cross between *The Canterbury Tales* and Chaucer's earlier experiment with a framed narative collection, *The Legend of Good Women*. All the stories focus on women, and all have love for their subject. A reader following Hengwrt's ordering of the tales will find himself on a journey inward (or downward) from heavenly love (Man of Law's tale) to romantic love (Squire's) and finally to a centrepoint (or nadir) of carnal appetite (Merchant's). Then the direction reverses — the Franklin's tale treats again of romantic love, the Second Nun's and Clerk's of heavenly — so that the reader ends where he began.[25] Such a pattern — where the outer members of a sequence image one another and frame the inner — is not unknown to medieval literature.[26] And the next tale in the manuscript, that of the Physician, may complete the pattern, since, as we shall see, it includes elements from each stage in the pattern. Nevertheless, we should not put too much reliance on such a pattern. Other arrangements produce very different patterns, equally plausible, scarely more authoritative.[27]

These observations draw towards a general point, already noted but worth repeating. Whatever its links with its fellows, the individ-ual tale derives its primary significance not from its place in the sequence (which need not be of particular moment) but from the idea of storytelling as enunciated in the framing narrative. While, each in its own degree, and some more obviously than others, each tale appears to continue the forward movement of the whole work, each tale also (again, to a varying degree) marks a new beginning in its own right.[28] At one and the same time, therefore, the individ-ual tale is subordinated to the total pattern, and a symbolic realisation or expression of that pattern. Our sense that *The Canterbury Tales* appears to be pointing in two logically opposite directions is a clear reflex of the unfinished nature of the work as we have it. Yet experience of parallel structures, like Boccaccio's *Decameron*, warns against placing too much weight on the struc-ture *The Canterbury Tales* might have become. Even when all its joints are formally articulated, the collection of stories within a larger story differs in degree rather than in kind from *The Canter-*

bury Tales as we now have it, and to a smaller degree than we might imagine. At best, the fully-formed frame narrative only papers over its own cracks more thoroughly than *The Canterbury Tales.*[29]

How then do we write about a work in two different ways at once? With difficulty. Analysis requires us to treat *The Canterbury Tales* either as the finished shape it was becoming, or as the raw material out of which it was being formed. The former approach commits us to the narrative line authorised by its outermost parts, and to a sequential reading of the tales within the agreed groups. The latter, which seems called for more clearly by the tales of the great middle, will look most easily to genre or theme for its frame-work.[30] All the same, whatever their logical status, pure matter and pure form (raw material and finished shape) are functionally necessary to one another and hence interdependent: as Chaucer says, in words which might have been written with *The Canterbury Tales* in mind, 'mater apetiteth forme alwey/ And from forme into forme it passen may/ ... as a welle that were botomles' (*Legend,* 1582-4). Therefore, our study must find some way of including them both: implying the one even as it concentrates on the other; or dividing its attention so that it considers now one, now another aspect. As it happens, practical considerations dictated simpler solutions to this problem. This study was to have considered the narratives of *The Canterbury Tales* both generically and, where possible — most notably, in the major groups — sequentially. I have been unable to realise so ambitious a project since, like the Squire, 'if I shal tellen al th'array/ Thanne wolde it occupie a someres day' (V, 63-4). The study of the outermost frame has therefore been deferred: and even in the great middle I have been able to consider only the religious narratives in any detail.[31]

The abandoned larger shape has, however, left several traces in the work. Since, for example, this study is considering the linked tales of group VI, and four of the tales of group VII, three of them also linked, it inevitably includes comment about the relation of these tales to one another. Such comments offer the skeleton of a reading of *The Canterbury Tales* in terms of its larger narrative lines. For a number of reasons, though, the present work could hardly make much of this approach. Represented though they are in the outer frame of the work by the Parson's tale and the 'retrac-ciouns', the religious narratives as a whole fit more loosely into its overall structure than any of the others. They are prominent among those tales which tangibly realise their independence from their immediate narrative context either because they want head-links (Physician and Second Nun) or because their head-links carry only a general reference to the context of the pilgrimage (Man of Law and Clerk). Then, too, while fabliaux and romance are generally treated in the couplet form used for all but one of the link passages, four of the nine religious narratives here studied use rhyme royal (Clerk, Prioress, Second Nun, Man of Law), one uses prose (*Melibee*) and one a unique eight-line stanza form (Monk). We can therefore approach the religious narratives as separate contributions to the meaning of the whole work: contributions, moreover, in which, to anticipate ourselves, the conflict between 'forme' and 'mater' — or, to stretch a point, between the outer and the inner sections of the work — will be most clearly realised.

Such an approach is ironically authorised by the poet himself. The head-link to the Miller's tale invites the *gentil* reader to 'turne over the leef and chese another tale' if he prefers something more edifying, like 'storial thyng that toucheth gentillesse/ And eek moralitee and hoolynesse' (I, 3177, 3179-80). Most modern readers take the invitation straight, even if, by one of the ironies of history, it is the religious 'leef' which they most often turn: and so did a significant number of medieval scribes, who selected material from the unfinished work for projects and purposes of their own.[32] They could the more easily remove tales from their immediate narrative context because of the already noted independence of the individual tales from one another. Major alterations to the pirated texts were therefore rare.[33] By and large, religious tales were likeliest candidates for removal from *The Canterbury Tales*. The fabliaux were never so treated; the romances only occasionally, and then always in company with those religious tales which could be read most easily as romances, those of the Man of Law and Clerk. (In MS British Library Harley 1239 a copy of Chaucer's *Troilus* partners five Canterbury tales, those of the Knight, Man of Law, Wife of Bath, Clerk and Franklin; in Longleat 257 a copy of Lydgate's *Siege of Thebes* partners the Knight's and Clerk's tales.) The best proof of this generalisation occurs in MS Naples XIII B 29, whose scribe, when making a collection of romances, chose the Clerk's tale as his representative of the genre from *The Canterbury Tales*.[34] Otherwise, the excerpted tales were always religious, as the present study will define the term. They were combined reasonably often with other material in compilations of

fairly heterogeneous sort (for example, MSS Bodleian Rawlinson
C 86, and Trinity College Cambridge R 3.19); but usually in
compilations of a clear religious bent, sometimes hagiographic,
sometimes didactic (more than half the surviving compilations in
which the religious tales were rehoused are of this cast). Six of the
tales in this study were excerpted in this way — that of the Prioress
and Chaucer's *Melibee* (five times), then those of the Clerk (four
times), Monk and Second Nun (twice) and Man of Law (once): in
addition, the Parson's tale, not here studied, was twice antho-
logised. But the best evidence of a reader approaching *The
Canterbury Tales* for its religious content comes in a manuscript
made shortly after Chaucer's death. The scribe of this manuscript
copied one minor religious piece by Chaucer, the lyric *Truth*, and
one major, the *Boece*. (This translation of the *De Consolatione
Philosophiae* of Boethius received pride of place in the 'retracciouns' and in the earlier list of Chaucer's works, in the prologue to
the *Legend*, as a work of 'hoolynesse'.) The scribe filled the
remainder of the last leaf with lines from the General Prologue,
'apparently from memory'. He had committed to memory not the
celebrated opening lines, nor the portraits to which modern
readers so readily turn, but the portrait of that heavily idealised
religious figure, the Parson.[35]

As with the scribes, so with one of Chaucer's most devoted
followers, John Lydgate. The prologues to Lydgate's works *The
Siege of Thebes* and *The Fall of Princes* contain particularly interesting references to *The Canterbury Tales*.[36] In the former,
Lydgate recognises the great variety of narratives in *The Canterbury Tales*:

> Some of desport, some of moralite,
> Some of knyghthode, loue and gentillesse,
> And some also of parfit hoolynesse,
> And some also in soth of Ribaudye ...
> Feyned talis ... þing Historial
> With many prouerbe diuers and vnkouth
>
> (22-5, 50-1)

The later *Fall of Princes* summarises *The Canterbury Tales* in very
similar terms:

> Summe off knyhthod, summe off gentilesse

And summe off loue and summe of parfitnesse,
And summe also off gret moralite,
Summe off disport, includynge gret sentence

(342-5)

It then describes three more stories in detail, all including 'gret sentence', and all included in this study:

In prose he wrot the Tale off Melibe,
And off his wiff, that callid was Prudence,
And off Grisildis parfit pacience,
And how the Monk off stories newe and olde
Pitous tragedies be the weie tolde

(346-50)[37]

The foregoing comments clearly explain the decision to include the tales of the Clerk, Prioress, Second Nun, Man of Law and Monk, and Chaucer's *Melibee*, in this study of religious narratives; they do not explain how three other tales, those of the Physician, Pardoner and Nun's Priest, came to be included. The latters' paradoxical status is indicated by their position at the end of this book. Other reasons have to be found to support their inclusion.

Granted, the tales of Pardoner and Nun's Priest are not too difficult to accommodate to this pattern. Whatever their deeper ambiguities, both can be readily located among the works for whose production Chaucer thanks Christ in the 'retracciouns':

of the translacion of Boece de Consolacione, and othere bookes of legendes of seintes, and omelies, and moralitee, and devocioun. (X, 1088)

On such a reading the Pardoner's tale would seem to be one of the 'omelies' in *The Canterbury Tales* (the other is the Parson's tale); the Nun's Priest's tale must surely belong to the class of 'moralitee', since it ends with a call to 'goode men' to take the 'moralitee' of the story, and with the traditional image of narrative 'fruyt' and 'chaf' which connects with two other religious narratives, those of the Man of Law and Parson.[38] The grounds for including the Physician's tale are more difficult to argue. The absence of head-link, though shared with the Second Nun's tale, is scarcely a defining property of religious narratives in *The Canterbury Tales*; the Shipman's bawdy tale also wants a head-link. More importantly if, as we have argued, the Physician's tale includes elements of romance and fabliaux traditions, it can hardly be a simple religious story.[39]

But what, in any case, is a religious narrative? Are we to define it in terms of its delivery by a speaker, its reception by an audience, or its content? On the first point: not every person professed to some form of religious observance tells a tale that can be called religious. Even though his work has the form of a religious story, the Friar is concerned less with the religious dimension than with using it to score points against an opponent.[40] Again, persons other than professed religious may tell religious tales (the Man of Law, the Clerk, Chaucer). Nevertheless, the religious story dictates a particular posture — more accurately, two such positions — on the part of the narrator. These are neatly summed up in the epigraphs to the first and second sections of this book ('the hand-maid of the lord', an echo of the speech of the Virgin at the Annunciation, Luke 1:38; 'Jacob wrestling with the angel', a detail from the story of the Old Testament patriarch in Genesis 32). According to the first, the narrator is humbly submissive to the story which he is faithfully transmitting — never more so than when he is actually producing a translation — without addition or comment of his own. The narrator relates such a work, so to speak, on his knees; if he acknowledges the audience at all, he will expect it to identify with his own posture. Hence he speaks in his own person, if at all, in a confessional vein, and addresses his hearers only as projections of himself (*we, us*). According to the second model, the narrator seeks to interpret the story to his audience by way of comment and exhortation: here the hearers are separate from, and subordinate to, the speaker (the *I* addresses a *thou* or a *you*). Now these two postures do not in themselves make a work religious. A joke dies if it has to be explained, and most of the fabliaux of *The Canterbury Tales* encourage a self-effacement on the part of their narrators the equal to that of the narrators of religious stories. Similarly, a self-consciously literary effort may require as active a narratorial presence as the most didactic religious work, and several of the religious tales here studied are also self-consciously literary exercises.

In the same way, the religious narrative cannot be defined simply as the production of a particular effect on its audience, or related simply to the preferences of a particular audience.[41] *The Canterbury Tales* twice acknowledges the force of the Pauline dictum (in Romans 15:14) that 'al that is writen is writen for oure doctrine' (VII, 3441-2; X, 1083). Secular narratives are therefore susceptible of religious interpretations, and certain categories of secular narrative were regularly so treated in the Middle Ages. The most obviously secular narratives in *The Canterbury Tales*, however, neither seek nor seem to generate such a reading. Different pilgrims have different things to say about the Miller's tale, for example, but mostly they take it in the spirit of its offering: 'for the moore part they loughe and pleyde' (I, 3858).[42] The preferences of the audience prove equally ambiguous pointers to a tale's meaning. One group of pilgrims, it is true, requests a moral tale; their expression of literary preference, as we shall see, probably owes more to social considerations than to religious. (Similar ambiguities obtain in medieval religious paintings, when the donors have themselves included in the painting in all their finery. They also recur in *The Canterbury Tales* when the narrator invites the *gentil* reader to 'turne over the leef and chese another tale'.[43])

Yet even if the religious work cannot be simply identified with the profession of the speaker or the preference of the hearer, it certainly dictates a particular attitude to itself different from that of any other story. Quite simply, a religious narrative is more obviously true and more immediately significant than any other work. Whatever the ironies attending its delivery and reception — and, as we shall see, these are many and profound — a religious narrative, as a narrative, is almost invariably, in intention, to be offered and received straight, and without irony.

But if we are then to define a religious narrative primarily in terms of its content, we confront a further problem, which the Physician's tale focuses very neatly for us. The Physician's tale begins with an imagined speech by Nature in praise of the virginal heroine of the story. As God's deputy, Nature has had a leading part to play in the creation of the heroine, and finds her creation an unfailing source of pleasure and delight (VI, 9-31). A little later, when the story is telling how all who loved virtue also sang the heroine's praises, the narrator qualifies this picture with a pointed comment:

> thurgh that land they preised hire echone
> That loved vertu, save Envye allone,
> That sory is of oother mennes wele,
> And glad is of his sorwe and his unheele.

The doctour maketh this descripcioun

(113-17)

Both passages are added by the narrator to his story. Both are clearly, if in very different ways, religious. The first has a larger, more comprehensive view of its subject. God mediates himself to man, it implies, through an unbroken system of dependent causes. The fact of physical existence thus images God, and connects man tangibly, if imperfectly, to Him. This formulation originates in the teaching of Plato and his disciples; it can be readily squared with traditional Christian teaching, as witness the impeccably orthodox twelfth-century writers who mediated it to Chaucer.[44] Such a view is concerned less with morality than with ontology; less with doing than with being; less with action than with understanding. To this essentially theoretical and mystical understanding of religion we oppose the practical bias revealed in the second quotation. Here the principal focus is on morality, and the principal source of authority not a pagan philosopher but the text of the Bible, as mediated by one of the Fathers of the Church (that is, the 'doctour': on this point see further below, p. 211).

If the personification of Nature grows out of a comprehensive awareness of God as the source and end of all life, the personification of Envy offers an opposed, exclusive view; God is the source not only of life but of a holiness expressed in moral imperatives, and makes His favour conditional on obedience to His dictates. Now, these opposing views are as necessary to one another as the earlier noted opposition of form and matter in *The Canterbury Tales* itself. All the same, the former is the more important. Religion is, first and foremost, a distinctive way of seeing.[45] Only as a consequence of that way of seeing does it generate a code of conduct: which, like any other, is, in greater or lesser degree, culturally and in many other ways, predetermined. When, therefore, Chaucer lists his religious writings in the *retracciouns* and the two versions of the prologue to the *Legend*, it may be significant that he gives pride of place to his *Boece*; for while Boethius ends his great work with an injunction to right living, 'syn that ye worken and don ... byforn the eyen of the juge that seeth and demeth alle thinges' (V, pr 6 309-12), his ultimate model is not the Bible but Plato, and his book moves in the direction not of right action but of right seeing or understanding.[46] And if *Boece* is accepted as a religious work, so too, presumably, the narratives in

The Canterbury Tales with pronounced Boethian echoes, like those of the Knight and Wife of Bath. The field of enquiry suddenly widens alarmingly.

To resolve this difficulty I have applied Procrustean measures, and deliberately resorted to the narrow view of religion implied in the Physician's invocation of 'the doctour'.[47] In practice, therefore, I have included only those narratives which explicitly invoke specifically Christian traditions as the source of ultimate author- ity.[48] Stories whose characters invoke Christian reference are included only when the narrator's identification with their point of view can be taken for granted.[49] Such considerations therefore rule out the narratives of the Friar, Summoner and Manciple, whose stories may be called religious in a wider sense (just!) but cannot be called so in the narrower.[50] We must also exclude the tales of the Knight and Franklin. The Knight treats religious questions seri- ously, but he does not actively engage with specifically Christian language or reference. Though actively present as a narrator, he disavows knowledge of divinity (I, 2811) and invokes Destiny (1663 ff.) and Fortune (2682), but no specifically Christian force, to explain human action.[51] Tales of pagan times — of which the Knight's is one — could be, and often were, accommodated to a Christian frame: such accommodation, though, implies, and prob- ably requires, an active narratorial presence in order to explain how what looks like a straightforward story is in fact a covert alle- gory of the moral life or some other Christian position.[52] I do not find clear evidence of this in the Knight's tale. On my reading, the Knight's tale is to be read as the symbol not of a specifically Chris- tian position, but of a general human dilemma. As in the Franklin's and Monk's tales, the paganness of the past is taken straight, not presented as a covert symbol or imperfect realisation of Christian values.

Likewise, when the Franklin refers to the pagan past of his story, he is far from Christianising it. On the contrary, he opposes its error ('as hethen folk useden in thilke dayes': V, 1293) to the truth of his own religious position, so as to secure himself against attack from his religious masters:

> swiche folye
> As in oure dayes is nat worth a flye,
> For hooly chirches feith in oure bileve
> Ne suffreth noon illusioun us to greve.
>
> (1131-4)[53]

The Physician's comment on Envy works very differently; it makes the pagan narrative exemplary of Christian teaching. A further comparison of the Physician's with the Franklin's tale, which it follows in the Ellesmere order, supports the decision to include the one and exclude the other. Dorigen, the heroine of the Franklin's tale, finds herself in an impossible situation very similar to that of the Physician's heroine, Virginia. Both women see no alternative but death to an enforced sexual liaison which will destroy the marriage of the one and the virginity of the other, and both remind themselves of heroines similarly placed to encourage themselves. But where Virginia invokes an Old Testament heroine, the daughter of Jephthah, Dorigen draws on pagan women for her models.[54] Such reasonings clearly support the inclusion of the Physician's tale in the present work.

All the same, our study must regularly imply the wider religious perspective which it can so seldom engage directly. Two areas in particular focus that wider perspective: imagery which is more open-ended, less one-dimensional, than the typical religious image; and a performance of the tale — this may include a pilgrim's response to it — which suggests the human context within which the tale's bloodless ideal must work itself out.[55] A particular fitness therefore attaches to the two tales with which this study concludes, those of the Pardoner and Nun's Priest, since they focus most clearly the problems of producing a simple religious narrative. These tales make up the concluding section of the book, and its epigraph 'water into wine' (an echo of the story of the marriage at Cana in John 2) suggests their achievement of a precarious balance between the two opposed perspectives. Their achievements can be most easily seen in imagery of metamorphosis (the rioter becomes his own death; the cock is given a human voice) and in narratorial postures which deliberately undercut any narrow religious reading of the stories.

Before this package can be inspected, however, a further difficulty must be considered. As noted earlier, Chaucer has treated the two narrative coordinates of time and space in a fairly casual fashion in the pilgrimage narrative. He has not been much more careful with the third, whose interaction with the others creates the narrative: that is, person, in this case the persons of the pilgrim-narrators. The narrators scarcely have any existence outside of the immediate context of their own narration. They come alive only when called on by the Host to speak. Once they finish speaking they return to an oblivion from which only our presumed familiarity with their descriptions in the General Prologue may preserve them. Granted, those who say little or nothing outside their stories are regularly brought alive by other means: nowhere better than when the Host is speaking in the Shipman–Prioress link. Almost in mid-sentence ('and with that word he sayde') the Host switches from the forthright language of the public bar to a polite and strangulated syntax ('as curteisly as it had been a mayde').[56] He has just been commending the Shipman for his tale; such language is hardly appropriate to request a tale from the Prioress:

> My lady Prioresse, by youre leve,
> So that I wiste I sholde yow nat greve,
> I wolde demen that ye tellen sholde
> A tale next, if so were that ye wolde.
> Now wol ye vouche sauf, my lady deere?
>
> (VII, 446-50)

If we except the self-effacing Knight in the General Prologue ('of his port as meeke as is a mayde': I, 69), and the Clerk in the head-link to his own tale ('ye ryde as coy and stille as dooth a mayde': IV, 2), other instances of men assuming the *curteisie* of a maid in order to have dealings with a woman have clearly ironic overtones: I think of Nicholas in the Miller's tale (I, 3202) and Jason in the *Legend* (1548).[57] This passage, then, does not tell us what the Host sees, merely what he thinks or wants to see. The syntax he appears to identify with the Prioress reappears in her tale as the property of a prayer, but whether real, or adopted in response to his expectation, there is no way of telling:

> 'O Lord, oure Lord, thy name how merveillous
> Is in this large world ysprad,' quod she;
> 'For noght oonly thy laude precious
> Parfourned is by men of dignitee,
> But by the mouth of children thy bountee
> Parfourned is, for on the brest soukynge
> Somtyme shewen they thyn heriynge.'
>
> (453-9)

The difficulty of deciding what is person and what merely the projection of another person, and where character stops and role starts — in the previous quotation, for instance, what connotes Chaucer's prioress of 'Stratford-atte-Bowe', and what merely the language of a woman praying ('quod she')? — finds yet clearer focus in three speeches in the link passages. The first is a comment on the unfinished Squire's tale. The speaker obviously can hardly comment in an informed way about a tale of which Chaucer has written, and he has so far heard, only part. He therefore does what many critics similarly placed might do: praises not the story but its execution, and talks generally of the wit and eloquence of a story-teller whose words are full of refinement and charged with feeling (V, 674, 678, 681). But the speaker does not stop there. Carried away by the Squire's resemblance to his wild young son, who provides so unfavourable a contrast, he finds himself the centre of attention and forced to tell the next story. To my ears, his speech in praise of the young man is not a little patronising, the kind of thing spoken by an older to a younger man who has professed great consciousness of his limited powers of oratory. Hence the speaker finds the Squire's achievement the more praiseworthy 'considerynge thy yowthe' (675), and reckons that none will surpass him in eloquence 'if that thou lyve'. (I take this to mean, if the Squire should live until he reaches the mature years of the speaker, or, possibly, if he lives long enough to improve on so poor a performance.)[58] The scribe of the Ellesmere manuscript (that used by Robinson for his edition and followed here) assigns these words to the Franklin. Hengwrt originally does not use them, but later assigns them to the Merchant. Similarly, the end-link to the Man of Law's tale, as already noted, includes a speech assigned variously, in the manuscripts which have it, to the Shipman, Summoner and Squire. Lastly, Ellesmere presents an exchange between the Host and Squire, before the latter's tale (V, 1-8). When this eventually appears in Hengwrt, it has been turned into an exchange with the Franklin, and introduces the Franklin's tale.

These examples are neither as problematic nor as conclusive as they seem. If, as is normally reckoned, Chaucer intended to cancel the end-link to the Man of Law's tale, the value of its evidence diminishes accordingly. Moreover, Hengwrt's ascription of the other speeches to the Merchant and Franklin respectively almost certainly represents a change to the more authoritative version found in Ellesmere, because the Hengwrt version mangles the metre, and the Ellesmere does not: for example,

Sire frankeleyn, com neer if it your wille be
And sey vs a tale, for certes ye
Konnen theron as muche as any man

(Hengwrt)

Squier, com neer, if it youre wille be,
And sey somwhat of love; for certes ye
Konnen theron as muche as any man.

(V, 1-3)[59]

Reliable or not as witnesses to what Chaucer wrote, though, these examples show how notional the tie between tale and teller could be. Inevitably, they lead to the conclusion that not the individual but the type is being realised in these exchanges with the Host.[60] In the first instance, the type is an older and socially self-conscious person, who looks with possible envy at the youthful representative of a higher class than he himself inhabits. In the second, as already noted, the speaker, who reckons to have neither 'philosophie/Ne phislyas, ne termes queinte of lawe' (in fact, he has 'but litel Latyn'; II, 1188-90) identifies himself with the *lewed* and against the *lered* members of his audience. In the third, a person is being addressed who is learned in the ways of love (El) or storytelling (Hg), and high enough on the social ladder to require polite handling by the Host; the latter's request, 'com neer, if it youre wille be', has a clear parallel in the earlier noted request to the Prioress to tell a tale 'if so were that ye wolde'.

Notional the tie may be between tale and teller, and general the social role which gives life to the telling of a story, but no scribe of the whole work ever broke that tie completely and reassigned one tale to another speaker. Wherever they put the tales, and whatever the genuine link-passages they used or the spurious ones they created, the scribes always assigned the same tale to the same pilgrim. Even so, doubts have been raised about this regular ascription of a tale to a particular speaker. Three tales contain internal features at odds with the given identities of their narrators, or with the words spoken by them in head-links. Feminine referents in the Shipman's tale, and masculine in the Second Nun's, have suggested to some readers that both tales were originally intended for, or spoken by, other characters (the Shipman's by the Wife of Bath; the Nun's by Chaucer before he began work on *The Canterbury Tales*).[61] The Man of Law declares that he will speak in prose, yet tells his tale in rhyme royal: consequently, some critics have argued, he must originally have been meant to tell the only other prose tale except the Parson's in *The Canterbury Tales*, Chaucer's *Melibee*.[62] Fortunately, these difficulties are more apparent than real. They spring from the same old-fashioned approach that could not brook inconsistencies like the one in *Macbeth* whereby Lady Macbeth has had children but her husband has not: one that really wanted to read *The Canterbury Tales* as a psychological novel. Yet that they were raised at all suggests that for Chaucer the relation of tale to teller was more formal, even haphazard, than the firmness of its ascription might suggest.

Our real problem with character, of course, has very precise origins in the descriptions of the pilgrims in the General Prologue. These descriptions are sometimes called the portrait gallery of *The Canterbury Tales*, but their real affinities are with the extended stage directions by means of which literary-minded dramatists like Bernard Shaw introduce their characters to the readers of their plays. To read them, as critics have often done, as authorising a particular approach to the pilgrim-narrators and their stories is to be misled. In the fictional scheme of things the narrator is writing about his fellow pilgrims with the benefit of hindsight. In the cast-list — as I shall call it — he is providing a digest or summary of the time he spent with them on their way to Canterbury. But any claim that the cast-list authorises a particular approach to the stories, which Chaucer tantalisingly seems to invite, is undermined, both by Chaucer's involvement in the events of the pilgrimage and by his inability to organise his impressions in any coherent and consistent way. There is, so to say, a gap between what the cast-list tells us about the pilgrims, and what the framing and framed narratives tell us about them. Sometimes this is an accidental consequence of the unfinished nature of the work. Characters appear in the cast-list who get no chance to tell a story and hence realise themselves as characters through a narrative. At other times the gap may be deliberate: R.M. Jordan has drawn particular attention to the gap between the Merchant of the cast-list and the narrator of the Merchant's tale.[63]

The gap between cast-list and the rest of *The Canterbury Tales* can be simply described. Written after the event of the pilgrimage, it is a different kind of narrative from the one which it prefaces. The illusion of *The Canterbury Tales*, we have said, is that of a journey faithfully recorded as it actually happened. (That Chaucer undercuts this illusion by studiously casual treatment of time and place is not in point.) By contrast, the cast-list is, in intention, an explicitly literary creation and the product of an active and ordering memory.[64] It thus operates several times at once: it blends beginning, middle and end of the pilgrimage narrative into a 'no-time' parallel to that of the pilgrimage narrative and peculiar to itself. On the one hand, it presents the characters formally not in terms of the relationships they are to form during the pilgrimage (mostly covertly or overtly antagonistic) but as groups of 'sondry folk' who met 'by aventure' at the Tabard at the start of their journey.[65] On the other, as writers have noted, it makes ample reference to the actual circumstances of the journey, notably, the characters' horses and horsemanship (or, in the case of the Shipman, lack of it). This blending of two times with a third time, the now of reminiscence and narration, has the immediate consequence that we cannot relate the cast-list to the pilgrimage narrative in any simple or direct way.[66] Even when the two echo one another (I am willing to read such echoes unambiguously only in the portraits of the Pardoner and the Wife of Bath) each has its own independent status. Normally, for example, and surely rightly, we read the account of the Wife's deafness, in the cast-list, in the light of her own story in the prologue to her tale. Yet it seems to me that the narrator's comment on her deafness — 'she was somdel deef, and that was scathe' (I, 446) — is not simply an anticipatory reference to the Wife's self-revelation during the pilgrimage. The context allows us the inference that, even before he learned the cause of her deafness, the narrator had experienced its effects (not simply her deafness, that is, but its consequence for the hearers — a loud and insistent voice — was 'scathe').

Inevitably, therefore, the two narratives — the pilgrimage narrative with its framed collection of stories, and the cast-list — have to be constantly checked against one another if positive inferences are to be drawn about the narrator of a given tale from his or her portrait in the cast-list. It will not do to read the individual tale simply as a reflex of the character in the cast-list: to do so is literally to 'maken ernest of game'. And since, in the fictional scheme of things, the cast-list receives its ultimate sanction from the pilgrimage which we approach through it, reading backwards to do so, I should have been tempted, if the present work had been able to study *The Canterbury Tales* in its entirety, to reserve a place somewhere near 'the hyndreste of oure route' for the cast-list.[67] As it is, the following pages will invoke the evidence of the cast-list directly only in the chapter on the Pardoner.

If character is problematic, so is voice, and the cast-list can also focus this difficulty for us. The simple question is: Whose voice are we hearing at any one time? That of a pilgrim, conceived as an individual or, more probably, a type? that of the poet, or that of one of his fictional *alter egos* (the character who 'moot reherce as ny as evere he kan/Everich a word'; the figure whom the *retracciouns* name 'the makere of this book' and its compiler[68])? The cast-list, I have implied, is the third of the fictional Chaucer's fictions in *The Canterbury Tales*. Yet its status as a story is not comparable with those told by him during the journey, and hardly comparable with any told by other pilgrims, not because he is telling it to a different audience, nor yet because he is recording personal impressions — though only the confessional prologues of the Wife of Bath, Pardoner and Canon's Yeoman approach it in this respect — but because it makes use of other voices than his own. In this respect the contrast is striking with the individual tales of *The Canterbury Tales*. Admittedly, narrators who translate from other works — and several of the tales are of this kind — will, in intention, subordinate their own voice to the voice of their original. Otherwise, speakers of the tales generally take pains to conceal the precise nature of their relation to speeches they have heard and books they have read. After he tells his story of the crow, for instance, the Manciple explains how he got it not from the 'olde bookes' to which he first refers for authorisation (IX, 106), but from his mother, who told him the story and offered a lengthy *moralisatio* upon it (317-62). Her words must have made a deep impression on the small child, for the grown man quotes them as his own conclusion to the story.[69] Within the confessional prologues, too, the speaker often repeats other people's words, or his/her words at another time. These examples apart, we must reckon to be listening to the voice of the speaker himself; the Man of Law, for instance, claims to have heard his story from a merchant, but no clear trace of the merchant's words can be observed in the tale.

The general unwillingness of the individual stories to authorise any voice but that of their own narrators contrasts strikingly with the readiness of the cast-list to take on other people's voices alongside, and even in competition with, the voice of its narrator. To start with, tone of voice regularly features in the cast-list as an

element in the description of a pilgrim. The Friar speaks sweetly
with a lisp (264-5), assumed rather like the maidenliness of the
Host's address to the Prioress; the Merchant in a grave, even
pompous, manner (274); the Clerk 'in forme and reverence/And
short and quyk and ful of hy sentence' (305-6); and so on.[70] More
important, on occasion the narrator records the speakers' very
words. We hear the Summoner's scraps of drunken Latin (646)
and pithy dismissal of the ecclesiastical machinery he is pledged to
support ('"purs is the ercedekenes helle", seyde he': 658). Elsewhere, we see how the narrator's view of a character is heavily
dependent on that character's actual words, almost as if he were
simply turning them into reported speech:

[of the Monk]	And I seyde his opinion was good
[of the Friar]	he hadde power of confessioun/As seyde hymself
[of the Parson]	Out of the gospel he tho wordes caughte And this figure he added eek therto, That if gold ruste, what shal iren do?
[of the Pardoner]	he seyde he hadde a gobet of the seyl.

(183, 218-9, 498-500, 696)

This fact of voices within a voice, if I may so call them,
confronts the reader with a problem not only of interpretation —
the situation is immediately familiar to anyone receiving a message
at second hand, or reporting a conversation — but also of description: which is my real quarry here.[71] To repeat the earlier question:
Whose voice are we hearing at any moment? Within the fictional
scheme of things, for how much of the wording of the cast-list are
the individual speakers responsible, and how much of it is the
narrator's own voice? Similarly, how much of the tale is to be credited to the named pilgrim–narrator, and how much to Chaucer the
'makere of this book'?[72] Some critics have resolved this problem
by denying its existence.[73] Others reckon it too gross a deception
to obtain except with the most gullible. Since they find Chaucer the
pilgrim scarcely more realised as a character than the pilgrims
whose words he claims to report, they conclude that the fictional
realm has absolute status only when directly activated by a formal
acknowledgement of its existence.[74] Whatever parts of the work we
then make over to the characters — and critics are most ready to
do this only when the narrations are supported by evidence in the

link passages — we are confident that, for the most part, we are hearing the voice of Chaucer.

This Chaucer can hardly be the fictional pilgrim, journeying to Canterbury, writing up the story after the event; that figure only once claims authority over his narrative, when, before it has properly begun, he interrupts it (I, 35-42) to give us the cast-list (43-714). Now, as earlier noted, the cast-list has a subtly different principle of organisation from that of the pilgrimage narrative; it is memory to the other's experience. Its opening words, therefore, appear to sanction a work structured about the idea of reason; that is, the cast-list will express or embody a social or literary decorum. By the time we reach the end of the cast-list, the fictional Chaucer has to confess that he has failed in his plan to set people 'in hir degree' (40, 744). The claims of art, which he now describes, by implication, in the words, 'telle his tale untrewe/Or feyne thyng, or fynde wordes newe' (735-6), have had to yield to the need to 'telle a tale after a man' and 'reherce as ny as evere he kan/Everich a word' (731-3). Specifically, decorum has been violated by plain speaking, a necessary consequence of his decision to 'speke hir wordes proprely' (729). This public disclaimer of responsibility for the offered literary production, and equally public embracing of the humbler role of reporter of other men's words and deeds, is as double-edged as anything we shall find in *The Canterbury Tales*. Yet, within the fictional scheme of things, it points to Chaucer's readiness henceforth to let his story tell itself, as it happened and, by inference, allows the conclusion that the fictional Chaucer will merely 'telle a tale after a man' (or rather, a sequence of tales after a number of men and women) and 'telle ... hir wordes and hir cheere' and 'speke hir wordes proprely'.

This reticence of Chaucer in the face of his narrative exactly characterises the framing narrative. Except for the disclaimer at the start of the Miller's tale, which makes plain that any editorial work on *The Canterbury Tales* must be undertaken by the reader, not the writer, Chaucer rarely intervenes to direct our reading: his only regular comment, marking the beginning of a story ('bigan his tale, as ye shal after heere': I, 858; II, 98: VII, 452, 3462) is one the pilgrims are equally ready to use themselves (II, 133; IV, 56; V, 728). That is, the pilgrimage narrative appears to happen without his control, almost to be telling itself. This displacement of the compiler—editor of the cast-list (and of the opening verse paragraph of the General Prologue) by the scribe—reporter of the rest of the work has a telling parallel in Chaucer's self-presentation as a storyteller during the pilgrimage. His first offering, 'the tale of Thopas', is an old-fashioned 'literary' performance, full of address to the audience ('I telle it yow', 'it is no nay', etc.) and attempting to secure a place for itself relative to other examples of the genre ('romances of prys'). When the story is abruptly terminated by the Host, Chaucer withdraws into the humbler role of scribe–translator for his second offering, the *Melibee*, and, as we shall see, scarcely intrudes himself into its textures.

Admittedly, this reticence of the scribe–reporter does not confer upon the pilgrim–narrators the absolute distance from their creator that we observe, and expect, in more recent ventures in the field, like Emily Brontë's *Wuthering Heights* or Conrad's *Heart of Darkness*. For one thing, the pilgrim–narrators frequently address their fellow pilgrims as projections of their own narrative. There are no 'queenes ... duchesses, and ... ladyes' present among the pilgrim band, no 'maistresses' of 'lordes doghters', no lords of court, no 'worshipful chanons religious'; but the Man of Law, Physician, Nun's Priest and Canon's Yeoman act as if there were, and address their hearers accordingly (II, 652-3; VI, 72-3; VII 3325-6; VIII, 992).[75] More important, the narrators sometimes speak of writing their story for other people to read.[76] This breaking of the fictional frame reminds us that the whole work is being written by Chaucer. Yet there never was any doubt of *that*. By this device Chaucer places himself squarely in and of the pilgrimage, and at the same time asserts his distance from it. In fact, he is like the puppet-master or the ventriloquist who controls a series of puppets, including one representing himself. He moves the strings so that the puppets appear to speak, but he does not too greatly mind if we see his lips moving as well.

All this is by way of saying that if the voice we hear in any individual part of *The Canterbury Tales* is more than that of its fictional speaker, it is also, at the same time not simply that of its actual creator.[77] Even when Chaucer has included an already existing work without change in *The Canterbury Tales*, as it is claimed he did with the 'lyf ... of seynt Cecile', its changed context changes *it* and obliges us to see it differently. It is no longer simply the production of a famous poet; it has become part of a much larger and more complex whole, the offering of a fictional character, the Second Nun — about whom, to be fair, the cast-list tells us almost as little as her own narration. We have therefore to describe the voices we hear in *The Canterbury Tales* in such a way as to suggest the cooperation of author and fictional characters in the final product. Analysis, however, finds this task every bit as difficult as its earlier attempts to describe religion in terms of both ends *and* means, and *The Canterbury Tales* as both form *and* matter. The circle simply will not square. In practice, therefore, I oppose the coolly sceptical approach of such as Jordan, which I see as a clear reflex of the poet-creator's own position, in the name of a cheerful credulity, the equally clear reflex of the author's carefully created persona and the guarantee of such autonomous life as his characters enjoy: and I shall normally credit the named individual pilgrim with the narration and 'authorship' of his or her own story.[78] Occasional inconsistency of practice in this respect will provide my only explicit acknowledgement of Chaucer's absolute responsibility for the whole work.[79] Chaucer invites us to watch his dummies appear to talk, and cleverly realises their narratives in very different ways, most notably by the creation of very distinct styles and tones of voice.[80] To respond like a child to his invitation need not be to read childishly.

Notes

1. All quotation is taken from *The Works of Geoffrey Chaucer*, ed. F.N. Robinson, 2nd edn (London, 1957).

2. On this point, see D.R. Howard, *The Idea of CT,* (Berkeley, Los Angeles and London, 1976), p. 61; J. Coleman, *English Literature in History 1350-1400: medieval readers and writers* (London, 1981), pp. 198-202; and A.I. Doyle and M.B. Parkes, 'The production of copies of *CT* and *CA* in the early fifteenth century', *Medieval Scribes, Manuscripts and Libraries: essays presented to N.R. Ker*, ed. M.B. Parkes and A.G. Watson (London, 1978), pp. 186-94. See also comments on 'narrative collections' in the late middle ages by R.W. Frank, Jr, '*LGW*: some implications', *Chaucer at Albany*, ed. R.H. Robbins (New York, 1975), pp. 63 ff.

3. For the most fully developed statement of this position, see R.M. Lumiansky, *Of Sundry Folk: the dramatic principle in CT* (Austin, Texas, 1955); the 'onlie begetter' was G.L. Kittredge, 'Chaucer's discussion of marriage', *MP* 9 (1911-12), 435-67; reprinted in *Chaucer Criticism I. The Canterbury Tales*, ed. R.J. Schoeck and J. Taylor (Notre Dame, Ind. and London, 1960), pp. 130-59, and *Chaucer: modern essays in criticism*, ed. E. Wagenknecht (New York, 1959), pp. 188-215.

4. Some critics read the completed journey as a two-way process, ending where it began: so C.A. Owen Jr. For the fullest statement of his position, see *Pilgrimage and Storytelling in CT: the dialectic of 'ernest' and 'game'* (Norman, Oklahoma, 1977). Others read it as ending at Canterbury, most importantly, Howard, pp. 28-30, 67-72.

5. For an important statement of this position, as well as one of the earliest, see R.F. Baldwin, *The Unity of CT*, Anglistica, 5 (Copenhagen, 1955). Criticisms of Baldwin's work (e.g. Howard pp. 71 ff.; R.O. Payne, *The Key of Remembrance: a study of Chaucer's poetics* (New Haven, London, 1963), p. 153; and N.E. Eliason, *The Language of Chaucer's poetry*, Anglistica, 17 (Copenhagen, 1972), pp. 211 ff.) regularly admit its importance.

6. For judicious comments on the narrative's treatment of its own temporal and spatial coordinates, see Howard, pp. 163-8; P. Boitani, *English Medieval Narrative in the Thirteenth and Fourteenth Centuries* (Cambridge, 1982), p. 245; and J. Norton-Smith, *Geoffrey Chaucer* (London, 1974), p. 96.

7. The scribe of the Lansdowne MS of *CT* provided SqT with a similar conclusion (see Robinson, p. 894). References to summer in SqT (V, 64) and Prol CYT (VIII, 568) might, if read literally, provide a further symbolic time-frame for a narrative which begins in spring (cf. Eliason, p. 233): simpler readings of both passages, however, are equally possible.

8. So noted, for instance, by P.M. Kean, *Chaucer and the Making of English Poetry*, 2 vols (London, 1972), II, ch. 4, and pp. 110-12, 165; and H. Cooper, *The Structure of CT* (London, 1983), ch. 4.

9. A point often noted: for example, by Howard, p. 245; C.K. Zacher, *Curiosity and Pilgrimage; the literature of discovery in fourteenth-century England* (Baltimore and London, 1976), pp. 102-3; V.A. Kolve, *Chaucer and the Imagery of Narrative* (London, 1984), pp. 219-20, 366-8; and R.W. Hanning, 'The theme of art and life in Chaucer's poetry', in *Geoffrey Chaucer: a collection of original articles*, ed. G.D. Economou (New York, 1975), pp. 28-9.

10. On the links between MLT and KnT, see T. Whittock, *A Reading of CT* (Cambridge, 1968), pp. 108 ff.; A. David, *The Strumpet Muse: art and morals in Chaucer's poetry* (Bloomington, Ind., 1976), pp. 120 ff.; and C.V. Kaske, 'Getting around ParsT', Robbins, pp. 159-60.

11. Also noted in Norton-Smith, p. 151. See also his p. 81 for judicious comment about the 'Aristotelian narrative structure' represented by groups A−B and H−I.

12. On ParsT, see, for example, Howard, pp. 74, 385-7; Zacher, pp. 122 ff.; P.G. Ruggiers, 'Serious Chaucer: *Mel* and ParsT', in *Chaucerian Problems and Perspectives: essays presented to Paul E. Beichner*, ed. E. Vasta and Z.P. Thundy (Notre Dame, Ind., 1979), pp. 89 ff.; and L.W. Patterson, 'ParsT and the quitting of *CT*', *Trad.*, 34 (1978), 331-80.

13. See further Howard, pp. 211-15.

14. For a similar metaphor, of a 'broken reel of film', see Baldwin (p. 75) and comment by Eliason (p. 221).

15. The Ellesmere manuscript, used as the basis of Robinson, so treats MerchT and SqT (Robinson, pp. 127-8, splits the respective end- and head-links).

16. They also created spurious links to complete the work (Norton-Smith (p. 82), and for a single example, see n. 7 above). Eliason (p. 220) finds only one instance 'where we would be aware of a gap in the text and be puzzled by it — the gap after the unfinished CkT'. But see Kolve (pp. 284 ff.) for further comment on this gap.

17. Cooper (pp. 61-2) argues for reading IX−X as a single group; against this view, see *CT by Geoffrey Chaucer ... the Hengwrt MS*, ed. N.F. Blake (London, 1980), p. 5.

18. In this we may see a consequence of the medieval predilection for carefully wrought beginnings and tolerance of (relatively) undeveloped middles. (The obvious parallel in ME is Malory's *Morte d'arthur*, a comparison implied in Howard, p. 61.) W.W. Ryding, *Structure in Medieval Narrative* (The Hague and Paris, 1971), compares the resulting structure to 'an accordion, flexible in the

middle and steady at both ends' (p. 48). Then, as now, hasty readers 'read somewhat more carefully at the beginning and at the end' (the phrase is Petrarch's: see *Chaucer: Sources and Backgrounds*, ed. R.P. Miller (New York, 1977), p. 137). J.B. Allen and T.A. Moritz, *A Distinction of Stories: the medieval unity of Chaucer's fair chain of narratives for Canterbury* (Columbus, Ohio, 1981), p. 8, reckon that writers were more careful about beginnings than about endings: contrast Petrarch, who finds the end of a book the place where, 'according to the principles of rhetoric, the most effective part of the composition belongs' (Miller, p. 138), and G. Josipovici, 'Fiction and game in *CT*', *CQ*, 7 (1965), 185-97, for the claim that it was traditional to end a collection of tales with a particularly moral one.

19. See discussion in *The Text of CT*, ed. J.M. Manly and E. Rickert, 7 vols (Chigago, 1940), II, 475 ff.

20. Noted, for example, by Zacher (p. 105), and Cooper (pp. 125, 134).

21. For fuller comment see A.T. Gaylord, 'Sentence and solaas in fragment VII of *CT*: Harry Bailly as horseback editor', *PMLA*, 82 (1967), 226-35.

22. So Howard (p. 287), comparing groups I, III and VII; Gaylord, *PMLA*, 82, 233; and R.B. Burlin, *Chaucerian Fiction* (Princeton, N.J., 1977), p. 228.

23. Compare Derek Brewer's distinction between horizontal and vertical contexts in narrative: 'Towards a Chaucerian poetic', *PBA*, 60 (1974), 219-52; reprinted in D. Brewer, *Chaucer: the poet as storyteller* (London, 1984), pp. 68-9.

24. For a modern edition, see Blake.

25. On the importance of these three categories, see Payne, p. 159; on the linking of FrankT and SecNT, Howard, p. 289.

26. I have in mind the episode of the battle of King Arthur against the 11 kings (Caxton, *Morte*, I, 16; *The Works of Sir Thomas Malory*, ed. E. Vinaver (Oxford, 1954), pp. 20-6). See also Ryding (p. 110) on symmetry in the Arthurian Vulgate.

27. For the most celebrated such pattern, linking groups III–V (the so-called marriage debate), see Kittredge (full reference at n. 3 above): elaborated by B.F. Huppé, *A Reading of CT*, rev. edn (New York, 1967), ch. 4 and p. 227 (including MLT at one end and NPT at other). Other shapes include the linking of KnT, *Mel* and ParsT: e.g. Zacher, pp. 116, 126; and T. Lawler, *The One and the Many in CT* (Hamden, Conn., 1980), pp.102, 107; of MLT, SecNT and ParsT, by way of their respective head-links or prologues: e.g. Kolve, p. 369; or — relevant to the purposes of this book — of *Mel*, ClT, SecNT, PrT, PhysT, MLT and ParsT: e.g. R.F. Green, *Poets and Princepleasers* (Toronto, 1980), p. 159. Another creates its own order out of a number of different manuscript groupings (Allen–Moritz). Still another links PrT, MkT and SecNT and suggests links with PhysT, MLT, ClT and NPT (P. Strohm, 'Some generic distinctions in *CT*', *MP*, 68 (1970-71), 323-4.)

28. Thus Kolve finds MLT linked by way of its prologue to the preceding group, and at the same time 'something like a rebeginning of *CT*' (p. 292).

29. On frame narratives, see H.B. Hinckley, 'The framing tale,' *MLN*, 49 (1934), 69-80; M.W. Bloomfield, 'Authenticating realism and the realism of Chaucer', *Thought* 39 (1964), 335-58; Boitani, pp. 114-17, 227 ff.; and Franks, Robbins, pp. 74-5. For comment on other frame narratives, see Cooper, pp. 28-30 (the *Decameron*; see also ch. 2, n. 35 below); Kean, II, 72 (the *Divina Commedia*); Hanning, Economou (1975), pp. 20-1 (Ovid's *Metamorphoses*, Gower's *CA*, the *Decameron*); and Boitani, pp. 123 ff., A.J. Minnis, *Medieval Theory of Authorship* (London, 1984), pp. 177-90; and E.D. Kirk, 'Chaucer and his English contemporaries', Economou (1975) pp. 112-15 (on *CA*).

30. For examples of the former approach, see Kolve, Cooper, Howard, ch. 5; of the latter, Allen–Moritz, and S.S. Hussey, *Chaucer, an Introduction*, 2nd edn (London, 1981), chs 4-5.

31. Hence the present study considers only in passing the concluding religious narratives of *CT*, the ParsT and the 'retracciouns'. For comment on the former, see Patterson, *Trad.*, 34 (1978), 331-80; on the latter, O. Sayce, 'Chaucer's "retractions"; the conclusion of *CT* and its place in literary tradition', *M AE*, 40 (1971), 230-48; and comment in Norton-Smith, p. 80, n. 2.

32. See further D.S. Silvia, 'Some fifteenth-century MSS of *CT*', in *Chaucer and ME Studies in Honour of R.H. Robbins*, ed. B. Rowland (London, 1974), pp. 153-63; and E.T. Donaldson, 'The MSS of Chaucer's works and their use', in *Writers and their Background: Geoffrey Chaucer*, ed. D. Brewer (London, 1974), pp. 94-5. For general comment, see Boitani, ch. 1, 'The Religious Tradition'.

33. For a noteworthy exception to this generalisation, see MS, Trinity College, Cambridge, R 3.19. The MS contains a copy of MkT conflated with material from Lydgate's *Fall of Princes*. The new work is then entitled 'Bochas', in clear recognition of its dependence on Boccaccio's celebrated example of the genre, the *De casibus virorum illustrium*. For comment about manuscripts cited in the next few paragraphs, consult Manly–Rickert, I.

34. On the basis of their appearing together in Harley and Longleat MSS, Silvia (Rowland (1974) p. 155) describes KnT, ClT and MLT as 'courtly works' in opposition to the 'moral pieces', PrT, SecNT, MkT, *Mel* and ParsT. For a truer understanding of the case, see ibid., p. 157 and n. 10. In support of the original view, however, see n. 37 below.

35. See Silvia, Rowland (1974), p. 155, for a rather different assessment of this manuscript (BL Add. 10340).

36. For Lydgate's comments, see *Chaucer: the critical heritage*, ed. D. Brewer, 2 vols (London, 1978), I, 44-59; or C. Spurgeon, *500 Years of Chaucer Criticism and Allusion, 1357-1900*, 3 vols (London, 1925), I, 26-32, 36-43.

37. By contrast, Lydgate's *Temple of Glas* links ClT, KnT, SqT, MerchT, FrankT, as stories of love, with stories of *LGW* and others from classical antiquity (*The Temple of Glas*, ed. J. Schick, EETS ES 60 (London, 1891), ll. 75-6, 102-10, 137-42, 184-5, 405-6, 409-11.)

38. I am using the term 'omelie' loosely. For criticisms of the term applied to PardT, see ch. 9, n. 9 below; and to ParsT, Patterson, *Trad.*, 34, 332 and n. 6. (Patterson classes ParsT generically with manuals for penitents (p. 338), but allows that the precise terminologies 'are not very important'.) On preaching as a basic function of the Pardoner, see G.R. Owst, *Preaching in Medieval England* (Cambridge, 1926), pp. 99 ff.

39. Several writers do, however, group PhysT with some or all of the previous group: e.g. Payne (p. 162) and Eliason (p. 153), with SecNT, MLT, ClT, PrT. To this list Howard (p. 175) adds ParsT, *Mel* and MkT.

40. Cf. Burlin (p. 159): 'though the genre may be professionally in order, its proper function is perverted by the speaker.'

41. The pagan authors, for example, were regularly understood to be chiefly concerned with ethical matters. On this point, see J.B. Allen, *The Friar as Critic: literary attitudes in the later Middle Ages* (Nashville, Tenn., 1971), pp. 40-5, 57; A.J. Minnis, 'The influence of academic prologues on the prologues and literary attitudes of late-medieval English writers', *MS*, 43 (1981), 373 ff.

42. For comment on the religious reference in MillT, see R.E. Kaske, 'The *Canticum Canticorum* in MillT', *SP*, 59 (1962), 479-500; and 'Patristic exegesis, the defence', in *Critical Approaches to Medieval Literature*, ed. D. Bethurum (New York, 1960), pp. 52-60. See also Kolve (p.159) and Allen (pp. 118, 123).

43. Another question — does the use of an avowedly religious source make a tale religious? — is subsumed under considerations of the narrator's motives and methods: the obvious example, of analogues in sermon literature for FrT, is discussed in G.R. Owst, *Literature and Pulpit in medieval England*, rev. edn

(Oxford, 1961), pp. 162-3; Coleman, p. 201; and S. Wenzel, 'Chaucer and the language of contemporary preaching', *SP* 73 (1976), 143.

44. Their orthodoxy, in fact, is more open to debate than my words suggest. For the affirmative view, see C. Wood, *Chaucer and the Country of the Stars* (Princeton, N.J., 1970), quoting a passage from the *Megacosmos* of Bernard Silvester, which Wood reckons (p. 214) 'an account of world history up to the time of the Incarnation'. For a qualified negative which translates the passage in question, see P. Dronke, 'Chaucer and the medieval Latin Poets', Brewer (1974), pp. 157-8; and G. Leff, 'Christian thought', in *Literature and Western civilization: the medieval world*, ed. D. Daiches and A. Thorlby (London, 1973), p. 224. Bernard's text receives further comment below, pp. 166 (ch. 6 n. 44), 200 (ch 7 n. 20).

45. This crucially important metaphor figures prominently in several of the tales, and receives fuller comment below, pp. 91, 121, 127, 211, 246.

46. The Christianity of Boethius in the *Consolation* has been questioned almost as often as that of the twelfth-century neo-platonists. For further comment, see C.S. Lewis, *The Discarded Image* (Cambridge, 1964), pp. 76-9; W. Wetherbee, 'Some intellectual themes in Chaucer's poetry', Economou (1975), p. 83; and C.V. Kaske, Robbins, pp. 151 ff.

47. For a narrower definition still, see Kean II, ch. 5 (p. 197, n. 2 excludes MLT, ClT, PhysT on the grounds that they are 'concerned primarily with the development of themes which are not, strictly speaking, devotional ones'). For the complete opposite, which regularly allegorises secular reference, see D.W. Robertson, *A Preface to Chaucer* (Princeton, N.J., 1963).

48. Saints' lives, especially SecNT, invoke the traditions in their very narrative textures. Other narratives do so only through direct or indirect address to their readers: PhysT is the obvious such example. Between the two extremes come the remaining tales of this study.

49. Thus January's paraphrase of the Song of Songs, in MerchT, is placed not only by the narrative context but by the narrator's comment: 'swich olde lewed words used he' (IV, 2149).

50. The Manciple's use of Wisdom texts (IX, 314 ff.) in his sermonising conclusion might seem to make a strong case for the inclusion of his tale in this study: the Wisdom texts probably go back to Albertano of Brescia (Robinson, p. 765; Blake, p. 591), whose *Liber Consolationis*, in a French translation, furnished Chaucer with the source of his *Mel* (discussed further Ch. 5 below). On the other hand, MancT is framed in an overt 'quitting' mould (see above p.4), and the worldly wisdom it preaches is remote from any clearly Christian position.

51. On the religious dimension of KnT, see, e.g. Kolve, pp. 145, 150-51; R.H. Green, 'Classical fable and English poetry in the fourteenth century', Bethurum, pp. 128-33; Kaske, Robbins, pp. 156 ff. (and p. 159, contrasting KnT and ParsT as 'philosophy and theology, giving us a Virgil at the beginning of *CT* to match the Beatrice at the end'); and J.D. Burnley, *Chaucer's Language and the Philosophers' Tradition* (Cambridge, 1979), p. 38.

52. This point is regularly made of medieval literature and of Chaucer in particular: so Brewer, 'Towards a Chaucerian poetic', Brewer (1984), pp. 56-7; C. Donahue, 'Patristic exegesis in the criticism of medieval literature', Bethurum, pp. 61-82; P. Beichner, 'The allegorical interpretation of medieval literature', *PMLA*, 82 (1967), 33-8; and Kolve, Harbert and Shepherd in Brewer (1974), pp. 145, 271, 317.

53. Cf. *Astr* II, 4, 57-60 on the 'rytes of payens', noted R.W.V. Elliott, *Chaucer's English* (London, 1974), p. 302.

54. Ironically, Dorigen's exempla derive from the *Epistola Adversus Jovinianum* of another *doctour*, St Jerome; but neither she nor her narrator

acknowledges this Christian context of her utterance. Burnley (p. 38) notes the 'uncompromisingly medieval Christian character' of an earlier speech of Dorigen, on the 'rokkes blake' (V, 865 ff.). This speech, a prayer to God, contains pronounced Boethian echoes (Robinson, p. 723), and shares the inclusive Christian character of the *Consolation*: on these grounds too FrankT has been excluded from the present study. Note further that K. Hume, 'Why Chaucer calls FrankT a Breton lai', *PQ*, 51 (1972), 365-79, finds the alleged source 'belongs to a genre characterised by non-Christian morality' (noted Kaske, Robbins, p. 161).

55. This metaphor is literally realised in SecNT and touched on in MLT (see below pp. 92, 139, 141). The logical consequence of the religious position has been well noted by Payne (p. 164) as 'a moral statement which will be immediately apprehensible emotionally and nearly incomprehensible by any rational or intellectual faculty'.

56. Regularly noted, e.g. Burlin (p. 186) and David (p. 209). For unironic readings of the speech, see G.H. Russell, 'Chaucer: PrT,' in *Medieval Literature and Civilization: essays in memory of G.N. Garmonsway*, ed. D.A. Pearsall and R.A. Waldron (London, 1969), pp. 211-12; and F.H. Ridley, *The Prioress and the Critics* (Berkeley and Los Angeles, 1965), p. 34.

57. On maidenliness in the Clerk, see J. Mann, *Chaucer and Medieval Estates Satire* (Cambridge, 1973), p. 76 (and n. 112 for the same contrast with MillT); for a slightly different account of Nicholas's maidenliness, see Kolve (p. 166).

58. For a more sympathetic reading of this passage, see Burlin (p. 197); D. Brewer, *An introduction to Chaucer* (London, 1984), p. 227; and C.A. Owen Jr, '"A certein nombre of conclusiouns"', *ChR*, 16 (1981-82), 64.

59. On this point, see Manly–Rickert II, 475-6. N.F. Blake tacitly opposes metrical regularity as a sure indication of Ellesmere's greater authority, in 'Chaucer's text and the web of words', Rose, pp. 224-5.

60. On this point see Mann (1973) *passim*, Howard (p. 184), and Kolve (p.219).

61. See Howard (p. 25), and Blake (pp. 373, 459). On SecN, see further Kean, II, 204-5 (as extreme a statement of the position as I have encountered); and David (p. 232) (entertaining but misguided). A simpler reading relates the references to their assigned speakers in *CT*: so Eliason (p. 148); Whittock (p. 251, n. 1); Norton-Smith (p. 99, n. 28); and P.M. Clogan, 'The figural style and meaning of SecNT', *M&H*, NS 3 (1972), 214.

62. See Kolve (p. 287 and n. 61) for comment on such views. Whittock (p. 106), reckons the word 'prose' 'an ironic remark emphasising the tale's greater seriousness after the preceding fabliaux'; Elliott (p. 397) argues persuasively that it refers to the speaker's normal practice, rather than to the offered tale.

63. *Chaucer and the Shape of Creation* (Cambridge, Mass., 1967), ch. 6. For other examples, see Kolve (p. 260 and n.) (the Cook's three appearances in *CT*); C.D. Benson, '"Their telling difference": Chaucer the pilgrim and his two contrasting tales', *ChR*, 18 (1983-84), 64-5 (the narrators of Gen Prol and *Thop* and *Mel*); and Brewer (1984), pp. 68, 137, n. 12 (the former on the Monk, the latter on the Squire).

64. On memory as the organising principle of *CT*, see Howard (pp. 139 ff.).

65. Howard (pp. 154, 169 ff.) has responded as well as any to the notion of 'group' as the key to Gen Prol and to the whole work.

66. See Howard (p. 156) for the two narratives as symbolic expressions of one another. My point is closer to that of Boitani (p. 240): 'the narrator of the pilgrimage uses memory, the pilgrim uses observation.' Norton-Smith notes, in the apparent objectivity of the Host's portrait of Chaucer in Prol *Thop*, a warning to the reader 'that any mechanical matching of prologue portrait to a given tale had better be revised' (p. 146).

67. For fuller comment on Gen Prol, see Mann (1973), and Norton-Smith (pp. 112-15).

68. For comment on these terms, see A.J. Minnis, 'Late medieval discussions of compilatio and the role of the compilator', *Beiträge zur Geschichte der deutschen Sprache und Literatur*, 101 (1979), 388-91, 408-16; incorporated in Minnis, 1984 (pp. 94 ff., 190-210).

69. I find here ironic echoes of PrT, in respect both of the Prioress's memory of the infant St Nicholas, and — so far as the Manciple's relation with his mother is concerned — of the relation of the 'clergeon' with his mother (see further below pp. 77-8). Norton-Smith (p. 152) sees 'mi sone' in this speech as ironically applied to the Cook.

70. Elliott (p. 371) notes that 'such labelling of the speech of his characters goes back to Chaucer's earliest poems.'

71. Cf. Howard (p. 108): 'all speak in verse. But we perceive them as speaking differently ... as we have tales within a tale, we have styles within a style.'

72. According to Howard (p. 84), 'one characteristic of the style is that we are often not able to tell what voice we hear, and are not meant to.' At the same time, 'unimpersonated artistry' (Howard's term, and see his Index sv for examples) provides a tool, in principle, for distinguishing the poet's voice from those of his fictional creatures. For an instance of the theory in practice, see ibid. (p. 362 n. 24); for criticism of it, the exciting paper of H. Marshall Leicester Jr, 'The art of impersonation: a general prologue to *CT*', *PMLA*, 95 (1980), 213-24.

73. I have in mind here Kolve (1984), developing an earlier article, 'Chaucer and the visual arts', Brewer (1974), pp. 309 ff. For Kolve, 'the image — in itself and in configuration with other images in the context of the poem — [is] the essential mode of poetic expression' (this phrase is Green's, Bethurum, p. 122). In spite of the caveat (Brewer (1974), p. 313) that a proper understanding of the image requires ' the sound of those words, the level of diction, the harmony of rhyme and metre, and the emphasis conferred by accent and rhythm and pause' (and cf. Bethurum, p. 132) the approach seems to work best with a narrative which appears to tell itself and reveals little sense of a speaking voice (so Kolve's study of SecNT, Rose, pp. 137-74). I am less happy with its application to a strongly voiced narrative like MLT (Kolve, ch. 7; and cf. my ch. 6 below). A correction to this partial reading would place more emphasis on 'voice'; see, for example, R.O. Payne, 'Chaucer's realization of himself as rhetor', *Medieval Eloquence*, ed. J.J. Murphy (Berkeley, Los Angeles and London, 1978), pp. 275-6, 284; Leicester, *PMLA*, 95, 213-24; and Howard pp. 63 ff.

74. So, for example, R.M. Jordan, *Chaucer and the Shape of Creation: the aesthetic possibilities of inorganic structure* (Cambridge, Mass., 1967) (p.206); and E. Salter, *KnT and ClT* (London, 1962), p. 62.

75. Like other inconsistencies in the tales (see above, p. 19-20 and nn. 61-2), these have been explained regularly as the traces of earlier versions incorporated virtually unchanged into *CT*. An actual audience is then made responsible for these eccentric features: so Eliason (p. 67) on PhysT, though he does allow that 'the occasion ... may be fictitious'; M.Giffin, *Studies on Chaucer and his Audience* (Quebec, 1956), on MLT, pp. 68 ff., 77, 86; 'Chaucer's audience: a discussion', *ChR*, 18 (1983-84), 177. Other 'occasional' performances — notably, sermons — will betray their origins in this way: see Owst (1961), p. 156; Coleman p. 173; and *Middle English Sermons*, ed. W.O. Ross, EETS OS 209 (London, 1940), sermon 39 and comment pp. xxxvi-vii. It is not necessary to invoke an actual audience to account for these features. Several of the stories in Robert Mannyng of Brunne's *Handlyng Synne* ed. F.J. Furnivall, EETS OS 119 (London, 1901) show a similar specificity of application. Two stories about the relations of parents and children end with an address to the children and their mothers (11. 1285-8) and fathers

(5033-40) among the audience; another about an unjust judge, with an address to judges (5481-8); one about a converted usurer, to usurers (5937-42). For an interesting variant of the pattern, see *Jacob's Well*, ed. A. Brandeis, EETS OS 115 (London, 1900) (a countess damned for pride furnishes the occasion for address to 'ȝe poore folk þat are prowde': p. 81). In other words, this particular feature is to be explained, when it occurs in *CT*, as a device appropriate to the telling of an exemplary religious tale.

76. E.g. I, 1201, 1380; VIII, 78; cf. Eliason, pp. 69, 147, 227; Kolve, p. 14. A related inconsistency concerns the Knight's failure to keep objective distance between himself and the object of his narration (I, 1918, 1995). In visionary literature, like *HF* 142 ff., or *Purgatorio* X, we should find this inconsistency matter for praise. (On the latter, see Thorlby, 'Dante's *Divina Commedia*', Daiches-Thorlby, p. 609.)

77. Cf. Brewer (1984), pp. 104-5 for an account of three interacting 'dramatic levels of speech': the traditional story (e.g. NPT) 'tells itself' moment by moment 'through' Chaucer, the Nun's Priest and Chauntecleer. This view makes the impossibility of distinguishing the voices the real point of their use. Writers therefore regularly compare the characters in the fictions and the narrators of the fictions, sometimes reading the one as a psychological projection of the other. I prefer, so far as possible, to keep the levels separate.

78. In practice, therefore, except when given clear indications to the contrary by the text, I shall formally credit each voiced level of the fictional realm where possible — Chauntecleer, the Nun's Priest, the pilgrim narrator, the source, the tradition (one might call this approach 'Jordan upside-down'). The labels I assign to each such level are both a convenience and a necessary concession to the fictional realm. (On this point and the preceding, see also Leicester, *PMLA*, 95, 218.) I ought also to admit that the pull of the traditional reading — tales told by 'characters' authorised by their portraits in the cast-list — is strong, and I cannot swear always to have resisted the lure.

79. Such inconsistency occurs when I refer to Chaucer as the author of MLT, and similarly when I credit authors of other frame narratives cited for comparative purposes — notably Jean de Meun, Boccaccio and Gower — with their own framed fictions.

80. On this point, see comments by e.g. Benson, *ChR*, 18, 61; Leicester, *PMLA*, 92, 221; Norton-Smith, pp. 116 ff. Elliott (pp. 109, 400-10) offers a categorisation of religious and secular tales according to their use of words like 'thing', 'expounden', 'doctrine' and 'laude'. Voicing is always more than a question of individual words; still, the examples are a pointer in the right direction.

PART ONE

THE NARRATOR AS TRANSLATOR

'I am the handmaid of the Lord',
said Mary (Luke 1:38)

2 THE CLERK'S TALE

The Clerk's tale is important not just as a very good instance of a particular type of religious story, the allegorical exemplum, but also because the exemplum focuses most clearly of all literary forms the tension between the content and meaning of a narrative.[1] And since this tension is a vital and informing principle of religious art, we do well to begin our study of the religious stories of *The Canterbury Tales* with that of the Clerk. The logic of the exemplum, like that of a detective story, is most clearly revealed in its ending, where it presents, almost as an appendix, a single and authoritative interpretation of the narrative; and, to change our metaphor, runs to ground the many hares which it has started.[2] Throughout the story the writer scatters significant clues to the meaning, most evident when the narrative sacrifices plausibility and coherence to foreground an unexpected element by overt recourse to traditional symbolism.[3] But the progress to this single reading is not smooth or direct.[4] If the writer reveals too great an interest in the narrative for its own sake, his conclusion will appear forced and false. Yet if he focuses too sharply on the clues in his narrative, he may produce a clear and single message, but no very interesting story.[5] The exemplum works precisely in the degree that the story and its formal interpretation are seen to challenge one another, and so enlarge our understanding of, or feeling for, the linked realms which we may experience as opposed: flesh and spirit. The Clerk is very candid about the difficulties he has faced in his story. According to the epilogue, he has told the story for the single purpose of encouraging people to 'be constant in adversitee' and 'receyven al in gree that God us sent'. God has both made and redeemed us, and therefore has a twofold right to test our love for him. The story of a peasant girl married to a nobleman, tested cruelly by him and 'so pacient/ Unto a mortal man' that eventually he restored her fully to his favour, is thus a clear exemplum of our need to put ourselves under the governance of God (IV, 1145-62).

The clues to this reading are scattered liberally throughout the work. The marquis rules over a fertile and secluded valley, where the cares of his ancestors have found tangible expression in the fine buildings they have left and the obedient and loving service of his subjects (59-67). Entreated by them to marry, and invited to accept their offer to choose him a wife 'born of the gentilleste and of the meeste' (131), he yields to the entreaty, but declines the offer, on the grounds that 'bountee comth al of God' (157). He thus demonstrates — what will prove most important for the narrative — his moral authority over them. As we shall see, the people 'have no greet insight/ In vertu' (242-3). Even when he has promised to marry, they are anxious for him to name a day, because they do not trust him to keep his word (179-82). On the wedding-day they are still in the dark about his choice, and give voice to private fears that he is deceiving them all (246-52). Only after the event do they recognise the wisdom of his choice (400 ff.). Later still, they waver in their loyalty to him when he appears to have acted first badly, then wisely. Their vacillation is a necessary element in the presentation of the marquis as an emblem of the divine ruler.

Walter's moral authority is further stressed by his choice of the peasant girl, Grisilde, for his bride. We have already seen her through the eyes of the narrator. He finds her life an expression of the very life of Christ, whose exemplary virtue, like hers, was hidden by the circumstances of a poor upbringing:

> Amonges thise povre folk ther dwelte a man
> Which that was holden povrest of hem alle;
> But hye God somtyme senden kan
> His grace into a litel oxes stalle
>
> (204-7; cf. Luke 2: 6-7)[6]

This picture is reinforced by the account of the first year of her marriage. Grisilde continues to grow in grace and goodness (395, 407-10). She so endears herself to the people by her virtuous behaviour (400) that the mere sight of her makes them love her (410-13). People travel great distances from 'many a regioun' nearby just to look at her (414-20). They can scarcely credit he~ humble origins:

> it ne semed nat by liklynesse
> That she was born and fed in rudenesse
> As in a cote or in an oxe-stalle
> But norissed in an emperoures halle.
>
> (396-9, cf. 168)

Similarly, they reckon 'that she from hevene sent was ... peple to save and every wrong t'amende' (440-1). Every detail of this description is modelled on the life of Christ, born, like Grisilde, 'in a cote or ... oxe-stalle', and like her, 'norissed in an emperoures halle', that court of heaven whence people thought she had come. Like her, too, Christ 'increased in wisdom and in favour with God and man' (Luke 2:52); preached so graciously that people could scarcely credit that he had a human father (Luke 4:22); and, according to legend, was so beautiful that the very sight of him gave ease to those who suffered.[7] Like the vacillating bystanders, the virtuous Grisilde serves in this opening part of the story to focus more clearly Walter's superior moral discernment, and thus reinforces his emblematic role. Walter, who marries 'lowely — nay, but roially' (421), is a clear emblem of the divine condescension, active most obviously in the Incarnation, and present as God's unfailing response to prayer. (Hence, for instance, the speech of the people's representative, urging Walter to marry, includes the Biblical phrase, 'and lat youre eres nat my voys desdeyne' [98; cf. Ps. 130:2] so that this detail makes him explicitly a type of the faithful Christian.)

The preliminaries to the marriage focus this emblematic role yet more clearly by making Grisilde a type of the Virgin Mary at the Annunciation. Having heard the news of the coming marriage, but innocent of any sense that 'for hire shapen was al this array' (275), Grisilde has hurried home from the well where she has been fetching water. She is planning to complete her household chores as quickly as possible so that she may stand with her fellows at the door of the cottage to welcome the new bride as she passes. The unexpected summons by the marquis, and the equally unexpected offer of marriage, disturb her and her father: the father, we later learn, because he fears for his daughter's future in such a marriage (904-10); Grisilde, because 'she nevere was to swiche gestes woned'(339). Nevertheless, both are quick to express obedient assent (319-22, 359-64), even though Grisilde reckons herself unworthy of the honour (359).

Now, several details of this narrative, notably the well from which Grisilde is returning, have their ultimate origin in a set of folktales dealing with problems faced by a human being who fell in love with a God.[8] Nevertheless, their immediate origin, and source of their significance, is the Gospel account of the Annunciation (Luke 1:26-38), as elaborated by later commentators and developed in Apocryphal traditions. One tradition has it that the Annunciation took place beside a well; another, that the humility of the Virgin drew God to become incarnate in her. So humble was Mary that she did not expect to become the mother of God, and prayed only that she might be permitted to serve the virgin who would receive that great grace. Even when the angelic salutation promised it to her, she regarded herself as unworthy of it, even though she knew that all things were possible with God. Like Grisilde, too, she reacted with fear to the angelic salutation because of its unaccustomed form: she had never before met an angel in human shape. The accumulation of these details clearly supports an emblematic reading of Grisilde, and implies a divine role for Walter.[9] Grisilde's acceptance of Walter's offer generates another action of profoundly symbolic meaning: her old clothes are removed and she is invested with royal attire (372 ff.). She later interprets this act (654-6) as the symbolic abandonment of her will, and acceptance of the 'plesaunce' of Walter. This moment also reminds us of the transformation of the faithful soul in heaven when it is clothed in what St Paul calls immortality (I Cor. 15:53-4); it also recalls the Assumption and Coronation of the Virgin, a subject immensely popular in art of the late middle ages.[10] All the signals, then, seem to be pointing in the same direction; Grisilde is an emblem of the faithful Christian, and Walter an emblem of the wisdom and condescension of God.

The harmonious relation between God and his creation, explicitly symbolised by the relation of Walter to his subjects and by his marriage to Grisilde, is also suggested by another feature of the narrative. Walter does not go outside of his secluded kingdom to find a wife; nor, though they recommend him to choose a noble woman, do his subjects urge him to look outside his own domain. Instead, he goes to a village which represents his kingdom in humble miniature: it is 'delitable' (199; cf. 62), and those who work the earth live well on its 'habundance' (203; cf. 59). The logic of this landscape within a landscape, if one may call it that, is the coexistence of greater and lesser worlds. This landscape thus speaks to us of the dependence of the human on the divine; of the former's limited but real autonomy; and of the certainty that man belongs to God, and will finally be united with Him. (To be sure, we could also read it more simply as a comment about housewifely dependence: a view which, as we shall see, the narrator appears to share.)[11]

This harmonious idyll, however, is not the main theme of the work. As the epilogue shows, the story focuses not so much on a relationship which brings master and servant together, as on the ways in which the servant experiences, and responds to, the initiatives of the master: God,

> Er we were born, knew al oure freletee;
> And for our beste is al his governaunce,
> Lat us thanne lyve in vertuous suffraunce.
>
> (1160-2)

Grisilde and her father know that their best must be 'as [him] best thynketh' (353). They show their 'vertuous suffraunce' in their ready acceptance of Walter's marriage plans. For his part, he insists that they will neither 'grucche ne stryve' against his choice (170); for theirs, they express that total identification with his will (319-22, 360-1) which he had earlier demanded (311-12). Whatever the relation of these early moments of the story to the epilogue, though, it seems clear that they serve primarily to facilitate an emblematic reading of the rest of the story, and prepare us for the unequivocal interpretation offered by the epilogue. The wedding contract prepares us directly for these later developments. Just as Walter demanded acceptance of his will in the matter of choosing a wife, so he demands of Grisilde, once she is his wife, the same unquestioning acceptance of his actions (351-7). Though terrified and ignorant of the full import of his words, she agrees to his demand:

> And heere I swere that nevere willyngly,
> In werk ne thoght, I nyl yow disobeye,
> For to be deed, though me were looth to deye.
>
> (362-4)[12]

She does not have to wait long for an occasion to carry out her promise. Within a year she has borne Walter a daughter. Walter, we learn, has already tested her faithfulness, not just in response to the offered marriage but in a time of testing immediately afterwards. What those tests were the story does not tell us, but Grisilde has come through them all: 'he hadde assayed hire ynogh bifore/ And foond hire evere good' (456-7). It is one thing to profess obedience, though; another to be obedient when circumstances smile upon a person, as the text implies they did; still another to live out the implications of such a profession, when difficulties begin to mount.

The first test concerns their daughter. Shortly after the birth, the marquis comes alone to Grisilde at night in the privacy of her room and reminds her of her humble origins, which he trusts her new status has not made her forget (466-78). This preamble is itself a kind of test: of Grisilde's readiness to remember what she was. If Walter and Grisilde have not forgotten her humble origins, no more, according to Walter, have his nobles. They can scarcely brook their subjection to one so basely born; if anything, their attitude has hardened since the birth of her daughter (479-85). And since Walter must always satisfy the legitimate demands of his people (after all, he married to satisfy them) he must do something about the daughter to bring 'reste and pees' to the community. He has no stomach for what he must do. He will, however, do nothing without first informing her. Whatever happens, he requires her, as she had promised, patiently to accept his decision (486-97). This speech is the more plausible because it reflects a truth about the people which the reader has already seen (their fickleness and self-regard) and because it cunningly reworks elements in the speeches of Walter and the people's representative before the marriage in Part I. Then, even though his people assured him that marriage was a 'blisful yok/ Of soveraynetee, noght of servyse' (113-14), Walter professed to resent the 'servage' of marriage (147); now, they resent their own 'servage' (482). They desired rest from their anxieties about the succession (112). He satisfied them by the marriage, but that very fact now constrains him if he wishes to 'lyve ... with hem in reste and pees' (487); consequently, he cannot now act as a free agent. What best he may do for his daughter must be 'as [his] peple leste' (490). Walter, then, arms himself, like Satan in *Paradise Lost*, with 'necessity, the tyrant's plea', to justify his actions against an innocent. (The testing of Grisilde will develop an exact parallel with the testing of another holy figure by Satan, that of Job.) Like other figures so tested, Grisilde could recriminate against the marquis, or against the inconstancy of the people; yet Walter's affected reluctance to take action, and professed willingness to consult with her, even though he tells her nothing of his immediate purposes, provide a reassurance that all may be well.

Grisilde has learned enough about Walter, after a year of marriage, to reply without any sign of anger (498-500), or with any of the fear that marked her response to the original offer of marriage (358). Unlike the people of Part I, whom Walter cunningly offers as a justification of his own behaviour and a possible model for her own, Grisilde does not offer her loyalty conditionally. In a speech which consciously develops her earlier words of acceptance, she declares that she loves the marquis for his own sake, offers up her child as a tangible sign of her dependence on him, and promises that not even death at his hands — that final test of her love, which she had asked to be spared (364) — will make her change. She gives no sign of the isolation she feels facing the test. Yet he comes to her alone, and reinforces her sense of absolute dependence on him by removing a subsidiary prop, the good opinion of the nobility. Nor does he explain his purposes; he merely reminds her of the context of her original promise. The familiar landmarks are all swept away; she has only her trust in the loving purposes of her lord to sustain her.

In the light of her profession of faith, the marquis commissions a servant, 'a maner sergeant' as loyal to him (519-21) as Grisilde has promised to be (he 'loved and dradde' Walter (523) even as Walter's subjects do (69)). This servant must go to Grisilde, take the child, and make her think that he has orders to kill it (533-6). He does so. In mitigation, he pleads the same necessity as drove Walter to his actions (527 ff.). Grisilde must know better than most, he says,

> That lordes heestes mowe nat been yfeyned;
> They mowe wel been biwailled or compleyned,
> But men moote nede unto hire lust obeye,
> And so wol I.

> (529-32)

The servant's expressed awareness of the arbitrary powers of great men is also providing a further occasion for testing Grisilde. One might expect her, if not to curse God and die like Job, at least to utter some reproach. Everything conspires to make her think her child will be killed. The servant has a bad reputation (540); what he says does not inspire confidence (541); the meeting is taking place in the dead of night (542). Nevertheless, Grisilde 'neither weep ne syked/ Conformynge hire to that the markys lyked' (545-

6). The obvious tests, that is, turn out to be a façade for the more important ones.[13]

That obedience is costly for wife and mother — that natural instincts are in conflict with her vow of obedience to her husband — is tellingly suggested by a few details. Grisilde does not at once reply to the sergeant's proposal (547), almost as if she is struggling to gain control over her reactions. When she does reply, she asks only for such favour for her child as is consistent with the expected execution of her husband's purpose; she asks to be allowed to bless the child before she is taken away, lays her in her lap and soothes her.[14] Then she asks that the body should be buried somewhere where 'beestes ne no briddes it torace' (572). This moment owes much to that icon of innocence betrayed, the massacre of the Innocents; elements of the Pietà enter into it as well.[15] But perhaps the best instance of Grisilde's victory over natural feelings in this passage comes when we hear her speaking to the sergeant 'so as he was a worthy gentil man' (549): investing with gentility, because he is obeying the command of her lord, a man of whom 'suspecious was the diffame' (540). Although her child will be, as she thinks, sacrificed, it is she who is the lamb (538) — and that because in giving up her child without complaint she is actually sacrificing a symbol of her own will.[16]

The narrative appears, at this point, to be moving in a tragic direction; but we ought to remember that Walter has taken his cue for the pretended murder from Grisilde's own words, and that he has acted until now as a symbol of the divine wisdom. We are therefore hardly surprised that the next episode (580-96) carefully defuses any tension, and shows him acting for purposes which, though we do not understand them, we may trust are benevolent. He commissions the sergeant to take the child, carefully swaddled 'in a cofre or in a lappe' to Bologna, where his sister lives. The sister must be prevailed upon 'this child to fostre in alle gentillesse', concealing her identity from everyone. We trust Walter the more readily at this point because his actions continue to inhabit the same emblematic context active in the earlier episodes of the betrothal and marriage. Far from acting like Herod and massacring the child, he has spirited the child to a secret destination, even as Christ was taken by his parents to Egypt to escape from Herod, in response to a command from God (Matt. 2:13-16).[17] And the child whose parentage will thus be a source of general wonder (594-5) — a detail whose full import will be realised only later in the story — repeats the emblematic function of Grisilde herself, one whose humble origins could scarcely be credited.

Like Grisilde's role in the narrative, that of Walter is not just symbolic. Though publicly he presents a 'drery ... cheere' both to Grisilde and to the sergeant (514, 79), he experiences the same conflicting emotions as everyone else in the story: joy and amazement at her constancy (512); an eager desire to see how she copes with her new situation (598-602); more important, a 'routhe' (579) which, at one point, almost deprives him of speech (892-3). His emotions are the more striking by comparison with those of Grisilde. In the present episode we depend for our knowledge of Grisilde's feelings on the detail of her 'sad face' (552; 'sad' probably carries the meaning 'serious' here[18]) and the suggested comparison of her feelings with those of a nurse or mother:

> I trowe that to a norice in this cas
> It had been hard this reuthe for to se;
> Wel myghte a mooder thanne han cryd 'Allas!'
> But nathelees so sad stidefast was she
> That she endured al adversitee.
>
> (561-5)

Set against the movement of feeling in Walter, her emotional steadfastness almost makes her, at this point, an emblem of the divine. At all events, it brings the two characters together as complementary expressions of the divine nature, the God who does and suffers all things equally.

The next stage of the narrative repeats this first one almost exactly, sometimes word for word. Four years pass, and Grisilde bears the marquis a son, amid general rejoicing (610-16). When the child is two years old — that is, the age invoked by Herod in the context of the massacre of the Innocents — Walter comes to his wife and tells her that now the whole country is discontented with the marriage. In particular, the birth of his son (626: Walter had spoken of the daughter (484) as Grisilde's) means that, when he himself dies, 'thanne shal the blood of Janicle succede/ And been ... lord, for oother have [they] noon' (632-3). Admittedly, his people have not made such complaints directly to him, but 'swich murmur' and 'swich sentence' cannot be ignored; they constitute matter for 'dreede', since they threaten not only his own, but the general, peace (634-8). Therefore, he will have to treat the son as he did the daughter, and once more he warns her in advance, so that she will not abandon herself to grief but keep patience (639-44). Grisilde's response is yet more exemplary. She repeats her earlier words (645) and develops them in a number of striking ways. She reminds him of the symbolic dispossession of her will, when she assumed the clothing he gave her, as a guarantee of her faithfulness now (654-8). (Just as a previous speech had prepared for the supposed death of her daughter, this passage prepares for the third and final test she will have to undergo.) If she could, she would gladly perform her lord's wishes even before he uttered them (659-61). She would gladly die if that would please him, for 'deth may noght make no comparisoun/ Unto youre love' (664-7: here too we note the development of a detail in the earlier speeches, which expressed a fear of death but accepted it as a possibility). She will even disavow her children, although his is the command that kills them, since she has no part in them but the pains of pregnancy and birth (648-51).

This constancy of hers runs against all modern notions. But we ought not to condemn it as a gross and sickly confection masking an unpalatable moral pill without reflecting that there were people in the Middle Ages who practised this role of saintly detachment in relation to their children, and that religious commitment, on whatever level, presupposes a detachment from the cares and pleasures of the world and a loving subjection to the will of God.

The actual 'murder' echoes the earlier one so closely —

> This ugly sergeant, in the same wyse
> That he hire doghter caughte, right so he,
> Or worse, if men worse kan devyse,
> Hath hent hire sone —
>
> (673-6)

that the narrative dispatches it summarily in two stanzas. Although the narrator gives our imagination free rein in the phrase 'or worse, if men worse kan devyse', he gives us very little actual detail to build on. There is an 'ugly sergeant' contrasted with a beautiful child, and a mother who 'no chiere maade of hevynesse' (678); and the servant's silence contrasted with the mother's prayer that the child's body be buried to protect it from wild beasts (684; cf. 573); and that is all. If Grisilde's 'chiere' is at all at odds with her inner feelings, so is the apparent harshness of the sergeant, compared with the gentleness with which he carries the child to Bologna (686). As before, Walter watches his wife carefully for any sign of change in her, 'but nevere koude he fynde variance' (710). Did he not know how she loved her children, next to him, 'best in every wyse' (695), he might succumb to the temptation of supposing her not only indifferent to them, but even secretly glad of their disappearance (687-95). In fact, she takes more pains to show her love, and 'ay the forther that she was in age/ The moore trewe, if that it were possible' (712-13). It seems as if they do, indeed, have only the one will (715-16).

Hence the logic of the final test, to separate Grisilde not from her life but from the one whose will she has learned to share and identify herself with. Walter does this by means of a forged Papal bull which permits him to divorce Grisilde and take a new wife. The alleged reason — 'to stynte rancour and dissencion/ Bitwixe his peple and hym' (747-8) — has been carefully prepared for in the earlier encounters; so too the very words the Pope is alleged to use: 'as for his peples reste/ Bad hym to wedde another, if hym leste' (741-2; cf. 111-12, 489-90). The commoners, who have earlier failed their own test and taken as proved the villainy of their master (722-32), now take equally for granted the truth of the bull (750-1), and approve their master's new choice. Their reaction is contrasted with that of Grisilde. Although she maintains the same constant disposition (754-9), it may be guessed, and the narrator does not hesitate to do so, that 'hire herte was ful wo' (753). Of course, she does not know, as we do, that Walter is having the two children brought back, their identities still kept secret (765-70), and is providing the daughter with all the trappings of a new bride. The previous part of the story (III) had ended on the twin notes of Grisilde's patience and the secret removal of the daughter to Bologna; this part (IV) ends similarly, with the secret return of the two children. The final and longest part, therefore, Part V, begins with the anticipation of their coming,[19] and provides Grisilde with a more painful and protracted period of testing than she has yet had to endure.[20]

Walter announces their coming, and hence the certainty of his divorce from Grisilde, at the very beginning of the section. This time he speaks to her, for the first time, 'in open audience/ Ful boistously' (790-1). For the first time, too, he declares himself well pleased with her virtue (792-4). But this praise, far from heralding better things, is merely the preamble to a restatement of the old dilemma and a final, dreadful, resolution. Walter reminds Grisilde of her humble origins (795) and his own 'servitute' (798). This 'servitute' has its origins not, as earlier claimed, in the constraints of marriage, nor in the humiliation which his nobles saw in his marriage to a peasant girl, but in the very obligations of governors towards those they govern (797-801). Unable to 'doon as every plowman may' (799), he must take another wife. He produces the consent of the Pope to guarantee his behaviour (802): a master-stroke which forces everyone, commons and Grisilde alike, to accept his decision, and, confirming the rumours which he has himself started, prevents public debate about the truth. Moreover, the new wife 'is comynge by the weye' (805). Let Grisilde, therefore, make way for her, and return to her father with her dowry, bearing the reverse with a strong and even heart (806, 11). After all, 'no man may alwey han prosperitee' (810).

As if realising that she has no greater test to face than this, Grisilde answers at greater length than ever before; where her earlier speeches were 1, 2 and 4 stanzas long, this one runs to 11.[21] As before (645), she tells him, what she has always known (814), that she was never worthy even to be his chambermaid, and has reckoned herself not his lady but only his humble servant. Consequently, she owes him thanks for the honours he has bestowed on her; having no other way to pay him for them, she will pray God to reward him. For herself, she will return home, there to live as a widow. (Grisilde's 'widowhood' is scarcely touched on in the story, but it speaks of the faithful soul's trust in God even in the face of his apparent abandonment of her. It takes its colour, as an emblem, from the many widows in the Old and New Testaments who assisted prophets and provided bystanders with an emblem of faithfulness.[22])

There is, however, a difficulty with his generous offer to return her dowry. Since she brought with her only her faithfulness and virgin nakedness, she has nothing of her own to wear when she leaves. Her old clothes might count as such a dowry, but will be hard to come by, both because they are 'moore of age/ By dayes fele than at hire mariage' (916-17) and because she did not bring them with her to the palace. Grisilde appreciates the symbolic appropriateness of returning naked, like Job, to her father's house (871-2; cf. Job 1:21). But she does not absolutely own her own body, and the shame of being so exposed to public gaze, though perhaps fit recompense for her unworthiness, will reflect not only on her but on the children whom she bore and the husband who fathered them (876-9). She is therefore forced to ask a favour for herself which is also a service to him: 'voucheth sauf to yeve me, to my meede/ But swich a smok as I was wont to were' (885-6). Grisilde's determination to find the sanction for her every action in the good will of her lord here comes as nearly into conflict with her own instinct for happiness and self-preservation as anywhere in the tale; we see her asking for the smock not just as a grace but almost as a reward for service. And, try though she will, she can hardly keep the note of complaint out of her voice. In an interruption to the orderly progression of her argument, as if her feelings insisted on breaking out, she reminds him how kind and noble his appearance, and his words, seemed on their marriage day (852-4). She offers a pointed gloss on his moralisings about the 'strook of Fortune':

> sooth is seyd — algate I fynde it trewe,
> For in effect it preeved is on me —
> Love is noght oold as whan that it is newe.
>
> (855-7)

(This reproach is the more unexpected and even, in one sense, unjust, because Walter never promised to be even in his treatment of Grisilde.) Lastly, she picks up the rhyme 'reste ... leste', earlier used to justify the exercise of Walter's will in relation to the well-being of the people (111-12, 741-2), to remind him obliquely of his own obligations to *her* well-being:

> For sith it liketh yow ...
> That whilom weren al myn hertes reste,
> That I shal goon, I wol goon whan yow leste.
>
> (845-7)

What follows is an emblem of that ultimate dispossession, the Crucifixion. So moved that he can hardly speak, Walter grants her request, and goes out. Then, in the presence of all, Grisilde strips herself down to her smock (just as, according to a later development of the Passion narrative, Christ stripped himself before his torturers)[23] and returns home. She is followed by a weeping crowd, who exclaim aloud against Fortune (897-8), even as a great crowd of mourners followed Christ on his way to Calvary (Luke 23:27).

In the midst of all this weeping and unbelief, her silence (900) generates the same emblem of constancy as the silence of Christ, contrasted with the noise and violence of his executioners. (So, for example, in the York play of the Crucifixion[24].)

Grisilde's father, hearing the noise of their approach, is convinced that his worst fears are being realised. If she found 'suspect' the coming of the sergeant to her (541), he has been 'in suspect' of the marriage from the beginning (905); but where she kept faith in spite of the appearances, he gives in to his fears at once. He 'curseth the day and tyme that Nature/ Shoop hym to been a lyves creature' (902-3). In so uttering the words of Job (cf. Job 3:3), he is continuing the identification of Grisilde with Job begun in her earlier speech. But there is a vital difference between his words and hers. She gets the words of Job to speak which show Job keeping faith with God; he gets the words of Job's despair. His despair on his own account contrasts strikingly with her faith on her husband's account. Just as, earlier, she was contrasted with Walter as an emblem of constancy, so she is now contrasted with her father. Her relation with her father is not that of Samson with his father in Milton's *Samson Agonistes*. There the unbelief of the father proves a spur to the son's recovery of faith. Since Grisilde has never publicly lost faith in her husband, that reading of the relationship of father and daughter is inappropriate here. Still, like Milton's hero, she finds it easier to remain constant in the face of others' recriminations than in the face of her husband's reasonableness.

The return home is a sort of symbolic burial (her father, weeping, covers her with her old robe) and a return to the hidden life of her beginnings. So far as she knows, with the death of hope, and her divorce from Walter, the time of testing has also ceased. Yet she continues to behave with exemplary self-control and modesty. Just as she seemed perfectly to accept the loss of her children, so now she gives no sign of remembering her 'heighe estaat', and reckons that she has received no offence (920-4). She can do this the more easily because 'in hire grete estaat/ Hire goost was evere in pleyn humylitee' (925-6); she never acquired the 'tendre mouth' and 'herte delicaat' (927) that go with rank, but retained the simple tastes of her early days (cf. 214-17). The episode ends with a passage added by Chaucer to his source, which gives the narrator the chance to expatiate on the symbolic identification of Grisilde with Job:

Men speke of Job, and moost for his humblesse ...
Ther kan no man in humblesse hym acquite
As womman kan, ne kan been half so trewe.

(932, 936-7)

If Grisilde goes further than Job or any other person (except Christ, never mentioned directly, but one of the chief models in the work), it is because she remained faithful to the end. Nevertheless, even Job, contend with God though he may, will be granted a happy ending: so too, we may hope, Grisilde. And so the tone of this last part undergoes a subtle change — at the point where some manuscripts begin a new part, Part VI — which helps to prepare for the happy ending: as a notable mark of this coming end, the narrator now leaves the story to tell itself without the help of his commentary.

The arrival of Walter's brother-in-law with the two children, and the general expectation of the coming marriage, lead Walter to summon Grisilde again to the palace. Taking his cue from her earlier profession of unworthiness even to be his chambermaid (819), he commands her, since she knows 'of old' what satisfies him, to see to the preparation of the house (960-6). This may seem the ultimate humiliation, but at least it marks a temporary end to the separation between Grisilde and Walter, and gives her the chance to do him a positive service; until now she has expressed her obedience only negatively, in taming the impulses of her own heart. Consequently, she undertakes the commission gladly, and, while urging the other servants 'to hasten hem', shows herself 'the mooste servysable of alle' (978-9).

And now, at last, in counterpoint to the labours of Grisilde, the wedding party arrives, and the crowd, Grisilde among them, rush to the gate to welcome the new bride. At this point Grisilde's isolation from all that might support her is complete. Even the crowd, who formerly approved her so warmly and so warmly lamented her casting off, are eagerly transferring their loyalty to the 'noveltee' of a new bride. They reckon her more beautiful and also younger (in which respect, at least, they are right); they think the new marriage will preserve the noble strain better than the first (988-91); they reckon Walter a wise man 'thogh that hym leste/ To chaunge his wyf, for it was for the beste' (986-7).

Not everyone is joining in the junketing, though. For the first and only time in the story, we hear a group of 'sadde folk',

shadowy figures whose existence this tissue of elegant fabrication
and cruel misunderstanding has never given cause to suspect (995-
1003). These 'sadde folk', at least, know the crowd for what they
are. Literally, the mob represents that 'strook of Fortune' which
Walter had counselled Grisilde to endure; a people 'delitynge
evere in rumbul that is newe', and, like the moon, given to 'wexe
... and wane'; they are full of noise, and careless of the quality of
their own utterance. The attitude of these 'sadde folk' to the crowd
contrasts with that of other 'sadde folk' in the story; and of the
narrator. Walter expects no great constancy from the people, and
makes use of their inconstancy in his testing of Grisilde, but is
nevertheless easy enough in his relations with them to be
approached directly by them in Part I. Grisilde no more shows her
sense of betrayal by the people than she recriminates against
Walter for 'sturdinesse' and lack of 'mesure' (622, 700).

As for the narrator, he finds the behaviour of the crowds
comprehensible and even forgivable: he uses the same phrase to
gloss their behaviour ('no wonder is') as he had earlier used to
justify Grisilde's amazement at an unexpected offer of marriage
and the incredible fact of her humility (337, 727, 750). The narrator thus creates a link between Grisilde and the people which the
latter are thoughtlessly repudiating. By contrast, the shadowy wise
ones, by their apostrophe, underline the distance between
Grisilde's quiet and patiently cheerful spirit and the noisy cheerfulness of the crowd. Their complaint effectively heightens her
isolation. If the people are voices from a comedy, the wise ones
come straight from stoic tragedy. Their presence here contrives —
and in a story where so much is contrived, I think they are among
the less successful creations — momentarily to disturb the overall
direction of the story, and suggest again, what we have scarcely
seen since the first test on Grisilde implied it, the possibility of a
tragic outcome. At all events, the narrator gives the 'sadde folk' no
further part in the story, and shifts his gaze to the welcome of the
guests by Grisilde. Just as the combination of her humble origins
and innate royalty of disposition had earlier amazed her subjects,
so now the guests are amazed that one so poorly clothed should
display 'so glad chiere ... swich honour and reverence, and ...
prudence' (1016-22). With no thought for her own appearance
(1011-22), Grisilde is serving the guests impeccably (1016-18):
she is particularly full in her praise of the new wife and her little
brother (1023-6).

As so often before, her words now give Walter his cue. Playfully, as if nothing hangs upon the question, he asks Grisilde for her opinion of his new wife. Possibly in the same spirit — for she has nothing to gain or lose by her answer — Grisilde warmly approves her master's choice and prays a blessing on the couple. In the same spirit, too — though the words might have a much sharper edge — she presumes for the first time to give Walter advice (1037-43). Let him not treat 'this tendre mayden' as he has done others, for, being more tenderly brought up, 'she koude nat adversitee endure/ As koude a povre fostred creature.'

And now, at last, the plot seems to have used up all its possible twists, and it is time for the knots to be untied and Grisilde to receive again all she had thought lost. In one sense, of course, the resolution is purely formal; the logic of the repeated test is not a resolution but the creation of an emblem of constancy.[25] In another sense, the final section has prepared us for the coming resolution by subtly changing the roles of both Grisilde and the marquis, in somewhat the way that a key change can do in music. The active role assumed by Grisilde in household affairs shows that patience is consonant with more than silent suffering and ritual expressions of farewell: patience, that is, is perfectly consonant with the 'bisynesse' (1008, 1015) of an active and ordinary service.[26] And the playful tone adopted by the marquis (1030) transforms those tones which he had previously assumed: tones which the unsteady multitude might read literally for a moment, and the *cognoscenti* harden into a dogma.

As with Shakespearean comedy, the moment of resolution takes place in utter silence and stillness.[27] Walter tells her 'this is ynogh' (1051; cf. 456) and 'hire in armes took and gan hire kesse' (1057). Wonder (1058) deprives Grisilde of all reaction: she cannot take in his words, and 'ferde as she had stert out of a sleep/ Til she out of hire mazednesse abreyde' (1060-1). Paradoxically, this resolution also goes some way towards undoing the work's tightly emblematic structure. Walter feels constrained not only to explain the plot to Grisilde, but also to defend himself against the misjudgement of the people (1072-5). Grisilde's mask of patient cheerfulness slips; she swoons twice over (1079 ff., 1098 ff.), weeps passionately (1082, 1084-5) and embraces her children with all the intense and tender feelings she has had, until now, to suppress (1081-5, 1100-3). The bystanders are so moved to tears by her emotion that they can scarcely bear to be close to her

(1105-6). At this point, Grisilde becomes a focus for all the tears which the narrative has so carefully suppressed. (Others' tears, as at 897 ff., were always placed relative to her quietness and neutralised by her self-control.) This disturbance to the emblem — or its replacement by another emblem, of maternal suffering[28] — is only momentary, like the disturbance created in the story by the appearance of the 'sadde folk'. Walter raises her from her trance; the crowd rejoices with her; she regains her steady countenance; and there is great 'cheere/ Bitwixe hem two, now they been met yfeere' (1107-13). Lastly, there is the ceremonial removal of her old clothes and her reclothing in royal ones (1114-20), and a celebration which eclipses that of the original wedding (1125-7). The idyll — for that it has now become once more — now draws to its conclusion (1128-34). The daughter and the son both have happy marriages; the son succeeds his father to the kingdom; and — a detail added to the original — Grisilde's father is brought to court for the rest of his life 'in pees and reste': that condition which Walter claimed to be advancing by his actions all through the work.[29]

Allowing, then, for a few expressions of a different order of experience — expressions principally of feeling, necessary if we are to believe in the characters as more than abstractions — the story appears to follow a clear and single line to a clear and single meaning: that man needs to put himself under the 'governaunce' of God.[30] Unfortunately, the message of the story is neither clear nor single. Our chief difficulties cluster round the presentation of Walter as an emblem of divine wisdom. Explicit evidence for this reading of his character, in the form of clear comment by the narrator to that end, is virtually restricted to the narrative of the betrothal in Part II:

> he noght with wantown lookyng ...
> but in sad wyse ...
>
> ... thogh the peple have no greet insight
> In vertu, he considered ful right ...
>
> Thus Walter lowely — nay, but roially ...
> ... lyveth ful esily ...
> A prudent man, and that is seyn ful seelde.
>
> (236-7, 242-3, 421, 423, 427)

As first presented to us, on the other hand, he is a very different figure:

> I blame hym thus, that he considered noght
> In tyme comynge what myghte hym bityde,
> But on his lust present was al his thoght.

(78-80)

At this point Walter's clearest affinities are with his fickle subjects: the 'sadde folk' accuse them of 'delitynge evere in rumbul that is newe' (997); the narrator accuses Walter of similar tendencies. The young Walter, that is, is an emblem of thoughtless devotion to the present object ('inconsideratio futurorum'). A certain inconclusiveness therefore inevitably attends the debate between Walter and the people's representative in Part I. Both sides preserve the appearance of an emblematic encounter between the subject and the sovereign (we have already noted the Biblical echo in the commoner's speech); but the fact that debate is possible between them necessarily reveals the limits of both points of view. If the commoner's understanding of marriage as a 'blisful yok/ Of soveraynetee' (113-14) is limited, Walter's is no less partial: 'liberte ... seelde tyme is founde in mariage' (145-6). At the same time, both speakers have an important contribution to make to the debate: the commoner, that time is the measure and death the end of human possibility; Walter, that God is the source of whatever humans can achieve (116-26, 155-8). Brought together, as a debate implies they must be, these separate views make up a single truth, that of the exemplum itself. (That is, the true meaning of an exemplum is to be found in the interaction of *all* its parts.)

The narrator's presentation of Walter, then, is inconsistent with the single meaning he later claims to find in him. He undermines this single reading most damagingly when he narrates the tests on Grisilde. In Part I he keeps a slight distance from the two protagonists, after the manner of satiric comedy. In Part II, by contrast, he identifies himself directly with the two protagonists in the way of romantic comedy. What follows, in Parts III–V, brings us almost into the realms of domestic, or sentimental, tragedy. Although the narrator continues to identify himself directly with Grisilde, he sets his face squarely, for the duration of the testing, against Walter. Immediately the testing begins, he enters with his own commentary. Far from being an emblem of the divine, Walter is merely a representative specimen of the monstrous regiment of tyrannical rulers (581), husbands (622, 698) and stubborn and unyielding people (701). We cannot expect the servants of such a man to be better than their master (521-2), and need not wonder that rumours of murder follow close after (727). What is to happen to Grisilde 'bifalleth tymes mo' (449), and is the worse because Grisilde's self-evident faithfulness has surely been amply demonstrated (456-7). The tests are therefore gratuitous ('what neded it': 457; cf. 461, 621); excessive (cf. 456, 622, 697); harsh and unbecoming ('yvele it sit' : 460; 'sturdy': 698, 700, 1049). Others may choose to praise Walter's 'subtil wit' (459) and appreciate that, far from being 'nedelees', such temptation had 'greet skile' (1152); but the narrator, at this point, is not one of them. In any case, those who praise the 'subtil wit' are men: they will read the story, as the Host appears to do, for its supposed confirmation of their actual or imagined relations with women. At the end of the tests, in a kind of coda, the narrator dissociates himself still further from the judgement of his peers. Men, he says, are always going on about the patience of Job, and clerics are very willing to praise him for his patience; but, though they have so little time for virtuous women, in truth,

> ther kan no man in humblesse hym acquite
> As womman kan, ne kan been half so trewe
> As wommen been, but it be falle of newe.
>
> (936-8)

The Clerk expects this misunderstanding of his story to be so prevalent that he has to dispose of it formally before revealing the true meaning:

> This storie is seyd, nat for that wyves sholde
> Folwen Grisilde as in humylitee
> For it were inportable, though they wolde.
>
> (1142-4)

Such behaviour is 'inportable' — cannot be borne.[31] An exemplum is not a psychological study whose findings can be applied to a hearer's situation, but a picture of the spiritual principles inherent in the processes of life: prophetic in the sense not of prediction but of proclamation.[32]

Unfortunately, the narrator can more easily criticise an imperfect reading than commit himself wholeheartedly to a reading of his own. He may seek to counter the view of the men in the audience by inviting the women to identify themselves with Grisilde (561-2, 696-700). This identification of one section of the audience (the women) with a protagonist who, it is reckoned, will engage sympathy by virtue of correspondences between her situation and theirs (rank, occupation, sex), is a common feature of *The Canterbury Tales*. Normally it is sought as a means of intensifying the experience of the narrative (so, for example, in the Man of Law's tale; see further below). Here it is being practised as a device to challenge an imperfect reading of the narrative (by the men). But the narrator does not remove prejudices simply by exposing them in others. There are always his own prejudices: the prejudices of a man and a cleric. They emerge in the tell-tale comments 'but it be falle of newe' and 'though they wolde' in the previously quoted passages; also in the concluding account of how Walter's son was also 'fortunat ... in mariage' (1137; cf. 422), though he didn't tempt his wife:

This world is nat so strong, it is no nay,
As it hath been in olde tymes yoore.

(1139-40)

This last comment, with fine and unconscious irony, repeats Grisilde's warning to Walter to treat his new wife more gently than he has treated her, since, 'fostred ... moore tendrely', the new wife 'koude nat adversitee endure' (1040-2). All three bring to the fore what the comments of the narrator in the central sections clearly implied, notions of time and choice as necessary elements in any interpretation of the work. Now, the exemplum, as such, inhabits an enclosed and self-contained world where time is largely symbolic. Any attempt to make a credible psychological narrative out of the temptation of Grisilde leads away from myth and symbol towards history. And history, according to the conservative narrator, is a process of decline from golden beginnings. The marriage of Walter and Grisilde was a 'strong' time. By implication, decline was already setting in in the next generation, when the son did not 'putte ... his wyf in greet assay'; and so it has continued down to our own time. This passage leaves crucially unanswered the question: What made this Golden Age so strong? Strong tests, or their strong endurance, or both? Is modern weakness to be seen in the inability of the husband to 'putte his wyf ... in greet assay', or of the wife to endure such an attempt, or both? A similar question arises when the narrator tells us that no man can be 'half so trewe/ As wommen been, but it be falle of newe.' What impact, we ask, has the march to modern times had on the constancy of the sexes? Has it made men more patient, or women less constant, or what? To put the questions like this is to see that they should never have been put in the first place.

More important, they did not need to be put. As an accidental consequence of the fragmentary form of *The Canterbury Tales*, the Clerk's tale comes with only a brief reminder of the larger context of the pilgrimage narrative, in the form of an exchange between the Host and the Clerk before the story begins, on the model of the earlier exchange between the Host and the Man of Law. As if fearful that in the midst of all the merrymaking, the Clerk's modest silence may represent a judgement on the moral and artistic standards of the group, the Host asks the Clerk to pitch his offering at a level, both literary and moral, acceptable to the group. The Clerk appears very willing to comply. He has a story, he says, learned from his master Petrarch. The Host has requested him to avoid 'heigh style' (18). The story he elects to tell was originally so written (1148); in particular, it begins with a 'prohemye' written in high style (41). The Clerk proposes to cut the prologue. His reasons for cutting his text, however, have nothing to do with deference to the Host's expectations. Indeed, he actively approves of the 'rethorike sweete' by means of which his master has 'enlumyned al Ytaille of poetrie' (32-3). He is cutting the prologue because it is too elaborate, and irrelevant to the matter in hand. That is, the Clerk is not so much responding to the Host as taking issue with his dead master concerning the best shape of the latter's work. This dispassionate exercise of editorial judgement has for object not the entertainment of pilgrims but the perfecting of a text. That is, the Clerk's obligations to his 'mateere' (55) are primary and absolute; his duties to his immediate audience secondary.[33]

Now, the story came to Chaucer from Petrarch (cited by the Clerk at the beginning and end of the narration, 27, 31, 1141, 1147) in conjunction with an anonymous French retelling of

Petrarch's version. Petrarch's version consciously reworks an earlier version by Boccaccio in *The Decameron*, where it features as the concluding story.[34] The logic of *The Decameron*, as is well known, is that of 100 stories told over 10 days by a group of wealthy young Florentines who have fled from plague-stricken Florence to the safety of a country villa. Storytelling is thus, by implication, a cultured and courtly pastime, on a par with dancing, singing and the other innocent and escapist pleasures of their sojourn in the country. Moreover — and this is one of the most inspired touches in the work — the stories are to illustrate a theme, set a day in advance by the leader for the day. A tale whose meaning is thus predetermined enacts the same tension between the narrative and its meaning as an exemplum generates, but brings that tension to the fore from the beginning. Such a prescription also allows for more attention to be given to the manner than to the matter of the tale; and it invites the narrator from the outset to adopt a conscious position relative to the present meaning of his narrative.[35]

It falls to Dioneo, who, most of all, represents the spirit of playful misrule in this idyll, to tell the story of Walter and Griselda. The chosen subject for the tales of the last day is 'those who have performed liberal or munificent deeds, whether in the cause of love or otherwise': the motive for this telling, to induce valorous behaviour and breed famous achievements (IX, 10; McWilliam, p. 731). Dioneo picks the tale for the purely formal reason that all the other tales of this last day have had noble heroes, and the marquis of his tale counts as such a person. At the same time, he argues, any other reading of the tale would strongly suggest its inappropriateness as an illustration of the theme; the hero's actions, 'even though things turned out well for him in the end, were remarkable not so much for their munificence as for their senseless brutality' (X, 10; McWilliam, p. 813). Dioneo blackens Walter's character very thoroughly. He stresses his careless youth, as also the glad eye he gives Griselda because of her beauty. What people reckon wisdom in him, his choice of Griselda, may have been only a fortunate accident. Dioneo also stresses the suffering which Walter's arbitrary behaviour causes Griselda. At each stage in the testing he shows her struggling with her feelings before she complies with the will of her lord.[36] All this leads Dioneo to find a very different meaning in the work from the one with which he started: 'celestial spirits may sometimes descend even into the houses of the poor, whilst there are those in royal palaces who would be better employed as swineherds' (ibid., p. 824). In the face of such meaningless and brutal treatment, he cannot but think Griselda should have found herself another lover.[37]

The story undergoes the first of its transformations at the hands of Petrarch. In a letter to Boccaccio accompanying his version of the story (Severs, pp. 290-2), Petrarch tells how he came by a copy of *The Decameron*.[38] Among its bawdier offerings, which for various reasons he was minded to excuse, he found several serious and edifying things. One story, the last of the set, pleased him so much that he committed it to memory and recited it to friends. It has since seemed good to him, and those who have heard his retelling, that the story should be offered to a wider audience than the original (since it was in Italian) could hope to reach. To that end, he has faithfully translated the story into Latin, making only slight changes to the wording consistent with the aim of producing such a translation. He has two reasons for undertaking the work, his love of the story and his friendship with the author. He now sends the new version, with thanks, to his friend, who may judge whether it has spoiled or improved upon his own work.

This letter has many important things to say about the criticism of a work of art: notably, that the right reading of a work depends on an awareness of the different contexts, or patterns of causality, that have combined to produce it (literary tradition, artistic ability, audience expectation). But the letter has a more immediate claim on our attention, in Petrarch's assertion that he has acted as a careful translator (the phrase comes from Horace), making only those minor changes to the original which the act of translation forces upon any writer. This claim so put is somewhat disingenuous. Boccaccio's meaning was inextricably bound up with his choice of narrative form: a story within a story on a pre-set theme. This form enabled Boccaccio to furnish his version of the story with two readings, and commit himself unequivocally to neither. Read in the light of its given subject, Dioneo's story tells of exemplary virtue on the part of Griselda and/or Walter; read in the light of the narrator's attitudes, it exposes a glaring gap between power and principle. When Petrarch removed the story from its context and made it a free-standing item, narrating it in his own voice, he lost the ironic possibilities of the Boccaccian form, and had to limit himself to one or other of its readings, or a new reading of his own.

He chose an exemplary reading: but not the one proposed by

the leader of the revels in *The Decameron*.[39] The latter had
provided a social and vaguely secular interpretation for the story;
Petrarch an explicitly religious, allegorical one. The hints for his
reading, paradoxically, came to him from Dioneo's version of the
story. Do what he could as a man of the world to create a plausible
psychological narrative independent of any formal religious frame-
work, Dioneo could not entirely do without conventional religious
symbolism. In his already quoted concluding remarks, therefore,
he made Walter and Griselda emblems respectively of the Prodigal
Son (cf. Luke 15:15) and the incarnate Christ (cf. Luke 2:6-7).
The latter figure seems to have given Petrarch the key to his own
view of the story. His retelling advances Dioneo's concluding
remark about Griselda to the point where she first enters the
narrative, so that her emblematic significance is clearly seen from
the very beginning; and it cuts Dioneo's unflattering reference to
Walter as a prodigal. Though, like Dioneo, he finds Walter's
behaviour more marvellous than praiseworthy, Petrarch reckons
the learned may be able to explain it, and judgement should be left
to them. Petrarch modifies Dioneo's presentation of Walter in
other ways, too, always with a view to making him an emblem of
the divine wisdom. Walter's 'inconsideratio futurorum' was,
according to Dioneo, only what you would expect of such a
person; according to Petrarch, it is a minor blemish in an otherwise
exemplary character, as noble in manners as in blood. Where
Dioneo saw Walter's interest in Griselda as frankly animal,
Petrarch insists that Walter looks upon Griselda not with youthful
lust but with the gravity of an old man: that is, as an emblem of the
incarnate Christ, who, as a child of twelve, astonished the Jewish
doctors with his wisdom (Luke 2:46-7).

This excursion into the most illustrious of the versions that
preceded Chaucer's shows, among other things, how literary traditions develop as the natural expression of a relationship between
one artist and another.[40] But I had a much simpler reason for presenting it. The Clerk acknowledges no obligation but to the
tradition, embodied in the person of his dead master, Petrarch.
Logically, therefore, like Petrarch's own retelling, his retelling must
both approve and challenge its original: let the original speak for
itself where it seems to work well, and modify it where it seems to
falter. As noted, the Clerk cites Petrarch at the beginning and end
of his retelling. At first, he opposes his judgement to that of his
master. Anyone reading Petrarch's prologue, he argues, will find it

at best marginal to the whole story. It merely describes the countryside round Saluzzo, and is a protracted and largely unnecessary piece of scene-setting. His summary of this prologue (42-51), and selective quotation from it at the start of the tale (57-63), bear witness to this conviction: Petrarch's prologue is merely a random collection of geographical items. The Clerk's confidence in his own judgement is, however, misplaced. As I read it, Petrarch's prologue carries an important weight of symbolism which dramatically enlarges our perspective on the religious dimension of the story. As he describes it, the happy valley of Saluzzo, a world in miniature, is joined to heaven both by the surrounding mountains and by a river which, rising in them, flows its length (a description which forcibly echoes Wordsworth's scene-setting in 'Tintern Abbey', and performs a very similar function[41]). This scene-setting effectively duplicates that in which we first meet Grisilde: a little village contained within Walter's kingdom and linked directly to his palace (by a highway, we infer). Now, the latter piece of scenery, we noted (above p. 40), assisted in the creation of an emblem of dependence and co-existence (Grisilde as Everyman to Walter's God); the former must function similarly too (Walter is now the Everyman figure, and God now symbolised by the enclosing mountains and the overarching sky). Obviously, Petrarch could not make much of this shift in Walter's emblematic role, in part at least because the isolation of Saluzzo, as a function of the plot, forced a concentration on Walter's Godlike role at the expense of his human one. Yet its presence in the narrative, in however undeveloped a form, makes a profoundly important contribution to the work's religious meaning: that same that we earlier observed (p. 45 above) when Walter reacts with a movement of natural feeling to the events he has instigated, and Grisilde, by contrast, reveals only her rocklike constancy. Walter's double role is readily paralleled in other religious narratives: most obviously, in the cycle plays, where Old Testament patriarchs receive commands from God, and then pass them on to their children. This dual role of the emblem establishes the interdependence of man and God, and, more importantly, points to man's limited, but real, autonomy under God. (This is not to say, of course, that a person will necessarily or even regularly *experience* his relationship with God in such beautifully harmonious terms. Life is not lived, for most of us, on that level of consciousness.)

The Clerk's reading of Petrarch's prologue, then, turns out to

be, at best, partial. The same partiality characterises his reading of
Walter's testing of Grisilde in the central episodes of Petrarch's
narrative. Ironically enough, Walter's dual role facilitated and
encouraged his misreading of Walter's character[42]. Reading the
emblem from a purely human perspective, for one element of its
complex meaning, he could hardly do other than blacken his hero.

The seeds of this critical reading of the hero were lodged in the
French translation that Chaucer was using in conjunction with
Petrarch's original.[43] Where, for instance, Petrarch left it to the
wise to judge of Walter's thoughts and actions, the French translation suggested that such judgements might be partial: and this
became the out-and-out condemnation in Chaucer — 'though som
men preise it for a subtil wit' (459).[44] Again, the Clerk's address to
the women in the audience (696-707), though originating in a
remark of Petrarch, owes its rhetorical force to the elaboration of
that remark into a question in the French text.[45]

The French version does not, however, authorise what happens
at the end of the tale. The narrator has faithfully translated his
author's closing words, which clearly expound the single, complex
meaning to be found in the story. Now, suddenly, he turns to the
audience, and commits himself unequivocally to the antifeminist
reading shared by his male readers and directly acknowledged by
him beforehand only in the inadvertent comment that women
could not imitate Grisilde even if they wanted to ('though they
wolde': 1144). The modern world (1164) — on one level the
unacknowledged theme of the retelling — will not bear comparison
with this mythical narrative: one can barely find 'in al a toun Grisildis thre or two' (1165: is there an echo here of the story of the
ten just men, in Gen. 18, on whose account God was persuaded to
spare the city of Sodom?) To the golden age of the narrative there
has succeeded a mixed and debased currency, mostly brass (1166-
8); fixed to their purposes, like Walter, women 'wolde rather
breste a-two than plye'. Faced by the usurped authority of this
monstrous regiment, the narrator takes refuge in irony (1170-6).
He calls on the Wife of Bath, the self-proclaimed authority in the
group, to license an envoy which will 'stynte of ernestful matere'
(1175) and return the pilgrims to the merriment the Host had
asked for (15). The envoy, of course, has the effect of confirming
both sexes in their *partis pris*. Since Grisilde is dead, and her patience with her, let no man look to treat his wife as Walter did, 'in
trust to fynde/ Grisyldis' patience (1181-2); and let the 'noble

wyves' demonstrate their prudence by being proud, noisy, angry, fearless and sensual (1183-1212). They need not fear that a man will write such lies about *them* as are related about Grisilde (1185-7).

This relativising, or undermining, of an exemplum by its ending is not without parallel in religious works. Robert Mannyng's vast collection of stories for confessors and penitents, *Handlyng Synne*, includes one so like the Clerk's tale as to give us pause. It tells (Furnivall 11. 1917 ff) of St Macarius and the two good women who lived in peace with their husbands. It concludes (1997-2008) that such women cannot now be found ('God wuld hyt were now so here!') Consequently, some writers have read the Clerk's envoy as if it were an address of this order[46]. There is, however, a great difference between the tone of Mannyng's envoy and that of the Clerk. A closer similarity exists, as I see it, between the Clerk's envoy and the ending of Ovid's *Ars Amatoria.* Books I and II of the *Ars* have instructed men in the art of seduction; Book III shows women how to turn the men's weapons against them. To read the Clerk's tale in this light is to see the sex war as a second, unacknowledged, theme of the narrative[47]: not at all the reading Petrarch was advancing.

The Clerk's tale, then, ends facing the opposite way to where it began. At first, it affected to ignore the claims of its audience in favour of the tradition: not the Host, but Petrarch, is to be the measure of the retelling. Increasingly, as it proceeds, it shifts the balance in favour of the audience. This involves the narrator in a sort of juggling trick, since there is no single audience view corresponding to the single view of the *auctour*, and a yawning chasm appears to divide the expectations of the sexes. (This very diversity of readings will reappear as a prominent feature of the last two tales in this study, those of the Pardoner and Nun's Priest.) In the event, the narrator plays a devious game, allowing his commitment to the male point of view to emerge only in ironic aside. By the end of the work, Petrarch's authority has been so undermined that it is necessary to recall it in order to support an interpretation in which the narrator seems to have lost confidence: and this interpretation is now firmly placed in relation to the authority of the audience, embodied not in the Host but in the Wife of Bath. Going through the motions of pleasing both *auctour* and audience — logic binds him to the former, instinct to the latter — the narrator contrives, actually, to satisfy neither: he preserves his own authority only by playing one side off against the other. This practice may be little more than a subtle form of the time-serving rightly rejected by the 'sadde folk' of the story. But it has several interesting side-effects. Producing a double reading of the tale, as did Boccaccio's original, the narrator makes the formal relationships of the tale an exact image of its content. For example, the debate between Walter and the commoner in Part I — whether Walter's marriage will be a sign of 'soveraynetee' or 'servitute' — has a clear echo in the open strife between the sexes in the epilogue: the terms of the one explain the battles of the other.[48] More important, this double reading of the story forces the conclusion that each such reading is, if distorted, a mirror-image of the other, and hence necessary to the total meaning of the work. Although the original *auctour* and the present audience appear to be at daggers drawn over the meaning of work, and although the two sexes are scarcely able to see one another, as they dig themselves more securely into their prejudices, each side needs the other for its understanding to be complete: which is, as we said, the burden of the exemplum. It may also be reckoned the burden of *The Canterbury Tales*.[49]

Notes

1. On ClT as a good instance of the type, see David (p. 159); and Salter (p. 38). J. Sledd, 'ClT: the monsters and the critics', *MP*, 51 (1953-54), 73-82, reprinted in Schoeck–Taylor, I, 160-74, finds (p. 173) that the tale 'neatly avoids the blunt opposition of mere sermon to mere story'. For a review of recent criticism of ClT, see D.W. Frese, 'Chaucer's ClT: the monsters and the critics reconsidered', *ChR*, 8 (1973-74), 133-46.
2. ClT is the only clear example of the genre in *CT*. For other examples, see *Gesta Romanorum*, ed. H. Oesterley (Berlin, 1872); Ross (pp. 77-82, 91-2); and Owst (1961), ch. 4.
3. On foregrounding (her word is 'heightening'), see Salter (1962), p. 55.
4. On the difficulties of the genre, see Howard p. 177 (on *Gesta Romanorum*), L.C. Ramsey, '"The sentence of it sooth is": Chaucer's PhysT', *ChR*, 6 (1971-72), 186, and A. Middleton, 'PhysT and love's martyrs', *ChR* 8 (1973-74), 27 (on PhysT); and Jordan p. 199 (on ClT).
5. Cf. comments by Cooper (p. 38) on the relation of tales and morals in *CA*.
6. Grisilde has regularly received notice as an emblem of Christ and (see further below) the Virgin Mary, e.g. Kean II, 126-8; and F.L. Utley, 'Folklore, myth and ritual', Bethurum, p. 94. For one of the fullest accounts, see F.L. Utley, 'Five genres in ClT', *ChR* 6 (1971-72), 217ff. The 'oxes stalle' of the quotation, an allusion to the Nativity, is Chaucer's elaboration of a reference in both Petrarch and Boccaccio (see further below pp. 59,61).
7. For the classic medieval view of Christ's great beauty, in an anonymous thirteenth-century text purporting to be written by a contemporary of Christ, see E. de Bruyne, *Études d'esthétique médiévale* (Brugge, 1946), I, 285-6; see also R.

Woolf, *The English Religious Lyric in the Middle Ages* (Oxford, 1968), pp. 63-4.
For the legend that Christ's appearance gave release from suffering, see *Revelationes Sanctae Brigittae* (Lübeck, 1492) (i.e. the *Liber Celestis* of St Bridget of Sweden, ob. 1373), VI, i: 'tanta pulcritudine preditus erat, vt quicumque eum inspiceret, consolabatur a dolore cordis quam habebat' ['he was so beautiful that anyone who looked at him was relieved from any heartache that he had']. Grisilde's beauty also parallels that of the Virgin Mary herself (on which latter, see Y. Hirn, *The Sacred Shrine* (London, 1912), p. 258; and Woolf, pp. 125-6.

8.   See J.B. Severs, *The literary relationships of Chaucer's ClT*, Yale Studies in English 96 (Yale 1942; repr. Hamden, Conn., 1972), p. 4. For further comment on the folk-tale origins, see Utley, *ChR* 6, 204ff.

9.   On the Annunciation beside a well, expressing 'a clear influence from the gospel of James' (i.e. the apocryphal gospel known as the *Protevangelium*), see Hirn (pp. 276-7); and G. Schiller, *Iconography of Christian Art*, trans. J. Seligman, 2 vols. (London 1971-72), I, 35. David (p. 165) and Miller (p. 152, n. 10) would see an echo of Gen. 24: 13-18; Utley, Bethurum, p. 94, of Gen. 29 (the latter is closer to the account in ClT; either or both may have influenced the *Protevangelium* account). On the Virgin's desire to become the handmaid of the mother of God, see the ps-Bonaventuran *Meditations on the Life of Christ*, trans. by I. Ragusa and R.B. Green (Princeton, 1971), p.11; *Ludus Coventriae*, ed. K.S. Block, EETS ES 120 (London, 1922), p. 72; and Woolf, pp. 142-3. On the Virgin's fearful reaction at the unexpected appearance of the angel in human form, a regular gloss on Luke 1:29 by patristic and medieval commentators, see Hirn (pp. 285-7), Block (p. 105), St Bridget, *Liber* I, x.

10.   See further Woolf, pp. 298-301.

11.   Compare the similarly-functioning temple (of Venus) in the garden (of Nature) in *The Parliament of Fowls*.

12.   David (p. 165) links these words to Christ's prayer in the garden of Gethsemane (Matt. 26: 39-44).

13.   A parallel of sorts with the testing of Sir Gawain, in *Sir Gawain and the Green Knight*, is sometimes noted (e.g. Utley, *ChR*, 6, 207 and n. 29).

14.   Salter (1962) p. 51 finds this human moment opposed to Grisilde's function as a religious emblem. But her evidence for this, that Grisilde '*begs* the sergeant to let her kiss the child instead of doing so spontaneously', seems to me to force the words of the text: Grisilde does not beg but — a very different thing — 'mekely ... preyde'.

15.   On the massacre of the Innocents, see below pp. 76-7; on the Pietà, Woolf pp. 392-4.

16.   Other writers — notably, Whittock (p. 145); Utley, *ChR* 6, 227; and A.C. Spearing, *Criticism and medieval poetry*, 2nd ed. (London, 1972), p. 99 — see in this moment an emblem of the sacrifice of Isaac by Abraham. The offered parallel does not convince; though both figures clearly represent obedience to God and the sacrifice of the will, Abraham is functionally active, Grisilde passive. See below, ch. VIII, n. 26, for a closer parallel with the sacrifice of Isaac.

17.   ClT does not at this point translate a detail found only in Petrarch, which reinforces the emblematic significance of the moment (for an edition of the Petrarch text, see Severs, ch. V, xiii-xiv, trans. Miller (pp. 138-51), or J.B. Severs, 'ClT', in *Sources and analogues of Chaucer's CT* (hereafter *SA*), ed. W.F. Bryan and G. Dempster (Chigago, 1941), pp. 288-331). According to Petrarch, *SA*, p. 314, the sergeant carried the child to Bologna upon an ass. The iconography of the flight of the Holy Family into Egypt regularly features Mary with the Christ child on an ass.

18.   On 'sad', see D. Brewer, 'Some metonymic relationships in Chaucer's poetry', (*Poetica* (Tokyo, 1, 1974), 1-20 reprinted in Brewer (1984), p. 43).

19. Some manuscripts, and some modern editions, but not Petrarch, create a sixth part at l. 939, possibly on the authority of a similar division — though at a different point in the story — in the anonymous French text used as a secondary source for CIT.

20. Cf. Ryding p. 91: 'in keeping with the principle of gradation, the final adventure must be the most perilous of all'.

21. Cf. Ryding, pp. 93-4, on patterning of speeches in the *Vie de St Alexis* ('repeated motifs arranged in a climactic order'); for another instance of the pattern in CT, see p. 90; for an ironic inversion, pp. 283-4.

22. For the obvious parallels in *CT*, namely PrT and NPT, see below pp. 77, 271-3.

23. So St Bridget, *Liber*, I, x: 'personaliter se vestibus exuit' ['he stripped himself personally of his clothes']. And compare Christ's stripping himself at the moment of the Crucifixion in the Old English 'Dream of the Rood' (l. 22).

24. For a similar effect in paintings of the Passion by Hieronymus Bosch, see *The complete paintings of Bosch*, intro. G. Martin (London, 1969), pls. 50, 62 (the paintings there reproduced are 'The crowning with thorns' in the National Gallery, London, and 'Christ bearing the cross', Musée des beaux arts, Ghent).

25. Cf. judicious comments by Jordan (p. 204): 'the reconciliation then is nominal rather than agonic ... the two [protagonists] are brought together by no inner propulsion ... but simply by the external demands of narrative structure.'

26. Writers sometimes miss this positive side to Grisilde's role (e.g. J.A. Yunck, 'Religious elements in Chaucer's MLT', *ELH*, 27 (1960), 252).

27. On this moment, cf. remarks of Ryding, pp. 121-2, on 'unprepared peripety' in the *Vie de St Alexis*.

28. This figure is treated more fully below, pp. 74-7.

29. Blake (Rose, p. 228), argues for the superiority of the Hengwrt reading of this detail: 'his wyues fader and his court he kepeth'.

30. That single meaning is reinforced by the narrator's use of a language and style appropriate to a religious tale. See important discussion of this point in Salter (1962) pp. 42-4.

31. On 'inportable', see Burnley p. 89, and, for an opposing view, Cooper p. 138 n. 23.

32. See further Sledd, (Schoeck–Taylor, I, 168-9), and general comments in Brewer (1984) pp. 42-3, 60, 64-6, 78. Even medieval readers sometimes missed this point. For contrasted contemporary readings of Petrarch's version, see Miller (p. 139), regularly noted by modern critics. Philippe de Mézières regarded Griselda not as a type but as a real person (see D.W. Robertson, Jr., 'WB and Midas', *SAC*, 6 (1984), 4 and n. 12). As Burlin notes (p. 143), the emblem is always easy to read literally and dismiss either as an intolerable fiction or as 'all too human in its apparent inhumanity'.

33. As Burlin notes (p. 144), Chaucer pays the Clerk 'the supreme compliment — unparalleled in *CT* except over the materials of his fiction'. Cf. Spearing (1972) p. 81, Huppé p. 139.

34. For editions of the Petrarch, see above n. 17; of the anonymous French rendering, *SA*, pp. 297-331, and Severs pp. 255-89; of Boccaccio, *Decameron*, ed. V. Branca, 3 vols (Naples, 1966) and modern translation, used for quotation here, *Decameron*, trans. G.H. McWilliam (Harmondsworth, 1972).

35. For comment on the *Decameron* — which Chaucer may not have known: see Cooper pp. 33-5 — see G. Almansi, *The Writer as Liar: Narrative Technique in the Decameron* (London, 1975); and other references, ch. I, n. 29 above.

36. McWilliam (pp. 818-20): 'albeit that she felt her heart was about to break'; 'secretly filled with despair'; 'with an effort beyond the power of any normal woman's nature, she suppressed her tears'.

37. Utley, *ChR*, 6, 216, 227, finds the Boccaccian version 'a strange mixture of pathos, realism and cynicism' revealing in Dioneo's cynicism 'ambivalence on the part of his author, who has chosen for the tale the noblest place of all in his hundred tales'.

38. For a translation of the letter, see Miller (pp. 137-8).

39. On Petrarch's fondness for exemplary narrative, see C.C. Morse, 'The exemplary Griselda', *SAC*, 7, pp. 59ff.

40. For briefer comment on these developments, see Utley, *ChR*, 6, 198-9, 202-3; see also p. 217 for the suggestive comment that Chaucer 'retains the drama and the realism of Boccaccio and the exemplum of Petrarch'. For another view of the relationship between Petrarch and Chaucer, see Morse, *SAC* 7, p. 81.

41. For further comment on this scene-setting, see Norton-Smith pp. 117-8.

42. In this literalminded reading of the emblem the Clerk is followed faithfully by many of his modern descendants. Thus Walter is the 'unconscious instrument' of divine providence (Kean II 125); embodies 'fate or cruel misfortune' and presents 'a psychological study of a man ... tempted ... to try and play the role of God' (Whittock, pp. 144, 7); is an emblem of the prodigal (M.J. Carruthers, 'The lady, the swineherd and Chaucer's Clerk', *ChR* 17, 1982-3, 221-34); is identified with the people he governs (Carruthers p. 226) and falls, like them, under the domination of Fortune (B. Bartholomew, *Fortuna and Natura: a reading of three Chaucer narratives* (The Hague, 1966), pp. 59, 61-2; Burlin pp. 144-5). Walter expressing the domination of Fortune depends on l. 69; Walter as an emblem of Satan, on the Clerk's comparison of Grisilde's testing to that of Job; as an emblem of the Prodigal, on l. 80 (though clear evidence for the latter is found only in the ultimate original, Boccaccio: see below p. 61). All the same, these misreadings make an important point, of which we may suppose the proponents unaware. God works not only directly upon man but also through ambiguous intermediaries; equally, the Christian may *experience* God acting upon him with the apparent capriciousness of Fortune and malice of the devil. (For further discussion of this point in other tales, see below pp. 149-50, 182-3, 276).

43. For comment on the uses made of the two sources, see Severs section IV.

44. Petrarch: 'cepit ... Valterium ... mirabilis quedam quam laudabilis (doctiores iudicent) cupiditas' (*SA*, p. 310; cf. Miller p. 145: 'Walter was seized with a desire, more strange than laudable — so the more experienced may decide'); *Le livre Griseldis*: 'je ne sçay quelle ymaginacion merveilleuse print ledit marquis, laquelle aucuns saiges veulent louer' (*SA*, pp. 311) ['some bright idea or other took hold of our hero, which the wise among us may wish to praise'].

45. P:'poterant rigidissimo coniugi hec benivolencie et fidei coniugalis experimenta sufficere' (*SA*, pp. 316-8, cf. Miller p. 147: 'these trials of conjugal affection and fidelity would have been sufficient for the most rigorous of husbands'); Fr: 'povoient, je vous prie, a ce seigneur ces experimens d'obeissance et de foy de mariage bien souffire?' (*SA*, p. 319) ['I ask you, don't you think these tests of obedience and faithfulness might have satisfied our hero?'].

46. So Huppé p. 141 and, more subtly, Salter (1962), p. 64.

47. On this point, see David p. 163.

48. Cf. Burlin p. 144: 'the ... effect of the comic address to WB ... has been anticipated in the clash of the earlier perspectives.'

49. A point often made of *CT*: see e.g. Brewer (1984), p. 110 on 'the principle of complementarity' in *CT*.

3 SAINTS' TALES: THE PRIORESS'S TALE

The saints' tales in *The Canterbury Tales* have much in common with the Clerk's exemplum. They share its emphasis on innocence tested and vindicated as a sign to the faithful, and its explicit dependence on Biblical archetypes. All the same, there is a vital difference between the two genres. The exemplum moves always towards the expression of an abstract truth: its twofold limits are the ingenuity of the narrator to lead his reader through a mass of extraneous detail to that single and necessary truth, and the wit of the hearer to follow the narrator's line correctly. The narrative line of the exemplum, that is, dramatises the experience of faith, and its interpretation the meaning believed to inhere in that experience. If the narrator opposes other readings of his narrative to the exemplary one, his work will reveal the inevitable arbitrariness that, in greater or lesser degree, attends any attempt to create coherent meanings out of experience.

With the saint's life the picture is very different. The experience *is* the meaning: the experience of one man's life and death is authoritatively declared to reveal a single, final meaning, regardless of contradictory evidence in that life (say, a misspent youth). The teller's ingenuity has little place here; the object of the narration is not to develop an understanding of complex intellectual positions, but to encourage prayerful participation in the narrated experience. Inevitably, details of the narrative carry a strongly exemplary colour; hagiographers were always very ready to replace a flesh-and-blood original by a plaster cast. Nevertheless, the saints are demonstrably real: not a deceitful appearance to be broken open in pursuit of a meaning and discarded, but an inextricable part of the meaning. And the saint embodies that meaning more fully for having passed beyond death into life. He is not primarily an object of theoretical speculation, not an example to be followed, but a person offering the encouragement of his own experience. (This also distinguishes the saint's life from that of the secular hero. We read about the hero; we meet with the saint.[1]) And what we say of the narrative of one man's life can be applied, with equal force and justice, to the narrative of the whole history of salvation, as, for example, presented in the cycle plays.

It may seem strange, therefore, to begin this section with the
Prioress's tale. Chaucer himself calls it a 'miracle' (VII, 691),
which, technically, it is. An innocent Christian child has so
offended the Jews of the city where he lives by singing an anthem
in praise of the Virgin Mary as he goes to and from school through
the ghetto, that they have him murdered, and throw his body into a
privy. The distraught mother, who has looked for her child in
every likely place, seeks him in the ghetto, and is directed by Christ
to call out for him at the very place where he lies hidden. At once
the dead child begins to sing his anthem again. Taken up for Christian burial, he continues to sing, until conjured by a holy abbot to
explain the miracle. He tells how the Virgin has preserved his life
as a reward for his love of her: in the moment of his dying she
'leyde a greyn' upon his tongue as a sign that she would not leave
him until the grain was removed, when she would fetch him away.
The abbot removes the grain, the child ceases to sing or speak, and
the dead body is given an honourable burial.

As a literary category, the miracle is formally distinct from the
saint's life.[2] It is a momentary occurrence; it may come unbidden
(though that in the Prioress's tale is clearly offered as a return for
the child's devotion); it does not presuppose a life of faith; it does
not even dictate particular sanctity on the part of the recipient.
One of its chief functions is to challenge those who experience or
witness it to become more saintly. All the same, the two categories
overlap very considerably. The miracle is the momentary expression of what the saint's life represents in fully extended form.[3]
Again, the moment of death itself provides the final confirmation
of a person's holiness. The holy close of a holy life will often be
attended by miraculous happenings. Even in the absence of such
happenings, though, we may still see death as the final seal on a life
lived in devout prayer and final resignation to the will of God.
Such a death may also transform a less dedicated life, as with the
martyr. (This figure will receive fuller attention later in the book,
in the tales of the Second Nun and the Man of Law.) Since the
present story tells of a little boy slain by Jews, comparisons inevitably suggest themselves with other innocents similarly martyred,
like Hugh of Lincoln (684), and even the saint to whose shrine the
pilgrims are journeying. If the little child is a martyr (579), dying
for a faith which he expresses in the anthem he persists in singing,
his story inevitably becomes a saint's life.

In any event, the child's martyrdom, with its accompanying

miracle, harmonises with all the details of his life up to that point. He is regular in attendance at school (504), where he is learning 'swich manere doctrine as men used there': namely, 'to syngen and to rede' (499-500). But he has already learned from his mother a more important 'doctrine', and observes it assiduously: whenever he passes an image of the Virgin Mary he kneels down and says an Ave Maria in her honour. What we might call the two learnings, secular and sacred, are not, in principle, opposed to one another. They breed no conflict while followed separately, the one at school, the other at home and on the way. But when the two take place at the same time in different parts of the school, interests may well conflict. Learning his primer, the little boy hears older children learning an anthem from their hymn books. Much too young to have learned Latin, and unaware that the anthem is being sung to honour the Virgin, the boy sidles up to the older group, under some threat of punishment if he is seen ('as he dorste': 520), and listens until he knows the words and music of the first verse by heart. Next he approaches an older student (525-9) for information about the song: if not an explanation of its meaning ('expounden ... in his langage'), at least an account of its regular use. Though his companion is learning singing, he is little better placed to translate the anthem; if the 'litel clergeon' has no Latin, he has only 'smal grammeere'. He has heard that the song is a greeting to the Virgin Mary, and a prayer for her help in a person's dying moments, but he knows no more (530-6).[4] This, however, suffices to confirm the little boy in the direction he has tentatively taken away from his primer. He declares that he will devote himself entirely to learning the anthem before Christmas is over.[5] If this means that he falls behind with his primer, and is beaten for it 'thries in an houre', too bad: the higher claim cancels out the lower (537-43). So his friend teaches him the anthem in secret, day by day, as they travel home from school until he knows it by heart.

Now he has a new custom. On his way to and from school he sings the anthem, the 'Alma Redemptoris mater'. He still does not know what the words mean, but the song provides an occasion for him to 'set ... his entente' on the Virgin Mary (544-50). Not wise in worldly learning, he is wise beyond his years in his devotion to the Virgin. He cannot stop singing to her because her 'swetnesse hath his herte perced so'. The song, that is, has expressed and engendered a fixed religious purpose, which he experiences as a pang in the heart (551-7).[6] As we have seen, this practice will bring about his murder by the Jews: but his death at their hands merely ratifies the covenant between him and his heavenly patroness, which his constant singing of the anthem has symbolised. Once he has fastened his 'entente' on the Virgin, once she has pierced his heart, literally nothing but death remains. And, though the narrator may grow indignant at the Jews' execution of their wicked purposes, the child's actual death is only the logical working-out of his spiritual death to worldly concerns, and not a little anti-climactic by comparison.[7] Hence the stanza which squeamishly describes the privy into which the body was thrown as a pit, and curses the Jews for thinking so to frustrate God's purposes (572-8), is immediately followed (579-85) by an apostrophe to the young child, forever sealed in virgin purity and forever singing to 'the white Lamb celestial ... a song al newe'.

We can put this another way. The instructor who might beat the child for neglecting his primer, the Jews who murder him for spiting their 'lawes reverence', are jointly instruments, or expressions, of a lesser vision which the saint must renounce in favour of the greater.[8] They are not in themselves bad. Hence the first picture we get of the Jews and their ghetto is not the claustrophobic and threatening one that we associate, for example, with Shylock. Granted, the narrator will not for a moment defend their 'foule usure and lucre of vileynye', which makes them 'hateful to Crist and to his compaignye' (491-2). At the same time, she recognises that their guilt is, partly at least, shared by the lord (presumably a Christian) who permits them to live there and carry on their trade (490). And the Jews have not cut themselves off from their neighbours; there is free passage through the street where they live: 'for it was free and open at eyther ende' (494). Not only are they not isolated in guilt; they are also open to whatever good inspirations may come their way (like a little boy singing an anthem).[9]

This picture of the authentic expression of a limited vision does not immediately spring to mind when we think of representations of the Jew in religious art. The normal image is that of the torturer or executioner of Christ and his followers. Hence, in the N-Town Passion Play, the Jews do everything to Christ that, according to the Gospels, the Roman soldiers did: they scourge him, mock him, crucify him, dice for his clothes, compel 'poer comonys' to erect the other crosses with the two thieves on them; most horribly of all, when Christ is crucified, 'þei leve of and dawncyn abowte þe cros shortly'.[10] A more symbolic representation considers not their violence but their spiritual blindness. Thus the window of the Church and Synagogue, in Bourges cathedral, opposes the Jewish faith at all points to that of the Church. Blindfold, its staff of office broken, the mitre falling from its downcast head, the Synagogue is error to the Church's truth.[11] But the Jewish people could be depicted in another way, which showed that, though limited, they had a profound contribution to make in the drama of salvation. Such, for instance, we see in an illumination of the Synagogue in a late twelfth-century copy of the *Liber Scivias* of St Hildegard of Bingen.[12] Once again the Synagogue has her eyes closed to the ultimate truth; but within the capacious folds of her dress we see the patriarchs of the Old Testament, all looking heavenward for the reality which they know their own practice cannot directly bring to birth. It is this world, rather than the simple world of violence and error, that the Prioress's opening description seems to evoke.[13]

When the two faiths come into active collision, however, and the lesser puts a wall about its own limited practice — shows that inflexibility and lack of imagination that the little boy may instinctively recognise in his teacher — we are forced to judge between them, to the obvious disadvantage of the lesser. Thus we compare the Jews' 'entente' unfavourably with that of the child (575; cf. 550); contrast the 'privee place', where they go to hire the murderer, with the instruction which the little boy receives 'prively' from his fellow (544, 68). Above all, we oppose to the reverence of the Jews for their own law that of a saintly child for Christ (515, 64). All the same, we had better not forget, when we side so easily with truth against error, the consequences of such a commitment. We commit ourselves to a child-like state which knows nothing of forbidden times and places, and wills its own death in the hope of meeting afterwards what here it sees only through a dark glass. One little human life thus encapsulates the whole life of faith: which, we said earlier, is what distinguishes the saint. On the one hand, he stands for us; on the other, he stands for a tradition which originates with Christ and which the saint himself mediates to us as its latest expression.

The saint stands for us, in the first place, by revealing what no bystander could have guessed, the meaning of his own life. The miracle, the symbolic and necessary *point final* to the little boy's life, is no more intelligible to an adult than was the hidden life of a small child going unexpectedly missing. The grown-ups look on with wonderment (615, 73). Even the little boy cannot tell exactly what happened to him ('me thoughte she leyde a greyn upon my tonge': 662); his limited understanding is of a piece with his whole life up till then ('I loved alwey, as after my konnynge': 657). But he witnesses authoritatively to a truth which he has directly experienced, and others must hear about (cf. 531) or read in books (652).[14] What the older student knew only by hearsay (that the anthem 'was maked ... hire for to preye/ To been oure help and socour whan we deye': 532-4), has been confirmed by a vision granted to the child in the moment of his dying (658-69). In sharing with the 'hooly man' this one moment of a life devoted to the service of the Virgin, the child is adding to the bystanders' store of hearsay evidence, confirming his own sanctity and encouraging them to become more saintly themselves. Not surprisingly, the bystanders react with expressions of wonder which temporarily increase their own holiness, if not their understanding. They weep copiously (674,678, cf. 621), fall to the ground as if transfixed (675-7: a literal 'rooting' parallel to the child's fixing of his heart upon the Virgin), and, as he did throughout his short life, break out into tears of blessing (678; cf. 618-19). In one of the analogues to this tale, they weep tears of joy.[15] Here, their tears may also acknowledge the distance they have yet to travel to be 'Ther he is now'.

This sense of separation is well caught earlier in the story in the person of the child's mother. She stands, we may say, for that aspect of religious experience which the child's life has not emphasised: a suffering unwilled, overwhelming and apparently meaningless. Her journey in quest of her son echoes in ironic counterpoint his in quest of the Virgin. 'With moodres pitee in hir brest enclosed' (593; an echo of 555) and half out of her mind 'with face pale of drede and bisy thoght' (589), she seeks him in all the likely places. All the while calling on the Virgin for help (597-8; cf. 556-7), she is drawn inexorably to the ghetto. She beseeches the Jews for information (600-2; an echo of 528-9, where the little boy entreats information of his older companion). When they refuse to reveal what they know full well, she receives a wordless revelation from Christ: an analogue of the revelation of the Virgin to the little child as he lay dying (603-4), which results directly in the discovery of the body and the publishing of the crime. At every stage in the story, then, characters are taking up positions which express their bewildered, and sometimes painful, identification with the saint in his exercise of faithful obedience.

But we cannot stop there. Like the little boy's testimony to the abbot, the narration itself becomes part of the hearsay evidence on which narrator and audience, as Christian people, must take their stand. Consequently, the story begins and ends with prayer. The final prayer unites narrator and audience in a re-enactment of the story: we pray to 'yonge Hugh of Lyncoln', a little child similarly martyred, so we believe, by the Jews, to intercede for 'us ... synful folk unstable' and secure the mercy of God 'for reverence of his mooder Marie' (684-90). This prayer finds expression at the very end of the story: 'Ther he is now, God leve us for to meete' (683). Elsewhere in the tale, the narrator takes for granted her audience's involvement in the tale and dramatises in her own responses the reading she hopes to generate. Hence she starts with a prayer which contains the story in embryo, and enacts it by anticipation.[16] The Psalm text 'Domine dominus noster' (Ps. 8), with which it opens, and which the first stanza paraphrases, speaks of the power of God to draw praise out of small things as out of great. The story that follows will therefore prove this saying true; offering itself 'in laude .../ Of thee, and of the white lylye flour', the Virgin Mary (460-1), it will realise the prophetic dimension of the original Bible verse. And since other Bible texts make explicit the opposition, latent in the paraphrase of the Psalm, between the learned of this world and the babe in arms (e.g. Matt. 11:25; Mark 10:13-15), the story will also create a further link with the Psalm text. It will tell of a little child whose wisdom surpassed that of his elders. Not only the telling, but also the subject-matter, of the story thus claims kinship with a Bible text. (With this laying of one's cards on the table at the very beginning, we might contrast the way the Clerk reserves his aces till the very end.)

Now, if the narrator is making her offering as an expression of the same impulse that made the mouth of children cry out in praise of God, and if the learned of this world are babes when confronted by the truths of the faith, the narrator, logically, has only one position available to her: that of the suckling babe.[17] This, after all, is how God sees all men. Hence, like a child, the Prioress will do 'as [she] best kan or may' (460), not expecting for a moment that her labours will 'encressen hir [the Virgin's] honour' (464): needing Mary's help if she is to tell a fittingly reverent tale (473). She is the bolder to ask for such help because she knows of the Virgin's

readiness to intercede even before men pray to her. (This enlargement of the Virgin's role in the story proper must give even the
hardened sinner hope.) Consequently, though 'ther may no tonge
expresse in no science' (476) her various qualities, and though the
Prioress's 'konnyng is so wayk ... that [she] ne may the weighte
nat susteene' (481, 483), she may trust to the Virgin to aid her
('Gydeth my song that I shal of yow seye': 487). Her identification
with the child is even made explicit: 'as a child of twelf month
oold, or lesse', she 'kan unnethes any word expresse' (484-5).

All the same, we ought to observe — what the tale itself will not
directly show — that the professed child-likeness is not the same
thing as childishness. A child in the eyes of God, the narrator also
has the language of the learned at her fingertips. Paradox and
Biblical imagery are all pressed into service to provide a picture of
the person in whose honour the story is being told. Mary, a lily
(461), mother and maiden (462, 467), the burning bush that
burned and was not consumed in Exod. 3:2 (468); Mary, the one
whose humility forced God, as by a rape, to enter her (469-70);
Mary, the source of all virtues by reason of her connection with her
son (465-6); the one who obtains for us the light to lead us back to
him (479-80), that same light which enlightened her heart when
she conceived him (471-2): the linguistic game is as dazzling as, on
the subject of prayer, Herbert's 'Prayer I'.[18] Only one detail
suggests (and then not very strongly) that, before this encrustation
of pious superlatives covered her, Mary might have been a young
woman, timid and unsure, at the moment of the Incarnation: if the
Incarnation lightened her heart, as she now lightens the hearts of
her servants, she too may have been like the little child on whom
the narrator models herself and about whom she tells her story.[19]

If, then, like all theologising, the prologue must commit itself to
the expression of that child-like view which unbelievers will readily
call childish, it nevertheless does so by way of all the learned traditions available to it. This sophistication is most in evidence in the
confident placing of the story in relation to a whole set of Biblical
archetypes and models of juvenile sanctity. The story thus proves
the earlier models, realises their prophetic implications, and re-
vitalises them by re-enactment. As already noted, the child is
compared to the infant martyr St Hugh (684-6), and to St Nicholas
as a child, 'for he so yong to Crist dide reverence' (515). More
important, there is a clear connection between the murder of the
child and the massacre of the Holy Innocents at the hands of

Herod (Matt. 2:16-18). The Jews who commit the murder are doing the first Herod's work all over again ('O cursed folk of Herodes al newe': 574). The inconsolable mother will be called a 'newe Rachel' (627) — St Matthew had so described the mothers of the children massacred by Herod, quoting from an Old Testament prophecy (Jer. 31:15) to show its fulfilment in his own time. The little child is explicitly compared to Herod's innocent victims (608) and to the company of virgin saints 'of which the grete evaungelist, Seint John/ In Pathmos wroot' in the Apocalypse (579-85). There is added significance, too, in the Psalm verse used in the prologue. As other writers have noted, this opens Matins in the Office of the Blessed Virgin, and was also used among the portions of Scripture read at Mass on the feast of the Holy Innocents.[20]

But there are other, less obvious archetypes at work here too. The little child who learns at his mother's knee has obvious parallels in the lives of many saints; the Virgin Mary, for instance, is commonly represented in art as receiving instruction, while still a child, from her mother, St Anne.[21] The pit into which the body is cast (571) reminds us of the fate of the Old Testament patriarch Joseph, the youngest but one child of Jacob and preternaturally wise; his jealous older brothers threw him into a pit and then sold him into slavery (Gen. 37: 18 ff.).[22] The grieving mother who goes in quest of her child has an obvious parallel in the life of the Virgin Mary, who lost Jesus for three days as a boy of 12, and later found him in the temple sitting with the doctors, listening to them and answering questions (Luke 2:46).[23] And Mary provides a yet more obvious icon of the suffering mother than the 'newe Rachel' of Old Testament prophecy and Gospel narrative, as she follows her son to Calvary and stands at the foot of the cross. Normally late medieval art depicts her, like our widow, with face 'pale of drede ... as she were half out of her mynde ... swownynge by the beere'. Even the detail of the widow's reluctance to be parted from the dead body of her son (626-7) has a parallel of sorts with the Virgin's unwillingness in such paintings to loose her hold on the dead body of Christ, lying in her lap in an awful parody of the birth, so that it can be prepared for burial.[24] Then, too, the mother is a widow. The Bible offers many instances of holy widows (for example, Anna in Luke 2:36), many of whom, like Hannah in I Sam. 1:9, have holy children. None is more important than the Virgin Mary herself. Technically married to St Joseph, she is always represented in paintings of the Passion, and of her own last days, as a widow.[25]

It is perhaps worth pausing over these archetypal images — several already noted in one or another version of the Grisilde story — so as to distinguish more clearly the features of the saint's life as a narrative genre. In the exemplum, the archetype provides a clear directive to an abstract meaning, and points us away from the temporal dimension of the narrative. In the saint's tale, the archetype anchors us firmly in time. Necessarily, the time thus created is not a sequence of unrelated moments, waiting to be made into a unity by the ingenuity of the narrator. Every moment provides the occasion for an individual to keep, or break, faith: to become more or less saint-like. Consequently, every moment becomes, directly or indirectly, the mirror-image of every other.

This assured manipulation of traditional iconography is part-nered by a child-like absorption in the tale by the narrator.[26] Every time she reflects on the story of how the little boy learned from his mother to worship the Virgin, she says, she cannot help comparing him with the infant St Nicholas (513-15). On the face of it, St Nicholas instinctively refusing the breast on fast days — so Robinson reads the reference, at any rate — does not readily twin with our little hero docilely receiving instruction from his mother; but, having once got hold of the idea, the narrator seems perfectly happy to repeat it as an original contribution to the story.[27] She can do this only if the original experience of the story remains sufficiently fresh to justify a simple restatement of that thought. But to repeat an earlier thought in the same random way of its first occurrence clearly indicates a simple and child-like attitude to the story. Not all the Prioress's asides are spoken in such breathlessly child-like tones. She explains to us, as one adult to another, the kind of education the child received at school (500-1); as one refined person to another, she describes the pit into which the Jews threw the body (572-3). But the most important of her comments have this same character of the ingenuously self-evident. She inter-rupts her narrative at moments of greatest tension to apostrophise the characters: the Jews (574-8), the little martyr (579-85), God himself (607-8). She is reliving the original experience so completely that she can even enter into dialogue with the charac-ters. Here too a certain randomness attends her utterance. She harangues the Jews as if afraid they might actually get off scot-free: 'mordre wol oute', she tells them, 'the blood out crieth on youre cursed dede'. Almost as an afterthought, she reminds herself that when 'th' onour of God' is involved — which it clearly is in this story — the outcome can never be in doubt. She tells the little child how fortunate he is to have preserved his virginity (that is, she is seeing him as a sign of immediate relevance to religious like herself: needless to say, the narrative does not require this narrow interpretation). At the climax, she repeats her own opening words:

> O grete God, that parfournest thy laude
> By mouth of innocentz, lo, heere thy myght!
>
> (607-8)

(This repetition makes an important point of which she is possibly unaware: in the prologue God's praise 'parfourned is' by adults and children alike (456); here it is God who 'parfournest thy laude/ By mouth of innocentz'.) As a last expression of child-like trust, she tells us that she does not know where the child is, but prays that she may come there herself (683).[28]

Chaucer is aware, however, as the Prioress seems not to be, of the dangers of a child-like story told in a child-like way. And he carefully distances himself from the speaker in the very moment when she is so volubly commending the martyr's chastity, by means of the little phrase 'quod she' (581: cf. 454). That little phrase warns us against identifying ourselves too easily with this teller and her story. The reason is not far to seek, and it has everything to do with the presentation of the Jews.[29] The saints may condemn their way of life (492), but the Jews are not necessarily worse than those they live amongst (490, 493-4). Historically necessary as an important stage in the drama of salvation, they fulfil their role finally, paradoxically, perversely, in murdering Christ and his disciples. This qualified endorsement of their role cannot prepare us for their fate in the story once the crime is discovered. They are bound physically (620; perhaps an ironic anticipation of 676) and tortured, torn in pieces by wild horses and then hung by due process of law (634). The narrator gives no sign of wanting to distance herself from this barbarism. She approvingly quotes a proverb, 'yvele shal have that yvele wol deserve' (632), which underlines her earlier attack on the Jews for this 'cursed dede'. If she sees no difficulties in this account, however, I do. On the likeliest reading of these lines, the lawful death comes at the end of a process of 'torment and ... shameful deeth': dead, that is, in all but name, the Jews are ceremonially strung up so that the law may operate. And these lines disjoint the tale in a far more damaging way. All along we have been invited to prefer the higher vision of the Christian saint (grace) to the lower vision of secular learning and Jewish practice (law). Yet here, when the Jews have shown unwitting mercy to their victim, the Christian provost shows them not mercy but rigour and then law.

This incongruous development becomes the more striking if we compare the form of the story in those versions most closely related to the Prioress's tale (Carleton Brown's 'texts of Group C').[30] Nine versions exist, dating from the thirteenth to the end of the fifteenth centuries, all but one of English origin. In only one are any Jews put to death.[31] That one, produced between 1458 and 1460 by a Jewish convert to Christianity living at Salamanca, has an explicitly apologetic purpose, as its title indicates (*Fortalicium fidei contra Iudeos, Saracenos, aliosque Christiane fidei inimicos*).[32] To convert his Jewish readers, the writer waves a big stick at their representatives in the story. Even so, for all that he has nothing good to say about his former companions, the poacher turned gamekeeper is careful to explain and limit the scope of the Christians' revenge. The big stick had better not be too liberally applied or the Jewish reader might complain of arbitrariness and injustice. Consequently, the narrator sets his story in England, as a partial explanation of the expulsion of the Jews from that country in 1290. When the English king learns of the murder of the little child, he adds it to the many other instances of Jewish malpractice that have come to his notice, and in council assigns a day on which any Jews remaining in the kingdom will be killed. It is not the mere fact of murder that condemns those who fail to accept the offered clemency. Rather, they are being judged for the many actions, of which the murder is merely the last and most spectacular, whose execution has revealed their hatred of Christ and the Virgin Mary. In another version, preserved in the Vernon manuscript, the distraught mother asks the mayor 'to don hire lawe and riht' (85). When the crime is revealed, the Jew is forced to 'knouleche his wrong' (105) and receive judgement for it (114); but the text does not specify what the nature of that punishment is.[33]

In the remaining versions one of two things happens. Commonly the Jews just fade out of sight after the discovery of the crime, leaving the focus squarely on the miraculous end of the child.[34] The one text which keeps the Jews on stage till the end

(C10; *SA*, pp. 480-5) reckons them devout but misguided; they see the murder as an immolation as, in another sense, it is.[35] In this text the little child is miraculously restored to life and prays for his murderer; as a result the latter repents and becomes a Christian and a fervent worshipper of the Virgin. Since this version is the latest of all ('end of the fifteenth and beginning of the sixteenth centuries') we might be tempted to dismiss its forgiving spirit as an aberration or eccentricity, were it not that some of the most celebrated saints' legends of the middle ages (the death of the Virgin, for example, or the finding of the true cross by St Helena) carry much the same stamp.[36] On such a reading, the Jews act according to their limited lights, and are converted when the mercy of God reveals the greater light to them. The respectful silence of the earlier texts of the group about the fate of the Jews, the compassionate care of the latter for their conversion: both approaches make possible their accommodation to the overall iconographic scheme of the work, as clear in the earliest as it is in the latest version.[37] The disruption to that scheme provided by the Prioress's account of their punishment (far from being abstract symbols, they are all too real figures of flesh and blood) is therefore the more disturbing, since nothing in the logic of the story, nor any emphases recorded in versions prior to Chaucer, required or justified it.

Like the Clerk's tale, then, the Prioress's tale is a religious story imperfectly realised.[38] In very different ways — for the one is as deliberately ambitious as the other is deliberately modest — the two narrations sell themselves short, the one by resisting what it recognises as the necessary reading of its hero, the other by its unreflecting acceptance of a racial stereotype. Both seem to want villains whom the hearer can vilify or delight to see punished, and victims to cry over. At the end, both retreat from the ambiguities they have uncovered into the safer waters of doctrinal orthodoxy and prayer. But in this we see the real interest and significance of the two narratives: they show the struggles of the narrator to transmit a true understanding of a received text. Put another way, the two stories become interesting to the degree that their narrators are ceasing to act as simple scribes, and are claiming for themselves — usually mistakenly — the rights of authorship. And this explains — to move the discussion forward — why most people find the genuine saint's tale, that of the Second Nun, such a bland and disappointing affair.

Notes

1. The links between romance hero and Christian saint (regularly noted in discussion of MLT, see below p. 163 (n. 6 to p. 126) may produce an overlap in an audience's response to both. According to D. Mehl, *The Middle English Romances of the thirteenth and fourteenth centuries* (London, 1968, p. 26), we respond to the saint's life with 'pious devotion and meditation'; to the romance hero with 'rapt attention and admiration'.

2. On miracle as a category, see A.T. Gaylord, 'The "miracle" of *Thop*', *SAC*, 6, 68-9.

3. We might usefully compare the initial 'shewing' to Julian of Norwich in 1373 and its later elaboration in two versions, 20 and more years apart; see B. Windeatt, 'Julian of Norwich and her audience', *RES*, NS 28 (1977), 1-17; and R. Ellis, 'Revelation and the life of faith: the vision of Julian of Norwich', *Christian*, 6 (1980), 68-71.

4. Whittock (p. 205) finds this moment comic in its earnestness (I do not), and concludes, rightly, that 'worship is more than wit'.

5. On the significance of this moment see Russell (Pearsall–Waldron, p. 219), who urges a connection with the feast of the Innocents (28 December), and hence finds an anticipation of the coming martyrdom. More prosaically, C. Brown, *A study of the Miracle of our Lady*, Chaucer Soc. 2nd series, 45 (London, 1910), finds the detail to mean that the child was in his first term at school (p. 113).

6. In this phrase I read an echo of Cant. 4:9, regularly used in mystical literature to express the mystic's transport of love for God or the Virgin: see W. Riehle, *The Middle English Mystics*, trans. B. Standring (London, 1981), ch. 3, and p. 36.

7. Russell (Pearsall–Waldron, p. 220) finds that 'the pace of the tale is quickened' at this point, and notes the brevity and compression of the narrative here as a characteristic of the genre. I cannot agree. Compare my comments on pace in PhysT, MkT and PardT below (pp. 181, 190, 212, 216, 243). The narrator's relation to the story, and its narrative values, seem to me at this point what they remain throughout.

8. So also David (p. 211): 'the violence of the murder,' though sharply contrasted with the school scene, is 'cut from the same cloth.'

9. For different readings of the openness of the ghetto, see Burlin (p. 192); Russell (Pearsall–Waldron, p. 217).

10. Block, SDs to pp. 294-8.

11. For a reproduction, see E. Mâle, *The Gothic Image*, 3rd edn, trans. D. Nussey (London, 1961), p. 189.

12. MS 1 Stadtbibliothek, Wiesbaden. For a reproduction, see *Vorgotische Buchmalerei*, ed. A. Boeckler (Königstein im Taunus, 1959), plate 50.

13. On the double representation of the Synagogue, see also D.W. Robertson, Jr, *SAC*, 6, 13; Kolve, p. 150 and Fig. 61; and, on religious tolerance towards Jews in the fourteenth century, R.J. Schoeck, 'Chaucer's Prioress: mercy and tender heart', *The Bridge, a Yearbook of Judaeo-Christian Studies*, II (New York, 1956); reprinted in Schoeck–Taylor, I, 253-6. An equally vivid realisation of this same relation of Old and New Testaments is provided by an iconographic cycle by Jean Pucelle illustrating the Calendar of the Belleville Breviary. Month by month one of the twelve Old Testament prophets dismantles the Synagogue, a stone at a time, and hands the stone over to his New Testament counterpart, one of the apostles. By the year's end 'the Synagogue is shown completely in ruins'. For a reproduction and comment, see *MS Painting at the Court of France, Fourteenth Century*, ed. F. Avril (London, 1978), plate 11.

14. Russell (Pearsall–Waldron, p. 224) notes the 'calm authority' of the child's speech, which 'makes the Abbot's mode of address look foolish'.

15. C10 in Carleton Brown's list, printed *SA*, pp. 480-5; the detail in question is on p. 484.

16. For detailed comment on the prologue, see Burlin (pp. 186-9), Kean II, 188-9; R. Pratt, 'Chaucer borrowing from himself', *MLQ*, 7 (1946), 259-64; and Ridley, p. 29.

17. Cf. D.W. Fritz, 'The Prioress's avowal of ineptitude', *ChR*, 9 (1974-75), 166-73.

18. On Mary as lily, as mother and maiden, and as burning bush, see Woolf (pp. 131-4); and *Medieval English Lyrics*, ed. R.T. Davies (London, 1963), Appendix (pp. 371 ff.); on her humility as the human cause of the Incarnation, Hirn (pp. 261-2). See also discussion of parallel material, in Prol SecNT, in Clogan, *M&H*, NS 3, 224-5.

19. On the Virgin at the moment of the Annunciation, see above, ch. 2, n. 9.

20. So M.P. Hamilton, 'Echoes of Childermas in PrT', MLR 34 (1939), 1-8; reprinted in Wagenknecht, pp. 88-98. See also J.P. Brennan, on PrT 11. 579-84, 'Reflections on a gloss to PrT from Jerome's Adversus Jovinianum', *SP*, 70 (1973), 243-51; Russell, Pearsall–Waldron, p. 222; and Robinson, p. 735 and nn.

21. For comment on this traditional figure, see L. Réau, *Iconographie de l'art chrétien*, 3 vols (Paris 1955-59), II, ii, 168-9. For a single example, see the Burgundy Breviary (BL MS Harley 2897 f. 340v).

22. For this comparison with Joseph, cf. C10 of the analogues (*SA*, p. 483: 'extrahitur ergo puer tanquam alter Joseph de cisterna'; ['the boy is removed like a second Joseph from the well']).

23. Possibly this Gospel narrative also influenced the conversation between the child and the holy abbot.

24. On the Virgin's reluctance to loose her hold on Christ, cf. *The book of Margery Kempe*, ed. S.B. Meech and H.E. Allen, EETS OS 212 (London, 1940), 194/11-22 (the parallel is not exact).

25. So, for instance, the illumination of the Annunciation of the death of the Virgin, by Fouquet; see *The Hours of Etienne Chevalier*, ed. C. Schaefer (London, 1972), plate 9.

26. It is also evidenced by a particular rhetorical feature, 'determinatio', often noted by critics: see, in particular, Payne, p. 162.

27. Other episodes from the life of St Nicholas have been advanced as likely explanations of this reference: see A.S. Haskell, 'St Nicholas and saintly allusion', Robbins, pp. 109-11.

28. See Brennan, *SP*, 70, 249, for an interesting speculation about the observed stylistic difference between the apostrophes and the rest of the narrative: the former were composed after the story and grafted on to it.

29. Writers divide on this point. Some see the presentation of the Jews as a criticism of an ignorant or sentimental narrator (so Schoeck, Schoeck–Taylor, I, 245-58, energetically contested by Ridley, p.12; Cooper, pp. 167-8; Howard, pp. 277-8). Others see no irony (Brewer (1984), p. 128; Kean, II, 205, n. 25; Payne, pp. 162 ff.). Ridley (p. 5), David (p. 209) and Whittock (p. 208), look to folk origins of the story, or the anti-semitism of the age, or 'fairy-tale justice', to bear some, or all, of the weight of adverse criticism. Though I do not agree with the latter, I accept the force of their position, particularly that of Ridley: and my understanding of the beautifully traditional nature of the tale leads me not to want to over-emphasise the negatives in the following pages of my own analysis.

30. For fuller discussion of the analogues, see Brown, *Study, passim*; *SA*, pp. 447-85; and, for the texts of group C, *SA*, pp. 467-85. See also Brennan, *SP*, 70, 248; and Ridley, p. 26 on the choice of 'Alma redemptoris' as the offending anthem

rather than 'Gaude Maria', which Brown (p. 72) reckons the likely original.

31. Even in the versions preserved in Brown's groups A and B the execution of the Jews is not the norm: only A2, 5, 9, 11 and B6 have it. Cf. David p. 212 and n.11 ('Chaucer has probably heightened the violence'). Ridley (p. 28), sees the punishment of the wicked as a regular feature of saints' lives, and (p. 32) draws telling comparisons with the fate of the villains in other religious narratives of *CT*. Her arguments are forceful, but result in the replacement of a more by a less complex emblem.

32. For the analogue, see *Fortalicium*, III, x; for a note on the author, *SA*, p. 477.

33. For this text, C5 in Brown's list, see *SA*, pp. 470-4.

34. One, C8, a text roughly contemporary with Chaucer, ends (*SA*, p. 477) with the text of the 'Alma redemptoris' for those who do not know the hymn, which implies a pedagogic function for the story analogous to the apologetic aim of the *Fortalicium*.

35. *SA* (p. 481): 'arbitrantur obsequium se prestare deo set ymmo ymmolabant demoniis' [they reckoned to be offering service to God but were in reality making sacrifice to the devils'].

36. On the role of the Jews in the death of the Virgin and the finding of the true cross, see *Legenda Aurea*, ed. Th. Grässe (Leipzig, 1850), pp. 303-11, 504-27. For a modern translation, see *The Golden Legend*, trans. G. Ryan and H. Ripperger (New York and London, 1941), pp. 273-5, 453-4.

37. For an example already noted from C10, see above, n.22. Others include the widow as an emblem of the Canaanite woman of Matt. 15:27, or, more probably, if strangely, Lazarus from Luke 16:21 (so C1, C8, C10); of the Virgin Mary who lost the Christ child for three days after travelling to Jerusalem for the Passover, in Luke 2:46, an episode prophetic of the Passion of Christ (C7); the capture of the 'clergeon' as an emblem of the betrayal of Christ (C10); the 'clergeon' as a lamb (C10) and the well-trained heifer of Hos. 10:11 (C10); the Jews as the devil, like wolves (C10) or raging lions (C9).

38. On this point, see also Whittock (p. 208) on 'the human imperfection to be found even in the heart of worship and wonder'; David (p. 208) on 'a tale of sincere faith but dubious religious import'. For comment which finds PrT the height of Chaucer's achievement in the so-called sentimental experiment, see Payne (p. 162): 'almost pure lyric, with the action scarcely narrated at all but only referred to in order to establish points of reference for emotional elaboration'.

4 SAINTS' TALES: THE SECOND NUN'S TALE

Like the Prioress's tale, the tale of the Second Nun is the story of an exemplary life and death, that of the Roman martyr St Cecilia, canonised in recognition of what we might call her openness to the Spirit and availability to the faithful during and after her life. Even near the end of her life, when 'half deed, with hir nekke ycorven' (VIII, 533), Cecilie continues to demonstrate that openness and availability. She encourages her disciples by her preaching (538-9), bequeaths them all 'hir moebles and hir thyng' (540), and entrusts them to the care of Pope Urban ('recomende to yow ... thise soules': 541-5). Most importantly, she leaves instructions for her house to be made 'perpetuelly a cherche' (545-6); and so it remains in use, the narrator tells us, 'into this day' (552). With this detail the work comes to a strangely muted end, quite unlike that of the Prioress's tale. In the Prioress's tale, the saint's availability, here and now, is concretely realised in the closing prayer. In the Second Nun's tale, on the other hand, the saint's availability is realised not in the here and now of personal encounter, but in a church where, from earliest times, men have prayed to her, and continue to do so. Faith presented as an immediate experience, as in the Prioress's tale, requires no justification: it justifies itself. Faith presented as a process in time, as in the Second Nun's tale, requires to be defended as an intelligible system. The prevailing tone of the Second Nun's tale, then, is apologetic.[1]

This explains a distinctive feature of the tale without parallel in the tales so far studied: a prologue (in particular, 11. 85-119) which provides an authoritative interpretation of the ensuing narrative.[2] It does this by subjecting the saint's name to a number of etymological interpretations, all traditional, ingenious and far-fetched, so as to discover in it those qualities which the tale itself will reveal. The prologue, that is, presents or contains the narrative in embryo. It describes Cecilie as exemplary by virtue of her teaching (93) and her other qualities (105, 109-12). It tells how she combines in her own person (95) the demands of both active and contemplative lives ('thoght of hoolynesse' and 'lastynge bisynesse': 97-8). It reckons her most important single attribute (not surprisingly, given the story's emphasis on the reasonableness of faith) to be wisdom (101, 105, 111). And it names another quality which will actually set the story in motion: Cecilie's 'pure chaastnesse of virginitee' (88). These general comments are reinforced by traditional metaphors. Dividing the name into two elements, 'Ceci' and 'Lia', the narrator interprets the first, three times, as 'heaven' — the source of the light by which men see, and an explicit symbol of wisdom (100-1, 110-12); and twice as its opposite, 'blyndnesse' (92, 100). And a subsidiary meaning can be found in the interpretation of 'ceci' as 'heaven', though it will not figure so directly in the tale itself: heaven is 'swift and round and eek brennynge' (114). Like the swift heaven, Cecilie was 'bisy evere in good werkynge' (116, echoing 98); the roundness of heaven symbolises her 'good perseverynge' (117; cf. 'lastynge', 98); its heat, her 'brennynge evere in charite ful brighte' (118).

The narrator's determination to provide a single and authoritative interpretation for her story is further emphasised a little way in. Two garlands of lilies and roses have been brought from heaven, by a guardian angel, to Cecilie and Valerian, the husband whom she has converted on their wedding night. Valerian's conversion from the paganism he has hitherto shared with most of his contemporaries means that he can now see the angel for the first time; and from the angel he learns that the garlands will be visible only to those who are 'chaast and hate vileynye' (231). Valerian asks for his brother Tiburce to receive the same grace. Tiburce enters the room and, though unable to see the flowers, smells them at once. Convinced that no actual flowers could smell more strongly, and certain that at 'this tyme of the yeer' such flowers could not ordinarily be had, he feels a change come over him which 'the sweete smel' seems to have produced (246-52). Valerian explains that he will not see the flowers until he 'bileve aright and knowen verray trouthe'. To prove the truth of these strange remarks, he will have to do as his brother did: 'reneye/ The ydoles, and be clene'. Then, and only then, will he see the angel of God (253-69).

The narrative continues with a conversation between Cecilie and the two brothers (284 ff.). At its end, Tiburce takes himself off to Pope Urban for baptism and the promised sight of the angel of God. But before that conversation, the story interrupts itself, in mid-episode, with a comment deriving from St Ambrose, 'in his preface' (271). The narrator calls on St Ambrose to explain 'the myracle of thise corones tweye' (270). St Ambrose obliges, and offers more than he was asked for. His words summarise the narrative up to this point (275-80); indeed, they refer only in passing to the 'corones' (279-80), as a sign of God's grace and a reward for the brothers' faithfulness (277-8).[3] They also alert us, as the prologue did not, to the outcome of the narrative, one already predicted for Cecilie and Valerian by the angel: 'the palm of martirdom for to receyve' (274; cf. 240). And they present the relation of Cecilie and the two brothers whose salvation she has secured (281) as an exemplum of the work's meaning, the great value attaching to 'devocioun of chastitee to love' (283); chastity, a state prayed for by Cecilie even on her wedding-day (135-7) and a necessary feature of her marriage with Valerian (155-60), is a condition of seeing the angel of God (161, 230-1).[4] But there is a more important point to notice. The narrator has removed the words of the preface from their original context so as to expose the lines of her own argument more clearly. As is well known, the 'preface' on which she has drawn is the preface ('praefatio') of the Ambrosian Mass for St Cecilia: that is, the prayer preceding the *Sanctus* in the canon of that Mass.[5] This prayer provides the narrative summary of the life of St Cecilia on which Chaucer's narrator has drawn, but no trace of its original form has survived in the new work: in particular, the concluding phrases, which clearly established that the speech was being addressed to God as a prayer, are all cut.[6] Not prayer, but proof, is the primary interest of this narrator.

'Seint Ambrose', then, is actually saying something more, and other, than the narrator wants him to say. But if her use of the Ambrosian preface reveals a certain waywardness on her part, its real importance is other. Like her willingness to explain the story's meaning before it starts, her readiness to interrupt it in mid-flow indicates that narrative values (suspense, for example) do not, as such, rate very highly in the work; by contrast, the Prioress's interruptions identify her with the protagonists and thus emphasise its narrative values. Untutored wonder cannot be given its head in a story which argues a case. Hence the narrator's one expression of doubt in the whole work, concerning her ability 'by ordre for to seyn/ How manye wondres Jhesus for hem wroghte', is passed over swiftly, and a narration offered which is both 'short and pleyn' (358-60). Within the story itself similar patterns are at work. Wonder, notably expressed by Valerian and his brother, never remains untutored for long. Valerian, 'corrected as God wolde' (162) when he learns how Cecilie's guardian angel will kill him if he approaches her 'in vileynye' (156), is still human enough to suppose that his wife may have invented the angel as a cover for a human lover (167-8). 'Taught by his lernynge' (184) he takes himself off to Pope Urban for baptism. The Christian expresses wonder: 'Urban for joye his handes gan up holde/ The teeris from his eyen leet he falle' (189-90). At the same time, Urban understands, what Valerian has yet to learn, the meaning of the latter's behaviour: his conversion from 'fiers leoun' to 'meke ... lomb' is the first fruit of the chaste seed sown in Cecilie by Christ himself. Valerian now meets an old man who materialises abruptly, carrying a book written with gold letters. His unexpected and miraculous appearance terrifies Valerian (204); the old man's equally sudden disappearance baffles him (216). Wonder, however, gives way at once to sound, if sketchy, doctrine. On the basis of what he reads in the book:

> O Lord, o feith, o God, withouten mo,
> O Cristendom, and Fader of alle also,
> Aboven alle and over alle everywhere
>
> (207-9)[7]

Valerian pronounces his belief in its teaching: 'sother thyng than this, I dar wel say/ Under the hevene no wight thynke may' (214-15).

His brother undergoes the same experience. Wonder at the sweet smell gives way to certainty as Cecilie repeats her husband's condemnation of idolatry (284-7). His growing conviction that she is speaking the truth (288-9) deserts him, however, when he learns that he must go to Pope Urban for baptism. He has good grounds for feeling insecure. The Christians, for the most part 'povre folkes' living outside the town (173-5), are a persecuted minority, practising their faith in secret; their chief priest, Pope Urban, has gone into hiding in the catacombs (185-6). Even Cecilie, though born into a noble Christian family and so a Christian from childhood (120-3), practises secret mortification on the day of her marriage to a pagan (131-3), and prays secretly to God during the ceremony itself for the grace to remain a virgin (134-7). On her very wedding night, when she reveals to her husband (and to us) the secret existence of her guardian angel (152-61), she has first to secure his promise not to betray her confidence (144-7).[8] While knowing nothing of Cecilie's intimate relations with Valerian, Tiburce understands the general situation of the Christians only too clearly. Urban 'woneth in halkes alwey to and fro' (311), under constant threat of death by fire, a fate which awaits the brothers too if they are taken with him (313, 318). Thus their quest for the God 'yhid in heven pryvely' will cause their own deaths! But here, too, untutored reaction is allowed its head only for so long as it takes Cecilie to instruct Tiburce in the truths of the faith. Instructed about the Trinity and the life and passion of Christ, Tiburce obediently accompanies his brother to receive baptism. He now becomes what he always was potentially, a sign of the work's meaning: that is, he symbolises conversion from pagan to Christian values, a movement from 'dremes' to waking (262-4), though to the darkened eye it must seem the opposite, and a subsequent conversion from this world to the next by martyrdom. (If God and the Christian jointly produce the first conversion, God works ambiguously with pagan instruments to achieve the second.)

And so the brothers come to their end. Brought before the Prefect and imprisoned for refusing to sacrifice to Jupiter, they convert their guards and the Prefect's adjutant (376-8), who weeps to see their plight and blessed release even as Urban had done (371, 401; cf. 190). Only death remains (398). But even before they die, the narrator is calling them 'seintes' (370, 372), as is Cecilie, who applies to them words of St Paul (384-5: cf. Rom. 13:12; 386-7: cf. 2 Tim. 4:7-8) and calls them 'Cristes owene knyghtes' (383) — a phrase used by the narrator (353) to describe Tiburce at the moment of his baptism. Their deaths, and the subsequent summoning of Cecilie to the Prefect for examination, signal a whole flurry of conversions, and one further martyrdom. The adjutant witnesses to having seen the brothers' souls ascend to heaven in the company of angels. His witness marks his own conversion, secures the conversion of others, and sends him to a martyr's death. The ministers sent to fetch Cecilie are also converted, not by miraculous signs but simply by her 'wise loore'; they too weep. A God who 'hath so good a servant hym to serve' cannot be false. Their declared readiness to die as well (420) is not, however, put to the test. The stage is to be left clear for the final show-down.

The form of the work requires this last encounter between Cecilie and the Prefect to produce not a convert but a martyr.

Authority will remain as constant to its beliefs as the saint to hers, the martyrs produced by the former as clear a sign of that constancy as the converts generated by the latter. Hence, though both sides go through the motions of attempting to change one another's positions, they are locked into a situation whose possibilities diminish as the argument proceeds, until at the end only martyrdom remains. (For a secular version of this, compare Sophocles' *Antigone* and its limp updating by Anouilh.) This logically suggests an inconclusive debate. Nevertheless, the martyr-to-be must have the better of any debate, so that the blindness of authority can be seen for what it is: culpable. This is done in two ways. Although the debate proceeds speech for speech, Cecilie has twice as many lines to speak as the Prefect, and her final speech — after which nothing remains to be spoken but her formal condemnation — is three times as long as the Prefect's longest. And the accused has a better time of it than the prosecuting counsel because she is able to answer his charges point by point. Defeated on the one point, he must turn to another or repeat an earlier charge. The Christian answers out of a whole world-view, which informs her every contribution; the judge must, perforce, regard Christianity as a series of unlawful acts and attitudes, and challenge now its refusal to obey secular authority, now its lack of respect for the gods.

The debate begins inauspiciously enough. The Prefect puts a question so ambiguously worded that the saint can avoid the expected answer, about her 'religioun and ... bileeve'. Forced to restate his question, and accusing her of fearing to answer it ('though it thee greeve'), he draws upon himself the counter-accusation of a foolish beginning (428-30). He attempts to determine 'of whennes comth [her] answeryng so rude' (432). Already the trial is moving out of his control, away from the general matter it was called to determine, into a morass of irrelevant detail concerned with his conduct of the case. It is the saint, unexpectedly, who brings our attention back to the real question. Paradoxically, her 'rude answeryng' was an effect of those qualities which have brought her to trial: 'conscience and ... good feith unfeyned'. The Prefect changes tack, and reminds the upstart of his powers (435-6): powers of life and death (472), which he exercises as deputy of the mighty princes (470), whose ordinances concerning the penalties for professing Christianity (444-8) he is pledged to uphold. Cecilie answers him point by point. Earthly power is no more than a 'bladdre ful of wynd' easily punctured with a pin. Since he has power only to kill (479-86), he is more fittingly called 'ministre of deeth' (485). The pagans are foolish (428, 463, 493-5), liars (451,479, 486) and mad (450, 467). Christians, innocent of every charge but the one which should not provide grounds for criminal action — their love of Christ and their bearing of his name (452-5) — cannot deny the name whose power they have had such reason to acknowledge (456-7). They oppose their truth (451, 477) to the lies of the court. They are not proud, as their accusers would have it, but steadfast (474-6).

Faced by this firmness of purpose, the Prefect tries another tack. The saint need not renounce Christianity: it will be enough if she sacrifices to the gods (459-60). Cecilie laughs him to scorn. The Prefect finally attempts to shift the debate from personalities to principles. He can bear philosophically any wrong offered to himself, he tells her, but he cannot sit by and hear his gods blasphemed. We have earlier heard Cecilie condemn the pagan gods as 'a thyng in veyn ... dombe and ... deve' (285-6). Interestingly, the interrogation has not yet itself provided any evidence in support of the Prefect's claim. His failure to observe legal niceties has, however, ceased to matter. Cecilie uses his professed devotion to the gods, whom she identifies with their stone images, to prove the existence of the true God 'in his hevenes hye' (508). The Prefect shows himself as good as literally blind by calling a god what everyone can see (and, though he cannot see it, he could himself feel with his hand) to be a stone. The blindness of the heathen is thus a distorted image of the blindness of the virtuous pagan. The one, it is alleged, makes what he sees into something it is not; he does not admit to so doing, and his is the greater blindness. The other admits his blindness, and may thus attain to the sight of the spiritual realm, which he will paradoxically understand by way of metaphors taken from the world of sense. (These categories are not perhaps as distinct as they appear, but it is no part of the defendant's case so to argue, and the prosecution is not permitted to make anything of the irony.)

The debate ends, then, much where it began. There is no resolving the points of view by argument and, equally, no reason why the debate should not continue for many pages. (Compare the debate between another virgin martyr, St Katharine of Alexandria, and her judge, in Capgrave's *Lyf of St Katharine*.[9]) And so Cecilie is marched off to her boiling bath. But even then she is not so easily subdued. Until now her life has expressed itself largely through traditional religious symbols. The chaste marriage which she induced her husband to share has parallels in the lives of other saints and, most notably, in Old and New Testament stories, for example, the marriage of the Virgin Mary to St Joseph; the angel whom only the believing partner could see has a parallel of sorts in the Old Testament story of Balaam and the ass (Numbers 22:22 ff.); Cecilie before the Prefect clearly re-enacts the trials of Christ and the apostles before the Jewish and Roman authorities in the Gospels and the Acts. The boiling bath is also a potent Biblical symbol; it takes us back to the fiery furnace of Daniel 3. This updated version of the three young men preserved in the fire by the angel of God explains why Cecilie can spend a night and a day in the bath in perfect comfort: 'it made hire nat a drope for to sweete' (522).[10] The inability of the authorities to frustrate the purposes of God is finally revealed in the bungled attempt to execute her by cutting off her head. Bound by pagan laws, the executioner cannot administer more than three strokes. When his statutory three strokes have failed to sever the head, he must leave her to die in her own way and time: which, as we have seen, she does, when she has had time to put her affairs in order and continue her ministry to her own people. The death therefore serves no other purpose than to prove, what the story has already told us, that God answers the prayers of his servants (542-3), working directly with their desires, even as he works indirectly with the secular arm, to bring about his good purposes. All through, then, the story moves away from the inconvenient immediacy of personal experience, notably doubt, to the realm of argument and proposition. Cecilie's last days may be described as a 'torment' (537), but she gives no sign of feeling the torment; nor do those who come to collect her blood in 'sheetes' (536). The draining-off of the life-blood so that it may become a symbol of the heavenly realm (it will be used as a relic) is an appropriate symbol for a religious story whose sights are fixed from the beginning on a reality not of this world.

This confident and increasingly bloodless narrative presents a much greater problem to the reader than those of the Clerk and Prioress. Since their retellings were both limited and flawed, albeit in very different ways, it was possible to fault the telling without impugning the authority of the tale, and to look for versions which might more fully realise the tale's religious implications. With the

Second Nun's tale, by contrast, the narrator hardly ever acknowledges the difficulties of making a good religious story.[11] We can hardly reject the authorised interpretations of the tale without attacking the very fabric of religion, since one of the two authorities called to speak on its behalf, 'Seint Ambrose', is a Doctor of the Church. Fortunately, this difficulty is resolved almost as soon as put. The narrator is far from claiming for herself the title of 'auctour'. She is, in fact, producing a translation:

> I have heer doon my feithful bisynesse
> After the legende, in translacioun
> Right of thy glorious lif and passioun.
>
> (24-6)

And, she claims, her version will seek no particular glories of its own, but only faithfully to transmit the 'wordes and sentence/ Of hym that at the seintes reverence/ The storie wroot' (81-3). Hence she will 'do no diligence/ This ilke storie subtilly to endite' (79-80). That is, we have been describing not an original but a translated narrative, whose source, as the marginal annotations to the prologue in many manuscripts point out, was a version of the legend of St Cecilia found in that important medieval collection of saints' lives, the *Legenda Aurea* of James of Varaggio.[12]

Now, since the translation exists only to open a door previously closed to its readers, it will not, by and large, seek to draw attention to itself; nor will it accompany its version with the kind of running commentary that the Clerk created when he reworked Petrarch. Consequently, the translation seldom departs from the wording of the original: such changes as there are (largely minor) result from the decision to render the Latin prose of the original into that elaborate verse form, rhyme royal. In the Second Nun's tale, as in any verse translation, these changes consist, for the most part, of added phrases. (In the following quotations, and in similar quotations in later chapters, such additions are italicised.) These additions fill out a line, and secure or create a rhyme.[13] They heighten the conversational tone or emphasise the meaning of the original.[14] We can see this most easily if we compare the opening stanzas with the original:

> This mayden bright Cecilie, *as hir lif seith*,
> Was comen of Romayns, and of noble kynde,

And from hir cradel up fostred in the feith
Of Crist, and bar his gospel in hir mynde.
She nevere cessed, *as I writen fynde,*
Of hir preyere, *and God to love and drede,*
Bisekynge hym to kepe hir maydenhede.

And whan this mayden sholde unto a man
Ywedded be, that was ful yong of age,
Which that ycleped was Valerian,
And day was comen of hir mariage,
She, *ful devout and humble in hir corage,*
Under hir robe of gold, *that sat ful faire,*
Hadde next hire flessh yclad hire in an haire.

(120-33)

Cecilia uirgo clarissima ex nobili Romanorum genere
exorta, et ab ipsis cunabulis in fide christi nutrita,
absconditum semper euangelium christi gerebat in
pectore et non diebus neque noctibus a colloquiis
diuinis et oratione cessabat, suamque uirginitatem
conseruari a domino exorabat. Cum autem cuidam iuueni,
nomine Ualeriano, desponsata fuisset et dies nupciarum
instituta esset, illa subtus ad carnem cilicio erat
induta et desuper deauratis vestibus tegebatur.

(*SA*, pp. 671-2)

In the translation, paired phrases are reduced to singles ('a colloquiis diuinis et oratione' becomes 'of hir preyere') and complex
expressions simplified ('absconditum … in pectore' becomes 'in
hir mynde'; 'non diebus neque noctibus', 'nevere'). Otherwise
every word of the original has been translated, and the additions,
usually occupying the second half of a line, remind us of the literary character of the source ('as hir lif seith'; 'as I writen fynde'[15]),
and emphasise the virtues of the saint ('and God to love and
drede'; 'ful devout … hir corage') or the decorum of the narrative
('that sat ful faire'). Sometimes, though not in these opening lines,
the extra material involves the creation of a doublet for a single
phrase in the original (e.g. 'comanded *and maad ordinaunce*':
445).[16]

These additions create a particular tone, heard also in the
speaking voices of the characters themselves. Its character is a subdued but positive emphasis, quite without ironic distance. This can

be easily demonstrated — to anticipate ourselves a little — by comparing the narrator's account of the mysteries of her heroine's wedding-night with a passage in the Man of Law's tale. Although he takes great pains to identify himself with his saintly heroine, the Man of Law adopts a more critical view when describing her wedding-night:

> They goon to bedde, as it was skile and right;
> For thogh that wyves be ful hooly thynges,
> They moste take in pacience at nyght
> Swiche manere necessaries as been plesynges
> To folk that han ywedded hem with rynges
> And leye a lite hir hoolynesse aside,
> As for the tyme — it may no bet bitide.
>
> (II, 708-14)

By contrast, the Nun describes Cecilie's wedding-night straight: 'The nyght cam, and to bedde moste she gon/ With hire housbonde, *as ofte is the manere*' (141-2). That added phrase allows for marriage to include just such a chaste relationship as Cecilie will presently enjoin upon her husband.[17] More generally, the additions emphasise that faith which is the subject of the original story: its object, the knowledge of a mystery; its process, the exercise of will; its end, the creation of the believers into a single, loving family.[18] Such additions sometimes involve repetition of details of the narrative, notably, in a character's opening words:

> *Withinne his herte he gan to wondre faste,*
> And seyde, 'I wondre ...'
>
> Almache answerde ...
> 'Of whennes comth thyn answeryng so rude?'
> '*Of whennes?*' quod she, *whan that she was freyned.*[19]
>
> (245-6, 431-3)

These practices constitute the most important 'original' element of the translation. To them we might add what looks like a greater liberty, when the narrator suppresses speeches between the brothers and the Prefect (cf. 363, 94) so as to clear the way for Cecilie's debate with the Prefect, and make hers the chief voice raised in defence of the Gospel. The phrase 'to tellen shortly the conclusioun' (394), suggests that the translator was responsible for the cutting of these speeches. Even so, the overall picture is little affected by this practice. In any case, such omissions might have first appeared in the copy of the *Legenda* used for the translation. To a very considerable extent, the translator has carried out her promise to translate the 'wordes and sentence ... and folwen hire legende'. Only the sternest would take her up on her request '[hir] werk [to] amende' (84); and such corrections would concern only points of detail, like occasional mistranslation ('necessitate' rendered 'nycete' at 463) or infelicities of expression ('as hym was taught *by his lernynge*': 184).[20] The general level of achievement is high.[21] It compares very favourably with that produced in the fifteenth century by Chaucer's disciple, Osbern Bokenham, who chose the easier medium of couplets for his version of the Cecilia story.[22]

But it is this fact of translation, no matter how accomplished its execution, which poses the greatest difficulty for modern readers of the story. Accustomed to mass-produced prose translations, they are unlikely to sympathise with a translator working in verse, or to appreciate the very considerable achievement represented by a successful verse translation.[23] Heirs of the Romantic revolution, they subconsciously reckon translation less significant than original work. On such a reading, translation is less expressive of an original personality and, at best, a limited recreation of it: better to read the original in its own terms than see it through another man's eyes. They therefore see the translator as a kind of mechanical drudge, nearer to a medieval scribe than to the 'auctour' of a work. Now, they can hardly deny Chaucer's lifelong interest in translation, and his reputation as a translator. Deschamps called him the 'grant translateur'; the *Boece* was used for a verse version within ten years of his death.[24] Nevertheless, because modern readers generally find Chaucer the original artist, especially Chaucer the ironist, more appealing than Chaucer the translator, they are compelled to find some explanation for the presence in *The Canterbury Tales* of a work hardly original and not at all ironic. They explain it as an early work, painfully literal, which Chaucer later incorporated virtually unchanged in *The Canterbury Tales*.[25] They are able to do so because the Prologue to the *Legend*, of which the earlier (F) version was produced *c.* 1385-87, includes, in a list of Chaucer's works written before that date, a 'lyf ... of Seynt Cecile' (F 426): the early work taken on board *The Canterbury Tales* as the Second Nun's tale. This argument, however, raises as many problems as it reckons to answer. The evidence of the two versions of the prologue to the *Legend*, for example, shows that Chaucer was very willing to rework earlier material not noticeably deficient or immature. Is it likely that he would have found room in his masterwork for an early translation as immature as it is reckoned, without making massive alterations to it? In any case, even if the Second Nun's tale in its present form goes back directly to an earlier life of St Cecilie by Chaucer ('earlier' here only means pre-1382, the earliest date possible for the composition of the F prologue),[26] it is only the first of several works by Chaucer to carry a traditional prologue explaining the translator's aims and methods, which show that, throughout his career, Chaucer found the question of translation worthy of serious — if not solemn — consideration.[27]

After the Second Nun's tale, the next work to talk about the translation is probably the *Troilus*. Chaucer must have reckoned the *Troilus* a major original work; yet he is perfectly willing to talk about it in terms readily paralleled in the prologues contemporary translators provided for their works.[28] In Book I the translator describes his version of the 'Canticus Troili' in terms like those used in the prologue to the Second Nun's tale. His version of the 'Canticus' will translate not only the sense, but 'every word right thus' of the original: he aims, that is, to produce as exact a correspondence between his own wording and that of the original as 'oure tonges difference' will permit (I, 393-8). In the proem to Book II, he apologises for infelicities of expression on the grounds that 'as myn auctour seyde, so sey I'. Lacking direct experience of the 'sentement' (the felt 'sentence', so to say) of his original, he must follow its letter, and hope that the 'sentement' will communicate itself through the letter of his translation. Therefore he aspires 'noon oother art to use' than 'to ryme wel this book til I have do' (II, 10-21: compare the Nun's rejection of 'diligence/ This ilke storie subtilly to endite'). Still later, in Book III, he realises that he may have deviated from this goal and, albeit for the best of motives, 'any word in eched'. He therefore urges the experts to correct his text where they find it necessary: 'encresse or maken dymynucioun/ Of my langage' (III, 1326-36).[29]

Interestingly, it is the *Troilus*, along with Chaucer's translation of *Le Roman de la Rose*, that brings him actively under correction, in the prologue to the *Legend*, by the one absolute authority on matters of love: the God of Love. According to the god, Chaucer has been guilty of 'heresye': among other things he has translated the *Roman*, a work which thoroughly debunked the courtly ideal (329-34). With help from the god's consort, Chaucer clears himself of the charges by emphasising the limited role of the translator. Very little better than a copyist, he cannot be blamed for the perversions either of his 'auctours' or the patrons who commissioned his work. He has always meant his work 'to forthren trouthe in love and yt cheryce', regardless of the original's given meaning, which a faithful translation must faithfully include ('what so myn auctour mente': 470-2). Though he actively disapproved of their 'sentence', he did not feel entitled to subject their words to any very wholesale revision. (We might usefully compare the Clerk's attitude to the prologue of the tale he is proposing to translate.) Won over by these arguments, the god himself now becomes a patron, and commissions a series of legends of holy women 'trewe of love, for oght that may byfalle' (561). But this commission will produce not so much a translation as a paraphrase or summary of the originals: with one eye on the clock (563), the patron is aware that a full version would prove 'to long to reden and to here' (572). This rider to the commission provides the poet with a defence of his own performance in the *Legend*. Regularly he tells us that he is abbreviating his text to save time and focus more clearly the single 'sentence' which the god expects to find in it. Nevertheless, he says, other things being equal, he could have produced a version corresponding 'word for word' with the original (1002).

Next in point of time (1391) is probably the prologue to *The Treatise on the Astrolabe*. Here, too, expert readers may need pacifying, though for a very different reason. Although Chaucer trusts the book will eventually come into their hands, and receive the recognition due to any work of his, he is writing, in the first instance, for a little child. Consequently, he can hardly aspire to 'curious endityng and hard sentence', and must settle, instead, for 'rude endityng' and 'superfluite of wordes' (43-5). The latter phrase, meaning that he will 'writen ... twyes a god sentence' (48-9), allows for elaboration to the text of the sort claimed in *Troilus* III; the former has clear echoes in both the Second Nun's prologue and *Troilus* II. Whether because he knows no better (*Troilus* II) or because his readership knows no better (*Astr.*), or whether because, as the Second Nun's prologue implies, graces of composition are simply not necessary, the translator makes no pretensions to art in his translation. Hence, Chaucer explicitly compares his own translation with the work of a compiler, on the grounds of their common pedagogic bias: 'I n'am but a lewd compilator ... and have it translatid in myn Englissh oonly for thy doctrine' (61-4). Nevertheless, though the translation is 'light' (51), its conclusions are as 'trewe ... and as subtile' as those 'shewid in Latyn in eny commune tretys of the Astrelabie' (51-5). Given the practical use to which the translation will be put, this defence of its methods is obviously necessary. (We might also note how revolutionary is the offered defence of the English language as a medium on a par with Latin for the expression of scientific knowledge.[30])

With *The Canterbury Tales* we move back into the world of fictional narrators, and the most important of these is Chaucer. 'Under correccioun' of Harry Bailly for his first offering, Chaucer offers the translation of a 'tretys lyte' (VII, 963), the *Melibee*, as his second.[31] Since we shall be studying the *Melibee* shortly, we need note here only that Chaucer is not aiming to produce a literal translation ('I varie as in my speche ... I nat the same wordes seye', 954,959). He will 'telle somwhat moore/ Of proverbes' (955-6), a specific instance of the 'in eching' spoken of in *Troilus* III, comparable with the practices to be followed in the *Astrolabe.* Chaucer's reasons for so doing are to 'enforce with th'effect of my mateere' (958). All the same, the 'sentence' of the translation will be absolutely consonant with that of its original. When, therefore, Chaucer compares his proposed changes with the minor variations between one Gospel account of the Passion and another (943-52), we can see that he is reckoning to produce a very close translation indeed; one, moreover, that his audience can check against the knowledge of the original with which he credits them.

Now, the dramatic contexts in which most of these comments occur should warn us against reading them too literally. Nevertheless, though produced at various stages throughout Chaucer's career, they are surprisingly consistent with one another. While they only occasionally admit of the possibility of a 'word for word' translation, they regularly require the translator to render both the words and the sense of his originals: to modify them only in response to the demands of the English language or the needs of a reader; and to set fidelity to the original above graces of execution in the translation. Such a view of translation receives regular confirmation from Chaucer's own practices as a translator.

If, then, Chaucer let the Second Nun's tale into *The Canterbury*

Tales virtually unchanged it was with good reason. Not only is it a good example of its kind. As a translation, it raises fundamental literary questions in a way that the Clerk's and Prioress's tales could not, concerned as they were with the telling of a particular kind of story and, more insidiously, with projecting the narrator's personality at the expense of the story. For the purposes of the literary experiment which we call *The Canterbury Tales*, the Second Nun's tale signifies hardly at all as a particular kind of story — we might call it religious apologetic — told by a particular narrator. She remains a shadowy and unrealised figure. It signifies because it is a translation.[32] As such, it offers a clear and unambiguous answer to the question whether 'experience' or 'auctoritee' should be the measure of the fictional world.

But there is another benchmark against which art has to be measured, one yet more important than the traditions which may have authorised it. Indeed, as the prologue shows, faithfulness to 'auctoritee' is intimately bound up with, and directly results from, adherence to this other standard. The artist is responsible not just for the inherited tradition, but for the effects his retelling produces: that is, he must take due note of the ethical foundations of his work. Other pilgrims occasionally acknowledge their responsibility, as both pilgrims and narrators, for this aspect of the journey and its partnering narrations. The Man of Law, for instance, sets up in competition not with a dead but with a living master of the craft, Chaucer himself (II, 45-89). Widely read in the Chaucer canon (he names an early book, *The Book of the Duchess*, and a recently issued work, the *Legend*) he dismisses the author as a hack versifier whose work makes up in quantity for what it lacks in quality. One aspect of his work, however, merits praise. Citing — at greater length, we may feel, than he needs — the story of Antiochus's rape of his own daughter, he praises Chaucer for refusing to include such 'unkynde abhomynacions' in his work. Dull Chaucer may be, and prolix: but he had *some* standards. I shall have more to say later about the ironies of this moment; here it suffices to note that the Man of Law's profession of art's moral dimension brings him ironically into line with the Nun. (We have earlier noted another ironic connection between the two tales; see p. 95 above.) What the Man of Law advances in passing — and with a playfully patronising air, which undercuts what he is saying — becomes the centrepiece of the Nun's literary aesthetic; the greater part of her prologue is given over to the question.

For her, literature is not pastime as it is for most of the other pilgrims, but business.[33] Such business is both lawful and faithful (5, 24). It demands the best labours and 'entente' of narrator and audience (6, 14); demonstrates the quality of our faith (cf. James 2:17) and helps in our salvation (64-6). To such business she opposes that 'ministre and ... norice unto vices', idleness, against which she warns her hearers repeatedly (2, 7, 10, 14, 17, 22). Her understanding is fundamentally opposed to that prevailing among the group, where business results not in the 'encrees' of salvation for which she looks (18), but in the payment of a bill or the winning of a supper (cf. I, 760,799). The idleness which she condemns, and whose offspring are sloth, mindless sleep and mindless consumption of food and drink (17-21), is that very condition with which individual pilgrims are totally identified, and about which, as we shall see, the Pardoner builds his tale.[34] In effect, this understanding subordinates art to morality. According to the Nun, the artist has a primary responsibility not to his craft — in relation to which, negligence is scarcely to be counted a sin (79-80) — but to the faithful transmission, or translation, of that reverent attitude which informs his original (82). Such an understanding, carefully reasoned, beautifully consistent, completely traditional, is the mirror-image of the position implied by the decision to produce a faithful translation. Not surprisingly, the Nun's is almost the only voice heard in support of this position. Not surprisingly, too, readers who are not readily drawn to the idea of translation will scarcely relish the Nun's insistence on art's moral dimension and the artist's responsibility for the effects he produces. Just as they preferred novelty to *auctoritee*, so they will prize pastime (or 'murthe') above morality ('solaas'). Preference, however, is one thing; proof another.

Notes

1. On the problem of authentication of saints' lives, see Bloomfield, *Thought*, 39, 344.
2. For extensive commentary on the prologue, see Clogan, *M&H*, NS 3, 218ff.
3. This passage implies, what the story never states, that Tiburce also received a garland. Most scribes changed the correct reading 'Valerians' to 'Cecilies' (Robinson, p. 750).
4. On this point, see Whittock (pp. 255, 257) (chastity as not contrary to the meaning of marriage); Clogan, *M&H*, NS 3, 235; and Kolve (Rose, pp. 150 ff.) (on 'spiritual procreation', p. 151, as the concomitant of chaste marriage: with this

motto, a commonplace of spiritual writing, cf. the motto of the 'spiritual son', e.g. Meech–Allen, 83/27-30).

5. M. Henshaw, 'The preface of St Ambrose and Chaucer's SecNT', *MP*, 26 (1928), 15 ff.

6. The cut phrases are: 'huius te, Domine, largente gaudia celebramus, et ea fide qua mundi caligo detersa est, ad aeternitatis tuae deprecamur praemia pervenire' ['we celebrate her joys — you, Lord, have bestowed them — and we beg that we may come to the rewards of your eternity with that faith by which the darkness of this world was wiped away'].

7. A close translation of Eph. 4:5-6 (Robinson, p. 758).

8. For a different view of this moment, depending on 'she sang' (l. 135), see Whittock (p. 255) (Cecilie's asceticism is 'a joyful abnegation of the false pleasures of this world').

9. *The Life of St Katharine*, ed. C. Horstmann, EETS OS 100 (London, 1893).

10. See Kolve (Rose, pp. 148 ff., 152 and n. 33) for comment on this image. He reads it (like the fiery furnace of Daniel 3 which probably inspired it) as symbolic of the fire of lechery, from which virginity preserves the three Israelite children in the Old Testament narrative and Cecilie in this one.

11. Cf. Kolve (Rose, pp. 156-7), on a tale 'uncompromised by irony, unmediated by larger context, and uncoloured by the idiosyncracies of a personal narrative voice'; and Lawler (p. 167): 'a strong personal presence would be an individuating obstacle to the authoritative message.'

12. Grässe (pp. 771-7). In the present work quotation is taken from *SA*, pp. 667-84. See also Miller (pp. 113-20) for a modern translation.

13. See further R. Ellis, 'The choices of the translator in the late ME period', *The Medieval Mystical Tradition in England*, Papers read at Dartington Hall, ed. M. Glasscoe (Exeter, 1982), pp. 36-7. For comment about the origins in the ME rhyming romances of these added phrases, see D. Brewer, 'The relationship of Chaucer to the English and European traditions' (Brewer, 1966, pp. 1-38; Brewer, 1984, pp. 8-36). See also Harbert, Brewer, 1974, p. 148, on a translation from Ovid (*LGW*, 1694-7); he finds such places 'weak poetry' and the mark of apprentice writing. For general comment on translation in ME, see E. Salter, *Nicholas Love's 'Myrrour of the blessed lyf of Jesu Christ'*, Analecta Cartusiana, 10 (Salzburg, 1974), ch. 6.

14. Muscatine (Brewer, 1966, p. 101), speaks similarly of phrases which 'both fill out his line or couplet and support his tone of easy colloquy'.

15. This pattern occurs only near the start of the translation; cf. l. 86.

16. On doublets, see Ellis, Glasscoe, p. 27; W.M. Thompson, 'Chaucer's translation of the Bible', *English and Medieval Studies Presented to J.R.R. Tolkien*, ed. N. Davis and C.L. Wrenn (London, 1962), p. 194. Another phrase that I would regard similarly as a doublet ('devocioun of chastitee *to love*': l. 283) is not so treated by Clogan, *M&H*, NS 3, 237 and n. 33.

17. Howard (p. 291) finds 'a hint of irony' in the phrase.

18. These categories interconnect. Examples include (i) knowledge: 'if that I shal nat lye' (289), 'that men may wel espyen' (500); (ii) mystery: 'he nyste where' (216), 'as I understonde' (222); (iii) exercise of will: 'and ye wolde it here' (145), 'trusteth me' (229), 'for good entente' (178); (iv) creating a family or stressing its unity: 'leeve brother deere', (257; cf.263, 321). On the importance of this last as a theme in the tale, see Kolve, Rose, p. 151.

19. Robinson and Blake both read ll. 303-4 in the same way (Tiburce asks where to go '"and to what man?"' / '"To whom?"' quod he [*sc.* Valerian]'). In fact, the Latin ('cui dixit') needs to be read not as an interrogative but as a relative pronoun; and cf. Miller (p. 116). For general comment on this feature, see Ryding (pp. 72-8, esp. p. 78): 'the procedure tends to be used at points in the story that constitute lyric peaks, moments of moral beauty'. Ryding may be right that such

were considered 'stylistic elegances', but in SecNT their appearance is partly to be explained in terms of restrictions of the verse form. See also P.E. Beichner, 'Confrontation, contempt of court and Chaucer's Cecilia', *ChR*, 8 (1973-74), 202.

20. See Harbert, Brewer, 1974, p. 146, for general comment on Chaucer's mistranslations.

21. Writers loud in their praise of SecNT include Huppé (p. 230), Whittock (p. 260) and Kolve (Rose, p. 139). Against, on grounds of slavish translation, Eliason (p. 163). Clogan (*M&S* NS 3, 215) distinguishes the early part of the text, up to the baptism of Tiburce, from the later, in terms of Chaucer's relations to his source(s).

22. *Legendys of Hooly Wummen by Osbern Bokenham*, ed. M.S. Serjeantson, EETS OS 206 (London, 1938), pp. 201-25.

23. The text shows a lively sense of the difficulties of producing a translation. A gloss in three MSS, including the earliest, quotes St Gregory 'in registro libro 10 ad Eulogium' (i.e. Epistles X, 39, *PL*, 77, 1099) concerning the 'gravem hic interpretum difficultatem ... ea quae translata fuerint nisi cum graui labore intelligere nullo modo valeamus' ['great difficulty of translators ... without great labour we cannot at all understand those things which have been translated'].

24. On Deschamps, see Brewer (1978) I, 40; on Walton, the versifier of *Bo*, ibid., I, 61; and see also *Boethius de consolatione philosophiae*, trans. John Walton, ed. M. Science, EETS OS 170 (London, 1927), pp. 1-lxii. For detailed comment on the *Boece*, see T.W. Machan, *Techniques of Translation: Chaucer's Boece* (Norman, Oklahoma, 1985).

25. On early composition, see Kean, II, 193; and Giffin, pp. 29 ff. Giffin offers the date 1383, but her evidence is circumstantial; Kean depends on all-too-easy circular argument (inferior or colourless because a close translation and therefore early).

26. In that year Richard II married Anne of Bohemia; hence the F Prol, which names 'the quene' (l. 496), was written later (Robinson, p. 839).

27. If the dream poetry gave Chaucer the chance to reflect on the powers and limits of the creative imagination (so A.C. Spearing, *Medieval Dream Poetry* (Cambridge, 1976), p. 6) translation also raised literary and linguistic questions of the greatest importance, notably, about matters of form and style.

28. Elliott p. 116 points to their origin in manuals of rhetoric. See also Ellis (Glasscoe pp. 21, 26-8, 31) Salter (1974, ch. 6) Fyler (p. 113), and, for comment on the following passages from Prol LGW, A.J. Minnis, *Chaucer and Pagan Antiquity* (Cambridge, 1982), pp. 66-9.

29. 'In eching' receives extended study in *Geoffrey Chaucer, Troilus and Criseyde*, ed. B. Windeatt (London, 1984), pp. 4-11. Like 'encresse or maken dymynucioun', the term may as well apply to the parallel role of the adaptor/compiler as to that of the translator.

30. Note also the prayer for the king 'that is lord of this langage' (Proem, 56-7).

31. Huppé's understanding of the word 'tretys' as relating to *CT* and not just *Mel* (p. 235) is not accepted by most critics.

32. Cf. Kolve (Rose, p. 138): 'the importance [of SecNT] ... is chiefly thematic and structural.'

33. In this detail writers see an important parallel between the narrator and her heroine, and between the process and the subject of her narration. See, e.g. Whittock (p. 252), and David p. 233.

34. Huppé reads this material (p. 227) as a reply to a 'basic criticism of the monastics, their lack of the busyness upon which the friars prided themselves'; Brewer (Intro., p. 78) as aimed at *RR* and 'the lovely portress of the rose-garden'. Quite apart from its more immediate relevance to *CT*, this passage has obvious links with penitential literature, already noted more than once as a source or analogue of the religious narratives of *CT*.

5 CHAUCER'S *MELIBEE*

The other translation in *The Canterbury Tales* already referred to, Chaucer's *Melibee*, raises problems of a different sort. Whether or not we approve of the world-view of the Nun's story, a lot happens in it: as in the cycle plays, its varied spectacle goes some way to atoning for the rigid and limited view advanced. By contrast, *Melibee* is a narrative pruned almost completely of narrative interest. Granted, there is a violent and bloody beginning. Melibeus, young, rich and powerful, leaves his wife Prudence and daughter Sophie at home alone and goes out for 'desport'. In his absence three of his enemies enter the house by the upper windows, beat Prudence and wound Sophie 'with fyve mortal woundes in fyve sondry places', and make good their escape. When Melibeus discovers the crime, he weeps 'lyk a mad man' and tears his clothes. This violent beginning is speedily neutralised by the sense that the narrative is not, in itself, the narrator's prime concern. The careful numbering of the foes, and the precise account of the parts of Sophie's body which they wound, invite an allegorical reading of the narrative as the wounding of the soul in its five senses by the world, the flesh and the devil. Such a reading is confirmed by the manner of the foes' entry, through the windows. According to the standard interpretation of Jeremiah 9:21 ('ascendit mors per fenestras nostras'), the windows are the senses by which temptation enters the soul.[1]

The narrative, however, is not a simple allegory of this sort.[2] Prudence explains that a divine economy has punished Melibeus, in the person of his daughter, for his own sin. The entry of his three enemies by way of the windows, and their wounding of Sophie in five parts of her body, literally represent the way in which Melibeus has allowed his spiritual enemies to enter his heart 'by the wyndowes' of the body and wound his soul through the five senses (1418-26). That is, we have an actual narrative, the wounding of Sophie, which symbolises another actual narrative, the sin of Melibeus. Since the 'outer' narrative functions chiefly as the symbol of the inner one, it does not need to be greatly developed. Hence the wounded girl rapidly disappears from view with Prudence's calm declaration that she 'with the grace of God shal

104

warisshe and escape' (982, cf. 1110). Thereafter, in the person of Prudence, the story sets about providing the wounded Melibeus with the cure he needs, which her counsel will both symbolise and effect.

The most obvious, indeed the only, expression of Melibeus's sick state in the story is his lack of 'mesure' (991, 1605, 1848), his want of patience and prudence, and his desire for revenge. Faced by a man who has lost self-control — the more she counsels calmness, the more he weeps — Prudence takes a long view, as he cannot, of the immediate happening. She remembers what Ovid and Seneca have said (976, 984-5) about allowing the mourner to grieve 'as for a certein tyme' before attempting to counsel patience. Her own patient waiting (980; cf. 1051, 1224, 1728, 1832) thus represents a clear alternative to the immediacy of reaction and sensation to which Melibeus is presently exposed. It will be her role, throughout, to lead him away from his sense of grievance to a truer understanding of things. Likewise, she will correct his all too literal understanding of what he hears, literal-mindedness being another sign of entanglement in the present. Thus, when the physicians, members of the motley council summoned by Melibeus to give him advice, urge him to 'warisshe werre by vengeaunce' (1017), he understands them to be authorising a 'contrarie' act, vengeance, in return for the wrong he has suffered (1279-82); Prudence has to explain that the permitted 'contrarie' to one wrong is not another wrong, but mercy (1283-94). Like Boethius in a vaguely similar situation, Melibeus has to learn to ignore the voice of his own limited experience in favour of the distilled wisdom of the ages offered by his wife.[3]

He is a slow learner. He acknowledges her authority more than once (1112-14, 1232-5, 1261-4), yet continues to resist all her reasoning, and finally accuses her of having no regard for his honour (1681). At this point, with formal rather than dramatic logic, Prudence loses her cool and treats her froward pupil to an angry face and apparently angry words (1687, 1697). Confronted by this hostility — which she later explains was merely a pedagogic strategy (1706) — Melibeus repents and puts himself wholly into the 'disposicioun and ordinaunce' of his wife (1725). Even then, in a sort of coda to the story, he has to learn that mercy requires him to do more than simply spare the lives of his enemies, now humbly repentant and ready to accept their punishment at his hand; his first thought, to exile them and seize all their goods, still smacks of the unregenerate worldling who wanted war and vengeance.

The triumph of Prudence is completed in two stages. She puts the adversaries through the same course of instruction (fortunately for us, in miniature), and gets them to give the same promise, as Melibeus (1765; cf. 1725). Then, she secures the appointment of a council to advise Melibeus; she sees to it that the councillors speak as with one voice, her own, and thus reverse the ill-effects of the council first summoned by her husband. Only then, when all the voices speak the one word, does she permit herself the luxury of a simple feeling (1779, 1793). Prudence, then, is the ideal counsellor, not least because she is the perfect demonstration of what she is talking about.[4] By this reading, the narrative belongs to that class of stories in which a young man learns true wisdom as a result of meeting with an older woman. The obvious parallel in *The Canterbury Tales* is the Wife of Bath's tale, where the young knight, unable to see beyond present pleasure (rape of a young woman) or present disgrace (enforced marriage to an old one), learns to look beyond the appearances of things and, as a tangible admission of his own limitations, puts himself under the 'wise governance' of his wife (III, 1231).

Melibee, then, is formally a story about the education of the hero, just as its immediate predecessor *Sir Thopas* was, and for all that the two traditions of philosophical treatise and courtly romance appear to be facing in opposite directions.[5] But there is a clear difference between the two stories. When interrupted, *Sir Thopas* looks set fair, even as the Squire's tale did, to produce an interminable narrative full of inconsequential happenings. *Melibee*, on the other hand, produces an equally interminable narrative almost entirely bereft of happening.[6] Its narrative is a front. Now, the source Chaucer faithfully followed, an adaptation into French, by the Dominican Renaud de Louens, of the *Liber Consolationis* of Albertano of Brescia, described its original as an old story which Renaud had found in manuscript (*SA*, p. 568). Both Albertano's original and Renaud's adaptation had a clear and overriding didactic purpose. Both were directed to young men (Albertano's youngest son, and the son of Renaud's noble patroness) with a view to their instruction and profit, and, according to Renaud, the profit of every other nobleman willing to read the work and keep it in mind. The young reader is therefore to put himself in the shoes of the young hero, and receive as if spoken directly to him the words of Prudence to Melibeus. The thinnest possible line therefore separates the resulting narrative from a protracted piece of fatherly, or priestly, advice. That advice depends not on immediate experience — after all, the young man has his own version of that to oppose to his father's — but on the presentation of authorities. Every piece of advice is buttressed by at least one quotation from authority. The work thus focuses the same dilemma as Chaucer's translation of the story of St Cecilia, and comes predictably to the same conclusion: not 'experience' but 'auctoritee' is the heart of a narrative.

The meaning of the work thus lies, to a considerable degree, in the relation of the assembled authorities to one another.[7] But the narrator's practice, tacitly at least, opposes such a view of the work. He seems to find authority so single and self-evident that he has only to cite *auctours* to prove his case. That the *auctours* might not speak with a single voice, and that his use of them might compromise his work's single and self-evident message, he seems not to consider. Yet his heroine shows a readiness to argue against the letter of the text in pursuit of a higher understanding which compels just such a conclusion. For instance, Prudence quotes Ecclesiasticus 33:20 to the enemies of Melibeus to urge them to put themselves at his mercy (1754-6). The quoted text actually warns people against giving power over themselves to members of their immediate family and close friends: which is how Melibeus read it earlier (1060) when seeking support for himself in his refusal to follow his wife's advice.[8] If Melibeus took the simple sense of the saying, Prudence twists it out of all recognition to make it square with an alleged higher understanding.[9] She is well aware of the difficulties thus created:

> now sithen he deffendeth that man sholde nat yeven
> to his broother ... myght ... by a strenger resoun he
> deffendeth and forbedeth a man to yeven hymself to his
> enemy. And nathelees ... mystruste nat my lord.
>
> (1757-9)

She might also have remembered an earlier piece of her own advice; the opinions of one group of people, she said, should not be represented in a lord's council ('the book seith that "no wight retourneth saufly into the grace of his olde enemy"': 1183). Yet she is later proposing that the enemies of Melibeus should do this very thing! Elsewhere in Chaucer — but hardly here — the opposition of authorities to one another, or of diverse understandings of a single authority, features prominently in narratives exposing human pretentions to infallibility. As we shall see, this opposition is at the heart of the Nun's Priest's tale: to take only a single example, that work shows Chauntecleer attempting to demolish Pertelot's 'Caton' with 'many a man moore of auctorite' (2975-6). And the one authority is easily turned inside out by different speakers: the God of Love quotes 'Valerye' and 'Jerome agayns Jovynyan' approvingly as texts in praise of virtuous women, and the Wife of Bath's fifth husband applauds them for their denunciation of wicked women (*Legend* G, 280-1; *CT*, III, 671-85).[10] The two positions can, of course, be harmonised with one another, even as, in a *Summa*, the master confirms what was of value in the two students' opposed citations of authorities, and at the same time makes a new thing out of their limited understandings and transcends them both. There is, however, no *tertium quid* in *Melibee*. We depend on the narrative frame to persuade us to accept an authority which, looked at from the outside, appears as random and arbitrary as that which it opposes. A narrative which appeared to exist only as a cover for didactic purposes thus turns out — paradoxically, perversely — the only guarantor of those purposes.

A faithful translation of this perverse narrative will obviously preserve its contradictions intact.[11] As earlier noted, Chaucer's translation aims to reproduce exactly the 'sentence' of its original, while allowing for some variation in respect of its 'wordes' and 'tellyng': specifically, Chaucer will tell 'somwhat moore/ Of proverbes' than his original. This last turns out to be true, though fortunately Chaucer has not enlarged his original's store of wise sayings to any significant extent. He actually introduces only three proverbs into his translation, and each of them merely supports an existing *auctoritas* or expands an abbreviated or implied reference to one.[12] (Additionally, he twice turns the witness of his own source into an *auctoritas*.[13]) For the most part, though, he contents himself with additions to the text like those in the Nun's tale — their main function, to give some sense of a speaking voice ('*wel I woot*': 988; '*as hertely as I dar and kan*': 1052) and, more importantly, to underline the meaning of the narrative, especially the virtues of Prudence ('*whan she saugh hir tyme*': 1051; '*gladly techen*': 1071; '*unto youre grete goodnesse*': 1744; '*to youre wommanly pitee*': 1750). Larger additions gloss the obvious literal sense of an *auctoritas* (e.g. 1584, 1709). Most of them are of the simplest sort, doublets for an existing phrase or word (e.g. 'thy will *and thyn entente*': 1149).[14] Curiously, the further into the translation we proceed, the more important the simple doublet becomes: in the following passage, near the end of the work, the translation is almost twice as long as the original by virtue of its doublets and other additions:

> And whan Melibees freendes hadde taken hire avys
> *and deliberacioun* of the forseide mateere, and
> hadden examyned it *by greet bisynesse and greet*
> *diligence*, they yave ful conseil for to have pees
> *and reste*, and that Melibee sholde receyve *with good*
> *herte* his adversaries to foryifnesse *and mercy*.
>
> (1787-90)

Chaucer is not doing anything by this means that his original did not sanction — not the least of its sins was a tendency to prolixity — but the increase of the gloss seems to call for comment. So too another feature of the translation which, similarly, the original appeared to authorise: that is, the use of an eccentric word-order. Unsurprising in a verse text, where constraints of metre and rhyme encourage a certain flexibility, this word-order is distinctly odd, at the time when Chaucer was writing, in a prose text.[15] The most obvious feature of this odd word-order is a reversal of the normal pattern adjective–noun (thus 'biens temporelz' is translated 'temporeel goodes' at 1554, but 'goodes temporels', with retention of French plural adjectival form, at 998). This pattern is too common in Chaucer's other prose texts (the *Boece*, the *Astrolabe*, and the Parson's tale) to excite much interest.[16] More interesting is the change to word-order when infinitives and compound tenses of verbs are called for. A past participle may precede its auxiliary: 'called was' (967), 'retourned was' (973), 'cleped is' (976). Some-times an infinitive is placed at the end of the phrase, after a dependent object: 'bisoghte hym of his wepyng for to stynte' (974; cf. 978, 986), 'youreself to destroye' (983), 'ne parties to supporte' (1014). Sometimes these patterns are observable even with simple verb forms like copula and adjective: 'hym that sorweful is' (988); or verb and direct object: 'his sermon hem anoieth' (1044), 'his olde foes han it espyed' (970). Sometimes the subject of a sub-ordinate clause follows the verb: 'after the loore that techeth us Senek' (991), 'as taughte Thobie his sone' (1117). An abstract noun can even acquire a definite article: 'in olde men is the sapience, and in longe tyme the prudence' (1164).

The French text authorised most of these practices (and extraordinary literalisms like 'manye of othre resons' (1109, cf. French 'moult d'autres', rendered more idiomatically 'manye causes' (1123)): but not all of them;[17] there is, for example, no precedent in the French text for the inversion of past participle and auxiliary.[18] These distortions to English word-order sometimes throw an emphasis on a word, usually a noun or verb, displaced to the end of the clause or phrase (in the examples above, 'Senek', 'destroye', 'supporte'): but not regularly ('called was'). Similar effects are produced when dependent phrases are interposed between the subject and verb of a clause: 'he, lyk a mad man, rentynge his clothes, gan to wepe' (973). Moreover, these distinctive disturbances to normal word-order are not found in this concentration in any other prose work of Chaucer, not even the *Boece*, the elaborately patterned Latin of whose original might have been expected to call them forth.[19]

Inevitably, we conclude that a stylistic experiment is taking place. Chaucer is attempting a prose version of the effects he produced, for example, in the Proem to *Troilus* III:

> ... man, brid, best, fissh, herbe, and grene tree
> Thee fele in tymes with vapour eterne ...
> Ye Joves first to thilk effectes glade ...
> Comeveden, and amorous him made ...
> Ye fierse Mars apaisen of his ire ...
>
> (III, 10-11, 15, 17, 22)[20]

Just as Chaucer's translation aimed to better the original in respect of its added proverbs, so, it seems — and this would not have proved too difficult — Chaucer aimed to go one better stylistically as well. Hence the phrases 'I varie as in my speche' and 'I nat the same wordes seye', in the prologue, relate not only to the content but also to the style of the translation, and partially explain its greater recourse to non-native word-order.[21] The experiment, if that is what it is, did not last long. Most clearly in evidence in the opening pages of the work, these distinctive stylistic features are much less evident thereafter;[22] in the last pages, where the glossing of the text is vastly on the increase, they are all but abandoned.

Their demise, coupled with the rise of that simpler stylistic feature, the gloss, suggests that the experiment proved more trouble than it was worth. That Chaucer made the experiment at all, when he showed no sign of wanting to experiment with the style of the Second Nun's tale, is, however, probably significant. Renaud's narrative, we have implied, is almost completely bereft of human interest. Chaucer set out to attract and keep the reader's attention by a heightened rhetorical style.[23] He rapidly became aware of the limitations of a highly wrought surface as a cover for the original's own poor narrative façade, and the experiment lost most of its impetus within 40 lines of starting. And when, in the end, he opted for the simpler stylistic expedient of glossing the text, Chaucer exposed his original yet more directly as the hollow thing it is: a pretence of a story, and the appearance of a serious engagement with important ideas.[24]

As with the Second Nun's tale, the importance of *Melibee* lies less in the tale itself than in the literary positions taken up in the prologue. The preceding analysis should have suggested, as earlier references to the prologue implied, that Chaucer gives himself slightly more licence as a translator than the Second Nun. Nevertheless, his prologue draws very similar conclusions to hers about the relation of the new work of art to an existing tradition. In one important respect, though, Chaucer diverges from her line. She links art to morality; he links it to truth. (This opposition, it will be noted, exactly matches the one earlier advanced in the introduction when we were attempting to create categories for this study.)

Chaucer's is not the only voice so raised. The storytellers of our next group all make a bow in the direction of the artist's obligations to the truth. The Man of Law and Monk choose from available versions of the text that one of whose truth they are persuaded, and suppress those whose truth they doubt. The Physician presents his work as 'no fable' but an 'historial thyng notable' whose 'sentence ... sooth is' (VI, 155-7). And the Physician's claim to be reporting the truth is echoed by other pilgrims, eager to claim for their narratives the status of truth (so, for instance, the Reeve). Such claims are, for the most part, fraudulent. Most of the offered truths either pay someone else back (as happens with several *cherles'* tales), or project the speaker's own personality (so the tales of the professionals in the next section). Truth is not well served in so competitive a climate.

Even so, one speaker besides Chaucer takes the question

seriously: the Parson. Single-minded in his approach like the Nun, the Parson shares many of her presuppositions. He allows that, since his competence reaches only to rendering the 'sentence' of the original, informed authority may better his efforts (X, 55-60). Like her, too, he denies literature an independent and self-sufficient existence, and actively deprecates the artist's craft considered as an end in itself. But where she took her stand on the epistle of James, he takes his on Paul's letters to Timothy and on the preaching of Jesus. St James authorises the Nun's attempt to rescue literature from the status of an idle pastime and press it into the service of morality. St Paul, by contrast, describes an encroaching pagan world in which lies are being passed off as truth (31-4; cf. I Tim. 1:4, 4:7; II Tim. 4:4); and the apocalyptic preaching of Jesus divides the wheat from the chaff, garners the former, and burns the latter (35-6; cf. Matt. 13:30). That is, literature is answerable not just to morality but, more importantly, to truth. For the Parson, therefore, the central opposition is between truth and lies. Hence, he all but rejects the literary realm. He will not even countenance verse because he finds it intrinsically unworthy for the presentation of serious matter (43-4). All forms of verse provide the occasion for hearers, so to speak, to wander by the way.[25]

Like the Second Nun, the Parson is attractively honest and singleminded. Logically, though, his position entails the death of literary interest and significance in pursuit of religious truth. Not surprisingly, his tale bears these comments out. Chaucer's *Melibee* is just such another, where literary interest is all but lost sight of in the quest for significant truths. But the prologue to the tale is a very different affair; the literary understanding there revealed, more complex than that advanced by any other pilgrim, might almost stand as an epitome of *The Canterbury Tales* (and, incidentally, of the present work as well). In his speech to the Host Chaucer declares himself, in principle, in favour of a multiplicity of versions as the condition of apprehending a story. He thus opposes the Nun's conviction that invention had no place in the work of art. He also opposes to the Parson's stark contrast of religious truth and artistic deceit a more complex contrast, between a 'sentence' and its 'tellyng' (947-8). Chaucer's reference to the Gospel narratives of the Passion proves as important in this connection for the creation of his literary aesthetic as reference to other Bible texts, in their respective contexts, for the Parson and the Nun.[26] Biblical scholarship was well aware of divergences between one Gospel and another, but also knew that substantial disagreement could not obtain between divinely inspired texts, and was ready to conflate all four texts into a single Gospel harmony.[27] Nor is this distinction between a *sentence* and its telling a matter only for theologians. Since the evangelists were, so to speak, translators of a divine word into a human language — this was a traditional metaphor[28] — one could turn to the related world of translation theory and practice (to which, as already noted, Chaucer was no stranger) to find the same distinction. Truth is perfectly consistent with diversity of translation, according to the author of the prologue to the Wycliffe Bible — and the view is a commonplace — 'for where oon seide derkli, oon either mo seiden openli'.[29] In any case, truth is not simply a question of approximation to or deviation from an ideal. The writer's reasons for writing, and the effects he aims to produce, must also be taken into consideration. The evangelists expressed their purposes diversely, that same prologue tells us, so that 'goode men [schulde] ben exercisid'.

Chaucer is therefore advancing a literary ideal, in which the true telling of a tale depends on a relation of mutual respect and cooperation between tale, teller and audience. Literary activity can then be seen as a symbol of moral activity; tale-telling becomes the perfect artistic equivalent of a religious pilgrimage.[30] It is hardly surprising that only Chaucer sees beyond the simple oppositions in terms of which all the other characters set up, or operate, their literary categories; nor that most of the other pilgrims choose either pilgrimage or pastime as their motive for storytelling.[31] (The tales to be studied in the last section of this book, however, come closest to resolving this opposition. They also focus most clearly the question of the artist's relation to both the truth and the effect (or morality) of his 'mateere'.)

Notes

1. See *The Cloud of Unknowing and Related Treatises*, ed. P. Hodgson, Analecta Cartusiana 3 (Salzburg, 1982), 9/6-7 and n.; also EETS OS 218 (London, 1944), n. to 15/19.
2. Not all writers have grasped this point. Those who have include Cooper pp. 174-5; P. Strohm, 'The Allegory of *Mel*,' *ChR*, 2 (1967-68), 32-42; C.A. Owen, 'The Tale of *Mel*', *ChR*, 7 (1972-73), 276-7; Howard, p. 311; and Lawler, p. 23.
3. Also noted Benson, *ChR*, 18, 72.

4. Lawler (p. 103) argues that Prudence herself grows in understanding as the narrative progresses.

5. On 'education' (or testing) as the theme of romance, particularly of the quest type, see Brewer (1974), p. 29.

6. Cf. David (p. 219): 'plot interest is negligible in both.' In a deep sense this is true; not on the surface of the narrative, though.

7. For a persuasive reading of that relation — which argues a development 'from a wholly prudential to a somewhat providential point of view' — see Lawler, pp. 104-5. My view is closer to that of Norton-Smith (p. 147), who talks of 'a multiplying briar patch of contending "sentences"'.

8. See judicious comments by Gaylord, *PMLA*, 82, 229, on conflict of authorities in NPT and between the gods in MerchT: 'to the untutored eye the "sentence" of a piece might be almost the opposite of what the surface sense seemed to imply; at least a certain agility in argument was called for.'

9. So also Cooper, p. 173.

10. On the God of Love as a literary critic, see David, p. 50; on the use of texts in Prol WBT, ibid., pp. 138-9. See also Gaylord, *PMLA*, 82, 233-4, on quotation from Eccl. 32:6, used in *Mel*, and misunderstood by the Host in Prol NPT.

11. Most analyses of *Mel* therefore relate not so much to Chaucer — except in respect of style, see below — as to Renaud or even Albertano. (Such comment is generally covert; for an exception, see Burlin, p. 228 on 'Albertano's pale imitation of Boethius'.) Approving comments on Chaucer–Renaud–Albertano focus on the medieval predilection for wisdom literature (Zacher, pp. 116-18; Burnley, pp. 45-7, 50-1; Ruggiers, Vasta–Thundy, pp. 86-90: Howard, pp. 309 ff.). Generally critics favourably disposed to *Mel* place it in relation not to its source but to *CT* as a whole (Howard p. 315; Ruggiers, Vasta–Thundy, p. 85) or, more contentiously, to the presumed original audience. On the political dimension of *Mel*, see, in particular, C.A. Owen Jr, *ChR*, 7, 267-80; Green pp. 142 ff.; Zacher, p. 119. Howard (p. 310, n. 101) concludes that *Mel* 'applies religious ideas to political circumstances and not the reverse' (the only tale clearly to do so, and hence less secure in this study than might otherwise have appeared). Various recipients of the translation are advanced: John of Gaunt (Owen), the young Richard II (Green). Few consider directly the problem of such literature as literature, though their praise is faint at best (Ruggiers finds 'an intellectual plot of sorts'; Howard 'an appalling number of quotations'). This point is more clearly taken up by the critics: e.g. Elliott, p. 173; Cooper, p. 172.

12. Ll. 1054, 1326, 1510 (*SA*, pp. 573/150-4, 588/541-3, 597/771-2); cf. Thompson, Davis–Wrenn, p. 185, n. 5.

13. Ll. 1177, 1264 (*SA*, pp. 580/346-7, 585/472-4).

14. On this feature of the work, see Cooper, p. 176; Eliason, p. 79; and Elliott, p. 174, who notes its increase later in the tale, and calls it 'bloated circumlocution' (p. 180).

15. This convenient generalisation requires fuller substantiation than is possible in a footnote; for fuller detail, see following notes. In support of it, Elliott (p. 69) comments on Chaucer's departures from 'the usual patterns of late fourteenth-century English'. According to N. Davis, 'Chaucer and fourteenth-century English', Brewer (1974), p. 61, devotional treatises and sermons accounted for almost all original prose until late in the century and bulked large until its end. (Coleman, p. 161 finds, to the contrary, that the widespread use of prose by the Wycliffites 'merely confirmed a trend'.) Note further that the increasing mass of translated prose at this time needs to be assessed with caution in the endeavour to establish 'usual patterns of late 14th cy. English', since its word-order may derive from that of its sources. Of original prose, however, there is

a surprising amount: in the category of treatises and sermons, works as diverse as the Wycliffite sermons, the writings of the ME mystics, Clanvowe's *Two Ways*. Then there is the prose of public and private record (Davis, Brewer (1974) p. 61: 'up to this time ... the language was not much written for ordinary business or private purposes'); for examples, see B. Cottle, *The Triumph of English 1350-1400* (London, 1969), ch. 3, pp. 111-12; or *ME Literature*, ed. A. Brandl and O. Zippel (New York, 1949), pp. 248-9 (petition of the London mercers of 1386). We have also to reckon with a consciously literary prose, represented, among Chaucer's contemporaries, by Usk's *Testament of Love* and, shortly after Chaucer's death, by the preachers of sermons 39-46 in Ross. If we except these last, and discount prose whose word-order suggests unfamiliarity with the production of written texts, we are left with a range of texts which, taken together, may provide substantiation for any claim about 'the usual patterns of late 14 cy English' against which Chaucer's practices in *Mel* may be set. See also N. Davis, 'Styles in English prose of the late middle and early modern period', in *Les congrès et colloques de l'université de Liège 21* (Liège, 1961), 165-81.

16. E.g. *Bo*, I, m.1, 15: 'heeris hore'; 21: 'deth cruwel'; *Astr*, I, 4: 'south lyne or ellis the lyne meridional'; ParsT 79: 'weyes espirituels'.

17. Examples of corresponding word order in Renaud: (i) inf. after dependent object: pour toy et ta maison deffendre (*SA*, ll. 103-4); (ii) vb. prec. by dir. obj. (esp. noun, since pronominal object regularly precedes): ceulz qui joye mainnent (40). Most of the examples given in this paragraph, however, are not directly dependent on Renaud's word-order: e.g. the prudence] Ren. prudence (324); ne parties to supporte] Ren. ne supporter partie (81).

18. Such is, however, found in French texts: so, for example, Christine de Pisan 'emprises ne seroient' (quoted D. Bornstein, 'French influence on fifteenth-century English prose as exemplified by the translation of Christine de Pisan's *Livre du Corps de policie*,' *MS* 39 (1977), 373).

19. *Bo* achieves what most readers take for the strongly foreign feel of its word-order by the retention of complex patterns of subordination, including absolute constructions. Few instances occur of the practices noted in *Mel*: e.g. III, m. 12, 40: 'despyseth the floodes to drynken', II, m 5, 28: 'be of blood ishad'.

20. As earlier noted, the patterns noted in *Mel* also occur in Chaucer's verse, in particular the inversion of auxiliary and p.p.: e.g. *CT*, I, 1355: 'comen was'; II, 154: 'as I shal yow devyse'; 172: 'they han this blisful mayden sayn'; *Tr*, I, 64: 'the ravysshyng to wreken of Eleyne/By Paris don'.

21. Greater recourse to non-native word-order also characterises Usk's *The Testament of Love* (see *Chaucerian and other Pieces*, ed. W.W. Skeat (Oxford, 1887), pp. 1-46. (Parallels with *Mel* include — p. 3: 'the philosophers ... many noble thinges ... writen'; 'the perfeccion by busy study to knowe'; p. 5: 'she that shulde me solace' (the ending of a clause with an inf. or other vb. form has almost become a stylistic tic with Usk, as, later in the fifteenth century, with Pecock). Other literalisms make common cause with *Bo*, on which Usk was dependent. But Usk goes further than *Bo*. Like Pecock, he treats compound words on the model of the Rolle Psalter (for comment on which, see Ellis, Glasscoe, pp. 29-30) e.g. p. 67, 'out-bringe'. Similar recourse to non-native word-order in sermons 44-6 of Ross led the editor to conclude (p. xxvi with examples) either that the sermons were translated from Latin or French or that the author was not a native Englishman.

22. The experiment has been regularly noted, but inadequately described. In the nineteenth century it was fashionable to claim that Chaucer had mixed blank verse with the prose of the opening pages (Spurgeon, I, 498-9; II, 223-4; III, 54). More recently, M. Schlauch, 'Chaucer's prose rhythms', *PMLA*, 65 (1950), 568-89, claimed that Chaucer was using Latin prose rhythms to end his clauses (the so-called 'cursus'). For criticism of the claim that OE used 'cursus' which, by

implication, refutes Schlauch's claim, see S.M. Kuhn, 'Cursus in OE', *Spec.*, 47 (1972), 188-206; Kuhn concludes (p. 206) that 'the things which pass for cursus in medieval Latin, ME and other languages' are probably mostly 'simple linguistic phenomena, having little or no connection with the true cursus.'

23. The heightened style is described as 'eloquent style' by M. Schlauch, 'The art of Chaucer's prose', Brewer (1966), p. 153, and as 'style clergial' by Bornstein, *MS*, 39, 373. Bornstein, indeed, claims that *Mel* set the fashion for many writers in the fifteenth century. Both accounts seem to me impressionistic. The stylistic features I have isolated in the preceding paragraphs seem surer signs of 'style clergial', if such a thing has an objective existence in English, than those features isolated by Bornstein. When not actually the stock-in-trade of free translation in the period ('forsothe', 'as it happeth oft', 'this is to seyn'), her categories are often difficult to quantify ('Latinate words, elaborate explanations, legal phrases, synonyms, reliance on the passive voice, and a grave, ceremonious tone'). For general comment on style as the real significance of *Mel*, in the wider context of *CT*, see Benson, *ChR*, 18, 71.

24. Cf.S. Justman, 'Literal and symbolic in *CT*', *ChR*, 14 (1979-80), 209: 'Chaucer took the letter [of *Mel*] but who can prove in what spirit? Perhaps, though, it was not the spirit of his "auctor". Perhaps the *Mel* is a perfect counterfeit.'

25. Cf. Kolve (p. 81): 'in verse his characters are as likely to misunderstand . . . those texts [they are translating] as to get them right, and the purposes of Truth are served only by indirection.' And see also S. Barney, 'An Evaluation of PardT', in *Twentieth-Century Interpretations of PardT*, ed. D.R. Faulkner (Englewood Cliffs, N.J., 1973), p. 95, on the question of 'writing good literature, or telling good tales' in the light of 'the doomsday perspective or [even] the perspective of natural reason'.

26. For comment about this passage, see Brewer (1984), pp. 72,74; Howard, p. 185; Norton-Smith, p. 83; and Benson, *ChR*, 18, 69.

27. On Gospel harmonies, see Salter (1974), ch. 4.

28. For comment, see Minnis, *MS* 43, 382, reworked in Minnis (1984), p. 167. Cf. St Bridget, *Liber*, V resp. ad q. 16: 'non mirum, si hii qui narracionem euangeliorum ordinauerunt, quod posuerunt diuersa, sed tamen vera, quia quidam eorum posuerunt verbum ad verbum, quidam sensum verborum, non verba. Quidam scripserunt audita non visa' ['it is no wonder if those who arranged the Gospel narrative did not provide a uniform record, yet all is true, for some recorded what had happened — the letter of their texts — and some what it meant — the *sensus*. Some, indeed, wrote by hearsay'].

29. *The Wycliffe Bible*, ed. J. Forshall and F. Madden, 5 vols (Oxford, 1850), I,59; and cf. I,56: 'oo gospeller tellith the thou3tis, and another . . . the wordis'.

30. I thus side with Kolve (p. 82), and Kolve, Brewer (1974), p. 317. He, I imagine, would also agree with David (p. 133): 'there are times when the aims of the conscientious artist and the conscientious Christian coincide, but their goals remain fundamentally different.' And cf. Josipovici, *CQ*, 7, 196, on *CT* as a game which 'aims at a redirection of the reader's will'.

31. The simplest of these oppositions is well treated in Gaylord, *PMLA*, 82, 226-35 and regularly noted. For an excellent statement of opposition in Chaucer, see P. Elbow, *Oppositions in Chaucer* (Middletown, Conn., 1975).

PART TWO

RELIGIOUS SUBJECTS, LITERARY INTERESTS,
AND THE SENSE OF A PERFORMANCE

There was one that wrestled with him until daybreak.
(Genesis 32:24)

6 THE MAN OF LAW'S TALE

So far we have been considering stories which, for the most part, faithfully translate the 'sentence' and even the words of their originals. Notwithstanding the failure of the Clerk's tale completely to realise the emblematic possibilities of its narrative, this generalisation holds almost as good for it as for the Second Nun's tale and *Melibee*, and were an actual source ever discovered for the Prioress's tale, might well hold good for it too.[1] We therefore appear to have evolved a clear model for our study of the remaining religious narratives of *The Canterbury Tales*.

Unlike the Nun and the pilgrim Chaucer, the Man of Law does not claim to be offering a translation. He explains that he has learned his story from a merchant, long dead, merchants being uniquely well-placed, by virtue of their wide experience of foreign parts, to 'knowen al th' estaat/ Of regnes' and to pass on 'tidynges/ And tales, both of pees and of debaat' (II, 128-30). Our fictional merchant may have taken up the story because it begins with Syrian merchants who travel to Rome 'for chapmanhod or for disport', and bring back tidings of the Emperor's daughter Custance to their master the Sultan. If so, he can have found nothing else in it to interest him so directly, because the merchants disappear after the beginning. In any case, although it can be read as a narrative of travel to foreign parts — Syria, Spain, Northumbria, Italy — the tale is not a traveller's tale, a narrative of monsters and the marvellous such as the garrulous Mandeville brought back from his travels.[2] It is a soberly religious tale, in line with the 'sobre cheere' (97) of the narrator, and stands in a close, if unacknowledged, relation to the Anglo-Norman *Cronicles* of Nicholas Trevet.[3] One passage of the tale in particular translates the original very closely indeed. A false accusation is being levelled against Custance (called Constance in Trevet's original) by the man guilty of the crime: suddenly

A voys was herd in general audience
And seyde, 'Thou hast desclaundred, *giltelees*,
The doghter of hooly chirche, *in heigh presence*;
Thus hastou doon, and yet holde I my pees!'

(673-6)

119

E a ceo dist vne voiz en le oye de touz: 'Aduersus
filiam matris ecclesie ponebas scandalum; hec fecisti,
et tacui'.

(SA pp. 171-2)

Except for the additional glosses, the duplication of 'dist' by the
phrases 'was herd' and 'seyde', and the rendering of 'tacui' by
'holde', this is extremely close translation. Study of the Man of
Law's tale must therefore consider what kind of narrative Chaucer
inherited, and what he made of it.

The key to Trevet's narrative lies in its exemplary colour. As
with the Second Nun's tale, we have a heroine who actively represents the Christian faith in a pagan world. Like the heroine of the
Clerk's tale, she undergoes what we might call the martyrdom of
many years' enforced separation from those she loves; by virtue of
her unshakeable faith — hence her name — she is reunited with
them. She is prepared from the beginning for her twin roles of
missionary and martyr. Her father's only child, she is taught the
faith and made an expert linguist, both clear requirements of any
would-be missionary. The pagan merchants arrive from Syria and
she converts them. Returned home, and brought before the Sultan
as renegades to Islam, they praise the agent of their conversion so
warmly that the Sultan falls in love with her. With true generosity
of spirit he sends the merchants back with his emir to ask the
emperor for his daughter's hand, and promises an alliance between
Christians and Saracens. And when he learns from his emissaries
that Rome's acceptance of the alliance will require his own conversion, he not only agrees, but goes further: he promises the
Christians peace and free passage throughout his territories, and
gives them rights of ownership over Jerusalem. In addition, he
authorises the general conversion of his people to Christianity.
Constance is then sent with a large following and a rich dowry. We
may imagine that she will play a prominent role in the conversion
of the Syrians. We reckon, however, without the Sultan's mother.
The Sultaness cannot accept her son's proposed destruction of the
Islamic code, and works secretly with 700 Saracens to massacre
every Christian, including her son, at a banquet before the wedding. Three Christian slaves escape at the first sound of the attack,
and return to Rome with the news that, as far as they know, all the
Christians, including Constance, are dead.

Constance is still alive, the only member of the ill-fated party not murdered. Her enemies have kept her alive, it seems, because they recognise in her the chief agent of a Christian imperialism, and they seek by various means — promise of wealth and threat of punishment ('bele promesse de richesse ... manace de peyne') — to persuade her to recant, and, presumably, become a Moslem.[4] When Constance remains unmoved by threats and blandishments, they put her in an open boat with her dowry and food enough for three years (an unexpectedly kindly attention to her comfort) and cast her adrift on the open sea. Constance's sea journey lasts nearly four years, during which time she is completely alone, dependent on God to direct her physical and spiritual course. Eventually the sea casts her up on the Northumbrian coast. She presents the strange spectacle of a beautiful young woman of clearly noble upbringing but 'descoloure' [sunburned] and dressed strangely, in a ship stuffed with rich treasure. Her earlier linguistic training comes to her aid: she speaks to the inhabitants in their own Saxon tongue so fluently that Elda, the constable of the nearby castle, thinks her a Saxon princess from mainland Europe. Her fluency is not matched by candour: she tells Elda only that she was married to a great prince, and exiled because she offended his nobles. She does tell him, though, that she is a Christian: which will prove significant, since before the beginning of the story the native Christians of Britain have been driven to the westernmost reaches of the island by the invading pagan Saxons.

The next step in the story is the conversion of the Saxons. Notwithstanding her secrecy about her origins, Constance impresses Elda as favourably as she had earlier impressed the Sultan and his merchants. He takes her in gladly, and guarantees the safekeeping of her treasure. In a few days she has regained her original complexion, and all see her clearly for the virtuous woman she is. The constable's wife, Hermengild, falls in love with this vision of unparalleled goodness ('en terre sauntz peer en vertue'). Constance preaches the faith to her for several days, and converts her. Hermengild cannot yet realise her religious purposes, though, because her husband is still a pagan. Her difficulty is resolved by the sudden appearance of a blind and prescient Briton who calls on her, in the hearing of both Constance and Elda, to pray over him and cure him. Constance encourages the fearful Hermengild to act boldly, and Hermengild, addressing the blind man in Saxon, cures him. Then both women take the opportunity of the general amazement to preach the faith to Elda and his company. All are converted and the Bishop of Bangor is sent for to baptise them. Elda at once destroys the heathen idols, as the Sultan had intended to do, and travels to his master King Alla to report about Constance, like the Syrian merchants to their master. Like the Sultan, Alla is greatly impressed by what he hears, and proposes to visit Constance privately.

During Elda's absence, however, Constance has been receiving the unwelcome attention of his second-in-command, one of the new converts, who has fallen in love with her as suddenly as Hermengild did and has attempted to seduce her. Rejected by her, and fearful of being reported to his master, he murders Hermengild in her bed the night before Elda is due back, and throws the blame for the murder on Constance, who is sleeping in the same bed, by leaving the murder weapon under her pillow. Aroused by the return of Elda, who comes to announce the arrival of the king, Constance attempts to wake Hermengild and discovers the murder. In the ensuing turmoil the murderer finds the hidden weapon and accuses Constance of the crime. Distraught though he is, Elda cannot readily believe evil of his friend: so the murderer seizes a Gospel book conveniently to hand — the women have it by them every night 'par devocioun' — and swears to the truth of his accusation. At this point, as earlier noted, a heavenly voice condemns the perjurer, and what looks to the bystanders like a closed fist fells him to the ground and knocks out his teeth and his eyes. After this, the execution of human judgement, deferred until the king arrives to deliver it himself, is a mere formality. Constance's second trial leads, by way of Alla's baptism, to marriage with the king.

But the relief is shortlived. Shortly after the marriage Alla is forced to leave his pregnant wife in order to lead an army to his northern borders to repel a Scottish invasion. He puts Constance in the care of Elda and the Bishop of Bangor, and directs them to send him news directly the child is born. Constance gives birth to a fair son, called Maurice, and the protectors send a messenger to Alla with the joyful news. On the way the messenger calls on Doumylde, the King's mother. Like the Sultan's mother, the dowager hates Constance: partly because she has been instrumental in destroying the old religion; partly because of her beauty; partly for her foreignness and carefully concealed origins. The dowager gives every appearance of joy at the news, but that night she drugs the messenger and replaces the original letter with a forgery. Constance, she writes, has changed since her husband's departure, and shown herself as the evil spirit she is by giving birth to a monster. So that no shame will attach to Alla's person, the monster has been locked away and another child baptised as the king's heir. Not even the messenger knows the contents of the letter. What are the deputies to do with Constance and her child? The forged letter expects, and seeks to produce, a violent reaction. But the king, though greatly distressed by the news, is as unwilling to proceed against Constance in the face of so apparent a treason as Elda had been. Indeed, but for his faith in the truth of his deputies, he would dismiss the news at once as incredible. In his reply, therefore, he instructs them to keep Constance and the child safe until he returns. When the messenger breaks his homeward journey at her castle, Doumylde discovers the contents of her son's letter by the means she had formerly used, and, finding it not to her liking, replaces it with another forgery. This time she writes, as from the king, how he has heard in a foreign land what no one in the court has dared to tell him; if Constance remains longer in the kingdom foreign peoples — of whom, presumably, she is the agent — will invade the kingdom and destroy it. Therefore the deputies must, within four days, furnish a ship with food for five years, and the treasure which Constance brought with her, and banish her with her son.

And so Constance must put to sea again. The general grief that accompanies her departure has a clear parallel in that of the Romans when she left for Syria — a notable structural feature of a work whose earlier episodes regularly anticipate later ones — but is more fully treated here than before.[5] This moment is also import-ant because it shows us, what until now we have hardly glimpsed, the human situation of the emperor's daughter. Hitherto Constance has been clearly in control: she has secured the conversion of others, or assisted them to demonstrate their faith-fulness and discernment. Very occasionally the narrative paints a different picture. Once, after the massacre, it describes her as 'degarre'; once, after the murder of Hermengild, she reacts 'a grant affray'. Otherwise, it has carefully avoided any consideration of the effects on Constance of her own desperate situation. Even now it neutralises this moment of high drama by describing Constance as full of faith and ready for God's purposes ('pleine deu e prest a toutes sez voluntez'). The news that the king has ordered her banished draws no tear or complaint from her, but it does throw her back on her confidently held beliefs. In the only speech of its kind in the story, she absolves her husband from blame, and declares a readiness to make virtue of necessity ('a bon gree le doys prendre') in the hope of that merciful end which only God can bring about. The sailors who lead her boat out onto the open sea commend her not to the four winds, as did the Syrian sailors when she was exiled from Syria, but to God. They pray that God will grant her a joyful return to the land. For once, she is on the receiving end of other people's prayers, and her faith in God, like her friends' faith in her, is truly the substance of things not seen.

Two years now pass, and Constance's ship fetches up on the Mediterranean coast of Spain close to the castle of a Saracen emir, whose steward is a Christian who has apostatised. Constance shows no willingness to lodge a third time with the pagans — this time, it seems, there will be no converts — and, once refreshed, chooses the open sea and the protection of God. Nevertheless, her graciousness greatly impresses the emir, who charges his steward to take care of her. Overjoyed, the steward comes to her at night with a great treasure. He declares a willingness to escape with her and, with her, to put himself once more into the hands of God: he acknowledges his apostasy for fear of death and greed of worldly honour ('pour peur de mort e pur coueitise de terrien honur': that is, his reasons for apostasy were those rejected by Constance when offered to her by the Syrians). As soon as they are at sea, however, his good purpose lapses and, like Elda's deputy, he tries to rape her. Constance feigns compliance with his proposals to encourage him to lower his guard, and, when his back is turned, pushes him overboard so that he drowns.

The punishment of this miscreant prepares the way for another. Trevet now takes us back to the return of Alla, to universal opprobrium, immediately after the banishment of Constance. Little by little, he unravels the treason, and traces its source to his mother. The violence she had sought to provoke against Constance returns on her own head. Like a madman, the wrathful son forces the terror-stricken mother to confess the crime, and hacks her in pieces. His violent anger will require expiation, but Trevet makes us wait for that, and the episode ends instead with another emblem of constancy: the king makes a solemn vow never to marry until he has proof that Constance is dead.

The story now returns to Constance. One day, three years after her Spanish adventure, her ship fetches up amongst the ships of the Roman navy, at anchor in a seaport. Brought to land, she recognises a Roman senator, Arsemius of Cappadocia, known to her (though she is not recognised by him) because of his close friendship with her father. Questioned about her identity, she is as careful as ever to conceal her identity under the story — true, so far as she knows — of an exile caused by her husband's disapproval of her; she even conceals her name under its Saxon form, Couste. Arsemius is more open with his information. The navy, he tells her, was sent to revenge the massacre of the Christians by the Sultan's mother, and has just returned; the one blot on this otherwise successful mission has been its failure to find the body of Constance, whom the Syrians reckoned drowned at sea. Constance does not disabuse him of his error. She accompanies him to Rome, and lives incognito in his house for 12 years. Now she resumes her earlier role of inspiring love in others who cannot penetrate her secrets. Though unaware that Constance is her long-lost cousin, Arsemius's wife Helena loves her as devotedly as did Hermengild, more than anything in the world. As a practical expression of that love, the childless couple make her son their heir.

Now that Constance is at Rome, the story brings Alla there, too, so that all three parties — Constance, her father and her husband — can be reunited. Alla comes to Rome as a pilgrim to receive absolution for the murder of his mother, and leaves the kingdom in the care of another son, Edwin, whom we now meet for the first and only time in the story. (Maurice cannot become king, because the narrative proposes another end for him.)

When Constance learns that Alla is coming to Rome and will be staying at a palace owned by her patron — a neat touch which will bring husband and wife once more under the one roof — she yields to her natural instincts and, like Griselda at a similar moment, swoons. This lapse, inexplicable to the bystanders, recurs ten days later when she witnesses Alla's arrival in the city; she has to pretend it results from an illness sustained during her sea voyage. But, though she cannot directly confront her husband, she has an ally who can, her son, now in his eighteenth year and very like his mother in looks. Constance instructs him to serve the king at a banquet Arsemius is preparing for him. Surprised at this remembrance of his dead wife, the king enquires about Maurice's parentage; draws his own conclusion when he hears the senator's answer; and asks to see the child's mother. When he does, he recognises her for his lost wife, and the couple are reunited in a joyous demonstration of mutual love that amazes the bystanders. What remains, the reuniting of Constance with her father, is similarly achieved. Maurice is sent to invite the emperor, for the sake of his daughter, to a banquet given by Alla. No less startled than his son-in-law by this living image of Constance, and still more by the naming of her, the emperor accepts the invitation. On the day of the feast, Constance rides out with Alla and Maurice to meet her father. As the two groups approach, she gets down and proceeds on foot with Alla and Maurice. As she draws level with her father, she thanks God for letting her live to see her father in health. This controlled and commonplace greeting adverts to none of the difficulties she has faced and finally overcome; it almost proves too much for the old man, who needs the help of Alla and Maurice to stay upright on his horse. What remains is 'grant joye'. When Alla returns home, Maurice is left behind, and made his grandfather's heir (the narrative thus realises a second, and more important, inheritance for the young prince than that earlier conferred by Arsemius). In a kind of coda to the narrative, we learn of the death of Alla within the year; of Constance's return to Rome to be with her sick father, who dies shortly afterwards; and of her own death, within a year of her return to Rome. Elda dies on his way back from Rome, whither he had led her for the last time, and is buried by his companion the Bishop of Bangor: and the stage is left clear for Maurice, who will become the most Christian emperor of them all.

This protracted summary of Trevet's narrative — one might, with justice, call it 'a long preamble of a tale' — aims to provide the basis for a detailed study of its relationship with two of the versions directly dependent upon it. At the same time, it easily reveals, as our opening remarks suggested, the strongly exemplary colour of the narrative. Its most obvious feature is the extraordinarily elaborate patterning. In whole or in part, every scene echoes every other. This patterning does not pay much heed to narrative plausibility. For example, Alla needs a second son to rule the kingdom during his absence, so the narrative gives him Edwin. Yet Constance has had no time to bear him a second child before her exile, and he has not remarried. Or again: following the logic of romance, and with some feeling for psychological as well as formal values, the narrative requires a final gathering-up of all the scattered members;[6] so Constance lives in Rome incognito until her newly-arrived husband can receive her embassy in the person of her son. (The testing of Alla in this scene, of course, echoes the various tests on Constance earlier in the story; in addition, though the story makes little of the point, the time-gap has the formal function of making Alla, though innocent of any wrong done to his wife, worthy to be reunited with her.) The deaths of the main characters, similarly, are arranged symbolically. Alla dies first, leaving Constance free to tend her father, so that father and daughter end where they began; then the father dies, leaving Constance symbolically to re-enact her years of solitary exile; and when Constance dies the remaining figures, Elda and the Bishop of Bangor, are summarily dispatched.

These formal patterns embody an exemplary meaning. Constance, an emblem of utter confidence in the purposes of God, converts Syrian and Saxon alike; uses her native wit to frustrate attempts on her virtue; is defended by God in every dangerous moment; and deserves to bring her sufferings to a happy outcome. The narrative underlines this emblematic reading in a number of ways. At the outset it makes Constance a type of the wise virgin: a clear, if implicit, parallel exists between the narrative of her youth and that of St Katharine of Alexandria, and between her mission-ary activities and those of such as St Cecilia and St Ursula.[7] Then it compares her second sea journey with that of Noah; and it makes the villains clear instances of diabolic possession. Elda's deputy is punished directly by God; the renegade steward, by contrast, through human agency. But even when God cannot be seen directly at work in the story, Trevet shares his heroine's confidence in God's purposes to the extent of explaining away each fresh disaster as a further occasion for God to keep her safe: 'neverthe-less, the providence of God did not fail therein, which in tribula-tion never fails those who have hope in him' (*OA*, p.10);[8] 'But God was her mariner' (Ibid., p. 12).[9] It's all a question of reading the signs correctly. A symbolic fitness therefore attaches to repeated references to eyes and sight: the faithful Briton has his sight restored, the faithless Saxon has his eyes knocked out; first Alla and then his father-in-law confront the lively image of the beloved wife and daughter in the person of her son; and so on. Seeing *is* believing, if you know how to look.

Of course, the narrative is not just an exemplum like the Clerk's tale or *Melibee*, but also a piece of history, like the Second Nun's tale; consequently, it cannot entirely write off Constance's human situation. Occasionally, for example, the narrative describes not what Constance sees but what she thinks she sees. When she is about to be rescued by Arsemius, she does not at first realise that the Roman navy is approaching; she thinks she sees a forest floating towards her. A more important sign of her human situation comes with her repeated concealment of her identity. This action tests the discernment of the bystanders, but almost certainly originates in her fears for her own safety. Then too there are moments of anxiety, when she must face the death of a husband or a dear friend (the Sultan, Hermengild) or contemplate a further period of exile; or a moment of high emotion, when the news of Alla's coming is announced to her, marking the end of her exile. The narrator uses a tell-tale phrase to describe her: she is one predestined by God to grace and virtue, to temptation and joy ('cele que dieux auoit predestine a grace e vertue e temptacioun e joye': *SA*, p. 169). The way to predestined joy, so to speak, lies in the exercise of virtue and through temptation. For that matter, as in any saint's narrative, the bystanders provide a context of doubt, misunderstanding and repentance which, while it highlights the saint's faithfulness, also speaks to us of the human context within which that faith had to be expressed. (Compare the role of the bystanders in the tales so far studied.)[10] Whether she presents herself in person or sends a likeness, those who see her are drawn immediately and mysteriously to her (the word regularly used is 'suppris') and, without knowing the precise nature of her appeal, fall instantly in love with her. They must, therefore, share in the martyrdom symbolised by her sea journeys, either directly (they suffer death because of their association with her) or indirectly, in that they bear a burden of grief on her account. But this psychological reading of the narrative, for so it is, is never allowed seriously to disturb the primary reading of the story. Very few of the possible psychological readings are actualised in the narrative. The beautiful ironies of the heroine's meeting with Arsemius, for instance, are passed over in complete silence. And even doubt itself becomes exemplary when, as here, it shows itself so ready for instruction.

The actual narration is of a piece with this required reading. For the most part, Trevet enters his narrative directly only to endorse its unshakeable faith in God's purposes, and speaks, therefore, not in his own voice but in the voice of the Church. The resulting blandness and impersonality of tone all but reduce disaster and joy to the accidents they presumably are in God's eye.

This confident reading, and colourless retelling, of the narrative, falter only occasionally. At the beginning and end of the story, though, we observe a different emphasis, which generates, potentially, a subtly different reading from either the exemplary or the psychological one. This change results from the genre of the work; an historical chronicle. Whatever the form in which he found the story, Trevet offers it not as a single and separate story, like those considered in previous chapters, but as an item in a history of the world from its beginnings to his own time. From the time of Christ, his work carries a running title 'lez gestes des apostoiles, emperours et roys' ('deeds of apostles, emperors and kings'): it also carries reference, fuller the nearer it comes to Trevet's own time, to the history of England.[11] These elements all figure in the Constance story: part of a history of Christian Europe (the Roman episodes) and England (the Saxon episodes), the narrative includes two 'emperours' (Tiberius and his grandson), two 'roys' (Alla and his other son Edwin), and a saintly 'apostoile' (Constance). Trevet's narrative, therefore, requires to be read in the light of earlier episodes. Indeed, it directs the reader to preceding chapters for further information about the emperor, and about the flight of the Britons to Wales in the face of the Saxon invasion (*SA*, pp. 165-6,168,170). This feature of the story also explains the unavoidable sense of anticlimax at the end, when the characters must all be dispatched summarily so that the overarching narrative may continue. But the most obvious sign of Trevet's historiographical ambitions occurs at the beginning of the work. Here he offers two versions of the Constance story, both derived from chronicles. He prefers, and will follow, that found in old Saxon chronicles ('les aunciene cronikes de Sessouns'); but he records the alternative, according to which Constance was given in marriage to a Cappadocian nobleman called Maurice, whom her father then declared his heir. By this light, the whole Constance story exists to show how the son of a Saxon king and future emperor could be said to hail from Cappadocia (by being declared the heir of Arsemius of Cappadocia) and how the alternative reading, though easier to accept (the *facilior lectio*, so to speak) was clearly erroneous. Trevet's resolution of this problem at the very beginning of the story, where Arsemius is confusingly called Tarquinius, shows him operating more as an historian than as a simple storyteller.

Further signs of the historian's activity occur in the details of the story. Constance takes two years to get to Spain, three years to get to Rome, and spends 12 years there; her son is in his eighteenth year at the end of this time. More important is the setting of the English episodes in the aftermath of the displacement of the Christianised Celts by the pagan Saxons in the sixth century. Trevet also gives Hermengild a speech in Middle English over the blind Briton (quoted below, p. 134) as the nearest thing he knows to the 'laungge Sessone' which she would have spoken. Factual, too, if less easy to date because they occurred so regularly in the middle ages, are the border clashes with the Scots which take Alla away from Constance; and factual, too, the places where Constance lands ('pres Humbre') and Doumylde lives ('Knaresbourth').

Logically, this interest in history makes for a subtly different reading of the narrative from the primary emblematic one.[12] Like the earlier noted references to the dangers of Constance's situation, which generate a psychological reading of sorts, these references to actual as opposed to mythic times and places go some way to creating an historical reading of the narrative. In our eyes these readings — the psychological, the historical and the emblematic — may be more or less subtly opposed to one another. Though largely unconscious of this opposition, Trevet occasionally reveals its existence. For instance, he presents events in his narrative in the light of happenings nearer his own time. When, as part of his marriage arrangements, the Sultan gives free passage to the Christians and rights of ownership over the Holy City, he is unwittingly justifying the Crusaders in their attempts to oust his descendants 600 and more years later.[13]

For all that, the historical reading of the narrative is scarcely better developed in real terms than the psychological one. Like human psychology, history was typically seen in the middle ages in the light of the Incarnation; that is, human actions — so too, historical and psychological processes — were seen, on whatever level, not just as things in themselves but as images of divine activity.[14] In any case, the Constance story is not strictly comparable with the other entries in the *Cronicles*. It is not simply subordinate to the overarching shape which contains it. In the prologue Trevet tells us that the general character of the individual entries, as of the whole work, will be brevity. By this means he aims to attract readers who find troublesome the prolixity of other chroniclers ('ennoyez de la prolixite destoires') so that they can more easily understand the stories and keep them fresh in memory ('e retenir

de plus viue memoire': *OA*, p. v).[15] Brevity characterises most of
the entries in the *Cronicles*, but not the Constance story, easily the
longest single item in the work. Very possibly Trevet added it to
his work at a late stage in its production: at all events, it sits rather
uncomfortably in the finished work, and invites consideration, as
almost no other item in the *Cronicles* does, as a separate story.[16]
So to read it is to focus squarely on its primary exemplary meaning. And since the historical frame is activated most clearly at the
beginning and end of the story, a later writer might easily return it
to the freestanding form in which Trevet presumably found it, by
cancelling the more obvious signs of the historian's activity — the
cross-references in the body of the text, and the prefatory note
about the sources.[17]

These remarks draw us clearly towards Chaucer's retelling of
the Constance story. First, though, we need to look at another
version similarly dependent on Trevet and roughly contemporary
with Chaucer's — indeed, its readings may have influenced his:
that is, the retelling in Gower's *Confessio Amantis*.[18] The *Confessio* is a vast collection of tales told by the God of Love to his
wayward disciple, the narrator of the poem, to instruct him in the
vices to be avoided by lovers. Inevitably, Gower abandons the
historical reading of the narrative in favour of a moral–exemplary
one. He has no interest in recording the existence of variant
versions of the legend. When he acknowledges their existence ('the
bokes sein': II, 1586), he focuses not on their potential disagreements, like Trevet, but on their speaking with a single voice. Then,
too, although he keeps the concluding narrative of the deaths of
Alla, Tiberius and Constance, he draws from it a moral absent in
Trevet: not history, but morality, is the point of the episode:

> But he which hindreth euery kinde ...
> The deth comende er he be soght
> Tok with this king ... aqueintance

> (1572-3, 1575)

The overall moral is subtly different, too. In Trevet Constance was
an emblem of trust in the divine purpose; in Gower the God tells
the story as a warning against 'false tunges' and 'enuie/ Which
longeth vnto bacbitinge' (1602, 1604-5). According to this retelling, it is envy (641) which drives the Sultan's mother to her 'fals
covine' (683-4) and motivates Elda's deputy, when Constance's

rejection of him turns his love to hate (810-11); similarly, Doumylde's treasonably 'false tunge' and 'bacbitinge' (957, 1281, 1299) lead Alla to banish Constance. Readily enough suggested by Trevet's version, this reading is not achieved without a sense of strain; envy does not immediately spring to mind as an explanation of the behaviour of Elda's deputy, nor are the forged letters of Doumylde most readily interpreted as signs of 'bacbitinge'.[19]

A more important change comes with Gower's greater emphasis on the human situation of the protagonists. When, for example, Alla learns that his wife may be still alive, Trevet says only that he became very thoughtful ('deuynt en grant pensee'). By contrast, Gower describes Alla as a man torn by intense and conflicting feelings, and realises this conflict in a traditional profession of inability to represent the narrative moment adequately:

> But who that cowthe specefie
> What tho fell in his fantasie ...
> It were a wonder forto hiere
>
> (1407-8, 1411; cf. 1563-5)

Similarly, when Constance's ship has come in amongst the ships of the Roman navy, he has her hiding herself fearfully from her rescuers, since she does not know who they are (1141-3). Most importantly, when she is banished from England, he gives her a scene not found in Trevet, which dramatically increases the emotional temperature. She prays to God to keep her and her child safe; lies in a heap, weeping, 'swounende as ded' (1063); realises that her child will die if she yields to the luxury of despair; and forgets herself in nursing him:

> And tho sche tok hire child in honde
> And yaf it sowke, and euere among
> Sche wepte, and otherwhile song
> To rocke with hire child aslepe
>
> (1078-81)

Other expressions of this impulse to make Constance a figure of solitary suffering are worth pausing over. The renegade steward, here a villain from the outset, keeps her on board ship alone, out of sight from others, so that he may more easily achieve his wicked purposes; Constance is saved from him only because she prays to

God. When she rides with her husband and son to meet her father, she makes the last stage of the journey alone; in a conscious echo of Christ's entry into Jerusalem, she rides upon a 'mule whyt amblaunt' (1506). A yet better instance comes when the murder of Elda's wife is discovered. In Trevet Constance herself makes the discovery. In Gower it is Elda who discovers the murder. He has entered the chamber quietly so as not to wake anyone; his cries then awaken Constance, who sees her mistress dead and faints with fear. If Trevet's version of this moment makes Constance the active expression of a Christian conscience, Gower's makes her a picture of innocent and vulnerable simplicity.[20]

Gower modifies Trevet in other ways, too. In particular, he creates a clear metaphoric structure — wanting in Trevet's version — by way of repeated images of fire and burning.[21] If love is a fire (1410), so is envy, the formal subject of the retelling. Envy lights a fire whose effects prove painful to those directly exposed to it (1274-5) and even to the bystanders (1047-8). Symbolic fitness therefore attaches to the punishment Alla accords his mother: he burns her alive (1292-3). Nevertheless, this symbolic fire will be eventually smothered (1556) and the truth of love's 'wel menynge' (1599) will out. This pattern focuses not at all on the divine logic of events, but rather on the human realm of cause and effect. It is reinforced by two additional 'characters' used by Gower to account for developments in the narrative: the 'vnstable whel' of Fortune (1226-7), and 'he which hindreth euery kinde' — death (1572-5).

Gower not only modified the 'sentence' of the original; he also took considerable liberties with its wording, in part, because his chosen metrical form — octosyllabic couplets — forced him to attend more closely to the requirements of rhyme than to the wording of the original. His version of the divine judgement of Elda's deputy, for instance, is far from the faithful translation that, as earlier noted, Chaucer produced:

> O dampned man to helle
> Lo, thus hath God the sclaundre wroke
> That thou ayein Constance hast spoke:
> Beknow the sothe er that thou dye.

> (880-3)

Only occasionally does his version reveal a close correspondence with the wording of the original, as in the following, when he versifies Hermengild's speech to the blind Briton:

> Bisene man, in Iesu name in rode ysclawe, haue thi
> sith.
>
> (*SA*, p. 170)

> And seide, 'In trust of Cristes lawe
> Which don was on the crois and slawe
> Thou bysne man, behold and se'.
>
> (769-71)

Gower's version, then, is more a paraphrase than a translation.

All the same, these changes to the letter and sentence of the original notwithstanding, Gower's version impresses by its general faithfulness to the overall structure and meaning of its source. In particular, the new version shares the colourless and impersonal tone of voice of its original. Sharing Trevet's confidence in the providential ordering of the narrative, Gower, for the most part, lets the story tell itself.[22] Normally he intervenes only at moments of high drama, and then he shows himself as ready as Trevet to invoke the heavenly *auctor* of the story so as to defuse any tension and reassure the reader: 'But what the hihe God wol spare/ It mai for no peril misfare' (693-4; cf. 714-16, 1064).

Notwithstanding the one instance of close translation so far considered in Chaucer's version, when the voice of God is heard over the guilty deputy, the Man of Law's tale is an altogether more complex affair. Chaucer probably had very specific reasons for translating so carefully at this point. The words come from the Vulgate (Ps. 49: 20-1, with substitution by Trevet of 'ecclesie' for its 'meae').[23] Trevet clearly acknowledges this borrowing, and all such borrowings in the *Cronicles*, by retaining the Latin of the Vulgate. Many of Chaucer's Bible texts, as Thompson noted, came to him embedded in other works; whether he translated those works faithfully or not, however, he always translated the embedded Bible quotations very carefully, most notably in the Pardoner's and Parson's tales. His careful translation of the Bible verses in the Man of Law's tale may therefore have less to say about the relation of the retelling to its original than about the absolute status accorded the Bible, whatever the form in which quotations from it were found.[24] We should not therefore too quickly conclude that Chaucer's faithful translation of the Vulgate text is typical of the whole tale.

We can more easily see the force of these observations if we compare almost any other passage with its original. Consider, for instance, what the merchants have to say about Constance to the Sultan. In Trevet they praise her for her part in their conversion, and her 'very high and noble wit and wisdom, and marvellous gentleness and nobleness of blood' (*OA*, p. 4).[25] In the Man of Law's tale they return, unconverted but greatly impressed by what they have seen of Custance (172) — and, more importantly, heard of her (150-68). Chaucer's brief summary of their report to the Sultan ('thise marchantz han hym toold of dame Custance/ So greet noblesse': 184-5) preserves only Trevet's account of the heroine's noble birth. Earlier in the episode, there is a fuller account of Custance delivered by the 'commune voys' of the Roman populace to the merchants (155); this report owes almost as little directly to Trevet as that by the merchants to the Sultan. Like Trevet, it stresses the heroine's youthful beauty: according to Trevet she is in her thirteenth year; according to the Man of Law, 'in hire is heigh beautee ... yowthe, withoute grenehede or folye' (162-3). Otherwise, the two versions follow subtly different courses. Trevet emphasises the heroine's wisdom; the Man of Law her 'goodnesse' (158) and 'vertu' (164) and the striking absence, in one so young, of any bad qualities to take the shine off her good ones. Lastly, the Man of Law has his commoners pray that God should 'in honour hire susteene' (160). These words prepare us more directly than anything in Trevet for the coming drama, where Custance will be in almost constant need of God's grace. It is this passage, and not the earlier noted translation of Trevet's Bible text, which typifies the Man of Law's tale: the whole tale yields only the one instance of close translation from the *Cronicles*.

The most immediate sign of Chaucer's departure from his original comes in the first episode. Here, as often noted, the narrator greatly increases the detail and alters the focus of the original. Although he will follow Trevet and make Custance a type of the Christian missionary, he does not give her this role, as Trevet did, in the opening episode. Instead, he makes her a courtly heroine, worshipped at a distance, fallen in love with by hearsay.[26] We make her acquaintance directly only on the day of her departure to Syria. At this point Trevet had allowed for the expression of a general grief, the natural result of anxieties about Constance's future far from home, among the barbarians. But he was carefully

silent about his heroine's reactions to what others might read as an
enforced exile. By contrast, Chaucer's version of the episode
focuses, almost from the start, on Custance's reactions. She is 'with
sorwe al overcome': pale, clearsighted about her probable future,
tearful. Her sense of impending isolation is heightened by the
narrator's reminder of present friends 'that so tendrely hire kepte':
in particular, her father who has 'fostred [hire] up so softe' and her
mother, her 'soverayn plesance/ Over alle thyng, out-taken Crist
on-lofte' (269, 275-7). The other versions make nothing of
Custance's mother. Though presented only this once by Chaucer
she adds to the pathos of Custance's situation. Custance goes,
expecting never to return (280), and maybe even to die (285),
praying Christ for grace to fulfil his commandments (284) and
obey the will of her father and the strange lord to whom he is sending her (287). Only after her speech are we made aware of the
general grief. Greater than the grief which accompanied the fall of
ancient civilisations like Troy, or that heard when the Carthag-
inians all but defeated the Romans, the grief of the bystanders
stresses Custance's isolation by suggesting its dependence on hers.
Put another way, Custance has first place in this episode by virtue
of her grief.

In this scene the emphasis has shifted sharply from an exemplary to a psychological reading of character. Gower's already noted
scene of Constance exiled with her young son from England
provides, if not the model, certainly an analogue for this shift of
emphasis: but the Man of Law's retelling goes much further
towards a full-blooded psychologising of its heroine than Gower.
At every stage it emphasises her suffering and isolation.[27] Hastily
banished from Syria (438-9), she prays to the Cross 'with ful
pitous voys' (449) to preserve her, even though she does not
expect to survive her ordeal(455), and help her amend her life
(460-2). She undergoes protracted exposure to poor food (466)
and 'wilde wawes' (468); in the face of such hardships death seems
inevitable (467). When eventually the sea casts her up on the
English coast, she is 'wery ... ful of care' and 'woful' (514, 522).
Unlike Trevet's heroine, she can speak only her own language, a
'maner Latyn corrupt' (516, 519); and she asks the foreigners only
for the mercy of a speedy death to deliver her from her misery
(516-18). Less forthcoming about her story than Trevet's heroine,
she refuses to reveal her identity 'for foul ne fair, thogh that she
sholde deye', and pretends to have lost her memory as a result of

her ordeal (525-7). The latter elements also figured in Trevet's narrative, but at very different places. The steadfast refusal to yield to threat or promise, even though death should result, comes earlier, when Constance is resisting the Saracens' attempts forcibly to convert her; the pretended loss of memory comes later, when Constance has to find some way of explaining the involuntary fainting fit brought on by the news of her husband's arrival in Rome. Chaucer's narrator brings these two elements together, at the point where Custance has just asked to be put out of her misery, and changes the context of the first. By this means he re-inforces his heroine's sense of isolation, and suggests that her story on land will involve the same suffering as her adventures at sea. Not surprisingly, her new friends are moved as painfully by the sight of her (528-9) as her former friends when they farewelled her. Coming or going, that is, Custance engages compassion.[28]

The story now enters upon a new phase. Mid-stanza we shift from 'routhe' and 'pitee', and receive a new picture of the heroine:

> She was so diligent, withouten slouthe,
> To serve and plesen everich in that place,
> That alle hir loven that looken in hir face.
>
> (530-2)

This picture prepares for the heroine's exercise of that active missionary function which had figured so prominently in Trevet. In respect of this role, the following episode goes further even than Trevet. Custance not only converts Hermengild, and encourages her to cure the blind Briton; she also explains the miracle to the astounded constable, and preaches to him, converting him by nightfall. In Trevet, Hermengild had explained the miracle to Elda, and the two women had jointly preached the faith to Elda over an unspecified period of time. Even so, there is an all-important difference between Chaucer's missionary and Trevet's. In Trevet, Hermengild's conversion grows directly out of her love for Constance and her express desire to model herself on her friend. Though not immediate, for it takes several days to effect, the conversion nevertheless demands little of the preacher beyond sensitivity to the situation of the catechumen. In the Man of Law's tale, the conversion takes at least as long to achieve ('Custance hath so longe sojourned there': 536). It also has its origins in the same love of Hermengild for Custance — a love directly inspired, we infer, from Custance's pitiable situation and attentive, diligent service (528-32). But it costs the preacher much more, and is not achieved without prayer and 'many a bitter teere' (537). Where Trevet, then, focuses on the outer world of behaviour ('gestes'), the Man of Law focuses on the inner world of feelings: prayers and tears.[29]

The patterns thus set up are now repeated, as in Trevet's narrative. The next episode, in which Custance will be accused of murder, opens with the tell-tale description of the two women asleep, 'wery, forwaked in hire orisouns' (596). Although this detail comes from Trevet, it acquires resonances in Chaucer wanting in the source. It tells us that the life of prayer now followed by the missionary and her disciple, like the painful prayers which helped Custance secure her friend's conversion (537), is wearisome. Moreover, the word 'wery' reminds us of Custance at the end of her long sea journey to England (514). That is, both prayer and the enforced sea journey, in different ways, symbolise the pain of the Christian's separation from God, and the labour of return. Of course, the sea is a traditional metaphor for what separates man from God: journey over the sea thus means exposure to the chances of the world as the Christian journeys to heaven.[30] Only retrospectively, by means of such a detail as this, does Chaucer's narrative make us aware of the religious meaning of Custance's sufferings. Trevet did not trouble to develop the implied metaphor of the sea in his narrative; for him the sea was merely the condition of moving Constance from one location to another. In the Man of Law's tale, by contrast, the sea provides the means of exposing Custance to one disaster after another.[31]

Not surprisingly, therefore, the present episode reminds us at several points of earlier moments in the story. Confronted after the death of her mistress by the suspicious circumstance of the bloody knife, Custance is at first reduced to a griefstricken silence which literally enacts her earlier pretended loss of memory (609; cf. 526-7). Fallen into 'disese and ... mysaventure' (616), Custance now stares death directly in the face, alone, as when the Syrians set her adrift on the open sea, with no 'champioun' but Christ to keep her from death (631-7). Indeed, her isolation is increased by the 'wrong suspecioun' (681) that others receive of her. Nevertheless, her innocent suffering creates the same powerful effect upon the bystanders as earlier on the Romans, when she departed for Syria. Most of them are moved with pity (621), convinced of her innocence (622-6). Even the king, though unable clearly to determine her innocence or guilt, is moved with pity (614, 628, 659-60) 'that from his eyen ran the water doun' (661). Once more Custance has no recourse but prayer. She knows she will die if her prayer is not answered (644), and she invokes the first of two Biblical emblems of innocent suffering to give her support. The figure with whom she identifies was not used by Trevet: it is the Old Testament heroine Susanna, falsely accused by the envious elders (639-40; cf. Daniel 13).[32] At this point the narrator underlines his heroine's sense of isolation by means of a vivid simile of a man condemned and being led towards his death:

> Have ye nat seyn somtyme a pale face,
> Among a prees, of hym that hath be lad
> Toward his deeth, wher as hym gat no grace,
> And swich a colour in his face hath had,
> Men myghte knowe his face that was bistad,
> Amonges alle the faces in that route?
> So stant Custance, and looketh hire aboute.
>
> (645-51)

The colour has fled from her face, even as on the day she first left Rome: which is merely to repeat that every episode is interchangeable with, or symbolic of, every other.

Of course, vindication is immediately forthcoming, and the episode ends with a general repentance (677-86). Custance once again assumes an active missionary role, mediates the Gospel to the king 'and many another in that place', and converts them. Even here, she stands alone, if to a very different end. While 'of this mervaille agast was al the prees' (677), she has no fear of the divine vengeance (679); likewise, we infer, only Custance has pity on the guilty man, who is at once put to death (687-9). The episode ends with a partial realisation of the prayer of the Roman populace, at the beginning of the story, that Custance might be 'of al Europe the queene' (161): Alla marries her, and 'thus hath Crist ymaad Custance a queene' (693). But her elevation has ironic overtones, too. We have already seen her enter Syria in triumph as another ruler's queen (391-2, using the same rhyme as at 160-1); and her triumph then was pitifully short-lived.

When next we see her, the security of her new position is being undermined by the plotting of her mother-in-law. Even before the full effects have reached her, she may have sensed the coming ill. In a passage which reminds us both of the earlier sleep from which she woke to a false accusation, and of her own earlier expressed understanding (286) that women must expect a life of suffering, the narrator reckons that she will have slept badly and had 'penance' in her dreams (803-5). The following episode incorporates material from both Trevet and Gower. Both describe the grief of Alla's deputies at having to enforce the directions of the forged letter; both, if at different points in the episode, give Constance an important farewell speech. In addition, Trevet describes the general grief that accompanies Constance's departure, which includes a universal outcry against the king; and Gower focuses on the concern of Constance for her little child. These elements are all used by the Man of Law. Characteristically, he makes much more of them. Admittedly, he dispatches the weeping bystanders in a single line (820); but, in a most important change, he allows their complaints to surface, in muted form, in Elda's exclamation about the injustice that permits 'wikked folke' to 'regne in prosperitee' (816); in Custance's tearful question to her child, ' "Why wil thyn harde fader han thee spilt?" ' (857); lastly, in her farewell to her absent husband: ' "farewel, housbonde routhelees" ' (863). Elda's speech clearly expresses the believer's painful sense of contradiction: confronted by the manifest evil of the world (812), an evil which preys on innocence and maintains the wicked in authority (815-16), the deputy is driven to question not only the justice of God (813-14) but the very survival of the world (811).[33]

Custance's reactions are more complex. As when she left Rome (320), she composes herself to take her fate 'in good entente' (824; cf. 867). She sets her face towards the sea, giving only a backward glance to the securities she must leave (862,864). Until now God and the Virgin Mary have been the objects of her devotion and trust; she has prayed to them at every critical moment (832), and they have preserved her from 'false blame' (827-9: she is probably thinking of the false charge of murder brought against her). She therefore trusts them to preserve her once more, even though — and this is a tell-tale addition — she cannot see how they will do so (830). In any case, not everything is lost. As she goes, Custance recalls to herself that cardinal Biblical picture of suffering womanhood, the Virgin Mary. A woman's enticements led Adam to sin, and brought about the death of Mary's son on the cross (841-5), the instrument of salvation to which Custance had earlier prayed. This implied equation of her own with Mary's situation holds true in one respect of which she is unaware: Donegild has deceived Alla into banishing Custance and her son, even as Eve deceived Adam into eating the forbidden fruit. But the parallel does not hold good at another point, and she knows it: the Virgin's sufferings, especially at the Crucifixion, were altogether greater than her own (846-7), and Custance still has her little child to comfort her (849).[34] Nevertheless, like the Virgin, Custance does suffer on her child's account, reacting 'pitously' to his sufferings (835) as others do to hers. Even more helpless than his mother, the infant is crying in her arms, needs to be hushed and lulled asleep (834,839,866), and requires protection from the elements with the very covering of her own head (837-8). Hence Custance asks mercy, first of the Virgin, then of the constable, not for herself but for her child (850-4, 858-61): if all else is unavailing, let the constable at least give the child the farewell kiss its father should have bestowed (861). All the same, her concern for the child is, on another level, displaced anxiety for herself. She may now have an object by means of which to distract herself from the thought, which until now seems to have haunted her, of her own death; but her situation remains what it was. There is no colour in her face; she still looks like one condemned (822).

The next stages in her story develop this picture in some degree. Custance remains 'in peyne and wo' (901); is 'wo...bigon' and cries 'pitously' (918-19) when the steward tries to force himself upon her; then journeys

> thurghout the narwe mouth
> Of Jubaltare and Septe, dryvynge ay
> Somtyme west, and somtyme north and south,
> And somtyme est, ful many a wery day.
>
> (946-9)

In this quotation the first phrase, 'narwe mouth', evokes the difficulty of her journey; the second ('west...north and south...est') not only suggests its wearisomeness but may also remind us how the sea was an emblem of the vagaries of Fortune. Found by Arsemius sitting 'pitously' in her royal ship, she resumes the role of fair unknown earlier adopted by her on arrival in England (970-3). For almost the first time, though, the narrative now offers this psychological reading less than wholeheartedly,[35] and prefers instead the simpler religious reading favoured by Trevet. Thus Custance struggles 'wel and myghtily' with the steward, and he falls overboard and drowns. This little moment of high drama is surrounded by moralising comment:

> But blisful Marie heelp hire right anon ...
> And thus hath Crist unwemmed kept Custance
>
> (920, 924)

Again, the final sea journey lasts only 'til Cristes mooder ... hath shapen ... to make an ende of al hir hevynesse' (950-2): at which point the narrative rightly proposes to 'stynte of Custance but a throwe' (953) and brings us up-to-date with the Roman vengeance. Lastly, her 12-year sojourn in Rome, an explicit echo of her time in England (979-80; cf. 530-2), proves the divine assistance of the Virgin whom she had earlier so piteously invoked, and makes her an exemplum of the happy end promised to all Christians: 'Thus kan oure Lady bryngen out of wo/Woful Custance, and many another mo' (977-8). For that matter, the sense that the last sea journey is a mirror-image of the second (Custance returns through the Straits of Gibraltar, which she had earlier passed through on her way to England, 465, 947) prepares us for the coming happy ending and a return to the *status quo ante*.

What follows, as in Trevet, emphasises this sense of the coming ending. Alla comes to Rome at the behest of the plot. Custance engineers the meeting with him by way of her own son — and Alla is greatly struck, as in Trevet, by the image of his wife. But Chaucer's narrative then goes further. It gives the senator a speech in praise of Custance (1023-9), which returns us to the speech of the 'commune voys' at the beginning of the story, and thus anticipates her reuniting later in the episode with her own father. The certainty of the happy ending permits the narrative a little self-indulgence at this point. Alla's reactions are developed as fully as in Gower. Struck with wonder (1016) by Maurice's vivid resemblance to his wife (1032), he sighs quietly and hastens away from the banquet (1035-6) so that, in private, he can reason alone with himself, and argue himself out of 'skilful juggement' into acceptance of a possible miracle: no greater, he tells himself, than was the miracle of Custance's first coming to him (1037-43). This important passage, though not the first to do so, brings the king clearly alive. It also focuses an implied temptation to unbelief and despair, analogous to earlier reactions to the forged letters, and shows the effort of will needed to leave behind the world of sense and enter the world of spirit. By contrast, both Trevet and Gower make the grieving king an emblem of constancy; Alla refuses to remarry until he has news of his wife, and therefore will be ready and watching for the happy ending. Granted, Gower gives Alla as important a part in this episode as Chaucer; as we have seen, his Alla experiences the same 'werre of yay and nay' as Chaucer's. Nevertheless, the end product is very different. In Gower, Alla recognises his wife's name under the Saxon form she has used, and 'somdiel smylende he lowh' (II, 1404); his constancy enables him the more easily to penetrate the mystery.

Not yet for Chaucer's protagonists the happy ending. Summoned to meet with Alla, Custance can barely stand upright (1050). Alla greets her fairly and immediately bursts into tears, 'that it was routhe for to see' (1052). For her part, able only to remember the experience of his unkindness (1057), she stands silent and reproachful (1055-6); then she swoons twice, which makes him weep all the more (1058-64). Far from being the joyful encounter for all parties that we see in Trevet and Gower, the meeting is a 'long ... sobbyng and ... bitter peyne'. The mutual complaint not only increases each partner's woe (1068) but even affects the bystanders similarly (1067). Only after the resolution of the whole process of misunderstanding does the narration permit itself the joy of a loving reunion surpassed only by 'the joye that lasteth everemo' (1076). And the same pattern is observed when Custance meets her father. As we saw, Gower suggested Constance's innocence and isolation when he gave her a white mule to ride. Chaucer stresses his heroine's isolation by transferring to her a detail assigned by Trevet to the emperor. According to Trevet, the emperor all but falls off his horse for joy when he recognises Constance; in Chaucer, it is Custance who falls on her knees before her father (1104) in a ritual gesture of humility designed to remind him of a daughter whom, so she thinks, he must have forgotten (1105-6). And where Trevet gave Constance a colourless speech of thanks, Chaucer's Custance reminds her father how he initiated the drama when he sent her to Syria (1108); tells him how she suffered on the 'salte see' (1109-10); and begs him to show mercy and not so treat her again (1111-12). 'Glade' they may be at the end of the story; the whole company will eventually sit down to meat 'in joye and blisse/ ... a thousand foold wel moore' than can be told (1118-20). But the first moment of recognition generates something else, a 'pitous joye' (1114). This moment is explicitly recapitulated by the return of Custance, after the death in England of Alla, 'for whom Custance hath ful greet hevynesse' (1145), to her father in Rome, and the final stages of her 'aventure' (1149-55).

In the character and situation of Custance, then, as, to a lesser extent, of her friends, Chaucer is not so much articulating and defending a religious system as exploring the consequences of belief in the life of the believer. Granted, there is more to faith than the single experience of suffering, to which Chaucer's narrative addresses itself almost obsessively. Nevertheless, that narrow focus throws clear light on the cost of belief. Faith, that is, is an exercise not first of the intelligence but of the will, and requires constant reaffirmation, often in the teeth of contradictory evidence.[36]

All this can be seen very clearly in the opening episode of the Sultan's conversion.[37] For Trevet the process of conversion was almost a matter of form. Each stage led naturally on to the next, and the whole was characterised by a generosity of spirit which proved the candidate's worth. Trevet's smooth and bloodless narrative wants any sense that conversion might involve a struggle and exact a price: but not Chaucer's. The Man of Law passes over the orderly process of a mass conversion almost in silence (in much the same way, later, he hardly refers to the mass conversion of the Saxons). Instead, he gives us the Sultan's determination, cost what it may, to have Custance. The description of Custance given him by the merchants has made him fall in love with her. He therefore summons his council, and presents them with a problem for which they must 'shapen ... som remedye': if he cannot have Custance he will die.

The obvious solution, marriage, is not come by easily. The council speaks with a divided voice (211-13), and some reckon that only witchcraft ('magyk and abusioun': 214) will provide the answer. This is because the obvious source of 'avantage' raises further problems: 'no Cristen prince', they tell him, 'wolde fayn/ Wedden his child under oure lawe sweete' (222-3). Taking their beliefs as the constant, they have to face the difficulty of converting the Christians to Islam.[38] Not for a moment do they consider the Sultan's conversion as a solution to the problem. But this the Sultan now proposes. If Custance cannot be had any other way, and given that his need for her is the constant, he will become a Christian. His proposed action is much more of a cast of faith, and his motives more ambiguous, than in Trevet.[39] In Chaucer the Sultan knows no more about Christianity than the machinery of initiation ('I wol be cristned': 226); he is interested rather in securing his own life and happiness than in discovering whether his new faith is true, and, if so, whether that makes the old faith false. The truths of faith, that is, are realised concretely only in ambiguous social, political, even geographical, contexts. Islam here confronts Christianity as a completely separate system of equal force. This opening episode expresses the political context of belief very clearly by reducing the various messages that pass between persons in Trevet to an expression of *realpolitik*: 'by tretys and embassadrie/ And by the popes mediacioun' (233-4).

But the opening episode does more, as we see when the Sultan's mother comes on stage. Partly in order to heighten the pallid purity of the suffering innocent, the narrator blackens the Sultaness more thoroughly than ever Trevet did: she is the 'welle of vices', the 'roote of iniquitee', the visible sign of the devil's presence in the world (358-71); she actually has ambitions to take over the country (432-4). The Christian must surely react with horror to the blasphemy of her pretended readiness to follow her son into baptism (351-4, 376-8) so as to lull him into a false sense of security and more easily bring about his death. At the same time, the son who proposes baptism almost as a matter of course so as to achieve his end, and the mother who accepts it in the same spirit to frustrate that end, are not simple moral opposites. If our own 'olde sacrifices' (325) and 'hooly lawes' (332) have been given to us by God (333), we need a more compelling reason than infatuation to make us abandon them. Since, moreover, every religion implies penalties as well as rewards, we can hardly hope, in this life, to escape the 'thraldom ... and penance' proper to the new religion; nor, in the hereafter, shall we be spared the pains promised to those who have apostatised from the old. So, at least, the Sultaness tells her council (337-40). Viewed from the outside, she implies, Christianity is only a sort of slavery ('thraldom'), or a system enshrining a set of bizarre rituals, most importantly, that of sprinkling 'coold water' over a person. In itself, the water cannot change a person. Let the Christians bring as much of it with them as they will; it will be put to better use washing away the blood which she proposes to shed (351-7). Now, the massacre of those whose beliefs differ from our own is the clearest possible judgement on the beliefs in whose name it was committed. Moreover, the Sultaness cannot understand the full import of her words. They are creating a connection between baptism and martyrdom which paradoxically validates the beliefs she is rejecting. As in the Prioress's and Second Nun's tales, this conventional agent of wickedness is ironically serving the purposes of the Christian God when she proposes to confirm an ambiguous baptism with the blood of a martyr.

But, though the Christian is clearly expected to read between the lines of the Sultaness's speech to discover its true meaning, he cannot altogether suppress the nagging question raised by this creation of an alternative perspective. If all beliefs are culturally and psychologically determined, what makes one religion superior to another? Isn't the experience of faith remarkably similar, no matter what the formal system created to contain it? The narrative hints at this heterodox understanding when it gives similar terms to Christian and Muslim to describe their experience of their own faiths. The Muslim law is 'sweete' (223), and the Christian 'deere' (237), to its followers. Another detail links Christian and Muslim, Custance and the Sultaness. About to depart for Syria, Custance describes her subjection to the will of her new husband as the 'thraldom and penance' (286) to which women are born: a thraldom dramatically realised in her father's disposing of her like a piece of real estate. Though neither party knows it, that phrase makes common cause with the Sultaness, who, as noted, reckons 'thraldom and penance' the penalty of embracing Christianity. Just as Custance's various experiences are presented as images of one another, so this repeated phrase implies a connection between Custance's journey to an unknown fate in Syria and the journey of the would-be convert to an equally unknown fate.[40] Nor is that all. When Custance lands on the coast of Northumberland, she can speak only her own language, a 'maner Latyn corrupt'. The pagan Saxons, though, are cosmopolitan enough to understand her, and the text may even credit them, by implication, with classical Latin.[41] That is, the story refuses the Christians the monopoly of virtue and natural feeling — or even simple knowledge.

This relativising of religious positions is one of the most important contributions the new version makes to the development of the story. But it is not the only one. There is also the important matter of the tone generated by the speaking voice of the narrator. Like the originals of the Clerk's and Second Nun's tales and *Melibee*, the versions of the Constance story by Gower and Trevet appear almost to tell themselves. As already noted, Trevet's narrative projects a steady confidence in the abilities of its matter to communicate the self-evident message that constant faith in God's purposes will not go unrewarded. At moments of high tension — when Constance is cast adrift on the open sea, for example — Trevet keeps the reader's gaze firmly on the exemplary religious meaning of the work. Constance is not alone; her situation is not hopeless. God comforts her in her own tongue, Trevet tells us, and guides her ship safely to land. At such points in the narrative Gower also readily invokes the heavenly *auctor* as 'he which alle thing mai schilde' (714). For the most part, therefore, he too allows the story to speak for itself. We receive little sense of a distinct speaking voice; his version has much the same impersonal tone as Trevet's.

In this respect the Man of Law's tale contrasts strikingly with the other versions of the story: we are constantly being reminded of the narrator's presence.[42]. To be sure, the contrast is not absolute. Like Gower and Trevet, the Man of Law uses heavenly figures — God, Christ, the Virgin Mary — in a kind of coda to each episode to validate the happy outcome. We have already noted two instances of this practice (11.693, 977-8: see above, pp. 139, 142); it is a vitally important feature of the retelling. At the beginning of one episode, similarly, the narrator presents Satan to explain an impending disaster (582). As in Trevet and Gower, then, Chaucer's narrator underlines the moral pattern of the story by this reference to, and invocation of, spiritual principles. But the practice takes him further into the story as an active presence than either Trevet or Gower: and in a subtly different direction. Trevet and Gower use their comments chiefly to defuse moments of tension. By contrast, Chaucer lets the narrative work out its own tensions first, and only then reads the narrative details as proofs of God's activity. And other examples of this practice in the narrative, far from reducing the tension, actually increase it.

When, for instance, the narrator tells how Custance, on her final sea journey, 'fleteth in the see, in peyne and wo/ Fyve yeer and moore, as liked Cristes sonde' (901-2), we may wish to read this reference to the good will of Christ, like similar references in Trevet and Gower, as authorising a happy ending. We have already seen how Christ's will brought the previous sea voyage to a happy end

('she kneleth doun, and thanketh Goddes sonde': 523) and gave
Custance a temporary respite from suffering ('the wyl of Crist was
that she sholde abyde': 511). Here, though, the narrator's choice
of phrase ('as liked Cristes sonde') produces a very different
effect to the parallel phrases in Trevet and Gower. It has to be seen in
the light of earlier moments, when characters are forced to believe
that what they experience as a disaster is in reality the expression
of God's good purposes. When he receives the first forged letter,
Alla replies, 'Welcome the sonde of Crist for everemoore' (760),
and prays:

> 'Lord, welcome be thy lust and thy plesaunce;
> My lust I putte al in thyn ordinaunce'.

> (762-3)

When Custance receives the burden of the second forgery,
similarly, she 'taketh in good entente/ The wyl of Crist', and prays,
'Lord, ay welcome be thy sonde!' (826). This link generates a
sense of her powerlessness, in the later episode, in the face of what
she experiences not as Christ's pleasure ('liked') but as a painful
('peyne and wo') and protracted ('fyve yeer and moore') exposure
to the elements.

The narrator's sense of his heroine's powerlessness leads him to
identify with her directly in ways that Trevet and Gower never did:
he calls upon God for a happy outcome (873-4, 908-10), and,
though Custance never cursed her enemies, curses them on her
account (602, 914). Only as his story draws to a close does he
speak consistently of God with a voice of calm and simple authority. Nearer the start of the story, he identifies himself so closely
with its tragic possibilities, and with the human situation of his
actors, that he only once speaks with this voice of calm authority.
Otherwise, his fear that the Sultan and his band of converts are
destined for a violent and undeserved end, and Custance herself,
as her own fears suggest, a painfully lingering one, so overpowers
his sense of God's hand in the narrative that he addresses God
only through his heroine: 'Now, faire Custance, almyghty God
thee gyde!' (245; cf. 447-8). Such interventions do not release, but
merely heighten, the tension. In any case, the chief actor in this
early part of the story is not God but the impersonal force which
men call destiny: to find out about the workings of destiny men
must ponder the ambiguous evidence of 'thilke large book/ Which

that men clepe the hevene' (190-1; cf. 261, 295-308). That is, the narrator identifies himself here not with his characters' beliefs so much as with their experiences; in particular, their struggle to find and keep faith. Inevitably, therefore, he models his accounts of the departure of Custance and the death of the Sultan not on Bible stories or saints' legends but on episodes from Greco-Roman legend and history: the fall of Thebes (200, 289) and Troy (288-9), the threatened sack of Rome by Hannibal (290-1); the triumphs of great men (Julius Caesar: 400-3);[43] their deaths, and the deaths of their enemies (Hector and Achilles: 198; Pompey and Caesar: 199). In the illustrious pagan company of Hercules, Turnus and Socrates, the Old Testament hero Samson makes his appearance as the sole exception to this generalisation (200-1). Yet he is not being presented as an emblem of the victorious Christ, nor even as a type of the Christian hero, fallen in sin and justified by faith. Rather, his affinities are with secular Renaissance iconography: he symbolises not the faith, but merely the death, of the hero (a view which receives further attention at the hands of the Monk: see below, pp. 191-3).[44]

Our sense of foreboding is further increased in this early part of the story by the narrator's address to other characters. He apostrophises Custance's father (309-15) and curses the wicked mother-in-law (358-64). He also exclaims against the malign influences to which the imprudence of the former bears implicit witness, and which the wickedness of the latter explicitly embodies: that is, he apostrophises the cruelty of adverse planetary conjunctions (295-308) and the malice of the devil (365-71).[45] These anxious invocations to earthly and heavenly powers separate Custance still more from the spiritual principles which the narrator has claimed to find embodied in her. Inevitably, they force a psychological–tragic reading of the situation upon us: one reinforced by an apostrophe, immediately before the massacre, to the 'sodeyn wo, that evere art successour/ To worldly blisse' (421-2). But they do something else too. They dramatise the necessary traffic between spiritual and human agents at the heart of religious experience: heaven and hell work with human instruments to achieve their ends. The paired apostrophes to the Sultaness and the devil show this collaboration most clearly. Satan tempting Eve is regularly represented in art with a woman's face and upper parts, and the lower parts of a serpent:[46] similarly, the Sultaness is a 'serpent under femynynytee' (360), concealing a fiendish interior by her feminine shape as surely as Lady Macbeth will do ('look like the innocent flower, but be the serpent under't'). Again, Satan's temptation of Eve (368; cf. 842-3) points to his use of other women, like the Sultaness, for the same end: to 'bigile' and 'brynge us in servage' (368, 371).

This pattern of double apostrophe occurs elsewhere in the work, and to similar effect, when the narrator blames first the messenger and then Donegild for their parts in the plot against Custance (771-84).[47] More importantly, it occurs when Custance is on trial for her life. Here we have, in rapid succession, an address to Custance (631-7), a speech to the reader (645-50) and an address to the noble ladies of the audience (652-8). Like his heroine, the narrator seems desperately to be seeking a way of escape. He prays that Christ will champion Custance's cause. After all, Christ 'starf for our redempcioun/ And boond Sathan (and yet lith ther he lay)' (633-4). The narrator's reminder to himself of the defeat of Satan counters the remark with which he introduced the episode ('Sathan ... evere us waiteth to bigile': 582), and echoes his own earlier comparison of the devil, the 'serpent depe in helle ybounde', to the Sultaness (361). But at this moment of tension the certainty of Christ's victory over the devil, dramatised earlier by the failure of the Sultaness to carry her plan fully into effect, does not convince the narrator. Nothing short of an 'open myracle' (636-7) will preserve Custance: this in spite of the fact that the narrator had earlier argued for just such a 'wonderful myracle' when she survived her second sea voyage (477). His address to Custance gives way to a moment of narrative (Custance on her knees, praying for her life), and is immediately followed by a total abandonment of the religious frame in favour of the psychological—tragic one. Addressing us directly for the first time, the narrator urges us to visualise Custance as an emblem not of grace but of its total absence: she is like a person 'lad/ Toward his deeth, wher as hym gat no grace' (646-7).

He is saying more than he knows. Like his comparison of Custance to an innocent lamb, earlier in the episode (617), this phrase reminds us of the prophetic description of the Passion of Christ in Isaiah 53 under the figure of a suffering servant led like a lamb to the slaughter. According to the prophet, the suffering servant had neither beauty nor grace in his looks, and was so disfigured that bystanders turned away from him in horror. Even on the literal level this figure hardly bears much relation to Custance's situation. Granted, she is alone, like the suffering servant, and on

the point of death; but, as we have seen, the bystanders do not turn
away from her. They identify completely with her desperate plight,
and make helpless and tearful protestation of her innocence. On a
deeper level the image actually turns inside out what the narrator
presents as a desperate situation. Though he may want all outward
grace in the moment of his dying, the servant's obedience to the
will of God confers on him a fulness of inner grace, and his death
looses that grace upon the whole world.[48] As with Christ, so with
his followers; as earlier noted, the deaths of the *litel clergeon* and
St Cecilia, in the Prioress's and Second Nun's tales, provide classic
instances of this outpouring of inner grace (and Cecilia symbolises
it by tangible reminders of herself which she bequeaths to friends).
Even were she to be executed, then, Custance's want of outer
grace merely symbolises, in ironic counterpoint, her fulness of
inner grace, in much the same way as the Sultaness's proposed dis-
gracing of her son by execution will paradoxically confer upon him
the grace of martyrdom. The narrator, though, seems not to appreciate that this moment is an occasion for rejoicing. Addressing the
noblewomen — readers whose sympathies are most likely to be
engaged by the plight of an emperor's daughter — he urges them
to spare a little pity for Custance, as she 'stant allone' with no one
to whom 'to make hir mone' (655-6). His appeal is misplaced to
the extent that, until now, we have seen Custance constantly
making moan to God, and being answered.

The presence of so much apostrophe provides a clear indication
of the narrator's commitment not to the given religious reading of
his story but to his own psychological–tragic reading of it. A
further sign of this preference is provided by his use of a startlingly
unexpected text to gloss key moments of the story: the profoundly
gloomy *De Miseria Condicionis Humane* of Pope Innocent III, a
work which describes 'the vileness of the human condition' so as to
humble the haughty (Lewis, p. 92). The narrator shows an easy
familiarity with the *De Miseria.* He translates five passages, which
almost form a digest or epitome of the original treatise; we have
sections on the pains of poverty (99-121; translating *De Miseria,*
I,14); the sad end of all human happiness (421-7; *De Miseria* I,21)
and its radical impermanence (1132-8; *De Miseria* I,20); the fearful consequences of drunkenness (771-7; *De Miseria* II,19) and
lust (925-31; *De Miseria* II,21).[49] These passages provide a
nucleus about which the psychological–tragic reading of the narrative can grow. Yet their character is as paradoxical as any of the

narrator's other additions to the original story.[50] They are inserted as randomly in the narrative, are as marginal to its overall design, as was the Prioress's recollection about the infant St Nicholas. Couched in the form of apostrophe or rhetorical question, they merely increase the emotional temperature; two of them (421, 771) actually heighten the sense of foreboding.

The first passage of all, on the pains of poverty (99-121), is still more ambiguous.[51] It serves as prologue proper to the tale. It describes the poor man in the grip of cold and hunger. Ashamed, but compelled by his need to ask for help, he is forced, in the absence of such help, to beg, borrow or steal (99-105). Hated by neighbours, friends and relations (115, 120-1), he would rather die than endure his wretched state (114). He blames Christ and back-bites his rich neighbour, who must have benefited at his poor neighbour's expense (106-9). In the next world, he gloats, this rich neighbour will learn the error of his selfish ways (110-12).[52] And then, in mid-stanza, and with no sign of incongruity, the narrator breaks free from the straitjacket of his source and addresses 'riche marchauntz'. Such men are noble, prudent and — because so widely travelled — wise; the source of gossip about foreign parts; authorities on 'th'estaat/ Of regnes'. Not for them the uncertain chances of the game of life which yield the losing throw on the dice; they may dance Christmas away (122-30). Such observations trivialise both the Man of Law's tale and the quotation from the *De Miseria.*[53] Though chiefly concerned with the pains of poverty, the latter had also spoken of the pains of the rich. One such pain — though clearly the rich would not so experience it — the *De Miseria* reckons the common misunderstanding that equates wealth and the possession of virtue, a judgement which may be undeserved and unfounded ('he is considered as good as he is rich'; Lewis, p. 116). Ironically, the Man of Law bears unconscious witness to this very misunderstanding, when he makes so approving an equation of riches and nobility, prudence and wisdom.[54]

The narrator, then, has not read the *De Miseria* very critically; he seems to have drawn from it only that message which corresponds to his own interests and, by implication, endorses his own sense of the status quo. Moreover, the prologue relates only marginally to his retelling of the story. True, like the poor man in the prologue, Custance is no stranger to undeserved and protracted suffering; true, too, the pains of the wicked figure in both prologue and tale; true, too, the poor man's back-biting of his rich neighbour has an equivalent, if not in the Man of Law's tale, at least in Gower, and could therefore have provided a frame of reference for the story which it prefaces. Yet the whole prologue seems merely to mark time, until the narrator can introduce us to the merchant from whom he claims to have got his story.[55]

As with the prologue, so with the epilogue. Here, at least, the narrator has not misunderstood the text of the *De Miseria*. He uses it, though, to describe the death of King Alla, and the end of his 'blisse ... with Custance' (1141) only a year after their reunion (1132-8). Conjoined with a reference (shared with Gower) to death that 'taketh of heigh and logh his rente' (1142), the quotation from the *De Miseria* tips the balance once more in the direction of tragedy. (In Trevet, by contrast, the death of Alla is merely an instrument for restoring Constance to the *status quo ante*.)

The narrator's pursuit of an alternative reading to the exemplary religious one, then, is shot through with ironies — not least that he often misunderstands and misapplies what he reads. There are other inconsistencies in his approach to the story. One concerns his view of its sexual elements. Generally, in religious tales, sex is noteworthy more by its absence than by its presence; licit sexual relationships figure, if at all, as an expression of obedient faithfulness or to account for the birth of a saint. A religious work which considers them in any detail runs the risk of turning into something else — a satiric comedy, a sentimental tragedy. The Man of Law does not entirely avoid the danger. Custance's fears at being sent to Syria to marry a man she has never seen provide the occasion for a knowing wink at the expense of that stock comic figure, the tyrannical husband:

> Housbondes been alle goode, and han ben yoore;
> That knowen wyves; I dar sey yow na moore.
>
> (272-3)

The narrator hardly needs to draw his audience's attention to the realities of arranged marriages: the married members of his audience will know of them at first-hand, and Custance herself is well aware of them (286-7). Then, in an attempt to right the balance in favour of the men among the audience (we might compare the Clerk's equally devious game), the narrator makes Custance on her wedding night a figure of comedy, a sort of holy tease:[56]

> They goon to bedde, as it was skile and right;
> For thogh that wyves be ful hooly thynges,
> They moste take in pacience at nyght
> Swiche manere necessaries as been plesynges
> To folk that han ywedded hem wyth rynges,
> And leye a lite hir hoolynesse aside,
> As for the tyme — it may no bet bitide.
>
> (708-14)

This extraordinary aside begins well enough, but coarsens as it goes. At first it views sexual relations in marriage as reasonable and lawful ('skile and right'). Then it reckons them a necessity imposed upon the woman of giving the man pleasure ('pacience', 'necessaries') — martyrdom of a lower order. Worse is to come. Marriage, it implies, gives men the occasion to take women down a peg or two, and make these 'ful hooly thynges ... leye a lite hir hoolynesse aside'. But since the phenomenon is purely temporary ('as for the tyme'), would-be saints should not find it too inconvenient. Crucially missing from this shabby exercise in logic-chopping is any meaningful sense of the sacramental character of marriage. The couple, it is true, have 'ywedded hem with rynges', but the narrator seems to treat this sacramental sign merely as a necessary item of ecclesiastical furniture. In this respect his position resembles the Merchant's jaundiced view of the marriage of January and May:[57]

> to the chirche bothe be they went
> For to receyve the hooly sacrement.
> Forth comth the preest, with stole aboute his nekke ...
> And seyde his orisons, as is usage,
> And croucheth hem, and bad God sholde hem blesse,
> And made al siker ynogh with hoolynesse.
>
> (IV, 1701-3, 1706-8)

Ironically, he seems to care as little for the sacramental character of those exchanged rings as the wicked Sultaness cared about the religious meaning of that other sacramental sign figured in the tale, the water of baptism. (Contrast the view of marriage advanced by more orthodox religious narratives, such as the Clerk's and Second Nun's tales.)

In fact, the narrator's interest in Custance's wedding night has more to do with his own psychology, we may infer, than with the requirements of the story. In an earlier conversation with the Host (57-89), he had shown considerable interest in love-stories, and reckoned that he would have told one himself if Chaucer had not already collared the best examples, particularly in his *Legend.* The love-stories of the *Legend*, of course, treat of pagan martyrs, women who have suffered and died for love (hence the title of the collection, 'the seintes legende of Cupide'). One could obviously so read the story of Custance, and bring to the fore its connections with the stories in the *Legend*:[58] exactly what the narrator's glancing references to a sexual element separate from the specifically religious dimension of the story seem to be attempting to do. Ironically, the fascination with the holy tease which this passage reveals may bring the narrator closer in spirit to the 'cursed stories' of Canace and Apollonius of Tyre, of which, in his conversation with the Host, he professes such a disapproval, than to the tale he ends up telling.[59]

Far from acknowledging these inconsistencies in his treatment of the story, the narrator takes pains to conceal them. He does this by accusing the audience of his own tendencies (the posture of many a moralist). He anticipates their lively interest in the splendid trappings of the story:

> Now wolde som men waiten, as I gesse,
> That I sholde tellen al the purveiance
> That th'Emperour, of his grete noblesse
> Hath shapen for his doghter, dame Custance
>
> (246-9)

And again,

> What sholde I tellen of the roialtee
> At mariage, or which cours goth biforn;
> Who bloweth in a trumpe or in an horn?
>
> (703-5)

He will not satisfy their curiosity. On the one hand,

> Wel may men knowen that so greet ordinance
> May no man tellen in a litel clause
> As was arrayed for so heigh a cause
>
> (250-2)

and on the other,

> Me list nat of the chaf, ne of the stree,
> Maken so long a tale as of the corn ...
> The fruyt of every tale is for to seye.
>
> (701-2,706)

In any case, a tale of incredible suffering and unimaginable grace will hardly commend itself to such hard-headed realists:

> Men myghten asken why she was nat slayn
> Eek at the feeste? who myghte hir body save?
>
> (470-1)

And there are further questions they may ask about her second sea journey:

> Who kepte hire fro the drenchyng in the see? ...
> Where myghte this womman mete and drynke have
> Thre yeer and moore? How lasteth hire vitaille?
>
> (485,498-9)

as about her surviving the attempted rape:

> How may this wayke womman han this strengthe
> Hire to defende agayn this renegat?
>
> (932-3)

Elsewhere the narrator has attempted to prove his case by adopting the calmly authoritative tone favoured by Trevet and Gower; these hard questions put him on the defensive, and require very different tactics. To confute the doubters and turn the tables on them, he produces a dazzling array of rhetorical counter-questions based on Biblical precedents. If we accept God's hand in these latter — and the signs are too manifest to admit of doubt — it is only logical to see him active, too, in the Custance story. This list of Biblical figures, the religious counterpart of the secular list earlier noted, originates ultimately in Trevet's earlier noted comparison of Constance's sea journey with that of Noah, but the Man of Law goes much further, and the tone of apologetic so produced is far removed from that of Trevet. In quick succession we get Daniel in the lions' den (472-6), Jonah in the whale's belly

(486-7), the 'foure spirites .../ That power han t'anoyen lond and see' (491-2) of Apoc. 7:1-3, St Mary of Egypt, who lived in the wilderness for years on what God sent her (500-1), then Goliath killed by unarmed David (934-8), and Holofernes killed by Judith, 'to deliveren out of wrecchednesse/ The peple of God' (939-42). Daniel, the sole survivor in the lions' den, foreshadows and authorises Custance's survival at a banquet where everyone else was slain. Jonah, kept safe in the whale's belly 'til he was spouted up at Nynyvee' by the same God who led the 'peple Ebrayk' dry-shod over the Red Sea (488-90), anticipates Custance's miraculous preservation during her long and dangerous sea voyage, as do the 'foure spirites of tempest', obedient to God's command to '[anoyen] neither see, ne land, ne tree' (494). If St Mary of Egypt could be fed for years in the desert by the same divine hand that used five loaves and two fishes to feed 5000 (502-3), Custance's food could surely last the three years of her voyage. And the deaths of Goliath and Holofernes show how Custance could survive the attempted rape.

The narrator presents these counter-claims from the position of a superior understanding, which will communicate itself irresistibly to the most dull-witted members of his audience. Granted, 'mennes wittes ben so dulle/ That no wight kan wel rede it atte fulle' (202-3): this remark, concerning our ability to read the 'large book/ Which that men clepe the hevene', can apply without strain to the difficulties of understanding the Man of Law's 'book'. Like the emperor, most of us, as readers, are 'to lewed or to slowe' (315). Nevertheless, the

> certein ende that ful derk is
> To mannes wit, that for oure ignorance
> Ne konne noght knowe his [God's] prudent purveiance
>
> (481-3)

is accessible to the scrutiny of the learned, and capable of proof positive, 'as knowen clerkis' (480): among which number, it seems, the narrator classes himself. His audience can be led to recognise for themselves the truths of the faith:

> Wel may men knowe it was no wight but he
> That kepte peple Ebrayk from hir drenchynge
>
> (488-9)

Wel may men seen, it nas but Goddes grace.

(938)

This phrase, 'wel may men knowen', was also used in an earlier
passage (see p. 155) where the narrator explains why he cannot tell
'al the purveiance' of the emperor for the departure of his daughter. That is, the truths of the faith are as self-evident as the circumstances of the narration. I find this juxtaposition very ironic. At
one point the narrator is willing to use his readers' knowledge of
the world to make good the gaps in his own narrative; at another,
he must challenge that worldly awareness in the name of a superior
religious understanding. Yet his claim to represent that superior
understanding is undermined by his own absorption in the actual,
as opposed to the exemplary, situation of his characters, which his
own reading so often reveals.

A similar irony attends his acknowledged relation to his sources.
As earlier noted, Gower makes nothing of disagreements between
his sources; Trevet almost as little, though he must at first resolve a
disagreement between the sources about the part played by
Maurice in the story, so as to explain the shape his own version will
take. The Man of Law does not use this material, but it seems to
have provided him with his cue.[60] When he airs disagreement
between the sources, he prefaces his discussion with a remark he
elsewhere uses to criticise his audience's imperfect understandings
of the story ('som men wolde seyn': 1009, 1086; cf. 'now wolde
som men waiten': 246). He thus implies that he intends the discussion to yield a reading of the story superior to those of his sources:
his own. Not surprisingly, he fails to make good his promise. Some
writers will have it, he says, that Arsemius took Maurice with him
to the banquet being held in Alla's honour in response to a request
by Custance. He cannot pronounce authoritatively on this difficulty ('I may nat tellen every circumstance'); but he does know one
thing ('sooth is this'). However Maurice was brought to the
banquet, he had been instructed about his behaviour there by his
mother (1009-15). This pretended resolution to a difficulty is, in
fact, a hollow sham. Trevet and Gower are not divided about the
manner of Maurice's coming to the banquet; neither version
considers the question as put by the Man of Law. What is more,
the narrator actually owes his 'solution' to an agreement of Trevet
and Gower, both of whom record Constance's instruction to her
son concerning his behaviour at the banquet. Slightly more signi-

ficant is the disagreement between the two sources — a real and not a manufactured one — concerning the role of Maurice in arranging Custance's meeting with her father (1086-92). In Trevet, Constance instructs her son to present himself to his grandfather; in Gower, Alla sends the child 'with thassent of Couste'. As the Man of Law sees it, neither version is right. Considerations of state argue against Alla's sending 'any child' on so important an errand (according to Trevet, the child is eighteen years old!): 'It is bet to deeme/ He wente hymself, and so it may wel seeme' (1091-2). This passage, however, reveals no very critical attitude to the sources: its real significance is other. Not for the first time in the work the narrator, who had earlier apostrophised queens, duchesses and ladies (652-3), and credited the wealthy and the noble with the possession of prudence and wisdom, is making the lives of the great the imaginative centre of his work.[61]

In any case, he cannot for long maintain this pretence of authority. These pretended resolutions of textual cruces come near the end of the work, when the narrator is retreating into the safer waters of orthodox symbol and interpretation. In that same part of the story we see him suddenly abandoning his god-like stance: no longer an editor, much less an author, he is rather the transmitter of another man's work. So, for example, he sends us to the 'olde Romayn geestes' for information which he cannot presently treat in detail:[62]

> This child Maurice was sithen Emperour
> Maad by the Pope, and lyved cristenly ...
> But I lete al his storie passen by;
> Of Custance is my tale specially.
> In the olde Romayn geestes may men fynde
> Maurices lyf; I bere it noght in mynde.
>
> (1121-2, 1124-7)

Again, the meeting of Custance's ship with the Roman navy in mid-ocean is authorised by the source:

> This senatour repaireth with victorie
> To Rome-ward, saillynge ful roially,
> And mette the ship dryvynge, as seith the storie,
> In which Custance sit ful pitously
>
> (967-70)

Like similar expressions in Trevet and Gower ('come dient les aunciene cronikes'; 'as the cronique seith'), such comments remind us of the narrator's dependence on an ultimate source of authority. They also point to his difficulties with the happy ending. How credible is it, after all, that two ships would meet in mid-ocean? How plausible that Custance, whom until now we have mostly seen reacting passively to events, should suddenly initiate so complex an action as the sending of her son, that living emblem of herself, to her father? For once, the narrator does not tackle the difficult questions head-on; he takes cover behind the source. Implausible though he may feel its account of events, he must report it faithfully or falsify the record: 'if I shal nat lye' (1007; cf. 694), 'but sooth is this' (1013). When difficulties cannot be satis-factorily resolved, because the source does not provide sufficient information (892, 905), he prefers to stress a point about which there can be no doubt, so as to preserve some vestige of his own authority: 'Th' effect is this ... that may men pleynly rede' (893-4); 'And wel rede I' (1095). Such phrases seek to maximise sup-port for his reading of the text. They reveal an uneasy awareness that, by himself, the narrator cannot be the measure of his own story. They constitute a tacit admission that the narrator's under-standing of the story exists only in relation to his source and to the situation of his audience. That is, authority resides in no one ele-ment of the literary process — narrator, source or audience — but, since all three are images of one another (albeit of a distorted kind), in the active interrelation of them all.[63] Inevitably, therefore, the story ends with a formal prayer, which identifies the narrator and his audience with the characters of the story, all under the 'sonde' of the one authority which requires no outside helps:

> Now Jhesu Crist, that of his myght may sende
> Joye after wo, governe us in his grace,
> And kepe us alle that been in this place! Amen,
>
> (1160-2)

The Man of Law's tale, then, is a much bolder experiment than either of its sources. Taking its cue from them, it magnifies their potentially conflicting elements, and leaves them in a state of almost unresolved tension. In respect of this feature, it approxi-mates to the total achievement of *The Canterbury Tales* more closely than any tale yet considered. The reasons for this boldness have less to do with the logic of a religious narrative, however, than with the exigencies of performance.[64] More than any other narrator yet considered, the Man of Law is conscious of the status of his work as a performance. In the first place, he is keenly aware of the time his story is taking to tell.[65] Begun, as earlier noted, shortly before ten in the morning, it lasts all day, like the elegant and protracted speech-making of the eagles in *The Parliament of Fowls* (484-90), and draws to a close only as daylight fades (1116-17). Consequently, the narrator takes pains to move his hearers briskly through the story. Sometimes the events defy description (419, 899, 1120); more often, he simply does not have the time to do them justice (250-2). Even were the hearers willing to stay up all night to hear of the tearful reunion of Alla with Custance — he could easily take so long over the episode — he is too exhausted by his own protracted exposure to their sufferings even to attempt it:

> I pray yow alle my labour to relesse;
> I may nat telle hir wo until to-morwe,
> I am so wery for to speke of sorwe.

> (1069-71)

Hence, throughout, he insists on the need for brevity. Regularly he rounds off episodes with phrases like 'this is the ende' (145). Rhetorical questions serve a similar function: 'What nedeth gretter dilatacioun?' (232); 'What sholde I in this tale lenger tarye?' (374). In a similar way, the narrator has to show himself controlling the separate episodes of the story. As he moves from episode to episode, he repeatedly declares that he is returning to the point, as if he feared to lose the thread (or 'fruyt', 'purpos', 'matere' or 'effect') of his story:

> But now to purpos lat us turne agayn.

> (170)

> And thus in murthe and joye I lete hem dwelle;
> The fruyt of this matiere is that I telle.

> (410-11)

> But now wol I unto Custance go.

> (900)

Now lat us stynte of Custance but a throwe

(953)

I wol no lenger tarien in this cas,
But to Kyng Alla, which I spak of yoore ...
I wol retourne, and lete I wol Custance

(983-4,86)[66]

The limits of his knowledge about a particular episode provide another convenient device for moving the narrative on: 'I kan sey yow namoore' (175; cf. 273), 'I kan no bettre seye' (874; cf. 881). Within the narrative he is constantly reminding of what we have heard or warning of what is to come: 'which ye shal heren that I shal devyse' (349), 'of which I tolde' (415), and so on.

Throughout the narrative, then, the sense of time passing and needing to be saved is playing a more prominent part than in any other story so far studied. The tale's insistence on its own duration is perhaps appropriate, given that earlier conversation of the Man of Law with the Host. The latter's playful observations about the dangers of wasting time (16-32) lead the former initially to profess his own inability to tell a 'thrifty tale' (46).[67] By the end of the tale, the Man of Law has won over the Host; in an echo of that earlier phrase, the Host finds the story 'a thrifty tale for the nones' (1165). But we need to consider, more carefully than the Host seems to do, the purpose of all this thrift. To what end, that is to say, is this time so conspicuously saved? The many references to time passing are not used to point a meaning or focus a structure; they are inserted as randomly into the narrative as the narrator's other comments. Rather, they give us the constant sense of a speaking voice in control of a performance. More important, the narrator's parsimony in regard to the details of his own narration is poorly matched by any modesty in the scope of his own commentary; as earlier noted, the commentary consumes time as conspicuously as the narration seeks to save it. We can hardly escape the conclusion that, where Trevet and Gower wanted others to hear their story, the Man of Law wants his audience to listen to the sound of his voice. And finely modulated effects that voice does produce. Hence beautifully turned phrases like

The day is comen of hir departynge;
I seye, the woful day fatal is come.

(260-1)

Hence the beautifully studied rhetorical questions, elegant apostrophe, and many other rhetorical figures not specifically noted
here. In other words, though the Man of Law provides now a
religious, now a psychological, reading of the narrative for his
hearers, he really feels no answerability to any greater authority
than his own sense of occasion. I avoid equating this performance
with that of a lawyer, just as I did not wish to equate what we
might call the way of opposition in the Clerk's tale with the voice
of a professional student: but I had better admit, too, that the
temptation so to read the two tales is strong.[68]

Notes

1. Green (p. 159) goes further than *SA* (p. 455) was ready to do and finds
PrT 'clearly taken from a Latin life of Hugh of Lincoln'. For a more judicious
estimate, see Wenzel, *SP*, 73, 142: 'we find analogues to PrT in a surprisingly large
number of works in Chaucer's England that are directly related to preaching.'
2. On links between Mandeville and *CT*, see Zacher, chs 5-6; on the
influence of Mandeville on *CT*, ibid., p. 130.
3. This work is still largely unedited. For an edition of the relevant portion,
see *SA*, pp. 165-81; for a translation, *Originals and analogues of some of
Chaucer's CT*, ed. F.J. Furnivall *et al.*, Ch. Soc. 2nd series, 1, ed. E. Brock,
hereafter *OA* (London, 1872), I, 2-53 (and cf. III, 222-50). For the suggestion that
the *Cronicles* influenced not only MLT but also PardT, see R.A. Pratt, 'Chaucer
and *Les cronicles* of Nicholas Trevet', *Studies in Language, Literature and Culture
of the Middle Ages and Later*, ed. E.B. Atwood and A.A. Hill (Austin, Texas,
1969), pp. 303-11, and particularly p. 306, n.4. For comment on Trevet and the
Cronicles see R. Dean, 'Nicholas Trevet, historian', in *Medieval Learning and
Literature: essays presented to R.W. Hunt*, ed. J.J.G. Alexander and M.T. Gibson
(Oxford, 1976), pp. 328-52; and P. Clogan, 'The narrative style of MLT', *M&H*,
NS 8 (1977), 222.
4. On motives for conversion to Islam, see D. Metlitzki, *The Matter of Araby
in Medieval England* (New Haven and London, 1977), p. 233, quoting Mandeville
(see *Mandeville's Travels*, ed. M.C. Seymour (Oxford, 1967), p. 103).
5. See comment above ch. 2, nn. 20-21; and in M.R. Paull, 'The influence of
the saint's legend genre in MLT', *ChR*, 5 (1970-71), 183.
6. The links between romance and hagiography both in general and in
relation to MLT have often been noted. See e.g. Mehl, pp. 12, 17, 26, 255; Burlin,
p. 138; Kean, II, 114; Clogan, *M&H*, NS 8, 219, 226 (the latter tacitly opposing
Mehl, p. 26 on identification of audience with the protagonists of the story); and
Payne, p. 161. See also Wood (p. 195) for an interesting view of MLT as a saint's
legend transformed by the style of its narration into a romance.
7. On St Cecilia, see above ch. 4; on St Katharine, ch. 4, n. 9; on St Ursula,
Ryan-Ripperger, pp. 627-31.
8. *SA* (p. 167): 'la purueaunce dieu ni faili poynt, qi en tribulacioun ia ne faut
a ceaus qi ount en lui esperaunce.'
9. *SA* (p. 168): 'dieu estoit son mariner'.
10. On the role of the bystanders in, for instance, the revelations of Julian of
Norwich, see Ellis, *Christian*, 6, 63-5.

11. The copy of the *Cronicles* in Oxford MS Bodleian Rawlinson B 178 indicates this feature of the text by the creation of separate rubrics for the English material.

12. For a stronger statement of this position see Burlin, p. 138: MLT 'has a generic conflict inherited from its source.' See also Mehl (pp. 20-1) on the distinction between romance and chronicle. (NPT will playfully appropriate the distinction: see below p. 291. As Mehl observes, the distinction is neither simple nor absolute.)

13. Recent history might have given special point to this observation of Trevet. In 1330 Philip VI of France demanded the surrender of Jerusalem and part of the Palestine coast (Metlitzki, p. 237).

14. On this point, see M. Keen, 'Medieval ideas of history', Daiches–Thorlby, pp. 290 ff; and Allen, p. 68, on 'the conviction that history existed as moral example'.

15. By contrast, the preface to Boccaccio's *De claris mulieribus*, a work discussed below, pp. 170-71, 193 ff, finds that women readers of history need more detail, not less.

16. Cf. Clogan, *M&H*, NS 8 (1977), 222: 'a romantic digression like his [Trevet's] Arthurian digression'.

17. Cf. Mehl (pp. 135 ff) on the relation of historical and moral–religious elements in *Emaré*, a romance long recognised as an analogue of MLT and sometimes offered as a secondary source (but unconvincingly, e.g. D.T. Hanks, Jr, 'Emaré: an influence on MLT', *ChR*, 18 (1983-84), 182-4). For an edition, see *The Romance of Emaré*, ed. E. Rickert, EETS ES 99 (London, 1906).

18. For the relevant part of *CA* (i.e. II, 587-1612) see *SA*, pp. 181-206. For the whole text, see *The Complete Works of John Gower*, ed. G.C. Macaulay, *The English Works* (Oxford, 1901), I, 146-73. Whether *CA* was a source or merely an analogue of MLT is a moot point. For comment see J.H. Fisher, *John Gower: moral philosopher and friend of Chaucer* (New York, 1964), p.290; C. Brown, 'ML headlink and Prol *CT*', *SP*, 34 (1937), 14; and N.D. Isaacs, 'Constance in 14 Cy England', *NM*, 59 (1958), 267. For reasons connected with MLT, 1086 (discussed above, p. 159), I incline to the view that Chaucer used Gower's version to supplement that of Trevet.

19. So Whittock (p. 112). Though scandal — the uttering of a slander — was the effect, it was not the motive of the villains' behaviour.

20. Elsewhere Gower uses the emblematic reading of Trevet for additions of his own: Constance grieving to find paganism rife in England when she arrives, for example (II, 744-6).

21. This metaphor may derive from Trevet's account of Alla confronting his mother 'tut enflaume de ire'.

22. Cf. Kirk, Economou (1975), p. 113, on Gower's 'plain style', and Whittock (p. 110) on the 'innocent directness' of the narration ('the tone of the poetry seems to say, quite simply, well, it happened like this; take it as you find it'). Cooper (p. 39), on the relation of the stories to the frame, finds a 'common tone ... an unvarying level of poetic competence ... and a consistency of style that smooths over the generic distinctions that the nature of the individual stories might suggest.'

23. Surprisingly overlooked, since noted by Robinson, in Thompson, Davis–Wrenn, pp. 183-99 (this account supersedes G.W. Landrum, 'Chaucer's use of the Vulgate', *PMLA* 39 (1924), 75-100).

24. It is tempting to suppose that political considerations may have played a part in Chaucer's decision to translate the Bible text so carefully. The question of vernacular Bible translation was a lively issue at the time. See also Thompson, Davis–Wrenn, pp. 192-3, on Chaucer's attitude to, and translation of, Holy Scripture.

25. *SA* (p. 165): 'trop haute e noble sen e sapience e ... graunde merueilouse biaute e gentirise e noblesce de saunc.'

26. Cf. Yunck, *ELH* 27, 250, on Chaucer's suppression in the opening episode of Custance's 'militant, self-assured often unpleasant proselytizing fervour not uncommon in the early saints' lives'.

27. In this light I find odd the assertion that Custance is 'confidently suffering', endowed with 'equanimity' (Wood, pp. 193,6), a 'childlike receptacle and instrument of divine guidance' displaying 'quiet and meek submission' (Yunck, *ELH*, 27, 252), 'steadfast, as her name suggests, in her love of God' (Brewer, Intro., p. 186). These views express the truth, but hardly the experience, of the story, and hence, in my view, short-change the meaning.

28. Cf. S. Manning, 'Chaucer's Constance pale and passive', Vasta–Thundy, p. 15: 'each character has his or her own space, which allows for reaction but inhibits interaction.'

29. Yunck, *ELH*, 27, 251, treats this moment similarly, but consistently makes more of Christ's part in the narrative than I am willing to do.

30. For extensive comment on this metaphor, see Kolve, pp. 326 ff.

31. Hence the difficulty I find with Kolve's reading. Not even Trevet goes as far as Kolve seems to do in reading the sea simply as an emblem.

32. See Yunck, *ELH*, 27, 253-5, for comment on the liturgical base of this comparison with Susanna (in prayers for the dying, and regularly in hagiographic accounts of martyrdom, hence doubly appropriate here).

33. Kean, II, 118 assigns this speech in error to the messenger of ll. 806-8.

34. For illuminating comment on these lines, see Kean, II, 192-3.

35. A feature also noted by Manning, Vasta–Thundy, pp. 18-19, though interpreted differently.

36. Contrast Kean's reading (II,122) that MLT focuses primarily on questions of freewill and Fortune, and provides the Christian complement to the philosophical solution of KnT.

37. For the literary background to the Syrian episodes, see Metlitzki, ch. 6 (references to MLT are pp. 153-6).

38. Cf. Metlitzki (p. 238): 'there is ample evidence of Christians turning Muslim to become full-fledged members of the court.'

39. Other writers judge the Sultan much more harshly: see Kolve, pp. 321-4, citing *MLT*, ed. N. Coghill and C. Tolkien (London, 1969), p. 35; Kean, II, 117. Kolve implicitly, and Kean explicitly, make the Sultan a parallel with the wicked steward, as an emblem of 'blinde lust'. So to read him is to ignore the strongly patterned structure inherited from Trevet, which had two loving husbands (the Sultan–Alla) and two false seducers (Elda's deputy–the steward). Chaucer's changes to the role of the Sultan do not, for me, succeed in breaking this pattern. Ambiguous or not, the Sultan's determination to become a Christian will be sanctified by his violent death. In any case, Saracen heroes regularly convert, on equally flimsy grounds, in medieval romance (normally, to be sure, at the end of the story). Their conversion proves their nobility (Metlitzki, pp. 182-3).

40. Like sympathetic presentation of the Jews (see above ch. 3, n. 13) this sympathetic presentation of Islam is not peculiar to Chaucer. See M.W. Bloomfield, 'Chaucer's sense of history', *JEGP* 51 (1952), 309-10; and Metlitzki, pp. 197 ff., quoting Langland. Zacher (pp. 143 ff.) quotes Mandeville, and brings to the fore an ambiguity in the Christian's position. On the one hand, he needs to 'chacen out alle the mysbeleeuynge men' (p. 132; and cf. the Monk's account of King Peter of Cyprus, noted p. 176 below); on the other, it is right to be charitable to those of other faiths. According to Zacher (p. 148), 'Mandeville's sense of cultural diversity [was] shared by Chaucer and by very few other English contemporaries.'

41. On this incident, see J. Burrow, 'A maner Latyn corrupt', *M AE*, 30

(1961), 33-7; Bloomfield, *JEGP*, 51, 306.

42. Cf. Howard (p. 51): 'if we are to understand the differences between Gower and Chaucer, then, we have to read both for tone, not content.' Strohm (*MP*, 68, 324) finds the essential difference in conception between MLT and SecNT and PrT 'is reflected in the manner and tone in which ML narrative is written'. Dronke (Brewer, 1974, pp. 158-60) talks of 'histrionic appeals ... to divine intervention' and finds three perspectives in the story — 'the fatalistic, the pious and the prurient' (all taken up in the following pages). Broadly, critics of MLT divide into those who find a gap between tale and telling, and those who do not (those who do, normally relate the gap to the persona of the narrator; those who do not identify the narrator with the poet). Extreme expressions of the former view are in Wood (pp. 193-5) and R. Delasanta, 'And of great reverence: Chaucer's ML', *ChR*, 5 (1970-71), 294-5. Important instances of the latter include Clogan, *M&H*, NS 8, 217-33; Yunck, *ELH* 27, 249-61; Paull, *ChR*, 5, 186-93. All three admit to doubts about the total effect of the active narratorial presence: Yunck (p. 260), talking of the 'titter at Custance's wedding night'; Paull (p. 193) when he describes the narrator 'as a separate character' in a plot whose overall purpose is 'developing the aesthetic of melodrama'; and Clogan (p. 222) comparing Trevet and Chaucer. I find the evidence for derivation of this narrator figure from hagiographical romance (Clogan, pp. 219-20) or female saints' lives (Paull, p. 186) doubtful: the precise configurations of the narratorial presence in MLT are without parallel, to my knowledge, in other examples, English or other, of the genres. Hence D. Pearsall, 'John Capgrave's Life of St Katharine', *M&H*, 6 (1975), 121-3, talks of a 'Chaucer–Lydgate tradition of embellished rhetorical hagiography' which was 'introduced into English by Chaucer'.

43. For comment on these lines, see Harbert, Brewer (1974) p. 143.

44. See Wood (pp. 208-19) for illuminating discussion of the relation of these lines to the source, the *Cosmographia* of Bernard Silvester. MLT has added Samson to Bernard's original list and — much more importantly — excised Christ from it, thus denying the source's clear understanding that pagan (and Old Testament) history culminated in the birth of Christ. See also D.B. Loomis, 'Constance and the stars', Vasta–Thundy, pp. 213-14. On Samson as an emblem of the victorious Christ, see *Aurora Petri Rigae Biblia versificata*, ed. P. Beichner, 2 vols, University of Notre Dame Publications in Medieval Studies 19 (Notre Dame, Ind., 1965), I, 241-3; Samson as an emblem of the Christian fallen in sin occurs in the *Glossa ordinaria* and the *Bible moralisée*. For an illustration from the copy of the latter executed for Jean le Bon *c.* 1350, see Avril plate 20.

45. For detailed comment on ll. 295-308, see Elliott, pp. 304-5.

46. See R. Woolf, *The English Mystery Plays* (London, 1972), p. 115 and n. 27.

47. This rhetorical figure also occurred in PrT (VII, 574-85) and will reappear, much more dramatically, in PardT (VI, 513-21; see also below p. 236). It also occurs in a speech of Custance before her banishment (II, 850-4, 858-61).

48. Huppé (pp. 101-2) rightly sees that Chaucer (if not his narrator) is aware of this 'concatenation of images evocative of ... Christ'.

49. We may also have to reckon with a link between the *De Miseria* and the *Cosmographia* of Bernard Silvester, earlier noted (n. 44 above) for its influence on MLT. Lewis (p. 292) reckons that variant readings in some manuscripts of *De M* (I, 25) may reflect the influence of the *Cosmographia*. See also Brown, *SP*, 37, 14-16, for the claim that the passages from *De M* were added to MLT when it was accommodated to *CT* frame: Brown, that is, ascribes inconsistencies between *De M* and MLT discussed below not to a bad narrator but to a careless author-compiler, Chaucer himself.

50. Giffin (p. 77) finds them appropriate on historical grounds; Yunck (*ELH*, 27, 257) finds the 'free use' of Innocent III 'thoroughly consonant' with Chaucer's

aim of presenting 'the greatness of divine power and the helplessness of man in the face of worldly vicissitudes'. David (p. 129) is closer to my reading when he talks of the 'gloomy impression of mutability ... even stronger than in KnT' that they produce.

51. See also Burlin, pp. 139-40; Wood, pp. 203-4.

52. This passage may echo material in *De M*, III,3, as also the parable of Dives and Lazarus, also used in *De M*, III,3.

53. So Howard (p. 175: the narrator may have missed 'the point of his own tale'); David, pp. 126-7; Huppé, p. 96; Hanning, 'Roasting a friar, mis-taking a wife', *SAC*, 7,7. But see also Burnley, p. 56, on the injunction to avoid poverty as an aspect of prudence.

54. So also Delasanta, *ChR* 5, 293.

55. Others explain this gap as an accident of the work's composition: Kolve, p. 294 and n. to p. 295; David, pp. 122 ff. The latter draws interesting literary conclusions from this observation.

56. For more sympathetic readings of this moment, see Kean II, 77, 93; David p. 127 and n. 14.

57. Also noted W.C. Johnson, Jr, 'MLT: aesthetics and Christianity in Chaucer', *ChR*, 16 (1981-82), 209.

58. On links of PhysT and *LGW*, see ch. 8, n.4. below. See also Kolve (p. 294) for suggestive comment about ways in which MLT might Christianise *LGW*, as it Christianises the tales of group I.

59. On the ironic relation of the head-link to the tale, parallel to the disjunction of prologue proper and tale, see David, pp. 126-7. His comment is apposite for my next paragraph: 'those who insist most loudly on morality in art are often morally insensitive.'

60. Burlin notes (p. 139) that MLT 'returning the story ... to an independent status, nevertheless retains much of the historical aura [of the original], most evidently at the conclusion.'

61. Cf. Burlin (p. 196): 'the piety he wishes to express is ... less deepseated than his love of "courtroom" oratory and respect for those values of the merchant class extolled in his Prol.' Yunck, *ELH*, 27, 260-1, speculates that the address to the noblewomen indicates that MLT was designed with the Prioress in mind as its narrator. That is, whoever narrates MLT, or was intended to, has an interest in a certain *class* of hearer over and above the specific religious message.

62. Conjoined with the dependence of MLT on the *Cronicles*, this phrase, and others noted in the previous paragraph, may explain the linking of MLT and SecNT in glosses in the Helmingham MS as 'cronica' (Strohm, *MP*, 68, 322, n. 5).

63. On this triad, see Gaylord, *PMLA* 82, 226; L.M. Leitch, 'Sentence and solaas; the function of the Hosts in *CT*', *ChR*, 17 (1982-83), 5-20 (a useful elaboration of Gaylord's article); M. Stevens and K. Falvey, 'Substance, accident and transformations: a reading of PardT', *ChR*, 17 (1982-83), 143 (they talk of 'the teller, the tale and the larger context in which it appears'); and Elbow, p. 128, on the 'paradoxical and at times transcendent relationship of participation between the poet and his sources'.

64. Burlin (p. 139) links MLT with what he calls 'psychological fictions', that is, those 'more concerned with the exposure of the narrator than with the apparent intentions of the narrative' (in my terms, with the telling than with the tale).

65. For comment on other parallels in *CT*, see Leitch, *ChR*, 17, 9.

66. For analysis of these traditional elements, see Mehl, pp. 24-5; R. Crosby, 'Chaucer and the custom of oral delivery', *Spec.*, 13 (1938), 413-32; Ryding, p. 70; Eliason, pp. 145, 147.

67. Kolve argues persuasively (pp. 286-7) that this passage links with Prol SecNT as a criticism of certain kinds of taletelling that do waste time.

68. Cf. Burlin as quoted n. 61 above. Delasanta, *ChR* 5, 294, yields to the

temptation ('he has pursued his extra-legal reading with an eye to intellectual posturing and didactic gesture'), and pp. 307 ff. reads ML as an emblem of the lawyer in the Gospel, Luke 10:25, who tempted Jesus. On the Clerk, cf. comments by Morse, *SAC*, 7, 83 ('the dialectical spirit of the university informs Chaucer's making of endings for CIT ... The Clerk adopts positions as a debater might').

THE MONK'S TALE

The process begun by the Man of Law is continued by the Monk. As we saw, the Man of Law took an exercise in hagiography and pushed it in the direction of a psychological study. The readings so produced — religious—exemplary, and what I have called psychological—tragic — occur in the tale in a state of almost unresolved tension. The Monk proposes a contribution which will achieve a similar blend of readings, but rather more easily. Taking his cue from the Host's original proposal that each pilgrim should tell four stories, two on the outward and two on the return journey (I, 791-4), he reckons to use up most of his allowance at once with 'a tale or two or three' (VII, 1968). At first he seems to toss this phrase off merely as a piece of self-advertisement: storytelling comes easy to him; why, he has several immediately to hand. But the phrase is more than a brag which he has no way of making good. If at first he proposes a single story, namely, a saint's life (1970), another choice immediately suggests itself to him: 'tragedies' (defined as 'a certeyn storie ... of hym that stood in greet prosperitte/ And is yfallen ... into myserie, and endeth wrecchedly' (1973-7)). Offered at first as an alternative to the saint's life ('or ellis'), these are immediately seen, with it, as part of the promised ration of stories: they will come 'first' (1971).[1]

The significance of this proposed double ration emerges from comparison with the double dose proposed or offered by the other pilgrims. There is the Cook, needled by the Host into promising a second story against 'an hostileer' (I, 4359-61) before he has begun his first. There are the narrators of group III, the Wife of Bath, Friar and Summoner. The first reckons her own life-story a 'tale' (586), though later she explains that the real tale is yet to come (828); the second proposes to 'telle of a somonour ... a tale or two' (842); and the third goes one better, reckoning to tell 'tales two or thre' at the Friar's expense. (In fact, the Summoner tells two, one after the other, though he calls the first and shorter one the 'prologe' to the second.)[2] Lastly, there is Chaucer himself, with *Sir Thopas* and *Melibee.* Except in this last case, the second tale, offered or delivered, breaks no new ground not already turned by the first, and mirrors its fellow's concerns more or less directly.

Thus the Summoner's two tales present the Friar in the same
unfavourable light as the arsehole of society (1690-8, 2145-51);[3]
the Cook's two offerings take place in a world of 'ostileers' and
'vitailliers' (I, 4366); the Wife of Bath's second offering represents
a symbolic transformation, a wish-fulfilment, of her first.[4] The only
storyteller to tell two tales one after another as distinct and separate offerings, Chaucer, does so only because his first has been
rejected, and he has been asked for something different.

Chaucer's two tales may have encouraged the Monk, who
speaks next, to offer two distinct and separate stories. Unlike
Chaucer, though — and unlike the other narrators who tell, or
propose to tell, two stories — the Monk makes his offer without
obvious external or internal compulsion. And his proposal has a
further significance for us. Just as *The Canterbury Tales* acquires a
meaning greater than the sum of its individual parts by virtue of
their interrelation — or, to take a religious parallel, Herbert's *The
Temple*, which includes poems widely contrasting in tone and style
and so enacts a whole religious life — so the tales proposed by the
Monk will generate a meaning greater than either could bear in
isolation. Moving with him from 'tragedie' to the saint's life, we
discover how intimately the two are connected; also, how the
limited perspective of the former is transformed, or overthrown, by
the latter's superior one. The Man of Law's tale contains the germ
of this understanding, in that it progressively reduces the scope of
the commentary as the narrative moves towards its close (that is,
the tale's authority is tacitly recognised as greater than that of its
retelling). A clearer parallel exists in the 'mixed' form used by
Boethius in *De Consolatione Philosophiae*: the limited perspective
of the opening books of the *De Consolatione* is overturned in the
closing books, and concretely realised in the movement from poetry
to prose as the dominant medium. The *De Consolatione* alternates
sections of poetry and prose — the form known as 'prosimetrum'
— but the poetry is less important in the later books; the work
begins with poetry, and ends with prose. What the Man of Law
and Boethius did within the frame of a single story, the one by a
commentary opposed in tone to that of his narrative, the other by
alternating prose and poetry, the Monk proposes to accomplish by
means of two separate stories.[5]

He has a precedent of sorts for this plan in a work of Boccaccio
which he uses in the tale: *De Claris Mulieribus*, a collection of
stories about famous women.[6] According to the preface of the

work (Guarino, pp. xxxvii-xxxix), the great women of the past have not normally received their due at the hands of male writers; yet their achievements are proportionately greater than those of the men commonly so celebrated, because of the greater difficulties under which they laboured. Boccaccio is therefore producing his collection as a way of setting the record straight. At the same time, he is clearly aware of one group of women whose achievements have been duly noted: the female saints of the Church ('Hebrew or Christian women'). These have been celebrated 'in special books, by pious men outstanding for their knowledge of sacred literature and for their venerable greatness'. This leaves the merits of the pagan women largely unsung. Boccaccio therefore restricts himself, in the *De Claris Mulieribus*, to this second group. He has good reason for so doing. The preference of the saints for 'true and eternal glory' raises them as far above the notice of the literary humanist as the desire of pagan women for 'this fleeting glory' sinks them below the notice of the professor of sacred literature. Set side by side, though, in two separate volumes, as the prologue implies they could be, they would reveal lines of continuity as striking as any differences. Boccaccio, that is, is claiming that his study will complement that of his religious counterparts in the same way as the Monk's offered ration of tragedies would complement the proposed life of St Edward.[7]

He has another model readily to hand, too, in a text used by the Man of Law: the *De Miseria* of Pope Innocent III. The prologue to that work, addressed to the Bishop of Porto, describes how, like Chaucer's Nun, its author used a period of leisure to improve his own moral state by producing a work on 'the vileness of the human condition'. At the same time, recognising the very narrow furrow he has ploughed, the author undertakes, if his reader approves it, to produce a partnering work, on 'the dignity of human nature, so that just as in this book the haughty man is humbled, so in the next the humble man may be exalted' (Lewis, p. 92). Of this second work the editor of the *De Miseria* has found no trace: had it been produced, it would have necessitated a changed reading of the first, in exactly the same way, I am arguing, as the Monk's second story would have enlarged the focus of his first.[8]

The logic of the Monk's position therefore suggests, and possibly requires, a careful separation of subject-matter and style in the two works, and a consistency of treatment within each, such that each realises its fullest effects only when set alongside its neighbour. This, however, reckons without the ability of the hearers to sustain the unrelieved gloom of the first work, and wait patiently for the unfolding of the complex purposes in the second tale. In the event, two of them grow restive. The Knight interrupts the story to ask for something different, and the Host asks for 'somwhat of huntyng' (2805), which he reckons the Monk knows more about. The Monk refuses the offered alternative to his own second story, and leaves it to another to 'pleye' (2806).

He is partly to blame himself for this unsatisfactory state of affairs. For his first offering he proposes not a 'tragedie' but 'tragedies', of which, he tells us, he has a hundred on his shelves (1972). That is, he will first relate a series of tales; each will depend on, and demonstrate, an initial definition, that tragedy is the wretched and miserable end of the great and prosperous. How these tales might be arranged relative to one another matters little — 'I by ordre telle nat thise thynges . . ./ Tellen hem som bifore and som bihynde/ As it now comth unto my remembraunce' (1985, 1988-9) — since the whole collection will generate a single view of human affairs against which the single story of the saint can be triumphantly set. Unfortunately, the promised reward takes too long to come. Hence a bold experiment, two contrasting stories, the first a sequence of stories in a single style, never gets off the ground. To see what the Monk is proposing we need to imagine what would have happened if Chaucer had made *The Legend of Good Women* one of his own contributions to *The Canterbury Tales*. Yet there is a vital difference between the Monk's tale and the *Legend*. Unfinished like the Monk's tale, and, like it, the expression of a single and limited subject-matter in a single and limiting style, the *Legend* has one great advantage wanting in the Monk's tale: a prologue describing the fictional circumstances of its own making. As earlier noted, the God of Love has commanded Chaucer to make a collection of stories about the good women 'trewe of love' whom he has seen in his dream (F, 481-91, 554-61); the god has also prescribed the manner of narration: 'reherce of al hir lyf the grete . . . sey shortly' (F, 570-7). The circumstances of patronage, then, explain and justify the failings of the *Legend*. The Monk has no such convenient *alter ego* on whom to off-load his own responsibilities. Moreover, the experiment that became the *Legend* is exactly analogous to what the Monk would have produced had he completed his project. Its two 'tales', prologue and 'legende', though causally related in a way the

Monk's two tales could never have been, function together precisely as his would have done: two different kinds of experience, two different kinds of story, even, possibly, two different styles of narration.[9] Wanting such a partnering text as the prologue provides for the *Legend*, we are forced to read the Monk's tale, for the moment, as a single and separate item.

This does not mean, though, that the resulting collection is completely uniform, particularly as regards its understanding of the subject-matter.[10] To be sure, the initial definition, already quoted, sets the tone of the whole work. In one way or another every tale echoes its description of the hero's tragic fall 'out of heigh degree/ Into myserie'.[11] The protagonists of the individual tales are exemplary not only in this sense, but also because they are possessed of exceptional personal qualities of one sort or another; in their own time, therefore, they are unmatched. If it sets the tone, though, the initial definition does little more. It describes a process or an effect; it does not consider causes. Repeating the terms of the original statement (1992-4), the opening stanza of the work goes one step further, and refers the reader to the operation of Fortune (1995), a motto which colours every tale in one form or another. Now, Fortune is often little more than a convenient personification of tragic effects; so understood, references to her in the tales enjoy no greater moral significance than attaches to any natural disaster. Such references therefore signify only the uncertainties attending all human actions, and the inability even of the virtuous to predict their own ends. But the first stanza does not end on that note; it warns men to 'be war by thise ensamples trewe and olde', and not to trust 'on blynd prosperitee' (1997-8). To describe human affairs as blind is to imply the responsibility of the human actors for their own tragedies: to invoke a moral dimension analogous to that propounded by Aristotle when he rooted the cause of tragedy in *hamartia* (a step taken in ignorance of the outcome, possibly the mark of pride or vanity).[12] And since the cycle of tales begins with Lucifer, whose fall, because he is an angel, cannot be blamed on Fortune (2001), we see that tragedy may be described as the deserved outcome of sin against God (2002). This understanding gives particular force to the repeated assertion that the protagonist was celebrated 'thurghout this wyde world' 'in his tyme' (2097, 2113); it also makes possible the inclusion of the Monk's tale in a study of the religious narratives of *The Canterbury Tales*.[13] Whatever its formal focus, then, the

Monk's tale forces the reader to reckon with three interacting causes of tragedy: God, Fortune, man.[14]

God's role is reserved exclusively for the Old Testament figures — Satan, Adam, Samson, Nebuchadnezzar and Belshazzar, Holofernes, Antiochus.[15] He is most clearly in evidence at the beginning of the cycle, as creator and judge of Adam (2008-9), and at the beginning of the story of Samson, whose miraculous conception points to his consecration to God in adult life (2015-17). The middles of some stories show God answering prayer and confounding pride in unexpected ways. Samson gets his drink from the ass's jawbone (2039-46); Nebuchadnezzar is punished for his pride by being turned into a beast (2167-82), Antiochus by an invisible wound that 'in his guttes carf ... and boot' (2599-2604). Such punishment gives a character the chance to repent and return to his former state (so Nebuchadnezzar). If a character will not learn from his own or another's experience, though, he will be brought to a fall, like Satan's, which there is no reversing. This pattern of persistent and culpable ignorance is also used of Croesus, whose story is marginally linked to the Bible narrative by mention of the Biblical Cirus who 'soore hym dradde', but wants other reference to the person or purposes of the Old Testament God. The pattern also figures most prominently in the narratives of Belshazzar and Antiochus.

Belshazzar refuses to learn from the example of his father Nebuchadnezzar, puts to sacrilegious use the temple vessels seized by his father during the sack of Jerusalem, and is visited by 'an hand, armlees, that wroot ful faste' upon his palace wall, the original of the closed fist in the Man of Law's tale. Daniel, who, as God's representative, had interpreted Nebuchadnezzar's dreams for him (2154-8), and resisted his idolatrous commands (2165-6), explains the mystery of the writing hand. First, he reminds Belshazzar of the fate that overtook his father (2210-22). No less than the act of sacrilege, Belshazzar's neglect of the warning embodied in his father's sufferings marks him out as 'rebel to God and ... his foo' (2225), and will bring about the downfall of his kingdom and his death (2234-6). This divine judgement overrides considerations of natural justice: Darius is made an instrument of God's purposes and seizes the kingdom from Belshazzar 'thogh he therto hadde neither right ne lawe' (2238).

Like Belshazzar, Antiochus is a poor learner. Punished by an invisible wound for his overweening pride (2583-7) and hatred of the people of God (2588-9, 2591-7), he refuses the correction and persists in his wicked purposes (2605-6). The terrible punishments that follow (2609-26) lead him, like Nebuchadnezzar, to the tearful acknowledgement that God is 'lord of every creature' (2621-2). This time, though, there is no second chance: 'thus hath this ... homycide ... swich gerdoun as bilongeth unto pryde' (2628-30). His punishment fits the crime in a totally reasonable way (2603): the mountains which he thought 'in balance [to] weyen' (2586) become the place of his death (2627).[16]

This picture of a punishment at once merciful and menacing — in that, though designed to induce repentance, it preludes total and irreversible disaster if resisted — is traditional enough. In both stories, though, it is complicated by reference to the operation of Fortune. Although the narrator does not oppose Daniel's interpretation of the Belshazzar story, he reads it more simply as an exemplum of pride going before a fall, and of the uncertainties of power; for him, the active force bringing about Belshazzar's downfall is Fortune (2189, 2241-6). Similarly, Antiochus's proud and overweening heart, which God will take away from him, was first given to him by Fortune (2583-7).

The story of Holofernes is yet more problematical. Rather like the Monk, the Man of Law had used Samson, Hercules, Caesar and Pompey as instances of tragic and apparently accidental death. In the figure of Holofernes, by contrast, he saw the power of God to save his servant and bring the unrighteous to a deserved end. The Monk's account of Holofernes focuses only on the deserved end of a renegade (2561) deceived by Fortune (2556-8) even as she deceived that other monster, Nero (2519-20, 2550). Nebuchadnezzar's example has no more effect on his chief-of-staff, Holofernes, than on his son. Holofernes persists in regarding his master as a god (2562-3). Like Nebuchadnezzar and Belshazzar, he sins in pride (2555), error (2561-3) and drunkenness (2568). But God does not act directly to confound him. A mere woman is made the instrument of vengeance (2571-4), and we learn of her only that she comes from a town whose inhabitants, like Daniel, are holding out against Holofernes' idolatrous purposes (2564-6). In this passage God is present directly only in the phrase 'Eliachim, a preest ... of that place' — not so much the agent of retribution as the object of priestly devotion.

Only two of these stories come armed with a moralising conclusion — they are the stories of Samson and Belshazzar. Far from endorsing the presence of God in the work, or even repeating the theme of the whole collection, these concluding remarks make Samson an exemplum of the virtue of not telling secrets to women (2091-4), and present Belshazzar as a man who loses his friends when he loses his wealth (2242-6: the story does not support this reading). Here, too, we see a certain inconsistency of approach.

The remaining stories divide into two: a set from pagan times (Zenobia, Nero, Alexander, Caesar and Pompey, Croesus and the mythological Hercules), and a set of more recent stories, the so-called 'modern instances', all but one virtually contemporary with the Monk's tale (King Peter of Spain and King Peter of Cyprus, both killed in 1369; Barnabo Visconti, killed in 1385; and Ugolino of Pisa, killed in 1289).[17] Ancient or modern, though, mythological or historical, these tragedies do not find it necessary to make God an actor in the drama, and hardly even refer to him directly. A no less striking feature characterises the modern instances, which, interestingly, provide the only instance in *The Canterbury Tales* of stories near the speaker's own time told specifically for their moral–religious dimension.[18] Except for the Bishop of Pisa, who appears as a figure of wickedness in the Ugolino story, the modern instances contain only one implied reference to Christian purposes: King Peter of Cyprus captures Alexandria from the Turks, makes 'ful many an hethen ... ful wo' (2392-3), and may thus be held to embody Christian values in opposition to those of the Turks.[19] This silence about the hand of the Christian God in the tragedies of modern kings and noblemen becomes the more surprising if we reflect on the shape produced by the Monk's blending of pagan, Old Testament and modern — hence Christian — heroes. Vaguely reminiscent of a traditional division of history into the periods of nature, law and grace, and more clearly paralleled in presentations of the Nine Worthies, the tripartite shape of the Monk's tale might have seemed to dictate specifically Christian reference in the modern instances.[20] It does not. The silence of the modern instances about the part played by God in the tragedies of Christian kings and noblemen partners a general reluctance to blame the protagonists themselves for their fall. Barnabo Visconti is described as 'god of delit, and scourge of Lumbardye' (2400): but what part, if any, these qualities played in Barnabo's downfall, the narrator no more knows than he knows the manner of Barnabo's death (2406). For the rest, the victims are worthy and heroic figures, plotted against and betrayed by evil men: King Peter of Spain by his brother and the latter's deputy (2378-90); King Peter of Cyprus by his 'owene liges' (2394-6); Ugolino by the 'peple', misled into revolting against him by the Bishop of Pisa (2415-19). The innocent victim achieves at best a 'pitous deeth' (2377), and the tragedy rises only to an acknowledgement of the power of Fortune 'hir wheel [to] governe and gye/ And out of joye brynge men to sorwe' (2397-8): that is, we have a tragedy entirely of suffering.

The narrator's unwillingness to invoke either human psychology or the Christian God to explain the tragic end of these modern great ones possibly reflects his sense that recent events are too tangled for causes to be easily discerned, and responsibilities apportioned, until either authority or their own antiquity confirms them. After all, when you don't even know how one of the victims died you had better not pronounce too confidently about the why of his death. A man who confidently finds the hand of God in recent events will often sound like a fool or a fanatic.[21] The narrator would, however, have received the powerful support of Dante, had he attempted such a reading of the modern stories.[22] The Monk's version of the Ugolino story comes from Dante (2460-2). Dante had made Ugolino one of his own modern instances in the *Inferno*. The moral and narrative frame of the *Inferno* expresses the clear conviction that God is at work in all of history: therefore, throughout the story of Ugolino's betrayal and death too.[23] The Monk could not well maintain Dante's chosen narrative frame — a first-person narrative cast in the form of a vision — in its totality. But, whatever the changes he had to make to the narrative frame, he had no need to abandon Dante's moral frame as well. But that he does. Co-author of the tragedy with Bishop Roger is not God, nor Ugolino himself, but Fortune (2413-14, 2456-7). Though Ugolino's youngest son utters what we might read as a prayer to God (2436), Ugolino addresses not God when the child dies, but Fortune (2445-6). His own end is 'langour' and despair (2407, 2455). The vividness of detail in this story has been justly, and often, praised — it is perhaps the most strikingly realised of all the stories in the Monk's collection.[24] Nevertheless, the narrative is offering not tragedy — not even tragedy of the order of Webster's 'I am Duchess of Malfi still' — but merely pathos.

With antiquity, of course, the case is easier, not least because centuries of Christian commentary on the stories of antiquity have helped to fix their moral structure in the mind of the narrator.[25] As with the modern instances, the narrator's approach to the stories from antiquity is more nearly single than his approach to the Old Testament stories. But there is a vital difference between the two sets of stories. If the modern tragedies imply the religious dimension only through the suffering of their heroes, the classical tragedies also imply it in their heroes' adherence to the moral system.

The first of the pagan heroes is Hercules. The chief grounds for his fame, in his own time and after, are his twelve labours (2098-110). He defeats the cruelty of a tyrant (2103-4) and of the Harpies (2100); destroys a poisonous dragon, a huge giant and a 'grisly boor' (2105, 2108-9); bears the very heavens on his shoulders (2110); and marks the limits of the known world with a 'pileer' at each end (2117-18). Placed immediately after Samson and, like him, victorious in combat with a lion (2098), he shares the former's moral no less than physical strength (in Samson, the two were images for one another):[26] not only 'strengthe' but also 'heigh bountee' makes him famous (2114).

Next to him comes Zenobia, a woman nobly born and unsurpassed 'in oother gentillesse' (2251; cf. 2298-302). Like Hercules, of one of whose labours, the struggles with the Nemean lion, we might reckon hers a domestic version, she fights wild animals barehanded and tears them apart (2260-3). Her native wildness serves as a practical expression, and safeguard, of her virginity. She lives in the open, and wrestles with the young men who wish 'in hir armes [to] stonde'; they no more prevail against her than do the wild beasts which she hunts (2264-9). Her friends eventually persuade her to marry a local prince, Odenake (2270-3). The marriage is a happy one (2274-8), blessed by children (2295); by Zenobia's diligent study of languages (2306-8) and of books which might instruct her 'in vertu' (2309-10); most importantly, by a series of military campaigns undertaken jointly by the couple against the Romans and the Persians (2311-20). When Odenake dies, she continues the campaigns against her enemies and lives to see her sons go 'in kynges habit' (2327-46). The morality of these later campaigns is thrown into question by the observation that she was cruel to her foes (2329). She remains throughout, however, what she was in her youth; her enemies have good cause to fear that she will treat them as she treated the wild beasts (2341) and, making peace with her, they leave her free to 'ride and pleye' (2334): almost as if she were, indeed, the natural force that her childhood showed her to be. But natural instincts are not always given their head. She carries into her marriage a sternly moral view of sexual appetite. She allows her husband 'doon his fantasye' with her (2285) only while she can be sure she is not pregnant. As soon as she conceives, she forces a regime of chastity upon him, be he 'wilde or tame' (2291), since sexual activity directed to other ends than procreation is 'lecherie and schame' (2293). On this question, at least, the child of nature turns out to have impeccably orthodox religious views.

Zenobia's story leads directly to the stories of Alexander and Caesar, and indirectly to Nero. Like her, Alexander and Caesar are great conquerors; the one wins 'this wyde world', the other 'al th'occident' (2634, 2674). Though one is nobly born, the son of King Philip of Macedonia (2656-7), and the other comes from 'humble bed' (2672), the virtues of the one have clear echoes in the life of the other. Granted, Alexander may be guilty of over-weening ambition (2666, a point neutralised by the following comment 'So ful was his corage of heigh emprise' 2667); unlike Zenobia, he can be readily turned aside from 'hye entente' by 'wyn and wommen' (2644-5). Nevertheless, he resembles her, and before her Hercules, in that 'the pride of man and beest he leyde adoun/ Wherso he cam' (2637-8). (Reference to his 'leonyn corage' (2646) may also remind us how Samson, Hercules and Zenobia showed similar courage against actual lions.) Even Nero, whom the narrator will thoroughly blacken, is allowed in his youth a master, Seneca, to teach him the 'letterure and curteisye' (2496) which Zenobia learned and taught her sons (2296). Under Seneca's good influence Nero was preserved for a long time from 'tirannye/ Or any vice' (2501-2). As a tangible mark of his respect for Seneca, the young Nero stood in his master's presence (2511-12).

As Nero begins, however, he does not continue. From the outset he is compared to the first character of the whole cycle, for he is 'as vicius/ As any feend that lith ful lowe adoun' (2463-4). His portrait concentrates the dark elements of the other portraits, and, in this respect, surpasses them. Nero shares the rule of the 'wyde world' (2466) with Alexander, but puts it to barbarous uses. By contrast with Zenobia, who, we shall see, has good cause to wage war against Rome, Nero burns his own city 'for his delicasie' (2479) and even kills the senators (2480-1). He also breaks the ties of nature and of nurture. In her relations with her sons, Zenobia embodied the twin roles of mother and teacher. Those bonds, represented for Nero by his mother and Seneca, he breaks, murdering both (2483-92, 2509-18). His motive for the former murder, sexual curiosity, is of a piece with his incestuous relationship with his sister (2482), and at the opposite pole from Zenobia's sexual modesty. Seneca, described as 'of moralitee ... the flour' (2497) and thus the moral equivalent of the all-conquering Alexander (2642), meets his death — so that the story of Nero becomes his tragedy, too — for equally simple reasons: Nero fears the disapproval of this good man, his master (2504-8), and resents having to show respect to him (2511-13). He is also guilty of the murder of his brother (2482). The catalogue of his crimes includes a love of fine array which he shares with Zenobia (2305), though he himself favours 'rubies, saphires and ... peerles' (2468). This love of finery quickly degenerates into the pursuit of novelty (2473-4): the same impulse sends him fishing in the Tiber 'whan hym liste pleye' with golden nets (2476).

Croesus is the only pagan character with no obvious positive moral qualities to set against the negative of a proud (2729, 2741, 2746, 2759), and vengeful (2742) spirit. He misreads his lucky escape from death (2729-33) as a sign that he cannot be killed by his enemies, and proposes immediate war upon them (2735-9). He misreads a dream as a sign of further favour, and is encouraged by it to set his heart on vengeance. He is the only one of the pagan heroes specifically to look for signs, and alone among them in misreading the signs he is sent. Hence he ascribes to the operation of Fortune his lucky escape from the fire (2737): an error parallel to the one that leads Ugolino to curse Fortune when his son dies. His life therefore dramatises the pagan want of God's grace (2733), and makes him the intellectual equivalent of the immoral Nero.

The narrative sheds no tears over their richly deserved ends. After the final outrage of Seneca's death, Fortune, as if embodying the reader's moral sense, determines no longer 'the hye pryde of Nero to cherice' (2520); accusing herself of foolish partiality (2522-6), she rouses the populace to massacre him. Out of his mind with fear, he approaches all his friends for help (2530-4), then calls on the gods (2539-40); lastly, since no help is forthcoming, he begs two peasants to kill him and cut off his head (2543-7) — a death which would make him the pagan equivalent of Holofernes, who dies with his head cut off by Judith in the very next story. In the event, he is forced to take his own life. Fortune finds the spectacle of his end richly comic (she 'lough, and hadde a game': 2550). But comedy, albeit of a black kind, and with a degree of pace seldom achieved elsewhere in the Monk's narration, has entered the story even as Fortune abandons her favourite. Nero knocks 'fast' at his friends' doors, they shut them 'faster'; the people, having risen up, are crying out and rumbling up and down;[27] he feels himself dying of fright and runs into a garden; there he is reduced to begging for death from 'cherles tweye', figures equivalent to the mere woman of the Holofernes story. Since the comedy works against the hero, we are in no danger here of losing our moral bearings.

In the tragedies of Nero and Croesus, then, Fortune performs a double role. Whether or not she acts directly to bring about the character's fall, she represents both a benighted view of spiritual reality (hence she calls herself 'nyce') and the punishment attending adherence to such a view. Elsewhere the pagan instances occasionally carry something of this double sense: in particular, the death of Hercules is made an exemplum of the need for self-knowledge (2137-42; and cf. especially 2139: 'ful wys is he that kan hymselven knowe'). But that story nowhere suggests that the want of self-knowledge contributed directly to the hero's death. The narrator is willing even to excuse the agent of his death, Dejanira, on the grounds that she might have given him the poisoned shirt in all innocence (2127-9): that is, circumstance rather than character generates the tragedy. The significance of the Hercules story lies, in fact, in the total harmony of the hero's death with the details of his life. Realising that death is inevitable, he chooses to meet it head-on, and instead of waiting for the poison to finish him off, throws himself into the fire (2132-4). The key to this tragedy lies in the firmness of purpose with which the hero opposes the random chances of life, and in his victory not just over wild animals and wicked men but even over his own instinct for self-preservation. The story is therefore tragic only in the formal sense of the initial definition, and, more loosely, in the sense that the ending of any life may be called tragic.

This same picture obtains with the death of Caesar. The victim of others' envy and falseness (2698, 2706), he meets his death with silent courage (2709, 2711), and with an exemplary modesty reminiscent of Zenobia's —

And as he lay of diyng in a traunce,
And wiste verraily that deed was hee,

Of honestee yet hadde he remembraunce

(2716-18)

he covers himself with his mantle 'for no man sholde seen his privetee' (2715). The role of Fortune in Caesar's story has clear parallels with that in the Nero story, already noted. At first Nero's friend (2478), Fortune finally turns upon the monster she has nourished (2519 ff.) and destroys him. In a similar way, Fortune first favours Caesar with success (2686), and makes him master of the East; at the same time she brings the former master of the East, Pompey, to a bad end (2693-4) with ironic echoes (2691) of the deaths of Nero and Holofernes. Eventually, she turns against Caesar as well (2678) and destroys him. Thus the two stories of Caesar and Pompey, mirror-images for one another as those of Nero and Seneca could never be, are completely summed up in the concluding phrase: 'Fortune was first freend, and sitthe foo' (2723).

The view of Fortune embodied in these pagan and modern instances, then, takes us clearly back to the bald summary of tragic processes offered by the Monk's initial definition. It either denies the tragic frame by asserting the hero's superiority to fate, or it reduces the tragedy to pathos by presenting an innocent victim destroyed by the wickedness of others. Overall, then, the Monk's 'tragedies' develop the idea of tragedy in a number of different ways, some overlapping, some clearly opposed. They present tragedy as a shifting relationship of three distinct causes: God, Fortune and man. Strikingly, the story of Antiochus refers to all three; normally a story focuses chiefly on one, though it may also imply the activity of a second. If Fortune is the chief cause of tragedy, the balance of the story tips in the direction not of action but of suffering. If man is the primary agent, we have what Aristotle understood by the term tragedy, that is, ironic reversal as the result of an action committed in ignorance. If God is the primary agent, as in the Belshazzar episode, we get neither pathos nor drama but theatricality, for God can be presented as an actor — and is regularly so presented in the English mystery plays — only by theatrical means like a magic hand. All the same, we ought not to force this distinction: in a very real sense, God, Fortune and man are all mirror-images for one another. Fortune, the link between God and man, behaves sometimes as men experience God, sometimes as men experience themselves; so too the other elements in the tragic process.[28]

The Monk's understanding of the subject, then, is excitingly diverse.[29] We cannot say the same for the tone of the narrative, which, for the most part, favours pathos: 'I wol biwaille, in manere of tragedie' (1991; cf. 2687). The stylised lament so produced turns the characters into static objects of tearful contemplation: 'who shal me yeven teeris to compleyne/ The deeth of gentillesse' (2663-4). This can be seen most easily in the repeated exclamations 'loo' and 'allas' (2015, 2123, etc.), also used in the speech of that most pathetic victim of the set, Ugolino (2429, 2445); it is also dramatised when the narrator addresses his characters directly, urging them to escape impending disaster or commiserating with them upon their falls (e.g. 2052 ff., 2375 ff., 2658 ff.). This kind of tone does much to flatten the ambiguous contours of the Monk's tale. It is also not a little two-edged. It may produce unintentionally comic effects — so, for instance, I read the denunciation of Fortune, as co-author, with poison, of the death of Alexander:

> Allas! who shal me helpe to endite
> False Fortune, and poyson to despise,
> The whiche two of al this wo I wyte?
>
> (2668-70; cf. 2660-1)[30]

It also highlights the essentially literary nature of the whole exercise. Tragedy, that is, is not so much a thing men do or suffer as a thing they read, or write, in books.

Bookishness, indeed, marks the whole enterprise, a bookishness largely indifferent to specifically religious questions. A relatively minor instance of this distinctive emphasis is provided by the narrator's cunning concealment of the identities of the assassins of King Peter of Spain:

> The feeld of snow, with th'egle of blak therinne,
> Caught with the lymrod coloured as the gleede,
> He brew this cursednesse and all this synne.
> The wikked nest was werker of this nede.
> Noght Charles Olyver, that took ay heede
> Of trouthe and honour, but of Armorike
> Genylon-Olyver, corrupt for meede,

Broghte this worthy kyng in swich a brike.

(2383-90)

Robinson's notes explain 'feeld of snow' as a reference to the coat of arms of Bertrand de Guesclin, and 'wikked nest' as a pun on the name of another opponent, Oliver Mauny. Such verbal gymnastics are not, in principle, out of order in a religious work. We think, for instance, of the riddling runes which identify the author in several of Cynewulf's religious poems; similarly, words used as an element of religious paintings sometimes appear in code form, and at other times upside-down or back-to-front. But in religious works verbal dexterity always serves clear religious purposes: it leads the viewer or reader to pray for the artist, and to acknowledge the existence of a religious dimension of life, difficult though it may be to interpret.[31] No such purposes are served, that I can see, by the Monk's rebusses. The focus of his interest, that is, remains narrowly literary.[32]

Support for this conclusion comes from the Monk's many references to the sources of the tales. He names these sources regularly — more often than any of the narrators so far considered — and with a casualness which shows their active presence in his consciousness.[33] He refers to two Old Testament books, Judges (2046, for the Samson story) and Maccabees (2579, 2655, for the pagan figures of Antiochus and Alexander); to Suetonius (2465, for Nero; 2720, for Caesar), Lucan and Valerius (2719-20, for Caesar); and, nearer his own time, to Dante (2461, for Ugolino) and Petrarch (2325, for Zenobia). The Hercules story includes reference to a source 'Trophee' (2117) and to unnamed 'clerkes' (2121, 2127); the Zenobia story carries added reference to unnamed Persian writers (2248, 2346).

Now, the citation of authority, and acknowledgement of a source, may be perfectly in keeping with the telling of a religious story: every tale so far considered has included explicit reference to an actual source (Clerk, Second Nun, *Melibee*) or indicated a general indebtedness to Scriptural or other traditions (Prioress, Man of Law). Such explicit citation of a source, however, can hardly be prominent in a religious story. A writer who constantly interrupts his story to consider its historical givenness runs the risk of making the story not a re-enactment of itself — the prime function of a religious narrative, I am arguing, analogous to the functions performed by the liturgy — but an object of historical or literary inquiry. Something of this sense is emerging at the end of the Man of Law's tale, which uses the historical frame of Trevet's original chronicle to generate speculation about the actions of the characters by means of the phrase 'som men wolde seyn', and the answering 'be as be may' (II, 1009, 1112). Both phrases are used by the Monk (2127, 2129). Another phrase used by the Monk ('what sholde I moore devyse?': 2652) also appears, in slightly different form, at the beginning of another very obviously literary production, the Clerk's: its narrator casts a coolly critical eye over Petrarch's prologue, finds it unnecessarily protracted and cuts it ('the which a long thyng were to devyse': IV, 52). It is this attitude — not religious, but an amalgam of literary and historical interests — which the Monk's tale documents very fully for us. The Monk's relation to his stories, then, reflects not religious but literary interests.

The consequences of this changed focus are profound. In the first place, the narrator affects a critical attitude to his sources which, whatever its appropriateness in other religious contexts, sits ill with the production of a religious narrative. The practical implications of this profession, however, do not add up to much. Since most of the stories are 'so commune/ That every wight .../ Hath herd somwhat or all' (2631-3), the Monk feels free to abbreviate them in the retelling, even as the Clerk cut most of Petrarch's prologue. Dante's version of the Ugolino story, he tells us, can hardly be bettered ('he kan al devyse/ Fro point to point, nat o word wol he faille': 2461-2). Nevertheless, he abbreviates it ('it oghte ynough suffise': 2458), just as he abbreviates the Zenobia story that he reckons to have found in 'Petrak .../ That writ ynough of this' (2325-6), and the Caesar story, of which Lucan, Suetonius and Valerius have 'writen word and ende' (2721). He also abbreviates the story of Alexander's conquests (2647-52): 'though I write or tolde ... everemo/ Of his knyghthod, it myghte nat suffise' (2653-4). This practice apart, the narrator demonstrates his superiority over his sources only when the existence of different versions of the same story compels the conclusion of likely error in one or other. Here, too, he is as unadventurous as the Man of Law confronted by a similar difficulty. When, for example, the sources disagree about the role of Dejanira in the tragedy of Hercules, he favours the one which presents her in a better light ('be as be may, I wol hire noght accusen': 2129).

The real purpose of this display is best seen, though, when the narrator recommends his version of the Caesar story to the Roman authors who provided him with it:

> Lucan, to thee this storie I recomende,
> And to Swetoun, and to Valerie also,
> That of this storie writen word and ende
>
> (2719-21)

Not even in his most 'literary' productions does Chaucer invoke the tradition so ambitiously. In *Troilus* he sends his 'litel bok' forth with the directive

> And kis the steppes, where as thow seest pace
> Virgile, Ovide, Omer, Lucan and Stace.
>
> (V, 1791-2)

In *The Legend of Good Women*, where Chaucer names his sources as regularly, airs disagreements between them as frequently, and cuts them as vigorously, as ever the Monk does, Chaucer only once addresses the *auctor* directly, and then with a properly humble sense of his own place in the tradition:

> Glorye and honour, Virgil Mantoan,
> Be to thy name! and I shal, as I can,
> Folwe thy lanterne, as thow gost byforn.
>
> (924-6)

In *The Canterbury Tales*, similarly, though the literary ambitions of the Man of Law lead him first to court comparison with Chaucer and with Ovid's 'epistles, that been ful olde' (II, 47, 55), a sense of reality rapidly takes over as he remembers the fate that overtook the daughters of King Pieros for competing with the Muses (91-3). Consequently, he leaves to Chaucer the field of verse, which, as earlier noted, he reckons Chaucer to have ploughed so inexpertly (47-52), and settles for the humbler medium of prose (96). No such modesty restrains the Monk: which shows all too clearly that, though his formal purposes in telling the tale may be religious, his real interests are literary.

Literary pretensions, however, are to be judged in the end by what they actually deliver. Put another way, can this reader of other men's books (*caveat scriptor*) tell a good story himself? Viewed as a whole, the Monk's collection has almost all of the weaknesses of *The Canterbury Tales*, and almost none of the strengths.[34] It makes no attempt to arrange the material thematically. Chronology hardly operates either as an organising principle. The opening tales of Lucifer and Adam set up an obvious historical movement, which the modern instances bring to a close in those manuscripts which place them at the end of the tale.[35] But the place of the modern instances is not beyond dispute, and the body of the tale proceeds by such random linkages as characterise the great middle of *The Canterbury Tales* (such connections include the already noted pairings of Samson with Hercules, and Nero with Holofernes).[36] As the Monk says at the outset, the collection does not owe its shape to the 'ordre' of historical ages (1985, 1987). Nor will it conform to the subsidiary pattern favoured by Trevet for his chronicle, which gives precedence to ecclesiastical over secular figures, and imperial over national ('of popes, emperours, or kynges': the Monk might almost have been recalling Trevet's 'gestes des apostoiles, des emperours et des rois').[37] Rather, the Monk will arrange his stories according to the order in which they come to mind (1989). Such randomness represents an explicit acknowledgement of the circumstances of the narration. Other characters of similar social standing in *The Canterbury Tales* — notably, the Knight, Squire and Man of Law — are equally frank about the circumstances of their own narrations, and keenly aware of the difficulty they face in attempting to carry their hearers with them throughout a lengthy and artistic narrative. That is, the tales of the Monk may signify, as a collection, not only as the offering of a bookish and antiquarian bent, but even as the offering of an upper-class ethos.

Another sign of randomness offers itself in the very uneven treatment accorded to the tales. Some are the merest outline of a narrative (Lucifer, Adam, three of the modern instances). Some attempt to make up in hyperbole for what they lack in detail. The longest runs to 16 stanzas, the shortest to eight lines. Most split into two uneven parts, one celebrating a great person, the other lamenting a fall; only the overall form provided by the original definition guarantees the unity of the individual tales. These limitations would not matter too much if individual tales were told with gusto and conviction. Unfortunately, with a few notable exceptions — the already noted death of Nero, for example — they are not.

Poorly organised overall, the stories are also poorly told. The narrator shows little feeling for pace, and no greater sense of direction than what an audience's presumed familiarity with sources might bring to bear.

We can see the force of these comments more easily if we compare the tale as a whole with the Boccaccian model, the *De casibus virorum ilustrium*, and then compare two of the longest stories — those of Samson and Zenobia — with their sources. Like some manuscripts of the Monk's tale, the *De casibus* sets its modern instances at the end of the work (Book IX); similarly, it alternates Biblical and pagan heroes in the body of the text. Admittedly, the formal division of the work into books, so as to give the reader a breathing space from time to time (I,19; p. 31), makes possible a patterning of the narratives denied to the Monk: pride of place can be accorded a Biblical hero at the start of a new book (so the story of Saul, II,1).[38] These formal patterns apart, however, the work is organised almost as randomly as the Monk's tale.[39] Yet its real affinities are not with the latter. Where the Monk's tale makes randomness a reflex of the narrator's limited organising powers, the Boccaccian form — not altogether happily called a dream vision by one critic[40] — builds randomness into the very fabric of the narrative. We can see this most easily if we consider Boccaccio's presentation of three famous pagan worthies, Oedipus, Thyestes and Theseus (I, 7-9). After narrating the Oedipus story, Boccaccio is planning to move on to Theseus, when Thyestes presses forward, claiming the right to have his story told because it is not less worthy of memory than that of Oedipus. Atreus then provides his own version of the events, and provokes a violent argument with Thyestes. Wearied by the story of their inhumanity, Boccaccio sends them packing and, at length, begins the Theseus story. I find this exciting writing. Strict parallels for this conflict of interest between the author and his creation — a creation already given life by earlier writers — are not to be found, that I am aware, until the work of Pirandello. But there *are* similar blurrings of the boundary between fact and fiction in any frame narrative: most obviously, in *The Canterbury Tales*. We need only reflect on the head-link to the Miller's tale for a comic analogue to the row between Thyestes and Atreus; or the head-link to the Man of Law's tale to see a character claiming rights over his author in the manner that Thyestes does. Boccaccio's *De casibus*, then, has deepest affinities not with the Monk's tale but with *The Canter-*

bury Tales as a whole.[41]

As with the Monk's arrangement of the tales, so with his narration of the individual tales. The story of Samson was so 'commune' that a certain casualness was possible in the treatment of the episodes: which probably explains a principal characteristic of the Monk's narrative, its presentation of a series of apparently unrelated incidents. At the outset, the angel of God announces Samson's birth 'longe er his nativitee', and so marks his consecration to God. When next we see the hero, he is on his way to his wedding, and killing a lion with his bare hands. Then his 'false wyf' is winkling his secret out of him, and revealing it to his enemies, sealing her defection by leaving him for another man. Her infidelity rouses his anger, and prompts an act of revenge which again demonstrates his strength and skill. He catches 300 foxes, ties them together by the tails in pairs, sets a burning brand between each, and looses them in the countryside. They burn all its crops. Immediately afterwards, it seems, he is massacring 1000 men with 'no wepen but an asses cheke', which will miraculously provide a source of water for the thirsty hero afterwards. Next, in despite of the Philistines living in Gaza, he uproots the gates of the city and carries them on his back to a hill 'whereas men myghte hem see'. These episodes represent Samson's triumph. They are summed up in lines (2055-60) which do two things: they remind us of the 'precept of the messager divyn', the angel of the opening stanza, who directed Samson's parents that their child must not take strong drink, or cut his hair; and they create a time-scale for the events (he rules over Israel for 20 years).

But the opening stanza, which presents Samson as an image of unparalleled 'strengthe and ... hardynesse', also limits his greatness to the time 'whil he myghte see', and thus explicitly anticipates his downfall: Samson yields to the blandishment of his wives, it tells us, and reveals his secret to them. This pattern is repeated in direct address to the hero after the narration of his exploits with the gates of the city (2052-4), and comments about him at the end of the stanza describing his rule over Israel (2061-2). The fall, thus prepared for, is immediately set in motion. Samson tells his 'lemman' Dalila how 'in his heeris al his strengthe lay' — the phrase repeats one used earlier (2058) — and, false as his first wife, she betrays his secret to his enemies (2065, 2068), and has his hair cut off while he sleeps in her lap. The enemy bind him and, putting out his eyes, make him work as a slave at the mill. At this point the narrator intervenes again to remind us how earlier warnings have come true; the narrative has now realised its hero's anticipated downfall:

> O noble Sampsoun, strongest of mankynde [cf. 2018-20]
> O whilom juge, in glorie and in richesse! [cf. 2060]
> Now maystow wepen with thyne eyen blynde [cf. 2061]
> Sith thou fro wele art falle in wrecchednesse [cf. 2022, 2062]
>   (2075-8)

Nothing remains to tell but the 'ende of this caytyf': not triumph but tragedy, as his enemies bring him to their temple on a feast day for their entertainment, and he pulls the temple down on himself and them.

Considered purely as a story, the narrative moves at a brisk but unvarying pace, with only such pauses as the narrator's reflections about its meaning, and his anticipation or recapitulation of its details, can generate. Considered purely as a story, too, the narrative proceeds in an extremely casual way. It remembers itself just in time, before the hair is to be cut off, to remind us how Samson's locks will be the visible sign of his triumph and tragedy. It fails to connect the early episodes with one another (that is, the killing of the lion, the first wife's betrayal, the act of revenge, and the massacre of the thousand) except as parallel expressions of heroic impulse. It only once personalises the enemies as Philistines (2048). It offers no motive for the wives' behaviour. It may imply that Samson's strength returned after he was blinded, when it describes him labouring at the mill, but it does not explain how he could pull the temple pillars down.

In defence of this casualness, the narrator presupposes an absolute familiarity with the Biblical source, which he calls 'Judicum' (Judges 13-16). 'Judicum' certainly makes good the gaps in the Monk's narrative. As one of the governors of Israel — Biblical scholarship interprets this term to mean 'the people's war leaders and deliverers' — Samson acts to free his people from the rule of the Philistines. What the Monk presents as the motiveless triumphs of Samson's early career, the Bible text links causally as expressions of this purpose. His first marriage, to a Philistine woman, provides an occasion for raising a quarrel with the enemy (Judges 14:4). The killing of the lion becomes the first step in this quarrel. He sets the wedding guests, all Philistines, a riddle which they cannot solve without knowing of his exploit with the lion, and places a bet on their failure to find the answer. They force his wife to get the answer out of him. Enraged, he kills 30 of their country-men, and presents their finery to the wedding guests in payment of the wager; then he leaves his wife, and the divorce is completed when her father gives her to the best man at the wedding. When, on his return to see her, he learns of her remarriage, he takes revenge on the populace by burning their crops. In return, they come in a body to take him captive. Delivered bound into their hands, he breaks the bonds and massacres the enemy with the jawbone of an ass. The ease with which he breaks his bonds — they become, the text says, 'like burnt strands of flax' (Judges 15:14) — has an ironic echo later in the story, when Delila is attempting to cajole his secret out of him, and he tells her that he can be captured if bound with new bowstrings or with new ropes (Judges 16:7,11). Both details give added point to the Monk's comment that while Samson kept his hair uncut 'ther was no boond with which men myghte him bynde' (2072). Moreover, at almost every stage of the Bible narrative of Samson's early exploits God is directly present as a character. He actively inspires Samson's marriage with the Philistine woman (Judges 14:4), and his spirit regularly fills the hero when a valiant deed is called for (Judges 14:6, 19; 15:14).

We need the Bible text, then, to make much sense of the Monk's narrative of Samson's early career. We also need it for a fuller picture of the hero's downfall and death. The Monk's narra-tive cannot meaningfully connect the picture of Samson labouring at the mill with that of the hero brought to the temple for the festival except by way of the element of compulsion common to both ('they made hym': 2074, 2081). To heighten our sense of the disjunction of the two episodes, the Monk interposes a lament over the fallen hero, which points only backwards. By contrast, the Bible story links the two episodes with a detail which clearly points forwards: the hero's shorn hair, it tells us, began to grow again (Judges 16:22). By contrast, too, with the Monk's view of a motiveless and ultimately meaningless death, the Bible story makes a profoundly satisfying end for the hero. The Philistines are hold-ing their festival to give thanks to their God for delivering Samson into their hands. As a practical and playful expression of thank-fulness, they call for Samson to entertain them. Once he has done their bidding, they take him to the two pillars supporting the temple, and leave him there. Now Samson seizes his chance; prays to God for strength to revenge himself on the Philistines for the loss of his eyes; and, crying out, 'May I die with the Philistines', pulls the building down. Not the least of the ironies in this finely controlled narrative is the awareness of a genuine, though misdirected, religious spirit among the Philistines. Equally, Samson is no mere religious abstraction. A man of violent passions throughout his life, he has consistently understood the work given him by God in narrowly personal terms. Even in the moment of his dying he looks not to free the people by his action but simply to avenge the loss of his eyes. These complexities are almost completely wanting in the Monk's narrative. The narrator, that is, reads a better story than he tells.

Nor can we argue, in his defence, that his chosen subject-matter, the tragic fall, keeps him from making more use of the material. Comparison with the version of the story in the *De casibus* (I,17), proves instructive in this regard. Like the Monk, Boccaccio reads the story of Samson as the tragedy of a great man brought low by Fortune, and of the limits inherent in the quest, however heroic, for the height of that worldly glory which passes with fools for blessedness (*SA*, p. 627). He also places Fortune's powers relative to those of the human agents of his story — a pattern also observed in several of the Monk's stories. Boccaccio allows Fortune to provide the ass's jawbone for Samson to use against his enemies: otherwise, he keeps her well offstage. Samson's early progress grows naturally from the miraculous annunciation of his birth — Boccaccio links the episodes of the story much more carefully than the Monk — and is symbolised from the beginning by his observance of the Nazirite vow. Boccaccio, however, will not claim for God the primacy he has denied to Fortune. He writes not as a moralist but as an historian; it is the historian whom we hear explaining how the Bible story uses the term 'judge', and reporting a superstition that equated Samson with Hercules, on the basis of the lion which each killed.[42] Now, the historian observes God not as the cause of human action but as the explanation commonly offered for it. Thus, according to Boccaccio, Samson, whose killing of the lion provides, so early, such a fine sign of his great nobility, further demonstrates his great character in ascribing to the power of God the works of his own hand. This nobility — also revealed in his determination to keep his own good deeds secret unless pressed by others to publish them

— requires no specifically religious explanation: it is consistent with a humanist view of man.[43] Boccaccio therefore invokes God explicitly only once,[44] as the provider of the drink from the ass's jawbone which chance had earlier thrown Samson's way. He thus takes a conventional medieval frame, tragedy as the operation of God and/or Fortune, and enlarges it by focusing on the human context of the action.

This humanist reading of the action comes plainly to the fore in Boccaccio's account of the hero's end: a mighty fall, he tells us, which a man of any other great spirit would not long have borne. Boccaccio does not attempt a religious reading of the end. He suppresses Samson's prayer to God. Though he retains the defiant final shout, he finds its origin in Samson's inward indignation at the offered humiliations. The story is thus one of ironic reversal and descent: as the final words tell us, the judge of 20 years' standing, despised and blinded by his enemies, 'mortem sibi constituit indignam'. But the word 'constituit' dramatically counters any impulse to pathos. Unworthy the death may be, but the hero chooses it for himself, and so turns tragedy to triumph, albeit of a secular sort.

To see how different this version is from the Monk's, we need only to compare its use of the word 'infelix' with the word which it probably inspired, the Monk's 'caytyf'.[45] For Boccaccio the word 'infelix', which we should perhaps understand as if spoken by the Philistines, is full of ironies — not least, the irony that Boccaccio had already criticised the idea that earthly glory could make men happy. The Monk calls his hero a 'caytyf' with no sense of irony, and with no greater purpose than the generation of pathos. Far from creating a whole new reading of the tale, like Boccaccio, the Monk must fall back on his original to make good the deficiencies in his own performance.

The case is subtly altered with the Monk's reworking of the Zenobia story.[46] Chaucer encountered this story in two forms, both by Boccaccio — the *De Claris Mulieribus*, from which the bulk of the story comes, and the *De Casibus*, used for the final stanza.[47] As already noted, the *De Claris Mulieribus* had the specific aim of praising famous women, and, where appropriate, drawing suitable lessons from their behaviour. According to Boccaccio, the women chosen for inclusion in the volume are all noteworthy for their 'manly spirit ... keen intelligence and remarkable fortitude', by means of which 'they have dared undertake and have accomplished even the most difficult deeds' (Guarino p. xxxvii).[48] But the stories will not only celebrate triumphs. They will also consider women who owe their reputations to infamous actions, and women made famous by 'Fortune's favour or enmity' (ibid.). This threefold reading of the characters' lives, as triumph, tragedies of character or tragedies of circumstance, shapes Boccaccio's whole work, and provides most immediate access to the Zenobia story.

For Boccaccio, the story is one of almost unbroken triumph. Like the Monk, Boccaccio begins with an account of Zenobia's childhood; this culminates in the account of her marriage to Odaenathus and — with all the appearance of an afterthought — a brief note about her physical beauty. He then considers her military career in greater detail than the Monk. Following the loss of the eastern empire to the Persians when Sapor defeats the Emperor Valerian, and realising that nothing is to be expected of Valerian's effeminate son, Gallienus, Odaenathus determines to conquer the eastern empire for himself. Zenobia assumes the imperial title and purple with him and with her stepson, and sets out with an army to oppose Sapor. The narrative gives her the lion's share of the action: chiefly responsible for the defeat of Sapor, she subsequently crushes a Roman attempt to regain the lost territories.

Odaenathus does not live to enjoy his conquests. A cousin kills father and son and assumes the throne. When the cousin is murdered in his turn, Zenobia takes over and rules on behalf of her sons by Odaenathus. Such is the threat she poses, and the fear she inspires, that not only the Roman Emperors Gallienus and Claudius, but the rulers of the neighbouring kingdoms, are glad to leave her unmolested.

The next episodes take place away from the battlefield, several in a domestic context (characteristically, Boccaccio's version of the story proceeds in this rather jerky way with haphazard changes of scene). Now we see Zenobia, in spite of her natural sobriety, drinking with subordinates and with visiting nobles 'to surpass them in wit and affability'. We see her care for her treasures forgotten when the occasion requires it: she mounts extremely lavish banquets. The little time she does not spend on hunting and fighting she devotes to learning. She commits to memory 'all the Latin, Greek and barbarian histories'; she even produces written digests of them. As in the Monk's version, Boccaccio stresses her sexual modesty: in addition to what the Monk says on this score, Boccaccio tells how she never admits men to her quarters unless they are 'eunuchs of sound morals and advanced age' (Guarino, p. 228). Occasionally, a less favourable note is struck. The narrative may be critical of her desire for adulation. It also criticises her for her desire to emulate Cleopatra: vessels once used by Cleopatra at a banquet given for the Romans make a regular appearance in the banquets she throws. Such criticisms, however, are neutralised by the context of their utterance: the former action was learned from the Persians; the latter was part and parcel of her familiarity with Roman manners.

The last episodes of Boccaccio's narrative return us to the battlefield, and describe Zenobia's defeat at the hands of Aurelian, emperor after Claudius and a man of great virtue. Aurelian proves a worthy opponent, and defeats her after a long and bitter struggle — which, however, shows Zenobia off to advantage, for, besieged, and in process of being starved out, she refuses all terms of surrender. Captured, she is brought to Rome with her children to grace his triumph. Pathos and irony centrally inform the account of the triumph. She comes on foot as a prisoner to the city she had hoped to enter as a conqueror — an ambition which the narrative now reveals to us, retrospectively, for the only time — and she walks behind the chariot in which she had hoped to make her triumphal entry. She bears the badges of slavery and the trappings of royalty: gold chains fetter her hand and foot and hang about her neck; she wears a crown and her royal robes are loaded with gold and precious stones. So great is the weight that, in spite of her great strength, she is often forced to rest, exhausted. Nevertheless, Boccaccio asserts, the celebrated triumph derives its chief glory from her presence; her greatness is marked even in defeat. Aurelian's greatness, that is, serves merely as a foil to hers. Though she is forced to become a private citizen, the Senate grants her an estate, where she lives to a ripe old age. And there, at least, she leaves the mark she had thought to make on the whole Roman empire: the estate is known locally for many years after her death by her own name.[49]

The Monk's retelling reveals a striking consonance with much of the foregoing. In respect of structure, indeed, the early sections of his version significantly improve upon Boccaccio. The Monk advances Boccaccio's afterthought about Zenobia's physical beauty to an introductory description of the heroine (2253-4), and brings together into one episode all the information relating to her married life, namely, her modesty (2279-94) and her careful bringing up of her sons (2295-6). Boccaccio introduces the boys to us only after the death of Odaenathus, as a way of explaining Zenobia's ambitions for the throne; her education of them appears much later, almost as an afterthought to the narrative's account of her own learning.

At the end of this episode, however, a note of anxiety creeps into the Monk's narrative wanting in the source. As if aware that such material, though necessary for the creation of a character, does not much advance an action, the Monk interrupts himself with the phrase 'but now unto oure tale turne we' (2297). He does not manage to realise this promise. He offers first a brief and general account of Zenobia's bravery in war, and then quits the battlefield to describe her splendid array 'as wel in vessel as in hire clothyng', and her attainments in learning. This confusion of material represents a partial return to Boccaccio's random narrative order in the central episodes (in sequence, Boccaccio had described Zenobia's modesty, regal splendour and love of learning). It also witnesses a continuing attempt by the narrator to organise the material. When the Monk tells how Zenobia was 'al cled in perree and in gold', he is anticipating a detail in Boccaccio's account of Aurelian's triumphal entry into Rome: there we learn how Zenobia wore her royal robes to grace the triumph.

As soon as he decently can, the narrator returns to the heart of his story, the account of Zenobia's military campaigns ('and shortly of this storie for to trete', is the phrase used to move us forward into the next section). At this point, in striking contrast to Boccaccio's narrative, the Monk's narrative falls apart. He refuses us information about the causes of the tragedy: 'how that al this proces fil in dede/ Why she conquered, and what title had therto' (2321-2). Subsequently he provides a summary of the action which observes neither chronology nor patterns of cause and effect. We learn that Zenobia conquers Roman territories in the East with her husband. These will later provide Aurelian with his only clear motive for action against her; she holds them during her husband's lifetime (2313-18). The latter detail ('ay whil that Odenakes dayes laste') suggests a decline in her fortunes upon the death of Odenake, but is flatly contradicted by the account of her achievements 'whan Odenake was deed' (2327) and is, therefore, meaningless and misleading. This offered pattern apart, we get only a sequence of kings, emperors and unnamed others whom Zenobia fought to a standstill and forced to respect her frontiers. 'Galien' comes, almost as an afterthought, after the man who succeeded him (2336). Boccaccio's careful patterning of his narrative makes sense of these various names: not so the Monk's. But then, he can afford to treat his material so casually, because his source, 'Petrak', has 'writ ynough of this, I undertake' (2325-6). Once again, then, the Monk is abandoning the attempt at authorship, and taking refuge behind the superior status of a received text.

The Monk's failure to make anything of the central episodes in the narrative leaves the concluding sequence, in almost every sense of the word, meaningless, a mere spectacle. And since the spectacle requires a tragic victim, the Monk does to Zenobia what he had earlier done to Samson. He abandons the Boccaccian view of Zenobia's life as a triumph; plays down the sense that Aurelian is, even in his own triumph, playing second fiddle to Zenobia; and makes her a pale reflection of his triumph. As she walks in procession, we see no trace of the enormous physical, and, by implication, moral strength with which Boccaccio credited her. Nor do we see her enjoying a quiet old age, well regarded by the Senate, making her mark locally. For his ending the narrator abandons the frame of the *De Claris Mulieribus*, and instead translates the tragic conclusion which the story carries, one similar in form to the already noted ending of the Samson story, in the *De Casibus*. This creation of two different endings for the one story, a tribute to the powers of the narrator, is not peculiar to Boccaccio. Chaucer did much the same thing with his two versions of the Dido story.[50] A story, however, which implies one meaning and then goes into reverse for its conclusion is at best an uncertain tribute to the powers of the narrator.[51]

The Monk's tale, then, is frankly disappointing. It begins excitingly, but fails to convince as an expression of either religious or artistic impulse.[52] In this respect, it invites comparison, already touched on (n. 19 above), with the tale which immediately precedes it, that other literary disaster in the set, the *Melibee*. The original of *Melibee*, faithfully translated by Chaucer, witnesses to the damage caused by the subordination of literary, and specifically narrative, values to the expression of didactic intent. It also witnesses, paradoxically, to the fact that, in a work of fiction, narrative values are the only safeguard of didactic intent (I shall have more to say about this point when we reach the Pardoner's tale). Now, the Monk's literary interests, in theory, subserve a clear didactic intent: the 'tragedies' he relates will signify both in themselves, and as a foreshadowing of the proposed 'lyf of Seint Edward', as exempla of the hand of God in the affairs of men. And his understanding of tragedy as an effect produced by a series of complementary causes (God, man, Fortune) is supple in much the same way as was the understanding, implied by the paired apostrophes of the Man of Law's tale, that destiny works jointly with human agency to cause the tragic events of that narrative (above p. 149). Yet this complex understanding yields neither religious nor literary fruit worth the tasting. The religious emblems it generates are one-dimensional cardboard cutouts, like those of the Second Nun's tale and *Melibee*, figures produced by an essentially one-dimensional understanding. They didn't need to be so flattened. I think of the dual role created for Walter by Petrarch, or of the sympathetic presentation of Jew and Muslim in the Prioress's and Man of Law's tales (pp. 62-3, 72, 144-6 above: such ambiguities seem easier to establish near the beginning of a story.) Nothing comparable happens in the Monk's tale. Yet the narrator's failure to generate any very complex religious emblem — that feature of the religious narrative to which all purely narrative values are subordinated — might not have mattered so much if he had shown a clear commitment to, or interest in, specifically narrative values. As we have seen, he does not. He consistently neglects the narrative values of his originals — pace, suspense, irony. He thus leaves the reader with the worst of both worlds. His effort represents the nadir of this sequence of religious narratives. What follows, in the Physician's tale, represents the eventual striking of a balance in favour of narrative values; and prepares the way for the more impressive balancing of religious and literary interests in the tales of the concluding section.

Notes

1. The St Edward, whose life the Monk proposes to relate for his second offering, is normally thought to be Edward the Confessor, or Edward the Martyr. Just possibly, a third royal Edward is intended: Edward II. According to Green (pp. 62, 183), Richard II commissioned a version of the latter's miracles and sent it in 1395 to Pope Boniface IX as part of the campaign for the canonisation of his ancestor. Lydgate refers to 'Seint Edward' in a work describing royal ancestors of Henry VI (*Minor Poems of John Lydgate*, ed. H.N. McCracken, EETS OS 192

(Oxford, 1934), 623). If Strohm's distinctions hold good (*MP*, 68, 323), the Monk's first offer of 'a tale or two or three' is generically distinct from the saint's life ('legende') and 'storie' of the tragic falls of the great. That is, the Monk first proposes something worldly and diverting ('tale'), and then corrects himself and offers material more in keeping with a man of his social and religious position. I am not happy with this reading: Strohm himself admits that the categories 'tale' and 'storie' are not watertight.

2. See further G. Olson, 'The terrain of Chaucer's Sittingbourne', *SAC*, 6, 105-6.

3. So noted Burlin, p. 166.

4. For fuller comment, see Fyler p. 127; Kean, II, 152; Howard, p. 253; Burlin, pp. 222-3.

5. On binary organisation in *CT* (other examples are the pairings MkT–NPT and PhysT–PardT: see further below) see Howard (pp. 319-20), who gives as key metaphors 'the facing pages of an open book', and, much more importantly, the two Testaments of the Bible. See also Patterson, *Trad.*, 34, 331-80.

6. I have consulted the 1539 Berne printing of this work. For a modern translation, see *Concerning Famous Women by Giovanni Boccaccio*, trans. G.A. Guarino (New Brunswick, N.J., 1963).

7. For similar comment on the preface, see Cooper, p. 31.

8. A point also made by Kolve, pp. 232-3. For another example of this diptych structure, see Andreas Capellanus, *De arte honeste amandi*, in *The Art of Courtly Love*, trans. J.J. Parry and ed. F.W. Locke (New York, 1957): Books I-II of the *De arte* consider carnal love; Book III spiritual. See also Mehl (p. 18) on the patterning of saints and romance heroes in the *South English Legendary*. Eliason (p. 176, n. 60) speculates that SecNT stands in a similar relation to *LGW*: one 'may have prompted' the other.

9. David observes (p. 39) that 'when we first encounter the heroines of *LGW*, we see their heavenly apotheosis, not their earthly misfortune ... What we see in the Prologue is surely the Heaven to which Cupid's martyrs first go.'(This exciting reading of the relation between Prol *LGW* and *LGW* thus ironically parallels that of Gen Prol and *CT*. Gen Prol is the 'mental heaven', so to say, in which the journey of the pilgrims comes finally to rest. The shape thus created reverses that proposed by the Monk for his double offering.)

10. Cooper (pp. 47, 177) to the contrary. Other writers note the absence of a uniform approach to the subject-matter (Lawler, p. 96: Whittock, p. 221), and seem to find it matter for disapproval.

11. See also the definition of tragedy in *Bo*, II, p 2, 70-2. Normally, but not always, the 'myserie' is completed by the hero's death.

12. On this point, see H. House, *Aristotle's Poetics* (London, 1956), pp. 93-6.

13. That is, MkT is not simply the negative of the proposed saint's life, as ShipT is of PrT.

14. On the role of Fortune, see H.R. Patch, *The Goddess Fortuna in Medieval Literature* (Cambridge, Mass., 1927), pp. 68-9.

15. Scribes regularly distinguished the two stories of Nebuchadnezzar and Belshazzar by means of separate rubrics. I prefer to see them as a single story with two contrasting figures, on the model, later in MkT, of the single story of Caesar and Pompey; and maybe also that of Nero and Seneca.

16. The obvious parallel with this pattern is Dante; parallels also exist in sermons (e.g. Owst (1961), p. 424 and n. 1).

17. *De Casibus*-type texts regularly place modern figures alongside classical (Green, p. 146). *SA* (p. 625) notes the presence of 'modern instances', alongside classical, in Raison's discourse to the lover about the perversity of Fortune in *RR*, which furnished the 'unmistakeable primary source' for the Monk's accounts of Nero

and Croesus (*SA*, p. 617). Boccaccio also includes moderns in his *De casibus*.

18. Compare parallel treatment of place in sermon exempla: Owst (1961), pp. 157, 65; *Handlyng Synne*, ed. Furnivall, ll. 2699, 3616-18.

19. For the historical King Peter, see T. Jones, *Chaucer's Knight* (London, 1980: rev. preface 1981), pp. xi-xii, 72-3, 221, and index. Jones reads MkT very narrowly as a tale whose criticism of the Knight forces the latter's interruption of it, on the basis p. 72 that Mk is set up (I. 3119) to 'quit' KnT with his own. Whatever political context MkT is presumed to activate (interestingly, it follows *Mel*, similarly explained in relation to a presumed political context: see above, ch. 5, n. 11), Jones's reading takes the dramatic theory of the Canterbury pilgrimage much more literally than the evidence seems to me to warrant.

20. For a recent note on the traditional division of history — a commonplace at least as ancient as St Augustine — see Roberston, *SAC*, 6, 7 and n. 16. The parallel with the Nine Worthies is also noted by Burlin, p. 184. Compare also the presentation of the pagan worthies in the *Megacosmos* of Bernard Silvester (noted above, ch. 6, n. 44).

21. For a parallel of sorts with the Monk's practice, see *Historical Poems of XIV-XV Centuries*, ed. R.H. Robbins (New York, 1959), pp. 184-6. This text, dated 'not later than 1466', uses the same stanza form as MkT, and acknowledges the tradition of 'Bockas'. If focuses on tragedies 'here in thys lande with-in the xx yere' (l. 14); like MkT, it offers its brief summaries in random order (l. 18). More important, except for a prayer for the dead Duke of Gloucester (l. 23) and a moralising address to the reader to 'trust in god and labour to doo wele' (l. 8), it invokes religion only in the ambiguous phrase 'suche was hys grace', describing the death of the Duke of Somerset.

22. Sermons often explain recent events in this same way; see Owst (1961), p. 226.

23. On Dante and the Christian–providential view of history, see Keen, Daiches–Thorlby, p. 305.

24. See, for comment, H. Schless, 'Transformations', Brewer (1974), pp. 220-3; Whittock, pp. 222-7; and P. Boitani, 'MkT: Dante and Boccaccio', *M AE*, 45 (1976), 50-69.

25. Thus Croesus imprisoned is read as an illustration of *opulentia* (Kean, II, 184); Hercules, as an emblem of the resurrection (in the *Ovide moralisé*, ed. C. de Boer, Verhandelingen der Koninklijke Akademie van Wetenschappen, Afdeeling Letterkunde, Nieuwe Reeks, 30 (Amsterdam, 1931-32), IX, 873-1029); his fight with Anteus (cf. MkT, 2108) as an emblem of resisting lecherous impulse (Ross, p. 212); Caesar and Pompey as, respectively, Adam and God (*Gesta Romanorum*, ed. Oesterley, tale 19). On Hercules, see also Owst (1961), p. 111 and n. 1; and Allen, p. 69.

26. For the offered comparison, see Owst (1961), p. 111, n. 2 (alleged source, St Augustine, and other English examples given). It is also found in Boccaccio's *De casibus*: *SA* (p. 627), 'nec defuerunt qui leonem a se [Samsone] occisum Nemaeum dicerent, et Herculem arbitrarentur Sansonem' ['there were those who said that it was the Nemaean lion which Samson had killed, and reckoned Hercules to be Samson'].

27. On 'rumble' as the property of an ill-informed multitude, see also CIT, 997, and (perhaps) HF, 1026.

28. Cf. Lawler (p. 96): 'Fortune is to God as experience is to authority (and as woman is to man)': and see comment on Walter in CIT as an emblem of Fortune in ch. 2, n. 42 above.

29. More so, say, than the typical medieval chronicle, for comment on which, see Keen, Daiches–Thorlby, p. 309.

30. With this doubling of causes, see above pp. 149-50 (MLT); and see further

below, pp. 192-3 (Boccaccio's version of the Samson story).

31. On this point, see J. Burrow, 'The poet as petitioner', *SAC*, 3 (1981), 61-75; reprinted in J. Burrow, *Essays on Medieval Literature* (Oxford, 1984), pp. 161, 166, n. 7; and R. Ellis, 'The word in religious art of the Middle Ages and the Renaissance', *Word, Picture and Spectacle*, ed. C. Davidson, Early Drama, Art and Music Monograph Series 5 (Kalamazoo, Mich., 1984), pp. 21-38.

32. The rebus also occurs regularly as a feature of political writing: see Coleman pp. 118-121, for examples; also *The Poems of Lawrence Minot*, ed. J. Hall (Oxford, 1897), 34/19. Its presence in the 'modern instances' may thus imply, or assist in the creation of, a political reading of MkT (on which see n. 19 above).

33. Individual tales normally name their sources only once (exceptions: Hercules, Zenobia, Caesar), but the accumulated effect of these citations is striking.

34. So Cooper, pp. 48-9.

35. The alternation of pagan and Old Testament figures thus produced in the body of the tale is, of course, a characteristic of the genre, as of the universal chronicle with which the genre has formal parallels.

36. Other patterns include those of W.C. Strange, 'MkT: a generous view', *ChR*, 1 (1966-67), 170, arranging the tales as five groups: Lucifer to Belshazzar, Zenobia to Ugolino, Nero to Antiochus, Alexander and Caesar, Croesus; Burlin, p. 184, characters in pairs: Lucifer–Adam, Samson–Hercules, Nebuchadnezzar–Belshazzar, Zenobia–Nero (with interruption for two modern Peters and two Italians, Barnabo and Ugolino), Holofernes–Antiochus, Alexander–Caesar, Croesus (linked with Chauntecleer of NPT). Thompson, Davis–Wrenn (p. 187), sees the pattern Adam–Samson–Hercules as repeating that in Jankin's book of 'wikked wyves' in Prol WBT.

37. Also noted Pratt, Atwood–Hill, p. 308; and see above p. 129.

38. Augsburg edn (1544), p. 33: 'quod in eius manibus, ante alios omnes, totius Reipublicae Hebraeorum gubernatio data est, ut huic libro daret initium libens assumpsi' ['I gladly determined to start this book with Saul because the government of the whole Hebrew Republic was given to him before all others'].

39. Variety of form and subject-matter characterises the work: III,1 is a fable remembered from youth; VI,1 is a colloquy of the narrator and Fortune, etc.

40. R.W. Babcock, 'The medieval setting of Chaucer's MkT', *PMLA*, 46 (1931), 205-13.

41. Boitani to the contrary: 'the body of MkT — the series of tragedies — is typologically related to Boccaccio's *De casibus*' (p. 228).

42. See n. 26 above.

43. Cf. A.D. Scaglione, 'Boccaccio, Chaucer and the mercantile ethic', Daiches–Thorlby, p. 585, on the story of Lisabetta in the *Decameron*: the outcome of the story 'is due to the violation of no other law but those of nature. Neither moralist nor theologian, Boccaccio reveals the "naturalist" drift in his sense of values.'

44. I exclude his oath, 'o bone deus!' for the same reason as I earlier excluded the oaths in MkT from consideration (see above, p. 177).

45. I thus oppose the conclusion of P. Aiken, 'Vincent of Beauvais and MkT', *Spec.* 17 (1942), 56-68, that there is 'no evidence ... of the influence of the *De casibus* on the Monk's tale of Samson' (p. 59). The word 'infelix' occurs neither in the Vulgate text nor in her offered source, the *Speculum historiale* of Vincent of Beauvais (The Samson story is in Vincent, *Speculum*, II, 67.)

46. For comment on the reworking, see Boitani, *MAE*, 45, 64-8.

47. For printings of both, see *SA*, pp. 632-6; for the former version, see also Guarino, pp. 226-30.

48. Berne 1539 printing, sig. iv^v: 'si extollendi sunt homines ... quanto amplius mulieres ... si uirilem euaserint animum, ac ingenio celebri, ac uirtute conspicua

audeant atque perficiant etiam difficillima uires extollendae sunt.'

49. By the phrase 'quae Zenobiana diu postmodum ab ea denominata est' (*SA*, p. 636), Boccaccio is referring to the generation that elapsed between the historical events and their recording by Trebellius Pollio and Flavius Vopiscus, whom he was using for his own version. See *The scriptores historiae Augustae*, with English trans. D. Magie, 3 vols (London, 1923-32), VII, 139-40.

50. See also Kean, II, 55 ff.

51. In both versions, moreover, Zenobia retires to her country estate (the extract from the *De casibus* in *SA* wants this material). The Monk, that is, has not simply chosen a tragic reading in preference to a triumph for his concluding stanza; he has also suppressed material authorised by both sources so as to create a starker end. In this respect we may see a parallel with the Hercules story which, at the Monk's hands, denies its hero the reward his last labour deserved (Boethius, *Consolation* IV, m. 7): metamorphosis in heaven among the glittering stars (Ovid, *Metamorphoses*, IX). Compare the similar avoidance of the happy ending in the story of Ceyx and Alcyone, this time narrated by the lovelorn poet, in *BD*.

52. On this point, see Fyler, p. 114.

8 THE PHYSICIAN'S TALE

The problem or question of religious narrative receives yet sharper focus in the Physician's tale, whose problematical status in this study has already been implied by comment on it in the introduction. The problem reduces to a simple question: what reading, or readings, of itself does the tale invite or require? Wanting the ambiguous helps that a head-link or a prologue — or, in the case of the Man of Law's tale, a head-link and a prologue — can provide, we have no option but to plunge into the text:

Ther was, as telleth Titus Livius,
A knyght that called was Virginius,
Fulfild of honour and of worthynesse,
And strong of freendes, and of greet richesse.
This knyght a doghter hadde by his wyf;
No children hadde he mo in al his lyf.

(VI 1-6)

The opening line reminds us clearly of the Monk's use of Roman historians for his tragedies of Nero (Suetonius), Caesar (Suetonius, Lucan and Valerius) and Zenobia (Trebellius Pollio and Flavius Vopiscus, though neither the Monk nor his Boccaccian source so names them). It also implies an attention to historical fact — in the same spirit, the narrator will later urge that his story 'is no fable/ But knowen for historial thyng notable' (155-6) — which has not particularly informed the tales of the preceding section: nor even, in this section, the Man of Law's tale (a point already urged in this connection, pp. 158-60 above).[1] The principal relationship to which we are introduced in these opening lines, that between a noble and honourable Roman and his only child — we learn much later that she is called Virginia — reminds us likewise of the Monk's 'tragedies', in several of which this relationship figures prominently (Nebuchadnezzar, Zenobia, Ugolino, Nero, Croesus).

Our growing sense of connection with the Monk's tale is, however, given pause by what follows: a long passage in praise of Virginia's physical beauty (7-38) and a slightly shorter one in praise of her virtue (39-58)[2]. The first, which describes her physical beauty in very traditional terms, does so very vividly, by way of an imagined speech put into the mouth of Nature herself (11-28). This figure, who clearly resembles her namesake in *The Parliament of Fowls*, tells how God, the 'formere principal', has given her, as his 'vicaire general', the 'cure' of all 'erthely creaturis ... under the moone'; how the creator and his minister are united in purpose and performance — what the one wills, the other performs perfectly; and how her work is God's worship, and her own pleasure. Pleasure and worship meet pre-eminently, and reveal the perfect union between God and his minister, in the person of the heroine, whose beauty Nature finds ample repayment for her 'sovereyn diligence'[3].

Nothing in the Monk's tale could have prepared us for this picture. The Monk's tale presents parent-child relationships as simple functions of its overriding theme. Thus the parent's fall involves the children whether they share the parent's guilt (so Belshazzar) or not (the children of Zenobia and Ugolino); alternatively, a wise child may offer warning advice to an erring parent (Phanye, the daughter of Croesus). The child's physical beauty is irrelevant to this picture. It is not, however, irrelevant to the portraits of other children in the stories so far considered: the daughter of a peasant in the Clerk's tale, of the Emperor of Rome in the Man of Law's tale, and of unnamed noble Romans in the Second Nun's tale. The Clerk, faithfully translating Petrarch or the anonymous French version of the story, finds Grisilde 'fair ynogh to sighte' (IV 209); the Man of Law speaks of Custance's 'heigh beautee' (II 162); the Second Nun, of 'faire Cecilie' (VIII 115). And, like the Physician, who tells us that 'if that excellent was hire beautee/ A thousand foold moore vertuous was she' (39-40), they describe their heroines' physical beauty as a natural outward mark of an inner, spiritual beauty. The Man of Law finds Custance unsurpassed 'as wel [in] goodnesse as beautee' (II 158, cf 162-4). For the Clerk, as for Petrarch, Grisilde's undeniable physical beauty pales into insignificance by comparison with her 'vertuous beautee', in respect of which she is 'oon the faireste under sonne' (IV 209, 211-12). And the same is manifestly true of the heroine of the Second Nun's tale. To read the opening moments of the Physician's tale in the light of these other tales is to expect similar narrative developments. Suffering and hardship in the course of the story will not result from a tragic fall, whether deserved or not, as in the Monk's tale, but provide the occasion for a display of constancy which will confer a greater reward, as in the other tales so far studied: not tragedy, that is, but a Christian comedy; not death, but some form of deification. (Hence we may see a particular fitness in the ordering of the tales in the Hengwrt manuscript, where, as earlier noted, the Physician's tale follows those of the Second Nun and Clerk.)

Unfortunately, this comparison proves almost as partial as that with the Monk's tale. The Man of Law and Clerk may emphasise their heroines' physical beauty, but neither is inclined to linger over it (and the Second Nun barely considers the physical beauty of her heroine). Each accords it only that attention consistent with the exemplary presentation of its heroine (even the Sultan, who falls in love by hearsay with the 'figure' of Custance, has been told principally of her 'noblesse'). That is, the Physician's concentration on his heroine's physical beauty does not readily square with the portraits of saintly and exemplary women that we find in the Clerk's, Second Nun's, and Man of Law's tales. It implies a connection between Virginia and the heroines of courtly romance (the Knight's, Squire's and Franklin's tales, *Troilus and Criseyde*, the latter part of *The Parliament of Fowls*) and courtly tragedy (*Anelida and Arcite* and the stories of the *Legend*[4]). This connection is made the stronger, in the *Parliament* and *Anelida*, by the depiction of Nature in thrall to the heroine's beauty (*Anel* 78-80, *PF* 372-8); and, in the *Legend*, by the statement that God, had he wanted a human lover, could never have chosen better than Dido (*Legend* 1035-43). Which of these two readings, comic or tragic, we are to expect still seems unclear: the narrator's assertion that Virginius has no other children (6) might read like an ironic anticipation of a tragic outcome, but Trevet, for one, made the heroine of his Christian comedy an only child, so either is strictly possible.

This uncertainty of narrative direction seems to require an explanation. A sympathetic reader might explain it as the generation of a particularly complex emblem akin to that provided by Petrarch for the opening of the Grisilde story, or akin to the totality of the narrative effects to be found in Trevet's and the Man of Law's versions of the Constance story. Like the three possible readings of that story (exemplary, psychological and historical) — the three elements in this one character — historical, exemplary and romantic — would similarly combine to present a picture of character as a dynamic interaction of contrasted but interdependent qualities. A less sympathetic reading would see, more simply, a narrator who was not yet clear about his overall direction: not so much the Petrarch of the Griselda story, more the hapless Monk. That this latter reading is the right one seems confirmed by a number of features of the narration. Though he has declared his dependence on a literary source at the outset, the narrator seems perfectly willing to deviate from the letter of history with an imagined speech by a character, Nature, who plays no further part in the narrative[5]. Our sense of the narrative's casting about for a direction is reinforced by a fair amount of repetition in the opening lines, which seems only to mark time while the narrator moves from one idea to another. Thus the phrase which introduces the section describing the daughter's physical beauty ('fair was this mayde in excellent beautee') is used again, at the end, as a bridge to the next ('and if that excellent was hire beautee'). Then, the narrative has barely begun when it is being suspended for Nature's imagined speech, and we rejoin it by way of a limp repetition of the phrase used to mark our departure from it ('as though she wolde seyn', 11, becoming 'thus semeth me that nature wolde seye', 20)[6]. Inside that speech we hear, twice within five lines, of the vain efforts of humans to imitate nature, both times with the same rhyme 'countrefete ... bete' (13-14, 17-18); there is even the phrase 'whan that me list' (13), reworked as 'right as me list' (22).

It is when the narrator gets clearly into his stride, however, with the extended account of his heroine's virtue, that the real difficulties of the narrative come to the fore. Here too the narrator's presentation of his heroine has much in common with the portraits of Custance and Grisilde. In the first place, all three are wise beyond their years. Custance has 'yowthe, withoute grenehede or folye' (II 163); Grisilde, a 'tendre ... age', which partners a 'rype and sad corage' (IV 218-20). Our heroine has the wisdom of Pallas Athene and needs no 'countrefeted termes ... to seme wys', expressing her 'maydens shamefastnesse' with perfect naturalness in a 'facound ... ful wommanly and pleyn' (49-55). Then, the young women all express their virtue in a life of active service. The initial description of Custance, it is true, says only that her hand, as 'ministre of fredam for almesse', was the natural expression of, and complement to, her holy heart (167-8). The implications of that phrase, however, are clearly revealed by the description of her time in the household of Alla, which speaks of her as 'diligent, withouten slouthe/ To serve and plesen everich in that place' (530-31). Similarly, although Grisilde's humble social situation, like that of the widow in the Nun's Priest's tale, leaves her little choice but a life that 'knew wel labour, but noon ydel ese' — like the widow, 'wel ofter of the welle than of the tonne/ She drank' (IV 215-17) — she actively accepts her lot as an occasion for growth in virtue ('for she wolde vertu plese', 216), and offers her father loving, obedient and diligent service (221-31). Both pictures accord with that of our heroine, who is always busy 'to dryve hire out of ydel slogardye' (57), and is as temperate, from choice, as Grisilde was from necessity (58). The lives of all three are therefore an open book to those who can read the signs correctly. Custance is 'mirour of alle curteisye' (II 166): to look upon her is to love her (532)[7]. Grisilde's virtue, at first hidden from general view, is widely publicised when her marriage to Walter makes it public property; those who see her cannot but love her (IV 413, a clear echo of II 532)[8]. Virginia's life, similarly, is an open book in which 'maydens myghten rede/ ... every good word or dede/ That longeth to a mayden vertuous' (107-9). Not surprisingly, she is widely celebrated 'thurgh that land' by all who love virtue (113-14).

As with his presentation of the heroine's physical beauty, the narrator at first makes much more of this moment than his fellow-authors did of theirs: nothing we have so far seen could have prepared us for the complex understanding generated by this presentation of a virtuous heroine. In an important deviation from his ultimate source, he claims that Virginia 'neded no maistresse' to supervise her moral development (106), but had a clear and innate moral sense, whose dictates she followed 'of hire owene vertu, unconstreyned' (61)[9]. Consequently, she 'floured in virginitee' (44). This image carries no sense of foreboding that I can see. Moreover, it implies an equation between moral and natural processes, such that physical and moral beauty can be seen truly as images of one another[10]. (In the same way, Virginia no more needs 'countrefeted termes' than Nature herself.) This complex understanding of virtue as a quality of life which draws towards its own perfection, and at the same time communicates its own sense of itself, easily and irresistibly, to observers, generates a strong contrast with the presentation of the heroines of the Clerk's, Man of Law's and Second Nun's tales. Custance and Grisilde, we recall, express their virtue primarily in reaction to adverse circumstances, by way of suffering and obedience[11]. Even the one unquestioned saint in the tales, Cecilie, does not do much more. Placed like

Custance and Grisilde in difficult circumstances, she does not share their passivity but goes onto the attack, and makes her very adversity the occasion for generating converts (contrast Custance, who converts people only when her personal circumstances have altered for the better). By contrast, our heroine's virtue is, for the most part, neither a passive response to adverse events — like the virtues of Custance and Grisilde — nor an active one, like the virtues of Cecilie. In fact, this picture reminds us once more of the heroines of romance. When, for example, the Physician describes Virginia as expressing maidenly qualities with a womanly wit, we think of other Chaucerian heroines whose innocent 'wommanly' spirit found easy expression in playfulness — notably, Dorigen in the Franklin's tale, which precedes the Physician's tale in the Ellesmere ordering[12]. All the same, there is a much darker side to this picture, and the narrator is not slow to force it upon our attention. Virtue must root itself, and grow, in a social context as ambiguous and compromising as the pagan worlds of the Man of Law's and Second Nun's tales. The heroine may not need to counterfeit the language of wisdom, but her need to avoid exposure to situations of dangerous looseness or levity has often driven her to practise the innocent deception of a pretended sickness (61-4). The people from whose company she thus seeks to preserve herself are not those who 'loved vertu'. At best, they are thoughtless, idle and prone to drunkenness and other 'folye'.[13] At worst, they are casting off their own innocence or, worse still, seeking to bring the innocent down to their own debauched levels. They do not see 'wommanly' behaviour, as she does, in terms of plain speaking allied to natural modesty; rather, they identify it with the 'booldnesse' which marriage teaches (71) and which, practised by the worldly Wife of Bath (III, 227), is visible in her very expression (I, 458).[14]

This picture of an innocence under siege and open to misunderstanding — like that of Fanny Price in *Mansfield Park* — figures prominently in the story, and is intensely ironic. Not the least of the narrative's ironies is that Virginia fails to inspire the disinterested spiritual love which Custance and Grisilde elicit from others; Nature falls in love with her physical beauty, and this, rather than her virtue, catches the eye of the Governor of the region and precipitates her tragedy. Yet greater is the irony that, having first read his story as a praise of innocence generating and communicating itself, analogous to the picture of Wisdom in Proverbs 8:30 and

Wisdom 7:22 ff., the narrator suddenly loses confidence in the emblem, and replaces it by the simpler one favoured by the Man of Law and the Clerk: innocence under siege. Like the worldly Man of Law when he speculated about the mysteries of Custance's wedding-night, or the Clerk, who in the Hengwrt manuscript copy has just told the men in his audience that he does not believe in his heroine except as a literary figure, the Physician is too well aware of the real world to give innocence its head. It is from him, and not from the narrative, that we learn of the

> feestes, revels and ... daunces,
> That been occasions of daliaunces.
> Swich thynges maken children for to be
> To soone rype and boold, as men may se,
> Which is ful perilous, and hath been yoore.
>
> (65-9)

The innocence earlier presented as a flower ('floured in virginitee') now turns into a fruit ripe for its own plucking: the lessons of the past ('and hath been yoore') and the experience of the present ('as men may se') point irresistibly in the same direction. The Physician reckons that his heroine will differ from her contemporaries only in coming more slowly to the sad lessons of experience; there will be time enough for her to learn them, he warns us, when she marries. (This detail also points to the likely outcome of the story. If Virginia's purity cannot survive into marriage, we need not expect the story to end with a marriage, or, as in the Clerk's and Man of Law's tales, the reuniting of a parted couple.)

The narrator also warns of the damage adults can do to innocents in their charge.[15] He turns first to the 'maistresses' among his audience. In their declining years they have been given authority over noblemen's daughters, either because they have preserved their own innocence or because they have now turned their backs on a long experience of their own 'freletee' and the 'olde daunce' of love (78-9).[16] They are best placed to warn the young from 'swich meschaunce' and 'teche hem vertu' (80-2). The much greater attention given to this second qualification than the first reflects the narrator's sense that it is much more likely to be realised than the first. Nor is that all. The tutor may actively subvert her charges by 'wikke entente'; she must be urged 'unto no vice [to] assente' and warned that 'of alle tresons sovereyn pestil-

ence/ Is whan a wight bitrayseth innocence' (87-92). This sententious and worldly-wise address is totally inapplicable to the actual
situation of the heroine, who, as we have seen, 'so kepte hirself hir
neded no maistresse'. Much the same effect is produced when the
narrator leaves the 'maistresse' to address her employers. In ultimate charge 'of al hir surveiaunce', parents must be reminded to
set a good example and warned not to spare the rod, so as to tame
the evil impulses of their young charges. How such reflections
might bear on the mutual love of a virtuous child and her worthy
father the narrator does not consider: the outcome of the story,
though, may make us wonder if Virginius hasn't taken the narrator's advice, in this regard, all too literally.[17]

No less pointed are the metaphors used to describe the relation
of the adults to their youthful charges: they are (83-6) of poacher
turned gamekeeper (the 'maistresses' who 'knowen ... the olde
daunce/ And han forsaken ... swich meschaunce') and (101-2)
the 'shepherde softe and necligent' who permits the wolf to attack
the flock (the parents whose 'necligence in chastisynge' makes
possible the moral or physical destruction of their children). First a
flower, and then a fruit — which, to adapt the Reeve, 'til [it] be
roten, kan [it] nat be rype' (I, 3875) — innocence is now a carcass
to be sold only at approved markets and served up only at
approved tables. We are back in the real world, where innocence,
like everything else, is a marketable property. Not surprisingly, the
metaphors echo the Wife of Bath's image for the arrangements of
the marriage bed: 'with empty hand men may none haukes lure'
(III, 415; cf. 389, 414). We cannot escape the sense of imminent
and spreading contamination. Virtue in retreat, compelled to feign
sickness; vice on the increase, consuming itself and battening on
the innocent, at best checked by confession and active correction,
at worst a pestilence which betrays and destroys.

Hence the irony that when we return to the story the narrator
continues as if the previous comments had not occurred, with a
further section in praise of his heroine (105-14). We are hardly
surprised, though, to find that not everybody loves her: there is
always 'Envye ... That sory is of oother mennes wele/ And glad
is of his sorwe and his unheele' (114-16). This allegorical figure
plays no greater part in the narrative than the earlier personification of Nature. Its presence merely puts another cloud on an
already lowering horizon. But it has a more immediate significance
for this study. It provides one of only two explicit references in the

story itself to the story's specifically Christian dimension. The narrator has not invented the figure of Envy; he claims to have taken it from 'the doctour', St Augustine.[18] This citation of the 'doctour' seeks to facilitate a particular and narrow reading of the narrative. Such a reading can easily accommodate the narrator's earlier and gravely sententious warnings against vice, but hardly his earlier hymn to virginal beauty (as earlier comments on this passage have shown, pp. 13-14 above); nor, without extreme ingenuity, can it square with the historical reading which the opening words of the story seemed to invite. To throw together Livy and St Augustine as authorising the narration, and Nature and Envy as characters in the fiction, is decisively to expose the moral and thematic incoherence of the narrative so far.

And so, at length, more than a third of the way into this very short work, the story gets under way. The heroine, never seen so far in public, leaves home and goes with her mother to town, making her way 'toward a temple'. Perhaps she is going to the temple, like Emelye in the Knight's tale, to offer sacrifice and prayer (I, 2278, 2332), as a further expression of her virtue and a specific 'bisynesse' designed to 'dryve hire out of ydel slogardye'. We never see her arriving at the temple. On her way there she passes by Appius, the Governor of the region, and innocently produces a devastating effect upon him. She is as ignorant of this effect as Dorigen when she falls under the gaze of Aurelius in the Franklin's tale (V, 936, 959 ff.), or Criseyde, who, though not pushing herself forward in the temple throng, nevertheless catches Troilus's eye (*Troilus*, I 271 ff.). Such a moment is not without parallel in the narratives of the Clerk and Man of Law. Grisilde is 'ful innocent' of the way in which Walter has 'ful ofte sithe ... sette his ye' on her (IV, 232-5); Custance knows nothing of the Sultan's falling in love with her by hearsay, at a distance, on the say-so of his merchants (who have themselves heard a great deal about her before ever they see her, II, 172). But the comparisons are once more of limited usefulness. Walter's often gazing on Grisilde proves that he is motivated neither by lust nor by infatuation (IV, 236-8); the Sultan's falling in love with Custance, sight unseen, is certainly closer to the spirit of romance, but serves chiefly to reinforce the emblem of faithfulness which he represents: the innocent passivity of the heroine thus focuses the insight of the one and the faith of the other. By contrast, Virginia's innocence provokes a reaction somewhere between infatuation and lust on the part of the governor. Now, unregenerate instincts do appear in religious narratives, but only as one of the trials besetting innocence (so, for example, in the Man of Law's tale, when Elda's second-in-command and the emir's deputy attempt, on different occasions, to seduce Custance). Such instincts cannot be given their head, and typically bring the guilty party to a speedy and deserved end. Nor are they prominent in the world of romantic comedy, however much the lofty ideas of the courtly lover may mask them from others and from himself. These base instincts receive much fuller treatment in satire and fabliau: so, for instance, in the Merchant's presentation of Damian and the Miller's of Nicholas (so too in Dioneo's presentation of Walter in Boccaccio's version of the Griselda story). They also occur, most obviously, in tragedies of innocence, like several of the Monk's tales and like what I have called the courtly tragedies of the *Legend*: and just such a tragedy the Physician's tale now becomes.[19] (Incidentally, this fact partially explains its place in this study immediately after the Monk's tale.)

The tragedy gets under way with the departure of the heroine — we do not see her again until the end — and the unfolding of Appius's plot. In Appius we find fully realised the narrator's earlier comments about the compromising moral context of his virtuous heroine. To the heroine's possession of her own virtue we now oppose the villain's possession by vice, personified (130) as the devil. He wants Virginia desperately, but he cannot hope to win her by bribes or force (133-4).[20] Virginia's 'confermed ... soverayn bountee' makes her proof against bribes, and since, like her father (4), she is 'strong of freendes', he can hardly attempt force (135-6). He therefore determines at once to work 'by slyghte'. Adding 'deliberacioun' to his initial delight — and thus marking his descent into sin — he summons a *cherl*, Claudius, 'subtil and ... boold' like the Wife of Bath (141).[21] Privately he concerts a plot with him, whose outcome will be 'that his lecherie/ Parfourned sholde been ful subtilly' (150-1). And now the narrative really takes off, with the twin characteristics, which it will maintain almost to the end, of speed and suspense: speed, in that the judge 'gooth now faste aboute/ To hasten his delit', and does not wait long to put his plan into action (158-60); suspense, in that we do not yet know the precise details of the conspiracy.

The conspiracy gets under way with the entry of Claudius 'a ful greet pas' (164) to the court over which Appius is presiding, with a bill of complaint against not Virginia but her father. Virginius is sent for, and the bill is read immediately. It claims that Virginius has come by, and is holding, property belonging to Claudius, a young servant girl stolen from him 'upon a nyght'. As if anticipating that the friends of Virginius will rise up to refute this testimony, Claudius offers to produce witnesses of his own (169, 185-6). The purpose of the conspiracy suddenly becomes clear when the plaintiff asserts that this servant 'nys his doghter nat, what so he seye' (187). Virginius is given no chance to disprove the allegation, nor to call other witnesses in his own defence (191-5), because the judge finds at once ('hastily': 192; cf. 196-7) in favour of the plaintiff, and makes the girl a ward of court (201), preliminary to handing her over to the *cherl* (199-202). What brute force could not achieve, confronted by Virginia's many friends, force of law (205) has effected by separating Virginius from the supporting testimony of his friends.

Virginius sees all too clearly the drift of the judge's ruling; Appius is renowned for his lechery (266). But no single individual can directly oppose the will of the court. So he returns home. There now follows a terrible parody of the earlier scenes, particularly the jumped-up trial. Sitting in his hall, like Appius in his consistory, Virginius summons his daughter (208), as Appius had summoned first Claudius and then Virginius himself (140, 173). When she comes, he looks upon her humble face (210) even as Appius had done (123 ff.). If her beauty produced a devastating effect on the heart of Appius (126-7), her humility produces a comparable effect on her father, 'fadres pitee stikynge thurgh his herte' (211). This phrase reminds us forcibly of the effect produced on the widow, in the Prioress's tale, by the disappearance of her little child ('with moodres pitee in hir brest enclosed': VII, 593); it also reminds us of the effect produced on the little child by his devotion to the Virgin ('the swetnesse hath his herte perced so': 555) — which, we remember, prefaced an actual stabbing. Our anxieties about the outcome of the present situation are not lessened by learning that Virginius is as fixed to his 'purpos', from which he will not 'converte' (212), as Appius to his (132).

Virginius now addresses his daughter, and the ironies multiply. He has always loved her greatly. His part in her upbringing has been a constant source of pleasure to him.[22] Flawlessly chaste, she has always been innocent of any wrongdoing for which she might expect to suffer the fate he now proposes. But he sees no alternative to a life of shame for her except death at his hand. It will kill him to have to kill her. Would that he had never been born. His last joy is now his greatest pain. Nevertheless, as a mark not of hate but of love, he must sentence her to death.

If the court scene, the first fruit of Appius's conspiracy, provided a concrete manifestation of that wickedness which the Physician reckoned so prevalent in the world, and so dangerous to the innocent, this parody of it realises the implications of the whole work in a far more terrible way. The delight of Nature in Virginia's beauty, transformed into the lust of Appius, now becomes for Virginius a painful pleasure which only memory can preserve. The call to parents to discipline their children so as to preserve them in virtue is now realised in the cruellest possible punishment, which must be administered if the father is not to prove 'softe and necligent' so as to preserve his daughter's virtue. Better a chastising which makes only the body 'perisse' than a negligence which will destroy the soul. The greatest irony of this self-pitying, self-regarding speech is focused by the parallelism between the sentence of Appius and that of Virginius (172, 224). The one purports to favour right, the other to act out of love; yet good and bad men between them, if for very different reasons, destroy innocence.[23]

At first, Virginia reacts neither as a plaster saint nor as an emblem of Christian fortitude but as a frightened young girl. Dependent on her father for life and favour, she flings her arms about her neck 'as she was wont to do', and bursts into tears, like a little child wanting to escape the rod:

> O mercy, deere fader! ...
> ... goode fader, shal I dye?
> Is ther no grace, is ther no remedye?
>
>   (231, 235-6)

But father knows no way out. Virginia is therefore forced to demonstrate her independence of a broken reed who, in a terrible parody of the Bible text, is proposing to bruise her. She asks for 'leyser' — this is the first time that we see her idle in the story — to bewail her coming death. After all, the Old Testament hero 'Jepte' (Jephthah, in Judges 11) did as much for his daughter, when he had to sentence her for no greater crime than that she 'ran hir fadir first to see/ To welcome hym with greet solempnitee' (243-4). This moment is barely plausible: no matter how virtuous she is, a pagan girl can hardly know the Old Testament. Its very implausibility reflects a clear attempt by the narrator to return his heroine to the emblematic role given her in the early part of his story. This Old Testament reference provides the only other evidence in the story for an explicitly religious reading of the narrative. All the same, the story of Jephthah, as presented, comes dangerously close to being not an emblem — though Peter of Riga so presents it in his *Aurora* — but merely an instance of tragic and undeserved death, like those listed by the Man of Law to explain the coming death of the Sultan, or those included in the Monk's tale.[24] Moreover, it has less relevance to Virginius's situation than at first appears. It hinges on a rash promise, made by Jephthah, which costs the life of his only child and unnamed daughter. Before a battle Jephthah has prayed to God for victory, and, in exchange, offered to sacrifice the life of the first person to meet him on his return. The daughter innocently puts herself in jeopardy out of love for her father by being the first person to meet the returning and victorious hero. Like Virginius, Jephthah is grief stricken at the dreadful turn of events, and pre-occupied by the cost to himself of his daughter's well-meant show of love ('what sorrow you are bringing me! must it be you, the cause of my ill-fortune!'). There is, however, a vital difference between the two fathers. Jephthah is bound by his vow to God, Virginius only by an unjust sentence. The character of Virginius, that is, stubbornly resists any simple emblematic reading on the basis of his daughter's comparison of him to Jephthah.[25] In any case, the obvious Biblical emblems speak of sacrifice averted (Abraham and Isaac, for instance).[26] The only clear parallel that I know of comes in late medieval art, with representations of God the Father punishing Christ,[27] or the Virtues crucifying him.[28] These emblems are more quaint — if not bizarre — than edifying, and only marginally relevant to the actual situation of Virginius.

But if the offered emblem of Virginius fails to convince,[29] the narrative does yield something positive in the way of an end for Virginia, which narrator and father can both use to justify their own lack of faith and which, strictly, neither deserves. Having uttered her complaint, Virginia falls into a swoon. When she recovers, she has lost her childish fears. Internalising her father's view of their relationship ('Dooth with youre child youre wyl') and accepting his understanding of the only possible resolution ('Yif me my deeth, er that I have a shame') she goes further than he was able to do, and blesses God that she will die a virgin. Then she swoons again, and the sorrowing father cuts her head off. Her faith, then, is put to the test and finally vindicated. Ironically, the human agent whom her belief thus vindicates never had the right to make this final demand of her.

While this episode has been taking place time seems to have been suspended, and the rapid pace of the narrative to have faltered, a feature regularly observed in emblematic narratives, where references to time are normally not functions of the plot so much as symbolic expressions of its meaning. But now the father, like a figure from a revenge tragedy, takes his daughter's head to the judge. Appius is still presiding over the court (257), so little time has passed in actuality between the departure and return of Virginius. Speed now returns to the narrative. Appius orders the immediate execution of Virginius; a crowd bursts in to save him, and throws Appius in prison, where he kills himself. Claudius is condemned to hang, but eventually pardoned by the intercession of Virginius and exiled (by a sad irony, which Chaucer's version shares with its sources, the life which the father's 'pitous hand' denied his daughter, his 'pitee' grants to a co-conspirator). Lastly, the narrative enlarges its focus and considers the end of others 'consentant of this cursednesse', the false witnesses whom Claudius proposed to produce (169), and who, in one of the sources, actually testified on his behalf. All of them are hanged.

This story, then, has an utterly distinctive shape, unlike anything so far seen. It falls into two broad sections. The first suggests a narrative of a fundamentally religious cast, but the Physician's address to what he sees as the real world, and choice of tragedy as the prevailing mode of his story, send it in a radically different direction. At the end, we look back over the preamble and see it as little more than holy window-dressing: its real significance lies not in the emblem it generates, but in the ways in which, directly or indirectly, its details anticipate or symbolise events in the narrative. Yet the narrator cannot leave his tragic narrative entirely free of religious considerations. He therefore concludes the story with a moralising passage, which claims the wages of sin as the real point of the work (277). Although a 'wikked lyf ... so pryvee be/ That no man woot therof but God and he' (281-2), the sinner's conscience is likely to terrify him by its unexpected operation ('agryse', 'afered', 280, 84). Hence we must be encouraged to forsake sin while we still have time ('er synne yow forsake': 286). After all, 'no man woot whom God wol smyte/ In no degree' (278-9). This material bears almost as tangential a relation to the tale as the conclusion proposed by the Monk for his version of the Belshazzar story. Certainly, the deaths of the conspirators speak of the wages of sin; the secrecy surrounding their plot (128, 143-4) inspires the comment about a 'wikked lyf ... so pryvee'. But the villains never once acknowledge the power of conscience over their actions. The injunction to forsake sin while there is time could, by implication, refer to the judge's settled course of sin — certainly it finds practical expression in the deaths of the villains — but the speaker is referring not so much to details in the story as to his own earlier words to the members of the audience (e.g. 87-8, 'looke wel that ye unto no vice assente/ Lest ye be dampned for youre wikke entente'). And his comment about the power of God to smite a man down is equally ambiguous. Appius is smitten by Virginia's beauty; Virginius reckons himself afflicted by misfortune. But the phrase probably refers directly to Virginia, on whom God visits first a powerful man of low instincts, and then a powerful man of the very highest instincts.[30] As a concrete expression of the power of God to 'smyte in [al] degree', the latter smites her head off (226, 255). Such a reading of the story makes Appius the central figure, and completely ignores the hymn to virgin beauty in the first third of the work.

The incoherence of this moralising conclusion, then, points to the moral incoherence of the whole work:[31] a point given unintentional substance by the Host's comments about the tale after its conclusion. Taking his cue from the closing words, the Host condemns the conspirators roundly; then, with a change of tack and tone, he warmly laments the death of 'this sely mayde', caused, as he reckons so often happens, by 'yiftes of Fortune and of Nature' (295).[32] To read the work in this way, as a tragedy of Fortune, is to attend insufficiently to the virtues of the heroine. It is also to give Fortune more prominence than she deserves. The narrator connects Fortune and Virginia's personal endowments only once, obliquely, when he has Nature describe her own sphere of operation, by implication, as the realm of Fortune, 'under the moone, that may wane and waxe' (23). Otherwise, it is not Virginia but her contemporaries, who, in their rush to acquire experience at the expense of their own innocence, unwittingly acknowledge the domination of earthly time and the reign of Fortune. Nevertheless, the Host's view of the Physician's tale engages more of it than the narrator's sententious and largely irrelevant conclusion.[33]

In the light of the foregoing remarks, it should not surprise the reader to learn how little in the tale can be traced directly to the named source, the *Ab Urbe Condita* of Livy, or that version of it found in the speech of Raison to the lover in the *Roman de la rose* and long seen as its main source.[34] The debt to the latter is clearly demonstrated by occasional instances of close translation. When Virginius declares that he is acting 'for love and nat for hate', he is appropriating Raison's words of him in the *Roman* ('par amour, senz haine': *RR*, 5635).[35] When the narrator rhymes the words 'storie' and 'consistorie' in the lines

As he sat yet in doom in consistorie.
And whan the juge it saugh, as seith the storie

(257-8)

he is virtually translating from the *Roman*:

Devant touz en plein consistoire;
E li juiges, selonc l'estoire.

(*RR*, 5639-40)

Other more important links with the *Roman* include the suppression of the heroine's fiancé, Icilius, to whom Livy assigns almost as great a role in the drama as Virginius; the failure to explain that the father is absent from court because he is on military service; and the ennobling of the father (a humble centurion in Livy, he has become a medieval knight in both de Meun and Chaucer). The most interesting example of the dependence comes when the father cuts off the daughter's head and presents it to the judge. The *Roman* credits Livy with this most stylised and theatrical moment in the story, and wonders whether he might not have made it up ('Se Titus Livius ne ment': *RR*, 5634). The ascription to Livy is without foundation. Livy's actual version was as dramatic as de Meun's is operatic; as concerned to create flesh-and-blood figures in a recognisable social and historical context as de Meun was to make a set of emblems. According to Livy, Virginius, powerless directly to oppose the sentence, pretends to acquiesce, secures the court's permission to question the nurse in the presence of the daughter, and, moving with them to one side, seizes a knife and stabs his daughter to the heart. Then he turns and howls curses on the judge. His action provokes a tremendous outcry against the judge from the bystanders. De Meun removes the bystanders and the whole historical context. Their absence imparts an eerie, unreal silence to the narrative, and isolates the central characters in studied and calculated postures, as the one figure presents the other with a literal image of innocence destroyed. The changed emphasis readily accommodates the story to the overall didactic purpose of the *Roman*. Raison is instructing the lover about the superiority of love over justice. She will do this most easily if she turns the figures of her story into emblems.

But if de Meun's version accounts for the strongly emblematic feel of the Physician's retelling, it does not explain its other distinctive features: the strong sense of impending doom; the speed of narration; and the tragic irony. These qualities, paradoxically, send the Physician away from the *Roman* and back to Livy.[36] Signs of clear dependence on Livy are few, and not, for the most part, as important for the development of the action as the earlier noted links with the *Roman*. Shannon noted some in his edition of the relevant parts of the *Ab Urbe Condita* (*SA*, pp. 402-7).[37] The most important such link, though, comes not in the story but as a part of the narrator's address to his audience. Livy gives Virginia a nurse who can accompany her to school at the start of the story and witness the horror of her death at the end. The *Roman* passes over this important figure in silence, and the Physician's retelling actively suppresses her. According to the latter, Virginia 'neded no maistresse'; consequently, on her way to the temple she is accompanied not by her nurse but by her mother, a figure completely absent in the *Roman* and present in Livy only in a shadowy relation of moral dependence on her husband parallel to that of her children on their father. Chaucer's narrator does, however, find a use for the nurse. She provides the inspiration for his sententious address to the members of the audience who have care of 'lordes doghtres' — just as his address to the noble parents derives ultimately from Livy's portrait of a humble centurion and his wife.[38] The ironies of these rewritings of the original are profound. They speak of a narrator with a very creative attitude to his sources — of which, to be fair, he has made relatively little use. Robinson's footnotes reckon almost half the story original: that is, the section describing the heroine's virtue and including the narrator's address to the audience (35-120), and the later account of the father's sentence and the daughter's ultimate acceptance (207-53). This account is factually inaccurate (according to Robinson,

Chaucer's first addition begins in mid-sentence, near the end of the section describing Virginia's beauty), and seriously underestimates the extent of the reworking. In particular, it fails to draw attention to the originality of the section describing the heroine's beauty and the imagined speech of Nature concerning her (7-38). Livy and the *Roman* provide the barest hint for this reading, the one with the phrase 'virginem ... forma excellentem', the other with the words 'sa bele fille'.[39] Nor do they make much, as the Physician does, of the heroine's spiritual beauty: except for a reference to her virginity, Livy says only that the father had brought up his daughter in accordance with his own high principles.

It is here, in respect of its treatment of the heroine, that the new version departs most widely from its originals. For both Livy and de Meun, the heroine is a function to bring together two strongly contrasting figures, the one embodying paternal love and devotion to civic duty, the other, lust and the tyrannical exercise of power.[40] While she is so presented, the ironies in her own role are minimal. Hence the *Roman* gives her no active part in the drama beyond an initial rejection of the judge and his lechery. She hardly has a bigger part to play in Livy's narration. Indeed, after her rejection of the original proposal, we see her as an independent agent only once, when Claudius is attempting to force her into the court; she becomes speechless with terror. When next the narrative presents her as a distinct character, she is once again the emblem of daughterly dependence: she comes to the Forum led by her father, her hand in his, and wearing rags as her equivalent of his mourning dress. In the Physician's tale this role is also imposed on Virginia once the story has begun: hence she is kept offstage almost until the end; hence, too, her tearful and child-like attempt to placate her father. Neither Livy nor de Meun, though, provides any hint of her heroic acceptance of her lot, which makes her her father's moral superior. Nor do they fall in love with her, as, in the opening section of the Physician's tale, both Nature and the narrator do.

The Physician's tale, then, is the most obviously literary offering so far studied. Like the other tales of this second section, it makes much of alternatives to its formal religious reading. It develops these alternatives more fully, and moves further in the direction of an openly secular reading of itself, than any tale so far considered. It invites comparison not only with the saints' tales — and comparisons have also been made with the *Legend*, that collection of tales of secular 'saints' — but with the tragedies of the Monk's tale, and with the genre of romance: we may even see overtones of that openly secular category, the fabliau. The Physician's tale therefore comes closer than any tale so far considered to symbolising, or epitomising, the total achievement of 'the book of the tales of Caunterbury'. Its centrality in *The Canterbury Tales* is suggested by a formal feature so far treated only in passing: that is, the verse form. Its use of rhyming couplets links it with the remaining tales of this study, and merits brief comment.

Until now, Chaucer has generally favoured rhyme royal for the religious tales.[41] Though not the most complex form available to him — one thinks, for instance, of the form favoured by an anonymous contemporary for that religious masterpiece, the *Pearl* — rhyme royal seems, in *The Canterbury Tales*, the verse equivalent of the brilliantly decorated surface of a medieval icon (I am thinking of the elaborate patterning so often tooled upon the gold leaf). It assists, so to say, in the creation of a holy object. Its rhythms are those of meditation and prayer; its, often limited, range of rhymes, as I hope earlier comments have shown, produce an effect akin to that of meditation.[42] Apart from rhyme royal, we have the eight-line stanza form used for the Monk's tale. This form is not used again in *The Canterbury Tales*, and may represent the attempt of a narrator keenly aware of the different verse forms used for tragedy ('exametron ... prose ... meetre, in many a sondry wyse') to provide a distinctive form for his very distinctive offering. We also have prose, chosen for the *Melibee* — and for the Parson's tale and the *retracciouns* — possibly because prose, the medium of instruction, can most clearly focus the penitential implication of the whole work. That leaves rhyming couplets for the Physician's, Pardoner's and Nun's Priest's tales — the form also used for the romances, the fabliaux and, most importantly, the overarching pilgrimage narrative. This choice would seem to be as deliberate as the other formal choices made by Chaucer in *The Canterbury Tales*.

For one thing, Chaucer's whole career shows a clear awareness of the distinctive effects produced by different verse forms — most notably, when he uses more than one verse form in a single work. For our purposes, the most important instance of such compound forms arises when an overarching verse form contains a secondary form: the latter is then given to one or other of the characters of the fiction to deliver, and provides an additional means of realising them as distinct characters.[43] Obvious examples include the roundel of the birds in *The Parliament of Fowls* (680-92), the ballade of the ladies in the G version of the *Legend* (G, 203-23), and the complaint of Anelida in the unfinished *Anelida and Arcite* (211-350). So presented, though both are obviously artificial, the two verse forms address two different levels of experience. The outer expresses or symbolises the objective reality in which the characters of the fiction find themselves, the inner a dependent world of subjective experience or fantasy. The relevance of this model to *The Canterbury Tales* should need no stressing. It carries the logical consequence that we find the couplet form used for the overarching pilgrimage narrative more immediate, closer to 'reality', than any of the variant forms used in individual tales. Now, individual tales using couplet form, logically, have no greater status in relation to the pilgrimage narrative than any of the others. In practice, though, their formal connection with it confers an authority on them wanting to the others. Therefore, we *feel* the Physician's tale, by virtue of its verse form, as closer to the physical realities at the heart of the pilgrimage narrative than the saint's tales: in the fictional scheme of things, the latter become a kind of glorious excrescence, a florid decoration in the margin of a manuscript. The choice of couplet form for the Physician's tale facilitates the tale's concentration on purely narrative values like speed, suspense and irony, in much the same way as the choice of rhyme royal, and other forms, for the tales so far studied, accompanies a relative neglect of those same values in favour of specifically religious ones — notably, the creation of an emblem.

And what is true of the Physician's tale is true in yet greater measure of the two religious tales which also use riding rhyme, and occupy a central place not just in this study of religious narratives, but in any study of the stories of *The Canterbury Tales*: those of the Pardoner and Nun's Priest.

Notes

1. On this point, see Minnis *Chaucer and Pagan Antiquity* (Cambridge, 1982) p. 29; and, on Chaucer's general readiness to follow the 'literal and historical' sense of his sources, Minnis (1982) *passim*.

2. On the source of these lines, and for comment about their effect, see T.B. Hanson, 'Chaucer's Physician as storyteller and moralizer', *ChR*, 7 1972-3, 133.4, Middleton, *ChR*, 8 16, Bartholomew p. 52, and Kean (II 180-82).

3. On the figure of Nature, see G.D. Economou, *The Goddess Natura in Medieval Literature* (Cambridge, Mass., 1972), esp. pp. 26-7; J.A.W. Bennett, *The Parlement of Foules* (Oxford, 1957), ch. 3 and appendix (according to which, p.

201, 'poets were quick to give Nature the special role of creating beautiful women'); Bartholomew p. 47. For a contrasting view of Nature, see below p. 281.

4. For suggested links with LGW, see Middleton *ChR*, 8, 28 ff, Howard p. 26 n. 6. (Though most easily read in themselves as tragedies of innocence betrayed, the tales of LGW acquire a very different significance from their connection with ProlLGW: see above, ch. VII n. 9).

5. Or rather, only an indirect and ironic part (contrast the role of Nature in religious narratives, such as the *De planctu naturae* of Alan of Lille: Economou (1972) *passim*).

6. Cf. Barney (Faulkner p. 87), and H.A. Kelly, 'Chaucer's arts and our arts' (Rose p. 110).

7. For parallels to this mirror image, see Economou (1972) pp. 90, 101, 106, 109, 114.

8. This echo is also noted by Cooper (p. 136).

9. Possibly Virginia needs no 'maistresse' because Nature is her 'maistresse': the *De planctu naturae* presents Nature as man's nurse, 'possibly echoing the *natura altrix hominum* of Prudentius and St. Ambrose' (Economou (1972) p. 78).

10. This image may connect with the presentation of the heroine in *RR*. See also Howard (pp. 199-206) for comment on the flower image; Kean (II 182) on the harmony between chastity and Nature, which allows for 'the perfections appropriate to marriage'.

11. Cf. Yunck, *ELH* 27, 252, comparing MLT and CIT as representatives 'not of an action, but of a passion'.

12. See also *BD*, 850, *Tr*, II, 1668, and Kean, II, 111-12 on the 'wommanly' ideal.

13. On the collocation of youth and folly, see Burnley p. 87.

14. On boldness, see also IV, 2269, VI, 141, VII, 1591, and contrast the boldness of the saint, IX, 319. For the comparison with WB, see Ramsey *ChR* 6, 196.

15. This point is also treated in sermon literature; see Owst (1961) pp. 465 ff.

16. Cf. Gen Prol portrait of WB (I, 476) and n. in Robinson.

17. For sermon material illustrating this point, often elaborating Prov. 13:24, see Owst (1961) pp. 461 ff: in particular, pp. 493, on Isaac as an 'ideal medieval son', and 464, on Deut. 22:18-21, describing how in the Old Law 'children that were rebelle and unbuxom to here fadres and modres were ypunysshed by deth'. See also above, ch. 1 n. 75, for parallel comment in *Handlyng Synne*, ll. 1285-8.

18. So the marginal glosses in several manuscripts (Manly–Rickert, III, 515). Blake identifies the 'descripcioun' of ll. 114-16 — as do most editors — as coming from St Augustine's commentary on Ps. 104:25 (*PL* 37, 1399: 'invidia est enim odium felicitatis alienae'), also translated ParsT (484), 'after the word of Seint Augustyn, it is "sorwe of oother mennes wele, and joye of othere mennes harm"'.

19. On this mixture of modes in PhysT, see also Middleton, *ChR* 8, 24-5. On unregenerate sexual instinct in MkT (the tragedy of Nero) cf VII 2482-90; and in LGW (the tragedies of Lucretia and Philomela) LGW 1745-56, 2288-93.

20. We might compare Constance's resistance to the bribery and force offered her by the Sultan's mother to secure her conversion to Islam in Trevet's original of MLT (above p. 121).

21. On 'deliberacioun' as a stage in the progress of sin, see S. Wenzel, 'Notes on ParsT', *ChR*, 16, 1981-2, 243-5.

22. In context these words might mean that Virginius' cares for her upbringing, though a source of pleasure to him, have been a constant preoccupation. If so, the words probably echo the ultimate source, Livy, which tells how Virginius had instructed his wife, and was instructing his children, in the same high principles as he himself followed (*SA*, p. 402).

23. On irony in the tale, see Hanson *ChR*, 7 136-8, and beautiful comments in Allen-Moritz, p. 161 and n. 47.

24. Beichner, I, 240. According to Peter of Riga, Christ is symbolised negatively by Jephthah and positively by the sacrificed daughter. Robert Mannyng of Brunne finds a simpler meaning: ' ȝoure wykked vowys shul ȝe nat fylle' (Furnivall, l. 2895: he is quoting St Augustine, which may give an ironic twist to the Physician's invocation of the 'doctour' earlier in the tale). See also Allen-Moritz pp. 161-2 and n. 51, and Owst (1961) p. 119.

25. In support of this point, see Leicester, *PMLA*, 95, 218. Against, Pratt, Atwood–Hill p. 308, who notes a similar 'admixture of Christian and pagan elements . . . altogether characteristic of the Middle Ages' in Trevet's *Cronicles*. The genre of 'universal history', however, to which Trevet's *Cronicles* belong, is providentialist in no narrow sense, and depends on the larger context of creation and Incarnation to secure a Christian reading of the pagan examples. Removed from that larger frame, their providential character cannot be taken for granted — any more than when ML quotes lines from the *Megacosmos* (see above, ch. 6 n. 44).

26. This emblem is as inappropriate, finally, to PhysT as to CIT (see above, ch. 2, n. 16); but A. Lancashire, 'Chaucer and the sacrifice of Isaac', *ChR*, 9, 1974-75, 321-6, has offered suggestive parallels of PhysT with the Isaac plays of the cycle drama.

27. Cf. Is. 53:4-5, Rom. 8:32, both used in a twelfth-century text by Peter of Celle (*PL*, 202, 1120): 'hunc unicum et dilectissimum Filium in quo sibi bene complacuit flagellis, imo durissimis scorpionibus absque ulla retractione velut inimicum . . .misericors Pater . . . cecidit' ['the merciful father slew his only and most dear son, in whom he so greatly delighted [cf. Matt. 3:17] with whips and most cruel scorpions [cf. 1 Kings 12:11] without any denial as if he were an enemy']. This passage lies at the back of a dramatic passage in the *Ancrene wisse* (see *Ancrene wisse Parts Six and Seven*, ed. G. Shepherd (London, 1959), 10/34 ff and n. to 11/5, for the reference to Peter of Celle).

28. For Christ crucified by the virtues, see Schiller II 138-9 and figs. 450-4. See also Schiller II, 228 and fig. 810 for a traditional allegorical representation of the Passion, conflating the crucifix and the winepress of Is. 63:3, such that God the father presses his son to death beneath the crucifix.

29. Others are, however, willing to take the attempt for the deed: so Bartholomew pp. 46-57, Kean, II, 179-85.

30. Ramsey *ChR*, 6, 196, sees the narrator's moralizing as the third violence done to Virginia.

31. A point regularly noted by opponents of the tale: eg Hanson, *ChR*, 7, 136, Whittock p. 183, Ramsey *ChR*, 6, 189.

32. For the claim that this phrase creates a link with PardT, see G. Joseph, 'The gifts of nature, fortune and grace in PhysT, PardT, ParsT', *ChR*, 9, 1974-5, 237-8, 241 ff.

33. Also noted Middleton *ChR*, 8, 13.

34. Relevant portions of both are printed *SA* pp. 400-7. For a modern edition and translation of Livy, see Livy *Ab Urbe Condita III-IV*, ed. and trans. by B.O. Foster (London, 1922), pp. 142ff. For a modern edition of *RR*, see *Le roman de la rose*, 3 vols, ed. by F. Lecoy *Les classiques français du moyen âge*, 92, 95, 98 (Paris, 1966-70); for a modern translation, *The Romance of the Rose*, translated by C. Dahlberg (Princeton, 1971). The use of *RR* constitutes a further link of PhysT with MkT (the latter uses it for the stories of Croesus and Nero). See Ramsey, *ChR*, 6, 190ff, for careful study of the sources.

35. Also noted Lancashire *ChR* 9, 323, Ramsey *ChR* 6, 192.

36. Cf. Middleton *ChR* 8, 11: 'Jean's distilling of the story is the one Chaucer

adopts; Chaucer's emphasis, however, is not Jean's.'

37. One not quoted by him is Virginia's resistance to money and promises ('pretio ac spe'). *RR* wants any such reference; in Chaucer it becomes Appius' realization that he will not win the girl 'by no force ne by no meede'.

38. For another way of reading the address, as a 'personal attack [of Chaucer] on his sister-in-law, Katherine Swynford', for neglecting her duties to her charge, John of Gaunt's daughter, see Coghill, (Brewer, 1966), p. 128; see also general comment ch. 1 n. 75 above.

39. On this point see Hanson *ChR*, 7, 134.

40. So also Middleton *ChR*, 8, 13.

41. The obvious exception, in ProlThop, may be explained as an imitation of the (short-lived) effect produced by the preceding PrT on its audience. On rhyme royal, see Payne (p. 165 n. 26), Brewer (Intro. p. 187), Leicester, *PMLA* 92, 221, and M. Stevens, 'The royal stanza in Early English literature', *PMLA* 94 (1979), 66-73.

42. On rhymes, see comments earlier on ClT and (implied) on MLT (pp. 47, 49, 139, 146-8), Burlin, pp. 163-4; C.A. Owen, Jr., 'Thy drasty rymyng', *SP* 63 (1966), 534; and caveat in Davis, Brewer (1974), pp. 67, 75 ff.

43. We might compare Shakespeare's use of a distinctive verse-form to realize the play-within-a-play in *Hamlet*.

PART THREE

TOWARDS A CONCLUSION

The steward tasted the water,
and it had turned into wine. (John 2:9)

9 THE PARDONER'S TALE

The tales of the preceding section have moved us further and further from the central area, or question, of this study: the communication of specifically religious truths in specifically literary terms. As we have travelled further away from our point of departure, the Clerk's exemplum and the two saints' lives, we have seen the balance of the two elements, religious and literary, tip one way at the expense of literary interest in *Melibee*; restored precariously in the Man of Law's tale; then tip the other way in the Monk's and Physician's tales. Indeed, the latter barely scramble under the wire as religious stories. The Monk's choice of Old Testament stories, and reference to the purposes of the Christian God, earn him a place in this study. The Physician owes his to his more calculated use of stray religious elements: a Biblical emblem, a citation of the 'doctour', a moralising conclusion. Neither is actually producing a religious story; the interests of both, we have said, are not primarily religious but literary. Both follow a lead given by the Man of Law and produce tragedies — that form before all others incompatible with a Christian literature. But their real importance lies not in the stories they tell but in the stories to which their own give rise. Just as the Monk had proposed to qualify his tale by a sequel, so Chaucer follows both stories with sequels which complement their limited perspectives and subject them to searching irony: the Pardoner's and Nun's Priest's tales.[1] This pairing of tales — Physician with Pardoner, and Monk with Nun's Priest — for specifically religious purposes, is unique in *The Canterbury Tales*. As earlier noted, other religious tales stand alone (Man of Law, Parson) or head their respective groups without an existing narrative to shape their own (Clerk, Second Nun);[2] the two that follow another narrative (the Prioress's tale, following the Shipman's, and *Melibee*, following Sir Thopas) seek not so much to complement the preceding one, since it is not in the least religious, as to oppose it.[3] Hence the Prioress's aside about the holy abbot of her story (VII, 642-3), usually taken as a veiled criticism of the monk hero of the Shipman's tale.[4]

Far from overturning the tragic vision of the Physician's tale, the Pardoner's tale at first looks to be reinforcing it. The Physician had placed his innocent heroine in a world of youthful excess: of sloth, drunkenness and 'folye'. The Pardoner's tale begins similarly, with

> a compaignye
> Of yonge folk that haunteden folye
> As riot, hasard, stywes and tavernes,
> Where as with harpes, lutes and gyternes,
> They daunce and pleyen at dees bothe day and nyght,
> And eten also and drynken over hir myght.
>
> (463-8)

The first two lines of this quotation clearly echo a detail in the Physician's tale ('for that she wolde fleen the compaignye/ Where likly was to treten of folye': 63-4): so too, with a downward lurch of the social scale, the young folk's dancing 'day and nyght' corresponds to the Physician's account of the 'feestes, revels and ... daunces/ That been occasions of daliaunces' (65-6). This downward turn of events is reflected clearly in the language. The Physician has a very literary way of describing the close links between wine and youthful passion (58-60); by contrast, though he keeps the Physician's image of the blazing fire, (481; cf. 60), the Pardoner speaks much more directly: not Bacchus, but 'glotonye' and 'dronkenesse'; not Venus, but 'lecherye' (481-2, 484). But these young people, living under the Christian dispensation, are incomparably worse than their counterparts in the Physician's tale. They may not know that their 'superfluytee abhomynable' is a sacrifice to the devil 'withinne that develes temple', the tavern or the brothel.[5] They may not know, though the text seems to suggest that they do, that when they laugh at one another's follies they are actually making light of their own sin ('and ech of hem at otheres synne lough': 476). They may not even realise that the band of camp followers whom their laughter seems almost to call into being,

> And right anon thanne comen tombesteres
> Fetys and smale, and yonge frutesteres,
> Syngeres with harpes, baudes, wafereres
>
> (477-9)

are the 'verray develes officeres' who will bring them to hell. They do know, however, that their oaths symbolically dismember Christ and re-enact his passion:[6] they playfully reckon to complete what the Jews failed to do ('hem thoughte that Jewes rente hym noght ynough': 475).

Almost nothing in *The Canterbury Tales*, outside of the Parson's tale, could have prepared us for this.[7] We come closest to it in the Cook's tale, whose youthful hero is addicted to the same vices, and described in very similar terms:

> For sikerly a prentys revelour
> That haunteth dys, riot, or paramour,
> His maister shal it in his shoppe abye,
> Al have he no part of the mynstralcye.
> For thefte and riot, they been convertible,
> Al konne he pleye on gyterne or ribible.
> Revel and trouthe, as in a lowe degree,
> They been ful wrothe al day, as men may see.
>
> (I, 4391-8)

'Perkyn revelour' gathers about himself a group of kindred spirits 'to hoppe and synge and maken swich disport .../ To pleyen at the dys' (4382, 4384). Sometimes he dances his way even into New-gate prison (4402). His master wearies of paying for his follies, and determines that this one 'roten appul' shall not infect the rest of his household — a metaphor also implied in the Physician's comment about children 'to soone rype and boold': so he is dismissed from his apprenticeship. He takes up with

> a compeer of his owene sort,
> That lovede dys, and revel and disport,
> And hadde a wyf that heeld for contenance
> A shoppe, and swyved for hir sustenance.
>
> (4419-22)

But even were this story, which Chaucer never finished, to have unfolded as a kind of Rake's Progress, it would hardly have yielded the stark picture of sin and damnation presented in the opening moments of the Pardoner's tale. Perkyn inhabits a world of thoughtless youth, with the generosity of youth ('therto he was free/ Of his dispense': 4387-8), to set against his conventional vices.[8] In any event, a story focused on a central rake figure is likely to follow a different path from one which identifies a group of young people, as a group, with conscious progress towards damnation. Practices which might symbolise youthful high spirits or, at most, warn the young to sow their wild oats carefully, are here invested with the lurid shapes and colours of hell itself. We start, that is, where the Physician's tale ended, with its gravely sententious warning to the audience to profit by Appius's fall and 'forsaketh synne, er synne yow forsake.'

The narrative has no sooner begun, with the entry of the 'develes officeres' on stage, than it is being interrupted for an extended moralising commentary. This commentary, which I shall also call the Pardoner's sermon, considers the principal vices thus far revealed: drunkenness and gluttony (480-588), gambling and oaths (589-659); lastly, lechery, mentioned in passing as an off-shoot of the first pair (481, 484, 549). With the sermon we leave behind the world of the Physician's tale.[9] The opening exempla present a father, Lot, who slept with his daughters because he was 'so dronke ... he nyste what he wroghte', and a stepfather, Herod. A 'governour' like Appius, Herod's ungovernable lust for his step-daughter led him 'whan he of wyn was repleet at his feeste' to order the execution of that emblem of virginal innocence, John the Baptist (485-91). Granted, the Pardoner does not treat directly of Herod's lust for Salome, nor of the active part played by Lot's daughters in their father's sin (they intoxicate him so as to make him sleep with them): but the domestic context of both exempla reminds us inevitably, and ironically, of that in the Physician's tale. And the sermonising creates a more important distance between the one tale and the other. In purely formal terms, the Pardoner's tale closely resembles the Physician's narrative, itself hardly under way when interrupted for a fictional speech (11-29) and an extended address to the audience (67-104). This distinctive pattern occurs elsewhere in *The Canterbury Tales*: in the Merchant's tale, for instance, which, after a brief narrative intro-duction (V, 1245-66), turns aside from the narrative to a protracted commentary (1267-392). Where, though, the Physician and Pardoner get their respective commentaries out of the way at the beginning, and then leave their stories very much to tell them-selves, the Merchant intrudes comments all through the tale, rather like the Man of Law and Clerk, so that the resulting structure of his tale is not strictly comparable with those of the Physician and Pardoner.[10] And there is a vital difference between the Physician's commentary and the Pardoner's. The Physician uses his to counter the idealism which until then has characterised the narrative; to throw an ironic light over his relation to the source; to prepare for the tragic outcome. By contrast, the Pardoner uses his to reinforce the meaning of the story. We may be uncertain what story will grow from this brief narrative preamble, but the sermon speedily dispels any lingering doubts about its meaning.

On drink and gluttony, the prevailing metaphor, as others have noted, is one of metamorphosis.[11] Drink and madness are interchangeable, with this difference, that 'woodnesse, yfallen in a shrewe/ Persevereth lenger than doth dronkenesse' (496-7). This phrase (which goes back to Seneca, probably by way of a thirteenth-century compendium of spiritual instruction, the *Communiloquium* of John of Wales)[12] probably also implies, what the sources did not, an equation of drink and madness with perseverance in one's 'shrewednesse': the settled commitment to sin displayed by the 'yonge folk' of the story. Similarly, the food a man eats becomes, by transference, the 'shorte throte, the tendre mouth' (517) through which it passes, a phrase which suggests beautifully both the impermanence ('shorte') and the fragility ('tendre') of the pleasures it engenders. It also becomes the 'wombe ... bely ... stynkyng cod' which absorb it, and the 'dong and ... corrupcioun' which it leaves behind (534-5). The interchangeability of food and the belly is well caught in a phrase of St Paul, which comes to the narrator either from the *De Miseria* or from St Jerome's *Adversus Jovinianum*:[13]

> Of this matiere, o Paul, wel kanstow trete:
> 'Mete unto wombe, and wombe eek unto mete,
> Shal God destroyen bothe', as Paulus seith.
>
> (521-3)

And if food becomes the throat on the way down, excess of drink may reverse the process and make the throat a sewer (527). In any case, before ever it comes to table, the food has undergone amazing transformations as a result of the 'greet labour and cost' of its production. Conspicuous consumption requires a whole army of men 'est and west and north and south/ In erthe, in eir, in water ... to swynke' (518-19). No ordinary fare will suffice: 'deyntee mete and drynke' are needed 'to make hym [the glutton] yet a newer appetit' (520, 546). In quest of something to stimulate the jaded palate, the cooks

stampe, and streyne, and grynde,
And turnen substaunce into accident,
To fulfille al thy likerous talent!
Out of the harde bones knokke they
The mary, for they caste noght awey
That may go thurgh the golet softe and swoote.
Of spicerie of leef, and bark, and roote
Shal been his sauce ymaked by delit.

(538-45)[14]

This passage, also from the *De Miseria* (Lewis, p. 10 and n. 52) repays close attention. The delicate bone marrow is carefully preserved to provide something easy to swallow; its blandness must then be covered by spicy sauces. In this process, the 'substaunce' (that is, the natural properties of the original foods) has become an 'accident' of the cook's art and the patron's palate: Nature has become art in the pursuit of novel sensation.[15] This denunciation of 'delices' may be a little attracted to the things it so forcefully condemns; but it is perfectly traditional. It has a powerful analogue in the classical picture of the Golden Age, known to Chaucer by way of Boethius and de Meun, and of which a defining element was a simple regime of food and drink. I quote from the *Boece*:

Blisful was the firste age of men. They heelden hem
apayed with the metes that the trewe feeldes
broughten forth. They ne destroyeden ne desseyvede
nat hemself with outrage. They weren wont lyghtly to
slaken hir hungir at even with accornes of ookes. They
ne coude nat medle the yift of Bachus to the cleer hony
(that is to seyn, they coude make no pyment or clarree)
... They ... dronken of the rennynge watres.

(*Bo*, II, m. 5, 1-10, 15-17)[16]

A practical expression of this turning of substance into accident, for the same profit motive, appears in the next section of the commentary. Vintners adulterate the better French wines with cheaper Spanish produce to immediate and dramatic effect.[17] The solid ground on which the drunk thinks to stand 'in Fysshstrete or in Chepe' has become the accident of his intoxication, and the scene of his mental delusion is not even 'the Rochele ne ...

Burdeux toun' but the Spanish 'toun of Lepe' (562-71). That is, he is twice deceived: once by drink itself, and once by the vintners' sharp practice. And this passage provides the ultimate images of metamorphosis. Earlier presented as a throat in the act of throwing up, the drunk is now seen as the 'verray sepulture' of his own 'wit and ... discrecioun' (558-9). As he falls into his stupor, he becomes 'as it were a styked swyn' (556): man finally into animal, as Boethius teaches in his moralising of the Circe story (IV, m.3), because he has forgotten his true nature.

This crucial metaphor, which will be fully realised in both the theme and the methods of the tale proper, has already been anticipated in the narrative preamble. There we saw the accident of the tavern transformed into what it substantially is, the 'develes temple'; the camp followers turned into 'verray develes officeres'; observed an equation between the practice and the circumstance of vice ('haunteden ... riot, hasard, stywes and tavernes'); and found lechery located in 'wyn and dronkenesse' (484). Of course, metamorphosis is not only image but also process; the process generates the image. Hence, the phrase parallel to that just quoted describes lechery as 'annexed unto glotonye': that is, lechery is not only coextensive, as image, with gluttony and drunkenness, but also grows out of them. Metamorphosis has the character of an ironic reversal, as both God and Nature take revenge on human presumption. The cardinal exemplum of this, third in the Pardoner's list, is Adam. According to the *Adversus Jovinianum*, which the Pardoner is here following, Adam was driven from Paradise because he would not abstain from 'the fruyt deffended on the tree' (508-10). Yet, if his gluttony initiated the processes whose effects the narrative will grimly realise for us, his successors easily outstrip him in sinning. According to St Jerome, Adam did not at first eat meat after he was excluded from Paradise, but followed a vegetarian regime in clear and close imitation of the food he had eaten in Paradise. God gave permission for men to eat meat only after the Flood, when they had proved, even to his satisfaction, their insatiable gluttony.[18] Even after the Fall, then, Adam's lifestyle is closer to that which he first knew than that which we now have. If Adam's fall exposed him to a life of labour (506) causally linked with that of his successors to gather and prepare food (519, 537), his labour of tilling the soil is closer to the 'labours' of the Golden Age, which he inhabited before the Fall, than to any of the corrupt sophistications practised by his present-day descendants. With their greater sophistication of appetite has come a whole crop of unforeseen illnesses:

> O, wiste a man how manye maladyes
> Folwen of excesse and of glotonyes,
> He wolde been the moore mesurable
> Of his diete, sittynge at his table.
>
> (513-16)

Whether we know what we are doing or not, for so long as we make our guts our God, in the words of St Paul (Phil. 3:18), we are 'enemys of Cristes croys' (532).

So far this performance has been in the nature of a soliloquy which we have been permitted to overhear. On our behalf (cf. 499-500, 512), the narrator has addressed now gluttony (498, 512), now the belly (534-40), now St Paul (521), and now a drunk man (551-7). The movement from one personification to another is like the Man of Law's cursing now Satan, now his incarnation the Sultaness, but it has a headlong vitality wanting in the Man of Law's narration: and, more important, brilliantly enacts the theme of metamorphosis — gluttony being realised concretely in a distended belly, metaphorically in a drunk man, and negatively in the testimony of 'the apostel wepyng'.[19] Then, while waxing eloquent about the vices of drink — drunkenness begins the sermon (485-97), surfaces during the attack on gluttony (520, 526-7), and resumes at 549 — the preacher suddenly shifts the focus of the address: 'But herkneth, lordynges, o word, I yow preye' (573). For the first time in the tale itself, the audience are being directly addressed. From now on, until the preacher resumes his narrative (660), the audience are aware of his eye upon them, as he exhorts them to attend to the exempla which he will relate ('looke': 579, 621) and confirm the truth of his words by reference to the Bible (578, 586, 634, 639). As a partial consequence of this changed focus, the second half of the sermon is simpler and less adventurous than the first.[20] When the preacher finishes with drink and turns on gambling, he roundly declares it 'verray mooder' of all manner of sins, including 'forswerynges' (591-4); but he actually realises this assertion only once, near the end, when he is drawing his comments on swearing to a close (629-55, 659). In a moment of beautiful colloquial vigour, the swearer, given to conventional oaths like 'by Goddes precious herte' and 'by his nayles', suddenly realises himself for us as a dice player, and shows how oaths, and murder, are causally linked to gambling:

'By the blood of Crist, that is in Hayles,
Sevene is my chaunce, and thyn is cynk and treye!'
'By Goddes armes, if thou falsly pleye,
This daggere shal thurghout thyn herte go!'
This fruyt cometh of the bicched bones two,
Forsweryng, ire, falsnesse, homycide.

(652-7)[21]

Otherwise, the preacher follows a surprisingly conventional course, for which the opening exempla (485-97) have prepared us: he proceeds entirely by exemplum and passages of generalised moral comment. In succession, we get Attila and Lamuel as exempla of the dangers of drink (579-87), and Stilboun and the King of the Parthians as exempla of wise men who would have nothing to do with dicing (603-26). There is an assertion

That alle the sovereyn actes ...
Of victories in the Olde Testament ...
Were doon in abstinence and in preyere.

(574-5,77)

There is the already noted passage claiming 'hasard' as the mother of all manner of vices. And there is a passage which uses Bible texts against swearing (Matt. 5:34; Jeremiah 4:2; and Exod. 20:7) to forbid 'gret sweryng', 'fals sweryng', and 'ydel sweryng' (629-47). The Pardoner treats the last of these to a perfectly traditional exposition. In 'the firste table/ Of heighe Goddes heestes .../ The seconde heeste' (that quoted in Exod. 20:7) forbids swearing — as everyone will know who 'his heestes understondeth'. Consequently, swearing is worse than 'homycide or many a cursed thyng' (640-7). For once, the preacher seems to have forgotten his theme of the interdependence of all sins, and to be operating a much simpler schema, namely, a hierarchy of sins.

The layout of this material confirms the impressions so far received. The earlier section largely wanted formal subdivisions; here they are clearly in evidence:

But herkneth, lordynges, o word, I yow preye ...

Namoore of this, for it may wel suffise.
And now that I have spoken of glotonye,
Now wol I yow deffenden hasardrye ...
Now wol I speke of othes false and grete
A word or two, as olde bookes trete.

(573, 588-90, 629-30)[22]

Paradoxically, this more limited performance, clearly instructing
and consciously addressed to an audience, represents a greater
achievement in terms of the total structure of the work (that is, the
narrative links at front and back of the tale, and the tale's formal
prologue) than anything so far seen.

A small point is perhaps worth starting with. Most of the time
the preacher addresses his congregation as a whole ('lordynges':
573; 'sires': 660; plural pronoun and verb forms, 'avyseth yow':
583). But at one point (648) he suddenly addresses the (generalised) individual member of the congregation: 'I wol thee telle al
plat'. This change of pronoun is not unparalleled in *CT*. In the
course of their narrations, the pilgrim narrators usually address not
an individual but the whole group ('lordynges', 'sires') or some
part of it, the latter normally a projection of it (for examples, see
above p. 25); but they occasionally acknowledge, the individual
hearer, personified as the Host at VIII, 1089, elsewhere by way of
a stock phrase like 'ther maistow seen' (I, 1918, 2128; IV, 60,
265). The model for this shift of address was probably not the
Middle English romances, on whose conventions of oral performance, as has been long recognised, Chaucer drew so freely for the
colloquial colour of his verse.[23] The Middle English romances
maintain the plural form of address with great consistency.[24]
Rather, I believe that Chaucer was modelling himself on the
practice of sermons, manuals for penitents and 'utilitarian, non-
religious handbooks', in which the shift of address from plural to
singular, and the reverse, occurs regularly enough, when writers
address their audiences directly, to be reckoned a stylistic feature
of such texts.[25] Such texts will declare truths common to all
members of the audience (*you, we*) and, at the same time, will
stress their relevance to each individual reader or member of the
audience (*thou, I*).[26] This shift of pronouns also characterises the
other 'sermon' in *CT*, the Parson's tale (e.g. X, 136, 155, 516) as
well as those parodies of a sermon, the Clerk's envoy and the
Merchant's sermonising preamble (IV, 1183-211, 1315-30).[27] The

Pardoner is probably taking his cue for his change of pronoun from the Biblical quotations just used: that from Jeremiah ('thou shalt swere sooth': 636-7) addressed the children of Israel as one person; that from Exodus ('take nat my name in ydel': 642) addressed the individual member of the congregation. (This pattern, too, is common in sermons and manuals).[28] We can therefore argue that this shift of pronoun provides another indication of the kind of work being produced.[29]

But this later part of the sermon contains more important material. In it the exempla receive a much narrower interpretation than the initial ones, and the moralising comments are slanted to make a very particular point. The death of Attila teaches us that 'a capitayn sholde lyve in sobrenesse' (582). The command to Lamuel has a message 'expresly/ Of wyn-yevyng to hem that han justise' (587). Addiction to dice

> is repreeve and contrarie of honour ...
> And ever the hyer he is of estaat,
> The moore is he yholden desolaat.
> If that a prince useth hasardrye,
> In alle governaunce and policye
> He is, as by commune opinioun,
> Yholde the lasse in reputacioun.
>
> (595, 597-602)

This last comment receives concrete expression in the exempla of Stilboun and the King of Parthia, which warn the 'gretteste ... of [the] lond' not to 'allyen [hem] with hasardours' (607, 618), and end:

> Lordes may fynden oother maner pley
> Honest ynough to dryve the day awey
>
> (627-8)

Now, the exempla chosen make possible this very specific application of the material to the situations of princes, justicers, lords and captains; but they do not, in themselves, provide a sufficient or necessary explanation of it. We are driven to the conclusion that the preacher is either expressing a personal interest in the lives of the great, like the Man of Law when he addresses the noblewomen in his audience, or responding to what he has identified as a major interest of his audience. The link passage between Physician's and Pardoner's tales helps to resolve this difficulty.

As happens elsewhere in the link passages, the Host has reacted powerfully to the Physician's story. Swearing 'as he were wood' by the nails, blood and bones of Christ (287-8, 314), and by St Ronyan (310), he declares he must have something different to lighten his heart: medicine ('triacle'), 'a draughte of moyste and corny ale', 'a myrie tale' (314-16). The connection between tale-telling and liquor has already been made at the outset of the Miller's performance, and does not point in any obviously moral direction. Nor does the request for a 'myrie tale'. Chaucer and the Parson both declare that such a tale may properly include grave and serious utterance (hence they describe their prose offerings in such terms). The Host hardly has that kind of merriment in view. His demand for a tale of 'myrthe or japes' recalls the Cook's description of his own tale as 'a litel jape' (I, 4343), and summary of the Reeve's tale, like the Host's of the Shipman's tale, as a 'jape' (I, 4338; VII, 439): none of these is immediately or obviously an edifying production. And it is the Pardoner of all people — the one whom Chaucer placed last in the portrait gallery in the General Prologue — whom the Host calls on, in a patronisingly familiar way ('beel amy'), to supply such a story. The Pardoner responds in kind: swearing the same oath (320; cf. 310), he reckons, before he tells his story, to 'bothe drynke, and eten of a cake' (322). This identification with the Host, on however mild a level, in two of the vices treated in the story — drink, and swearing — may give an edge to what I have called the Pardoner's soliloquy on the vices of drink and gluttony. It hardly explains the sermon's later concentration on the practices of the great.

As it happens, though, the terms proposed by the Host and accepted by the Pardoner are not the complete measure of the tale delivered. The *gentils* now press forward to oppose the idea:

> Nay, lat hym telle us of no ribaudye!
> Telle us som moral thyng, that we may leere
> Som wit, and thanne wol we gladly here.
>
> (324-6)[30]

They have not needed to react in such a straitlaced way before, because other proposed ribald offerings have generated an opposition which expresses a personal animus in the language of conventional morality, and hence confirms the moral status quo: hence, most notably, the Reeve opposes the Miller with

> Lat be thy lewed dronken harlotrye.
> It is a synne and eek a greet folye
> To apeyren any man, or hym defame.

(I, 3145-7)

It is only in the face of what they see as a coalition of carnal interest that they are compelled to wave the flag for decent Christian values. Their protest is the more surprising because they give no sign of disapproving of any of the bawdy offerings on the journey. They are almost certainly among the 'moore part' that 'loughe and pleyde' after the Miller's tale, and clearly included in the general laughter which the Host's coarse discomfiture of the Pardoner later provokes. What, then, are we to make of their protest? One thing, at least, is clear. Whatever the *gentils'* motive for making it, the protest effectively isolates them from the group, much as they self-consciously isolate themselves at the end of the Knight's tale when they register their approval so prominently for the offering of their chief representative (I, 3110-13). Their words give the Pardoner his second cue.[31] He promises them 'som honest thyng' (328) 'that shal by reson been at youre likyng' (458). And he fulfils his promise. He does this, in the first instance, once he has acknowledged the existence of his audience, by angling the sermon in the direction of the *gentils'* preoccupation with their own status. This material, then, brilliantly demonstrates the crucial connection between audience expectation and performed narrative: to revert to our image of metamorphosis, the double audience (Host and *gentils*) is absorbed into, and becomes, the sermon. Each can find what it wants there.[32] Those seeking japes will find them in the sharp practices of the vintner and the exotic productions of the cook, in the literal downfall of the drunk man, in belching and farting (536), in vomiting, in the put-down of the great (Attila dies of a nose-bleed in a drunken stupor; Demetrius is sent a pair of gold dice 'in scorn'). Those seeking 'som moral thyng' can turn to Bible stories and wise sayings, and to the narrator's undoubted control of the rhetoric of the pulpit. The two readings overlap. The one attends only to the surfaces of the sermon, ignorant of the learned traditions within which it operates; the other can claim to appreciate its deeper meanings. The one reader, for instance, might show a lively interest in the camp followers as camp followers; the other could expect to approve their condemnation:

> tombesteres
> Fetys and smale, and yonge frutesteres,
> Syngeres with harpes, baudes, wafereres,
> Whiche been the verray develes officeres.
>
> (477-80)[33]

But if one section of the audience has 'become' the sermon in a very specific and limited way, the story itself, which now unfolds, implicates the whole audience, the narrator included, in much more complex and all-embracing ways. In part this is a consequence of the interruption of the narrative, before it is properly under way, for the extended moralising commentary. Viewed simply as an interruption to the story, the commentary creates a space between the narrative preamble and the narrative proper, and loosens the necessary links between the two. Normally, a narrative grows out of its own beginnings as the particular, sometimes ironic, expression of a general truth embodied in those beginnings. In one sense, for instance, *The Canterbury Tales* represents the realisation of the general truth, contained in its opening lines, that

> Whan that Aprill with his shoures soote
> The droghte of March hath perced to the roote ...
> Thanne longen folk to goon on pilgrimages ...
> And specially from every shires ende
> Of Engelond to Caunterbury they wende
>
> (I, 1-2, 12, 15-16)

Narrative therefore operates on two levels at once, literal and symbolic or particular and general. This is as true of a religious as of any other narrative. No matter how implausible its surface detail, or how sketchy its treatment of the three coordinates of time, place and person — elements whose interaction we have argued creates the narrative — the narrative must also inhabit a literal dimension before it can be read symbolically: has to be the particular sign or effect of a general cause. Now, the Pardoner's narrative realises its own literal dimension more thoroughly, and more vividly, than any so far studied. We see the protagonists on the point of climbing over a stile. With them we hear the sound of a passing bell as a corpse goes by outside. Throughout, there is the same masterly control of pace that the Physician's tale displayed. At the same time, the narrative fails to locate these strongly realised moments relative to its own beginnings, 'in Flaundres whilom' with 'a compaignye/ Of yonge folk' who give themselves over day and night to 'riot, hasard, stywes and tavernes'. The first scene takes place in a tavern, early in the morning. We are in the company of three rioters, who seem prepared for a steady drinking session (at all events, they are raging drunk when they leave: 705). The narrative presents these rioters to us as if we already know all about them ('thise riotoures thre of whiche I telle'[34]): but we know neither who they are nor where the action is taking place. Flanders, conventionally associated with drunkenness, has become a tavern; the group of young folk, three young rioters (we learn only later of their youthfulness: cf. 759).

The narrative's deliberate dislocation of this opening moment from its own origins makes it a powerful symbolic restatement of them: its letter, that is, becomes its own symbol. One detail seems to dissolve into another as we listen.[35] To start with the rioters themselves: vividly realised in speech and action though they are, they inhabit no clearly defined space. We do not even know their names. One is 'proudeste' (716), one 'worste' (776), one 'yongeste' (804): but which is which we cannot tell. The youngest, also described as possessed by the devil (847-8), might also be the proudest; the proudest, who treats the old man in the story so discourteously, might also be the worst.[36] Only when the coalition of interest proposed by one of them near the beginning, and symbolised by their drinking together, has broken down in the face of the unexpected heap of gold coins, do the 'riotoures' realise themselves as distinct characters. Even then we see them only as the originators of plots against one another; the youngest plots to kill the other two, and they plot to kill him. That pattern apart, the narrative does not realise them as distinct and separate figures: it calls them simply 'that oon' (666, 802, 807), 'the firste' (819, 824), 'this/that oother' (807, 816, 822).[37] It presents them, in other words, as interchangeable signs of youthfulness, pride and wickedness.

The opening also realises its own dislocation for us in its offered time-scale: 'Longe erst er prime rong of any belle', the rioters are drinking in the tavern. Both literally and metaphorically their drinking dislocates the time, just as, in the sermon, drink was said to dislocate a person's consciousness of place. Like the gluttons who, according to the Parson, 'ete byforn tyme to ete' (X, 828), these three are drinking when they ought to be asleep or, if awake, working: others, a serving boy and the innkeeper, must already be up and working to maintain them in their excess.[38]

But the narrative has a far more powerful way of realising this dislocation for us. It sets up a series of images which reflect back on the primary image of youthful riot and are the chilling transformations of it. The first such image is heard rather than seen. It is the sound of a passing bell outside as a corpse goes by for burial. Ordered by one of the rioters to discover the dead man's identity, the boy has his answer ready. He has already heard that the dead man, a drinking companion of the speaker, died the previous night 'fordronke, as he sat on his benche upright' (674: no so badly drunk, one might have thought, as the supine and unconscious figure of the sermon: 556, 580). His death sets the story in motion. The rioters determine on vengeance. But the dead man also presents the rioters with a terrifying image of themselves. Admittedly, they are alive, as he is not; but in making 'sepulture' of their own wits they are realising symbolically what he embodies literally. Their dislocation of time and place in their own consciousness makes them an exact image of the dead man, and the parallel is made the stronger by their friendship with him and their recourse to the probable cause of his death, drink.[39]

The innkeeper and the serving boy, their wits not fuddled by drink, appreciate the warning note thus struck and the judgement thus threatened. The boy ascribes the death of the drinking companion to the operation of 'a privee theef men clepeth Deeth'. He and the innkeeper report how everyone 'in this contree' is being killed off (676), most notably by a recent visitation of the plague which has despatched 1000 people (679); within the past year, a great village about a mile from the tavern has lost all its inhabitants in the same way (686-6). Both speakers warn the rioters, in scaled-down versions of the Pardoner's own sermon, to reflect on their end:

> . . . er ye come in his presence
> Me thynketh that it were necessarie
> For to be war of swich an adversarie.

Beth redy to meete hym everemoore;
Thus taughte me my dame.

(680-4)

To been avysed greet wysdom it were,
Er that he dide a man a dishonour.

(690-1)

And the boy's comments have added point. His account of death invokes what the Bible calls the day of the Lord — that is, the day of Christ's Second Coming and judgement of the world, regularly described as coming like a thief in the night (e.g. I Thess. 5:2,4). The rioters pay no heed to the offered warning. In a clear expression of drunkenness and unreality one proposes a pact of brotherhood in pursuit of death, the others agree, and, like a grotesque parody of the Trinity, off they set, uttering dreadful oaths as they go.[40] The ironies of this moment are no more lost on the narrator than on the Knight, whose tale tells how a similar vow between two young cousins (I, 1129-39) proves the first casualty of romantic infatuation, and survives only in the care taken by each to arm the other before a projected battle to the death (I, 1651-2).[41]The ironies are underscored by the oaths accompanying the pact. By contrast with the mild asseverations of the boy ('pardee') and the innkeeper ('by seinte Marie'),[42] the leader of the gang — if he is that — peppers his speech with the oaths reprobated by the Pardoner in his sermon ('Goddes armes': 692; cf. 654; 'Goddes digne bones': 695; 'goddes dignitee': 701). Loyally seconded by his fellows as they set out, these oaths are literally realising the crucifixion of Christ, just like the oaths of the young folk in the narrative preamble:

And many a grisly ooth thanne han they sworn,
And Cristes blessed body al torente —
Deeth shal be deed, if that they may hym hente!

(708-10; cf. 473-4)[43]

The rioters meet not death, but another symbol of death, which they cannot read and once more have to have explained to them, this time by the symbol himself. When they meet the old man they are once more on the point of turning into symbols of themselves. Not quite half way to journey's end — the deserted village which the innkeeper had reckoned the dwelling-place of death — they are poised to climb over a stile. In that moment the narrative detaches them once more from any larger context than the moment implies, and thus leaves them suspended, poised almost literally between life and death, heaven and hell. If this moment clearly embodies a central Biblical understanding, that of pride going before a fall, it acquires the greater symbolic force because it has no clear or secure connection that I can see to any Biblical image.

The same is true of the old man who now materialises abruptly and meets the rioters with a prayer of blessing on his lips.[44] The suddenness of his appearance matches the effect of dislocation carefully produced by the description we are given of him by one of the rioters. Except for a 'pale and welked ... face' he is a shadowy figure, covered from head to toe. Not until his greeting has been returned as a curse accompanied with impertinent questions, which use the condescending singular form of the pronoun for their address, does the old man come out of the shadow, so to speak. Then he looks the speaker directly in the eye. Like the meeting of the mariner with the wedding guest in Coleridge's poem, the moment is profoundly symbolic, not least because of the importance of sight as a metaphor for religious belief. (Trevet's version of the Constance story made much of the metaphor; so too — though our analysis did not consider its development there — the Man of Law's tale.) Yet the moment is as ambiguous as it is symbolic. It features prominently in Shakespearean comedy at the point when the narrative tangles begin to unravel (I have in mind the heart-stopping moment near the end of *Twelfth Night* when Viola and Sebastian suddenly come face to face and realise the happy ending prepared for them from the beginning of the play.)[45] Yet this moment of eye contact also occurs prominently in Shakespearean tragedy at a point of greatest narrative tension, and to very different effect. (Here I have in mind the injunction of Claudius to Hamlet, in the opening court scene, to remain 'here in the cheer and comfort of our eye', which, on my reading, is a clear directive to a producer to create a moment of static eyeball-to-eyeball confrontation.) The old man is presenting something of the same challenge to the young bloods. At present, though, they are still too fuddled by drunken rage to read the sign correctly.

Nor do they understand the explanation he .offers for his advanced age. As with the answer given by the boy to the original question, the old man's words give further impetus to the quest, which his appearance seems momentarily to have displaced from the consciousness of the rioters. He reveals that 'deeth, allas! ne wol nat han [his] lyf', and that he seeks the quiet of a grave and a shroud for his bones. So reminded of their own quest for death, one of them, reckoning that the old man is death's spy ('oon of his assent') tries to frighten him into revealing death's whereabouts. Then the old man points them in the direction of the third and final emblem, which will truly become their deaths, the heap of coins. But his speech does not only advance an action, it also symbolises it. The old man is the most haunting and disturbing of the three symbols thrown up in the path of the rioters. He is poised yet more ambiguously than they between life and death: forever ageing and on the point of vanishing away (732); wishing, yet never permitted by God (726), Death (727), or Nature — if Nature is the 'mooder' whom he addresses (731) — to 'chaunge' his present state for the grave or for a return to his own youth (724, 734). He is restless, cast out, condemned to stand outside his 'moodres gate' knocking with his staff for admission.

The profundity of this emblem is well demonstrated by the conflicting elements which it contains. On the one hand, the old man quests for renewal of his own youth — according to the prophet (Isaiah 40:31), the reward promised to the faithful. In his patient submission to the divine purpose the old man then symbolises the believer, waiting for death in the hope of his own resurrection. The image of the old man leaning on his staff at the door of the grave might also express this same meaning: in similar vein, the patriarch Jacob, reckoned by Hebrews 11:21 an emblem of faith, blessed Joseph's sons as he was dying, and leaned on his staff as if bowing in prayer. The old man therefore embodies a warning to the rioters to amend their lives, akin to that earlier offered by the boy and the innkeeper. He embodies this warning literally, when he tells them that their discourteous treatment of him condemns them, and may cut short their lives (745-7),[46] and again, yet more starkly, in his parting words: 'God save yow, that boghte agayn mankynde,/ And yow amende' (766-7).

But the old man is not simply an emblem of faithfulness. He is also seeking a release from suffering, but in vain: seeking death, who flees from him. In this respect he is realising a prophecy in Apoc. 9:6, itself dependent on the cry of Job for a death that will not come (Job 3:21), which many medieval writers reckoned one of the greatest pains of the damned in hell.[47] The other side of death, that is, is not only resurrection but damnation: hell, as well as heaven. This aspect of the old man's character provides a terrible realisation of the implications of the earlier emblem of the corpse. The second rioter speaks truer than he knows when he reckons the old man the 'espye' of death, 'oon of his assent', and applies to him the phrase earlier used of death by the boy: 'thou false theef' (758-9).

The ambiguities carry over into the next episode. The old man reckons that death will be easy to find:

> turne up this croked wey,
> For in that grove I lafte hym, by my fey,
> Under a tree.
>
> (761-3)

Within two lines, to nobody's surprise, the tree has materialised into an oak in full view of the rioters (765). This landscape is as profoundly symbolic as was the place where the rioters met the old man. The 'croked wey' up which they are directed is too obvious a symbol of deviation from the right to need comment; the grove and its partnering oak, where death will be found, are more ambiguous. After all, as our earlier quotation from the *Boece* revealed (above, p. 234), the oak provided both shelter and simple food for the people living in the first age of the world, and could therefore be read as a sign of that Golden Age. It can hardly function in that way here: the Golden Age of the Pardoner's tale proves a very different affair. This emblem seems rather to depend on Old Testament narratives, which regularly present the grove, sometimes metonymically under the form of a pole or timber, as the sign of the holy place of a pagan religion. Israel's regular recourse to this sacred grove symbolises its backsliding from the true God; its return to the true faith requires the destruction of the grove. Such sacred signs were not always opposed to the true faith. Oak trees regularly mark the place where the Israelites met with one another, or with representatives of God. A prophet meets the man of God, and Gideon an angel, sitting under a terebinth tree (I Kings 13:14; Judges 6:11). So too the oak of Moreh: in Genesis 35:4, Jacob is striking camp with his family, and leaving behind all signs of pagan practice, which he does by burying the pagan idols owned by the family beneath the oak. Later Joshuah ratifies a covenant between God and Israel by means of a great stone which he erects under its branches (Josh. 24:26). Yet if these passages show Israel meeting God under the oak, destroying the idols and accepting a new covenant, another passage will show a very different meeting between God and his people. According to the prophet Ezekiel, the people have profaned the holy places with those idols which they ought to have destroyed, and God is about to visit them in anger. When that happens, their dismembered bodies will lie, with the idols they set up, under every leafy grove and spreading oak (Ezek. 6:13). Like every other sacred sign, and like the old man himself, the object under the oak turns out to point in two opposing directions: towards life, if it marks repentance and obedience; towards death, if it marks continuance in unbelief and sin.[48]

Once we find the heap of gold under the tree, we can hardly doubt the thrust of the narrative towards the latter reading. For though gold can symbolise an innocent and prelapsarian state, a literal heap of gold is likely to symbolise the Fall. According to Boethius, the Golden Age was so named partly because man had not yet mined for 'the gobbettes or the weyghtes of gold covered undir erthe and the precyous stones that wolden han be hydd' (*Bo*, II, m.5, 34-6). Until now, the narrative has only once referred to gold, when the sermon described the 'paire of dees of gold' sent as a mark of scorn to a king addicted to gambling; but the conspicuous consumption of the glutton and the drunkard does not pay for itself. That consumption is literally or metaphorically interchangeable with gold. In liquid form, gold can be taken internally as a medicine (so in the portrait of the Physician in the General Prologue, where the ironies depend, in the first instance, on a literal reading of the phrase 'gold in phisik is a cordial'). Metaphorically, gold can be exchanged for things that 'go thurgh the golet': hence characters in Jonsonian comedy regularly part with money with the injunction 'drink [or eat] this'.[49] The final irony of this complex symbol is once again reserved for, and realised among, the damned, who receive the literal satisfaction of their spiritual appetites over and over; in one version of the pains of hell, the avaricious receive the gold they so greatly coveted as a molten liquid poured down their throats.

As usual, the rioters see none of the complex meanings attaching to the symbol. Momentarily deflected from the object of their quest by their meeting with the old man, they now lose sight of it completely (772). For the moment, action gives way to contemplation. In an echo of the opening moment of the story, when they were 'set hem ... for to drynke', they settle down about the 'precious hoord'. The gold has a marvellously sobering effect on them and on the narrative. The first to speak makes plain that drink has not dulled *his* wits: 'my wit is greet, though that I bourde and pleye' (778). Tacitly he is inviting his fellows to see the whole action till now — drinking, swearing, gambling (cf. 751) — as 'bourde and pleye'; a passing, or wasting, of time till the main chance should appear. Our wild young men turn out, as so often, to have the instincts of city bankers. As a practical sign of this change, oaths disappear from their language from now on. All but one of their previous speeches had included oaths or cursing, on average once every three or four lines; now, except for a single oath, crafted out of earlier material ('Goddes precious dignitee': 782; cf. 651, 701), the tone is sober and the speaker concerned to calculate possible courses of action. He does not need to question the meaning of the sign: it is a treasure given by Fortune (779) as a mark of 'fair ... grace' (783); it has become their property (786); if they can get it safe under lock and key, it will confer 'heigh felicitee' upon them (787). They can spend it 'in myrthe and joliftee .../ lightly as it comth' (780-81), live 'under the trone/ Of God ... murye' (842-3), and use it for gambling and to satisfy all their other wants (833-4). Calculation enters in, though, with the thought that others will want to explain this sudden change in their economic status very differently, as a result of theft. They will then find what they have now stopped looking for, death, since they will be accused of being, what they called the old man and the boy called death, a thief:

> Men wolde seyn that we were theves stronge,
> And for oure owene tresor doon us honge.
>
> (789-90)

The palpable injustice of such an outcome leads the speaker to propose delaying the moving of the gold until nightfall. In the interim, let one of them — the one who draws the short straw in the 'cut' — go to town for provisions to keep them going until then; meanwhile, the others will 'kepen subtilly/ This tresor wel'. At night they will carry the treasure to the place they all reckon safest 'by oon assent'.

This calculation of probability is, of course, a judgement on them. Their labour in carrying the gold home, for instance, is ironically opposed to the labour undertaken by others on their behalf in exchange for it (520, 874). Fortune, grace, 'heigh felicitee', 'the trone of God': the terms consistently operate an alternative frame of reference of which the rioters are completely unaware, and provide a clear judgement on their dislocation of spiritual reality.

The next step is the breaking of the bond which until now has constituted the only positive, admittedly an ambiguous one, which we might oppose to the rioters' commitment to unreflecting excess. As soon as the brotherhood is physically broken, with the departure of the youngest to town for provisions, it begins to fall apart spiritually. One of the two left behind proposes to his fellow to cut the youngest out of his share, so as to do a 'freendes torn' to his fellow. He invokes the compact of sworn brotherhood to bind the two of them together. More significantly, as when Appius concerts his plot with Claudius in the Physician's tale (142-4), he invokes secrecy (819, 823). So far as they know, secrecy enters the story with their own calculation ('wisely ... slyly': 792; 'subtilly': 798). They will not be like the drunk who 'kan no conseil kepe' (561). We know more; all along, God has been acting in secret (675) through the ambiguous signs presented to the rioters. Once again, their calculations imply more than they realise. The plan to remove the youngest centres on the deliberate confusion of 'ernest' and 'game' which has characterised their behaviour, if not their consciousness, throughout. When the youngest has returned and 'is set' with them once more (so that this moment will resume earlier moments when they sat down, first drinking, then gazing at their gold), let the other get up as if wanting a playful fight (827-9): in the ensuing fight let him stab the youngest, and the speaker will do the same. Then, indeed, there will be time for games (834).

This plan reckons without the capacity of the youngest to act on his own behalf. Like Appius in the Physician's tale, he cannot get the image of 'the beautee of thise floryns' out of his heart (838-9; cf. 126-7); like Appius, too, he falls immediate prey to the suggestions of the devil (844; cf. 130), and acts in haste to achieve his purposes (851, 869; cf. 158).[50] He buys poison from a druggist and pours it into two of three large bottles, which he fills with wine, intending the poisoned drink for his fellows and the other for himself. The poisoned wine points possibly to Deut. 32:33, where

Moses describes the enemies of God as drinking poisoned wine; possibly, in ironic counterpoint, to the new wine of the Gospel (Matt. 9:17); it also represents, almost certainly, a terrible parody of the true wine administered in the Eucharist.[51] The 'fair grace' which the gold seemed to promise (783) has undergone its final ironic metamorphosis, and become the 'sory grace' (876) which the rioters returned, in answer, to the old man's greeting (717).[52]

The narrative has now exhausted its possibilities, and dispatches the villains summarily. The youngest returns and is murdered; his fellows sit down and pass the poisoned bottle from hand to hand as a gesture of fellowship and merrymaking preliminary to the burial of the body. This moment precisely repeats the opening moment of the story, when the rioters were sitting drinking in the vicinity of the corpse of another friend. Unexpectedly, we find ourselves returned full circle. The poisoned wine realises literally, decisively and finally the implications of that opening moment, and of every emblematic moment in the narrative till then. Though not greatly developed, the ironies of this final moment are many. Most notably, the narrative allows chance, whom the rioters had credited with their undeserved windfall, to determine the deserved outcome: 'it happed hym, par cas/ To take the botel ther the poyson was' (885-6). Substance into accident, indeed.

The narrator now draws his own predictable conclusions. He inveighs against the sins so far presented in the same exaggerated tones used at the beginning of his sermon. Here too, then, the whole work seems to return upon itself. A formal benediction follows, whose terms are borrowed from the speeches of the boy and the old man:

> Now, goode men, God foryeve yow youre trespas,
> And ware yow fro the synne of avarice.
>
> (904-5; cf. 682, 767)

and we are, it seems, at an end. Throughout, the pilgrim audience have been powerfully, if indirectly, implicated in the tale.[53] After all, in their own story of the pilgrimage they have witnessed drunkenness (Miller and Cook), heard oaths uttered heedlessly (Host, Miller, Cook) and taken part themselves in a game of chance (the 'cut' to see who will start the storytelling) spurred on by the desire for an unexpected windfall (the prize for the best story). At least two of them have a keen and informed interest in the production of exotic food (Franklin and Cook in the General Prologue). And there are minor links, too, between their own story and that of the three rioters. The old man put down by the younger closely parallels the Parson put down by the Host and Shipman in the cancelled epilogue to the Man of Law's tale, and possibly that moment when the Pardoner ironically opposes his youth to the greater experience and age of the Wife of Bath. The old man's retort against the youthful rioters echoes the Franklin's comment to the Squire after the latter's tale (noted above, p. 18). Above all, the unstable coalition of carnal interest which leads, in this tale, to the violent death of all parties, has its echo not just in the links created between the Host and the Pardoner at the start of the tale, but in the instability and ambiguity of all the relationships generated by the pilgrimage. Certainly, we shall not see murder on the pilgrimage: though we see characters looking murderously at opponents (the Friar and the Summoner at one another; the Cook at the Manciple), the violence is entirely verbal. But we see everything else, in one form or another, that the Pardoner inveighs against.[54]

The audience so addressed are being directed to read the tale in its entirety as the moral and honest offering requested by the *gentils*: to see the dynamic of its parts, even when they dissolve disconcertingly into one another like a dream, as a call to repentance. They will hardly find much evidence of the 'myrthe or japes' requested by the Host. Elsewhere in *The Canterbury Tales* the term 'jape' means an action morally dubious (as at V, 1271), with an unexpected and ironic outcome (I, 4338; VII, 439) whose full effects the protagonist could have avoided had he been 'wel ... avysed' (I, 4333): we may therefore call a story constructed about such an action, by extension, a 'jape' (I, 4343; cf. 4207).[55] In these terms, the Pardoner's tale can certainly be classed as a jape. The strain of such a reading becomes clear, however, when we compare the tale with the real 'japes' of *The Canterbury Tales*, the fabliaux. The latter furnish ample matter for the mirth which the Host equated with japes. In the Pardoner's tale, by contrast, the comedy is at best incidental, and invariably grim.[56] (In addition, the treatment of time and place is subtly different.)

But the Pardoner has another way of making his tale a jape. He lets himself be seen in the act of performance, and invites his hearers to approach the tale as an exemplum not just of its subject-matter but of its own processes, or techniques of performance. This study has referred more than once to the tension between subject-matter and process in a religious narrative. Only the translated works do not generate such tensions on their own account — and they faithfully reproduce any such tensions in their originals. All the other tales here studied manifest this tension in greater or lesser degree in their own performance. At the same time — if we except the Prioress's tale — they also take pains to conceal it; their performances allow us to infer, but never to prove, their narrators' motives. The Pardoner makes this tension a crucial element of his work. He does this, in the first instance, by a prologue very different from those so far considered, and different even from those with which it has close formal affinities (those of the Wife of Bath and the Canon's Yeoman).[57] The prologue to a religious tale generally introduces the audience to the theme and/or subject-matter of the tale, such that the tale itself becomes a simple and unequivocal exemplification of the prologue. By contrast, the Pardoner's prologue focuses primarily not on subject-matter but on process, concerning which, if we except a few obvious instances of authorial direction, the tale is almost completely silent. The Pardoner's prologue relativises his tale both implicitly, by creating a context of common practice against which to view it, and explicitly, by offering it as an example of that common practice (461). Yet the prologue has closest links with the portrait of the Pardoner in that secular entertainment, the cast-list in the General Prologue: it provides few clear links with the narrative detail or methods of the tale itself. Its most important link with the latter comes with the repeated declaration that the invariable theme of the sermons preached is 'Radix malorum est cupiditas' (333-4, 425-6).

This observation throws a vivid new light over the tale. Read without reference to the prologue, the tale simply presents a series of arresting images of death. Like the Pardoner's sermon, it speaks of the interchangeability of one sin with another, and of the sinner with that ultimate dislocation of his own consciousness, his death ('he that haunteth swiche delices/ Is deed, whil that he lyveth in tho vices'). Read in the light of the stated theme, the narrative turns upon the heap of gold coins, and the sins realised in its opening episode — drunkenness, swearing, disrespect to an elder — merely prepare for the real sins of greed and murder. (This reading was also implied in the sermon, which, as earlier noted, considered not only the interchangeability of the sins but also their relative rankings.) The prologue also explains the use, in the body of the tale, of

> ensamples many oon
> Of olde stories longe tyme agoon.
> For lewed peple loven tales olde;
> Swiche thynges kan they wel reporte and holde.
>
> (435-8)[58]

This connects with material in the tale proper, just such an 'ensample'. In particular, the sermon contains 'ensamples many oon', and the Pardoner's account of swearing is taken, if not from 'tales olde', from 'olde bookes' (630). Additionally, the prologue uses the same device as the sermon to move the audience on: 'of this mateere it oghte ynogh suffise' (434; cf. 588). At the same time, the reference to the 'lewed peple', in the previous quotation, decisively distinguishes the prologue from the tale. For though, we have said, the tale can be read as a jape — and, by implication, those who so read it will be 'lewed' — it does not readily admit of such a reading. Quite apart from the sermon's active engagement of the interests of the *gentils*, the whole work operates a learned language and symbolism remote from the interests or capacities of a 'lewed' audience. In sharp contrast, the prologue describes the Pardoner preaching in a very different way to a very different audience.

To begin with, he is preaching in a church. The prologue certainly shows him in a secular environment when not on duty ('I wol drynke licour of the vyne/ And have a joly wenche in every toun': 452-3), and the prologue and tale are delivered in just such a setting (321); but the report of his practice in the prologue restricts its exercise to a religious setting. He stands in the pulpit, and the 'lewed peple' sit to hear him, an action ironically echoed in the tale — and possibly, if scholars are right in tracing 11.467-9 to a Bible verse quoted in the *De Miseria*, in the sermon as well. Like Chauntecleer in the Nun's Priest's tale, or a dove on a barn roof (397),[59] he stretches his neck out and prepares to perform (unlike Chauntecleer, he looks 'est and west' over his audience, his eyes wide open for the main chance). Hands and voice work together (398); he knows all the arts of performance, including (330-1) voice projection; his preaching voice is clearly distinguished from his normal speaking voice, 'as smal as hath a goot' (I, 688).

But it is the content, rather than the style or context, of the performance that distinguishes it most sharply from the tale itself. The preacher delivers the tale without other visual and verbal aids than its own immediate context generates. By contrast, his performance in the prologue grows directly out of an impressive array of visual and verbal aids. First, there are the bulls which authorise his practice (336-43) and silence opposition (339). Then come a few words in Latin 'to saffron with my predicacioun/ And for to stire hem to devocioun' (345-6). And then there are the relics, or what the 'lewed' will reckon such. The dismissive reference to the learned language as mere tricks of the trade — a little local colour, no more — contrasts strikingly with the mastery of that language revealed by the translation of Bible texts in the sermon proper — a point already made in passing (p. 134) — and warns us that the 'sermoning' of the prologue may be a much simpler business than the preaching in the tale itself.[60] In fact, the sermon in the prologue is a performance expertly geared to the needs and capacities of a rustic audience, and focused exclusively on the magical properties of the Pardoner's relics. They have diseased animals? They would like to 'multiplye' their beasts or their crops? The women have suspicious husbands? Here is a bone from the sheep of a holy Jew to cure all that. Wash the bone in water, and give the water to the afflicted animal to drink; use it to make the husband's broth, or let the householder who desires increase of his goods drink a draught of this water every week, fasting at the same time, and the desired effect will be produced. Additionally, 'heere is a miteyn eek, that ye may se'. Put the glove on, and the grain you sow will multiply. The graces are for sale, in exchange for 'pens, or elles grotes'.

This sermon is tailored so resolutely to the needs of its peasant audience that it makes only oblique and ironic connections with the tale itself. Rather in the way that Jonson's *The Alchemist* presents the minor figures of Dapper and Drugger in the first Act, and delays until Acts II and III the appearance of the big spenders, Mammon and the Puritans, so as to present its gulls in an ascending order of significance, the preaching in the prologue represents a scaled-down version of the appetites inveighed against in the tale. It is silent about the vices of gambling and swearing. As for gluttony, it substitutes for the exotic food of the sermon a 'potage' made by the wife for her husband. The labours involved in turning 'substaunce into accident' in both sermon and tale have an equiva-

lent here only in the absurdly comic dipping of a bone in well
water to make a magic potion. In fact, the prologue sermon
considers only one vice in any detail, adultery (370-1, 381-2), and
then chiefly as a device to neutralise incipient opposition and
encourage the congregation to come forward in a body with their
offerings. By contrast, sexual sin appears in the tale as the
outgrowth of drunkenness, exemplified, in the commentary, by the
story of Lot.[61] Moreover, the manner of the Pardoner's address to
the rustic audience realises it as a distinct group of people very
different from the pilgrim audience being elsewhere addressed. He
addresses both men and women in the rustic audience; for the men
he uses a term of address hardly used elsewhere in *The Canterbury
Tales*, that is, 'goode men' (352, 377, 904; cf. 361). By contrast,
he addresses the pilgrim audience without differentiation as
'lordynges' and 'sires' (329, 454, 573, 660, 915, 919), terms
regularly used by other pilgrim narrators.[62]

So limited and different an address to so particular and different
an audience from that of the Canterbury pilgrims invites the latter
to adopt a stance to the prologue very different from that proper to
a religious tale, which, this study has argued, seeks to break down
the barriers between audience and subject-matter. The prologue
contains blatant hints of the difference between the performer's
calculation, and the rustic audience's credulous acceptance of,
theatrical effects ('to saffron with my predicacioun .../ Relikes
been they, as wenen they echoon'). But just in case any members
of the pilgrim audience are pious, or naive, enough to read this
sermon straight, as the 'moral thyng' asked for by the *gentils*, the
Pardoner underscores its real meaning with direct comment about
his own motives and practice:

> ... many a predicacioun
> Comth ofte tyme of yvel entencioun;
> Som for plesance of folk and flaterye,
> To been avaunced by ypocrisye,
> And som for veyne glorie, and som for hate.
>
> (407-11)

Again (this time he is telling how he isolates opposition by picking
the offending party off in the course of the sermon):

Thus spitte I out my venym under hewe
Of hoolynesse, to semen hooly and trewe.

(421-2)

And again:

For myn entente is nat but for to wynne,
And nothyng for correccioun of synne ...
I preche of no thyng but for coveityse ...
Thus kan I preche agayn that same vice
Which that I use, and that is avarice ...
I preche nothyng but for coveitise.

(403-4, 424, 427-8, 433)

Since he started business, he has made 100 marks a year with this 'gaude', one of the 'hundred false japes' he has in stock with which to con the peasants. His account of his own practices is echoed in Chaucer's portrait of him in the cast-list, written, according to the fictional scheme of things, after the Pardoner's delivery of his own prologue and tale; the many echoes of the prologue in the portrait are most sharply focused in the words 'with feyned flaterye and japes/ He made the person and the peple his apes' (I, 705-6). In describing his preaching to the peasants as 'japes', the Pardoner meets the Host's demands for 'japes' more clearly than he will do in his tale. He can the more easily invite this reading of his prologue because the peasantry is scarcely represented among the pilgrim audience; because other members of that audience as presented in the cast-list, notably the Friar and the Reeve, treat the peasants in much the same way; and because almost all of them share the Pardoner's basic assumption that 'al is for to selle' or to consume conspicuously ('for no cost wolde he spare'). No articulate or powerful opposition is therefore likely to be voiced by any of the pilgrims. It seems, then, that we are to read the prologue as the 'jape' requested, and the tale as the 'moral thyng'. Ironically enough, this double ration of stories makes common cause with the Monk. Like the Pardoner, the Monk reckoned to have 100 stories to draw on (VI, 394; VII, 1972); unlike the Pardoner, he could not realise his promise to tell two tales of very different calibre.[63]

This tidy division of the two 'tales' — one reinforced, I have argued, by the clear signs of disjunction between them — emphasises the fundamental religious cast of the whole enterprise, in contrast, say, to the pattern favoured by classical Greek theatre, which follows 'ernestful mateere' with 'jape'.[64] Or rather, it would, were it not being systematically undermined on all sides. The rustic audience is once addressed, like the pilgrim audience, as 'sires' (366).[65] More importantly, the Pardoner's self-exposure in the prologue ironically endorses the truths which his practice flouts, and, by the same token, criticises the worldliness of his hearers.[66] It is with good reason that he expresses his distaste for the peasant's life of honest toil in terms taken from the rule books of monastic and mendicant orders.[67] Both groups of religious profess to 'lyve in poverte wilfully' and 'the apostles countrefete' (441, 447). The monk achieves this identification with the example of his founders by a life of manual labour; the friar, by contrast, literally imitates what St Francis saw as the poverty of Christ, and goes out to 'beggen ydelly' (446): dependent on charitable offerings for his very life. The Pardoner's rejection of both courses of action implicates the Monk, who refuses the regime of manual labour in favour of hunting, and the Friar, who, as 'the beste beggere in his hous', is adept at screwing the last farthing out of the peasants. In any case, good results may come from actions undertaken for the worst of motives:

> But though myself be gilty in that synne,
> Yet kan I maken oother folk to twynne
> From avarice, and soore to repente ...
> For though myself be a ful vicious man,
> A moral tale yet I yow telle kan.

> (429-31, 459-60)

That is, the Pardoner himself becomes a sign pointing both ways, like the old man in the tale. To read the prologue simply as a 'jape' is to find the laughter returning on one's own head.

The formal ending of the tale works in the same way to undermine any neat categorisation of prologue and tale as, respectively, 'jape' and 'moral thyng'. Having reached his own 'journey's end' with a blessing on the bystanders and a warning against avarice, the Pardoner suddenly returns to the frame of the prologue, as if the whole tale had been delivered simply as an exemplum of the processes described in the prologue: as a typical sermon addressed to a rustic audience. Let the audience now come forward, he says, with 'nobles or sterlynges/ Or elles silver broches, spoones, rynges', and bow their heads under his holy bull. Let the women offer their wool (910), part of the cash in kind which he had earlier declared himself ready to accept from 'the povereste wydwe in a village' (450). As they do so, he records their names in his roll and guarantees them absolution. This abrupt change of gear, openly acknowledged by the concluding phrase, 'and lo, sires, thus I preche', presents the pilgrim audience with a clear challenge, both intellectual and moral. Are they, in fact, to read the story not as the moral thing which its telling seemed to warrant, but simply as a vastly extended and elaborate joke?

The challenge to the pilgrims' understanding can be simply put.[68] In so carefully framing the narrative, the Pardoner denies authority to any single reading of it, and invites the difficult conclusion that storytelling is, at one and the same time, utterly frivolous and deadly earnest: a wasting, and a saving, of time. (A similarly complex literary understanding is implied, as we saw, in the prologue to the *Melibee*, delivered by another professional storyteller). The intellectuals may be able to hold these two views in a state of tension with one another. But the long shadows cast by these opposed positions over the pages of formalist and moralist critics, the heirs, did they but know it, of Chaucer's pilgrims, remind us — if we should need reminding — that the circle does not square easily.

In any case, a religious narrative cannot rest content with the production of an aesthetic effect, no matter how complex. It must always move its audience to an act of faith. And that the Pardoner now proposes to do. If we except the Parson, whose narration explicitly seeks such an outcome (and maybe secures it, if we regard the *retracciouns* as the response of the pilgrim narrator to the Parson's tale), only the Pardoner throws down so explicit a challenge to the pilgrim audience to turn their laughter into a prayer: to internalise that corporate devotion which the prologue invited them to mock, but the tale has shown to be no laughing matter.[69] First, therefore, the Pardoner offers not the trash he has just reportedly sold to the peasants, but the pardon of Christ himself:

And Jhesu Crist, that is oure soules leche,
So graunte yow his pardoun to receyve,
For that is best; I wol yow nat deceyve.

(916-18)

And then, with yet another change of gear, he offers the 'relikes and pardoun' in his bag! How can so gross a deception hope either to amuse anyone, or take anyone in? After all, by presenting them exclusively as stage props, the Pardoner has invited the audience to reject them as worthless. The presenter of the cast-list, for one, is unable to resist the tempting offer, and opposes to the Pardoner's public view of the relics ('he seyde') a coolly critical account of what he himself saw:

> For in his male he hadde a pilwe-beer
> Which that he seyde was Oure Lady veyl;
> He seyde he hadde a gobet of the seyl
> That Seint Peter hadde, whan that he wente
> Upon the see, til Jhesu Crist hym hente.
> He hadde a croys of latoun ful of stones,
> And in a glas he hadde pigges bones.

(I, 694-700)

So to conclude with the 'reportour' is to reckon without the ingenuity of the preacher, who angles his appeal to the actual situation of the pilgrim audience as carefully as he did his appeals to the situation of the rustics in the prologue. Just as the various emblems in the tale have showed the pilgrims indirectly to themselves — poised, like the rioters, mid-way on their journey to an uncertain end — so now, for a moment, the Pardoner lets them see themselves clearly, in the physical context of their pilgrimage. By and large, they have avoided looking at themselves as pilgrims during their time together. Taking their cue from the Host's original proposal, they have cut themselves off from the real world through which they are travelling, and coccooned themselves in their own interests, and passions, concretely realised in an act of communal storytelling, rather as the rioters have done by drink. Hence they rarely admit to any sense of being on a literal journey, except near the end of their stories, when they can report that they are nearing a town as night is falling — and, by implication, that supper and security are not far off. Their refusal to face their own physical circumstances gives the Pardoner his cue. For a start, he is almost the only narrator who concretely realises the passage of time in his narration: his prologue is coextensive with the drinking of a 'draughte of corny ale' (322, 328, 456: as in the tale itself, this juxtaposition of drink and storytelling makes the two activities mirror images for one another). And at the end, he disarms possible rejection of his relics by reflecting to the pilgrims their own unspoken fears about the physical circumstances of their journey. Anything could happen to them as they ride along together in the open country; one or two might even fall off their horses and break their necks! What good fortune therefore that he is actually among their number, 'a suffisant pardoneer/T'assoille' them. This coolly calculated sales pitch is ironically realised when the Cook does fall off his horse, though fortunately he suffers no worse after-effects from the fall than further recourse to the drink that caused it (IX, 46-9, 87-93). If they are to claim the offered 'seuretee', though, the pilgrims will have to part with more than money. They will have to settle, after all, for a simple moral reading of what they have heard. The last laugh will be yet more profoundly on them. The free spirits will turn out, after all, to be children afraid of the dark.

In the event, they are spared the choice, because the Pardoner turns to the Host, as the person 'moost enveluped in synne', and invites him to be the first to kiss the relics for the amazingly low price of a groat. This attempt may reflect the Pardoner's stated practice of isolating opposition so as more easily to secure a general acceptance of his trickery. Clearly, the Host is so central a figure that, if the Pardoner can win him over, the others should follow his lead. Possibly, too, the Pardoner is looking to get his own back on the man who singled him out at the start in such condescendingly familiar terms.[70] Such behaviour would be in character with his self-revelation in the prologue:

> For whan I dar noon oother weyes debate,
> Thanne wol I stynge hym with my tonge smerte
> In prechyng, so that he shal nat asterte
> To been defamed falsly, if that he
> Hath trespased to my bretheren or to me ...
> Thus quyte I folk that doon us displesances.
>
> (412-16, 420)

(Admittedly, the tone of his address to the Host is rather different, but the effect is much the same.) Whatever his reasons for singling out the Host, the attempt miscarries. Harry Bailly has as keen a nose as the preacher for counterfeit coin, and rejects the offered 'honest thyng', retorting with a jape of his own against the speaker, which provides, if the pun can be excused, a cutting *argumentum ad hominem* that reduces the Pardoner to aloof (966) and angry silence (956-7, 963). The Host follows this up by metaphorically turning his back on him ('I wol no lenger pleye/ With thee, ne with noon oother angry man'); and the Knight, taking his cue from the general laughter that the whole moment has provoked, engineers a reconciliation between the two so that the pilgrims may once more 'laughe and pleye'. The two kiss, 'and ryden forth hir weye'.

Up to a point, the Host is behaving completely in character here. In very similar vein, he dispels the sober tone generated by the Prioress's tale with a jape at the expense of another pilgrim: one whose peculiarities of physical appearance similarly enable others to treat him as an outsider (VII, 691 ff.). At this point, as in the end-link to the Prioress's tale, he is seeking to restore a status quo (in the Knight's words, 'as we diden, lat us laughe and pleye') seriously threatened by the preacher's appeal to the fears and scruples of the audience. The reaction of the bystanders to the Host's words suggests a similar reading of the episode. Spared the proposed test, they can read the Pardoner's challenge, and the Host's rejoinder, simply as a jape; theirs, as I read it, is simply the laughter of released tension (961). But the status quo cannot be so easily restored. Aloof and angrily silent, in an echo of the Reeve's physical separation from the Miller at the start of the journey (I, 622) and an anticipation of the Cook's angry and fuddled silence in response to the Manciple near the end (IX, 46-8), the Pardoner refuses the offered return to the game structure. He thus pointedly dramatises the limits of laughter and merrymaking as expressions and instruments of community.

Ironically, the status quo is undermined more thoroughly from within, in the very terms of the Host's speech to the Pardoner. That speech rejects the offered visual emblem as a fiction (the 'olde breech' offered as 'a relyk of a seint'). It offers to replace it with a fiction of its own devising (the Pardoner's elusive cullions, to be cut off and 'shryned in an hogges toord'). In between, it invokes a visual emblem whose truth as a relic there is no denying ('the croys which that seint Eleyne fond'). Like the Pardoner's drinking, the relic is a mirror-image for the taletelling with which the Pardoner normally combines it in a single package.[71]. The Host's comments can therefore bear as well on the offered verbal as on the visual emblem. When he opposes his own fiction to the Pardoner's, the Host is therefore arguing, by implication, that fiction is defensible only as it approximates to the truth: the necessary condition of any religious narrative. But the Pardoner's fiction is a truthful expression not primarily of itself but rather of the perversity of the narrator (almost every tale here studied has realised the tension between these two positions in greater or lesser degree). Such fiction must therefore be opposed, in the name of that truth which it embodies so obliquely. Yet if the Host's irony deliberately exposes the Pardoner's fiction as a fiction, he can prove the superior status of his own fiction only by sheltering under that very truth which he claims to find so poorly realised in the Pardoner's narrative. Like the Physician, that is, he authorises his own 'fiction' by explicit religious reference (ironically, since the Pardoner reprobated swearing, he does so in the form of an oath).

The Host seems not to appreciate the larger ironies of his position. Within the space of a few lines, he is reacting to the Pardoner's angry silence rather as he has earlier reacted to his own intense involvement with the Physician's tale: or, to take a closer parallel, as the Cook has reacted to being teased by the Host about the quality of his food and the cleanliness of his shop (I, 4346-52). As if fearing that his teasing words might backfire or the whole joke get out of hand, the Host reminds the Cook that 'a man may sey ful sooth in game and pley'. The Cook tartly caps this proverb with another — 'sooth pley, quaad pley', that is, truth is bad play (4357) — and thus reminds us of the limits of game-playing as an instrument for the expression of truth.[72] Something like that seems to be happening in the present moment. Confronted by the real anger of the Pardoner, the Host restates his belief in 'pleye' as the condition of the pilgrimage: which, since pilgrimage is co-extensive with storytelling, implies a view of storytelling at odds with that just advanced. That is, the Host retreats from the large questions of truth and fiction, into which he has stumbled, into the simpler world he knew at the outset. In the deepest sense of all, the last laugh in the narrative is at his expense.[73]

The Host's withdrawal parallels that of the pilgrimage narrative itself. Having suggested the possibility of a reading which might incorporate both truth and fiction, 'pleye' and 'moral thyng', the narrative now retreats from its own implications and realises only its plot. Neither repentance nor judgement awaits the two combatants. The peace is engineered not by the moral but only by the social superior of the group, and he has waited for the group's laughter to give him his cue to proceed.[74] Like the symbols about which the Pardoner constructed his tale, the kiss, the sign of the patched peace which guarantees the forward movement of the pilgrimage, is profoundly ambiguous. It points, on the one hand, to the kiss of peace in the Mass; on the other, to the kiss of the betrayer. There is, however, an important difference between the narrative's use of this symbol and the Pardoner's use of symbols in his tale. The reader may be uncertain of the precise meaning (*in bono* or *in malo*) attaching to a particular symbol in the tale (the old man is the prime instance of this difficulty). He can have no doubts about the overall direction and meaning of the story; the vividly realised details express a single and coherent religious position.[75] By contrast, the vividly realised detail of the two combatants kissing and riding off together goes nowhere. Though it permits, it does not compel, a simple religious reading of itself:[76] the narrator is unwilling or unable to authorise such a reading of it. Consequently, the episode concludes with the pilgrims as emblems not of some superior religious position, but just of themselves.[77] They ride off: but to what end? Salvation, or damnation? The narrative does not tell us.

This reticence of Chaucer's narrative of the Canterbury pilgrimage — a feature shared, as earlier noted, by one of the narratives he tells in his own person — reflects an awareness that religion is both more and less than the particular forms it chooses for its own expression. This awareness is realised whenever the stories move towards a rounded presentation of their religious symbols (like the Sultan in the Man of Law's tale, or the Jewish ghetto in the Prioress's). It also figures prominently in the final story of our study: that of the Nun's Priest.

Notes

1. On Pard–Phys links, see e.g. Cooper pp. 154-6; Hanson, *ChR*, 7, 139; Barney, Faulkner, p. 84 (followed by Burlin, p. 241); and J. Adelman, 'That we may leere som wit', Faulkner, p. 97.

2. Of course, the envoy to ClT acknowledges Prol WBT; Prol SecNT may also be read in relation to the pilgrimage narrative: see above p. 101, and ch. 4, n. 34.

3. This is not to say that the opposition of religious to partnering secular narrative will not yield rich returns by way of comparison on a deeper level: notably, comparisons of SecNT and CYT, ClT and MerchT.

4. Sometimes also read as a criticism of the Monk pilgrim (so A.B. Friedman, 'PrT and Chaucer's anti-semitism', *ChR*, 9, (1974-75), 120.

5. A traditional figure: see Owst (1961), pp. 93, 438.

6. Another traditional moment: see Owst (1961), pp. 415, n.1, 418-20; Woolf (1968), Appendix G; Elliott, pp. 270-1.

7. Links of PardT and ParsT are often noted: Adelman, Faulkner, p. 104; Payne, Murphy, p. 275.

8. For useful comment on CkT, to which the present passage is indebted, see Kolve, ch. 6.

9. The word 'sermon' should not be read too literally here. For criticism of those who do so read it, see Wenzel, *SP*, 73, 139-40 and n. 4.

10. Barney, Faulkner, p. 88, followed by Burlin, p. 241, describes this as a 'bipartite structure ... "auctoritee" followed by "plot machine"', and writes of 'talky beginnings and swift, eventful endings' of tales using this pattern. On this general point, see also Payne, p. 162; David, p. 194; and Justman, *ChR*, 14, 206, 212 and n. 21. Lists of such tales include only two that I find strictly comparable: the twin narrations of the Wife of Bath (so Barney). Other offered parallels either locate their 'talky beginnings' *within* the fiction, not in the act of narration (MillT, SummT of Barney, *Mel* of Justman) or provide a running commentary all through the narrative (MancT, MerchT of Burlin) or reserve their commentary for the end of the narrative (NPT).

11. Barney and Adelman, Faulkner, pp. 91, 100-1 (the latter with a super-subtle pun on Host—host); Stevens—Falvey, *ChR*, 17, 142-58, arguing the primary such metamorphosis as that of the narrator into his tale: to this common view of the tale I shall be adding the metamorphosis of the audience into the tale.

12. On the influence of this text on PardT, see R.A. Pratt, 'Chaucer and the hand that fed him', *Spec.*, 41 (1966), 631-2; for comment on the *Communiloquium*, Minnis, *Beiträge*, 101, 402-3.

13. On this point see Lewis, p. 9 and n. 50. For comment on the *Adversus Jovinianum*, see Brennan, *SP*, 70, 243-51.

14. For parallels, see Mann, pp. 19 and n. 10, 154 and n. 29, 169.

15. See also Stevens—Falvey, *ChR*, 17, 154 and n. 16; and Owst (1961), p. 446 and n.1.

16. For comment on the background to this idea, see A.O. Lovejoy and G. Boas, *Primitivism and Related Ideas in Antiquity* (Baltimore, 1935), noted, with comment on Chaucer's *Form Age*, by Howard, pp. 126-8. For parallels in sermons, see Owst (1961), p. 442.

17. An ironic echo of the marriage at Cana (John 2:10)? And note further the ironic anticipation of the story itself (11. 868-78).

18. *Adversus Jovinianum*, II, 15; *PL* 33, 305-6.

19. Cf. David (p. 197): 'free and often incongruous association in this sermon ... jumbles together realism and scriptural allusion, the wines of Fishstreet and the blood of Christ.'

20. Also noted Muscatine, Brewer (1966), p. 94, n.2.

21. This connection is sometimes made in sermon literature: see Owst (1961), p. 418.

22. This material generates clear parallels with ParsT, in particular, the subdivision of sins, and detailed comments on swearing; for the latter, see X, 591-5.

23. Crosby, *Spec.*, 13, 413-32; Brewer (1966), pp. 1-38 or Brewer (1984), pp. 8-36; J. Burrow, *Ricardian Poetry* (London, 1971), pp. 47, 52.

24. Admittedly, I am talking of a tendency rather than of a fully realised distinction. Romances sometimes use the sg. form of address to secure a rhyme (so, for example, Rickert, *Emaré*, 11. 46, 96, 144) or even in the body of a line; so a small, but significant, number of times, in *Kyng Alisaunder*, ed. G.V. Smithers, EETS OS 227 (London, 1952). Nevertheless, most romances either avoid

completely address to the audience in the body of the narrative, or restrict themselves to the pl. form of address, normally to mark a new section of the narration.

25. See, in particular, the sermons in Ross (e.g. Ross 12/20–13/6), particularly interesting in this respect because their composite nature (Ross, pp. xix-xxvi) permits us to contrast various speakers/writers in respect of favoured forms of address. For an early example of the practice, see *Selections from EME 1130-1250*, ed. J. Hall, 2 vols (Oxford, 1920), I, 79/7-80/63. Similar practices obtain in contemporary penitential manuals, e.g. *Jacob's Well*, ed. Brandeis, 1/6-12; *Handlyng Synne*, ed. Furnivall, 11. 1017, 1287; *Speculum Christiani*, ed. G. Holmstedt, EETS OS 182 (London 1933), 12/5, 122/13; *Memoriale credentium*, MS BL Harley 2398 f. 61ᵇ (source, Owst (1926), p. 285). I owe my understanding that such practices also obtain in 'utilitarian, non-religious handbooks' to the kindness of Dr Helen Spencer. Though such handbooks require an enlargement of my original terms of reference, their very utilitarian bias brings them much closer to sermons and penitential manuals than to the romances earlier noted: all of them are concerned with producing particular *effects* in, and on the behaviour of, individual hearers.

26. A better reading of the sg. form of address might discern in it the intimate, or authoritative, tones of a confessor to a penitent, or a teacher to a particular pupil. Mannyng favoured the form over the pl. forms (and sometimes over the 3 sg. and pl. pron. forms) of his French original (e.g. Furnivall, 1017: þou hauntyst/Fr hante3; 1049:3yf þou be/Fr si ceo seit). Chaucer seems to have proceeded similarly in ParsT, so far as one can judge from the texts offered for comparison in *SA* and by S. Wenzel; see his 'The source of the remedia of ParsT', *Trad.*, 27 (1971), 433-54; and 'The source of Chaucer's seven deadly sins', *Trad.*, 30 (1974), 351-78. So too the Kentish translator of the homilies of Maurice of Sully (see *EME Verse and Prose*, ed. J.A.W. Bennett and G.V. Smithers (Oxford 1966), 218/128-39; and the original, *Maurice of Sully and the Medieval Vernacular Homily*, ed. C.A. Robson (Oxford, 1952), pp. 90, 11. 41-52). Of course, even if a text wants clear signs of address to a group ('iche of 3ou', '3oure hertes', 'sires'), we can read its pl. forms as a polite form of address to an individual. When the text does not direct us so to read them, however (e.g. by the use of a partnering phrase like 'dere frende': for other examples, see A. Hudson and H.L. Spencer, 'Old author, new work: the sermons of MS Longleat 4', *M AE*, 53 (1984) 226-7), I think it better to read them as addressing the whole congregation; and, in a treatise, as aimed at a more general audience than is created by the use of the sg. pronoun (compare, for instance, though the parallel is not extact, the 'double' readership, disciple and 'half-mekyd soulys', of *The Book of Privy Counselling*, Hodgson 84/5-11, 33-41).

27. On the difficulties of reading ParsT as a sermon, see above ch. 1, n. 38.

28. So, for example, Ross, 118/14-16; *Speculum Sacerdotale*, ed. E.H. Weatherley, EETS OS 200 (London, 1936), 4/11-16; and Holmstedt 2/14, 26-8.

29. Simpler explanations may be possible for the practice. (i) The sermon/manual is translating a source where these inconsistencies first appear. (ii) Texts are being translated whose pronominal usages are inconsistent with one another (for a parallel example in WBT, see Blake, Rose, p. 237). (iii) The preacher may be addressing not merely a listening individual in a group but a solitary reader. As Dr Vincent Gillespie points out, in an unpublished paper, 'Sermons in context', the line between public and private reception and performance of religious texts is difficult to draw; see also Owst (1926), ch. 7. On the other hand, this third explanation holds clearly only in a limited number of cases, where a text comes with clear directives from a *writer* to a *reader* (so Hudson–Spencer, *M AE*, 53, 224, 227 and n. 23). (iv) The sg. form of the

pronoun represents address by the Pardoner to the Host (Elliott, p. 258: against this view, the Host is usually named when directly addressed, as at VI, 943; VII, 2816; IX, 1089).

30. On this moment, and for comment on the role of the *gentils*, see David, p. 195; for a very different view of their role, Huppé, p. 210.

31. Barney, Faulkner, p. 87, sees the Pardoner as a good listener, shaping his tale to the weaknesses of PhysT and the Host's response to it.

32. So Adelman, Faulkner, p. 96. See also N. Owen, 'The Pardoner's introduction, prologue and tale: sermon and fabliau', *JEGP*, 66 (1967), 541-9; and R.W.V. Elliott, 'Our Host's "triacle": some observations on Chaucer's Pard T', *REL*, 7 (1966), 67-9.

33. See Howard (p. 353) for comment on a similar double reading of what I shall call the 'jape' of PardProl: in the prologue the Pardoner tells the *gentils* 'the most honest thing he can think of: he is a fraud and a scoundrel.'

34. Elliott, 'The Pardoner's sermon and its exemplum', Faulkner p. 29, reads the phrase 'these revellers, three of whom I am talking about': a 'legitimate rendering', but unlikely.

35. See further Burlin, pp. 173-4; Howard, p. 358; and Barney, Faulkner, p. 90.

36. So also Elliott, Faulkner, p. 31.

37. So also Cooper, p. 157.

38. Cf. Owst (1961), pp. 443-5.

39. See Howard (p. 359) for nice comment on the speech of the rioters as an imitation of drunkenness: 'they talk in non-sequiturs and repeat *idées fixes* as drunks do.'

40. See also E.R. Hatcher, 'Life without death: the old man in PardT', *ChR* 9 (1974-75), 247.

41. Also noted Cooper, p. 232; Elliott, p. 255, adds FrT, 1404-5.

42. On these oaths, see Elliott, pp. 261, 268. He reckons them the mark of a vulgar speaker.

43. On oaths see Owst (1961), Index for the many references to this topic.

44. For a convenient summary of the many interpretations of this figure, see Hatcher, *ChR*, 9, 246, n.1. See also G.R. Coffman, 'Old age from Horace to Chaucer', *Spec.*, 9 (1934), 249-77; and J.M. Steadman, 'Old age and *contemptus mundi* in PardT', *M AE*, 33, (1964), 121-30; reprinted in Faulkner, pp. 70-82.

45. See above, p. 53 for a Chaucerian parallel in C1T.

46. On respect the young owe the old in obedience to the third commandment, see Ross 23/24.

47. See, for instance, *De M* III, 8 (Lewis, p. 214, corresponding — so Lewis pp. 51-2 — to III,12 in early editions, and so presented by Miller, p. 490). For the link with Apoc. 9:6, and earlier claimed link of PardT with I Thess 5, see Barney, Faulkner, p. 92; for the old man as like those in hell, Adelman, Faulkner, p. 98; for the link with Job, Boitani, pp. 261-2.

48. Cooper (p. 129) reads the grove only *in malo*: 'symbolic associations of the forest are with wilderness, savagery ... even ... chaos.' Most writers read the oak simply as a tree, hence as a parody of the cross or as 'the tree which brought death into Eden' (Adelman, Faulkner, p. 99; Howard, p. 361). David p. 201 links it oddly with the pear tree in MerchT. For a notable exception to this generalisation, which provides classical and patristic readings of the oak *in bono* and *in malo*, see J. Dean, 'Spiritual allegory and Chaucer's narrative style: three test cases', *ChR*, 18 (1983-84), 277-80 and n.22.

49. Sir Epicure Mammon's ambitions reach further: 'nay, we will *succumbere* gold' (*The Alchemist*, IV,i,30).

50. A link also noted by Barney, Faulkner, p. 86.

51. For this point, see P.G. Ruggiers, 'Platonic forms in Chaucer', *ChR*, 17 (1982-3), 369.

52. So also Barney, Faulkner, p. 93.

53. Cf. Adelman, Faulkner, pp. 102, 104 and n.13.

54. Zacher (p. 54) notes that 'in addition to harmful gossip and sexual promiscuity [the latter realised in the pilgrimage narrative only in the Host's comment about the drunk Cook, IX, 18] almost all forms of sensual indulgence tempted the pilgrim.'

55. For comment on this term, which links PardT and CkT, see Kolve, p. 279 and n.43.

56. Owst (1961), pp. 162-3 cites an analogue for FrT, in BL Harley, 4894, and translates a phrase from it relevant here: 'this narration ... although partly jocose, is none the less revocative of certain vices.'

57. PardProl is a reworking of the character of Faus Semblant in *RR*. For detailed comparison with the original, see Kean, II, 96 ff. For another model for PardProl, the so-called 'liar's confession', see L.W. Patterson, 'Chaucerian confession: penitential literature and the Pardoner', *M&H*, NS 7 (1976), 163.

58. Cf. Coleman (p. 194), quoting Robert of Basevorn's view that '*amplificatio* by *exemplum* ... is most appreciated by the laity.'

59. David (p. 193) sees here a parody of the Holy Spirit and the dove of peace.

60. On the use of visual aids in preaching, see Owst (1926), pp. 349-52. On the Pardoner's two styles — in particular, the learned Latinate diction of the sermon — see Elliott, p. 418. The disjunction between the two can be usefully compared with the gap between the portrait of a pilgrim in the cast-list in GenProl and narration assigned him (see above, p. 20): in particular, compare the Summoner's scraps of drunken Latin in the cast-list (I, 638-40, 646) and careful translation of Bible texts in his tale (noted by Thompson, Davis–Wrenn, p. 184).

61. A traditional collocation: see Owst (1961), p. 429.

62. Outside of PardT, 'good men' is used only by the Host (e.g. II, 1164, 1174), Summoner (III, 836), Merchant (IV, 2416), and Nun's Priest (VII, 3440); 'lordynges' chiefly by the Host (I, 761; II, 16; X, 15), but also Wife of Bath (III, 4, 112), Friar (III,1645), Summoner (III, 1668), Clerk (IV, 1163), Franklin (V, 1621) and Monk (VII, 3429): on the term, see Brewer, Intro., p. 201. 'Sires' is used by the Reeve (I, 3903), CYeom (VIII, 1176), Host (VII, 799) and Manciple (IX, 41). 'Lordynges', the commonest form in *CT*, occurs only once outside it, in *Rom*, 5877 (the speech by the God of Love to his barons); 'sires' occurs in *Tr* and *PF*; 'good men' not at all. See also Elliott, p. 417.

63. A further link with the two tales is provided by the phrase 'of this mateere it oghte ynogh suffise' (VI, 434; cf. 588; VII, 2458).

64. For a (very vague) medieval parallel with this latter, cf. Zacher, p. 131, on *Mandeville's Travels*: in the second part 'the devout pilgrim metamorphoses into the wide-eyed curious wanderer'.

65. On this point, see Adelman (Faulkner, p. 102): 'in the course of his old story, the distinction between the pilgrims and the church audience is blurred: by the time he addresses the church audience as "lordynges" (573) the two audiences have become one.' I have followed a slightly different tack — the church audience seems to me realised as an audience only in the prologue (and epilogue, 11. 904-15): but Adelman's basic point stands.

66. Cf. Howard, p. 372 and n. 31: 'he reflects back to us the evil we dread in ourselves.'

67. For the most important monastic rule, one of the two cited by Chaucer in the portrait of the Monk (I, 173), see *The Rule of St Benedict*, trans. J. McCann (London, 1952, repr. 1970), esp. ch. 48 'of daily manual labour'; for developments in monastic observance during the later middle ages, see D. Knowles, *The*

Religious Orders in England, 2 vols (Cambridge, 1948, 1955). On the mendicants, see Knowles ibid., I, chs. 11-16; II, chs. 5, 7, 10; and A. Williams, 'Chaucer and the friars', *Spec.*, 28 (1953), 499-513.

68. Cf. Green, Bethurum, p. 128, on similar complexities in FrT: 'I doubt that contempt for the contemptible friar ... and all the delightful ironies of the story itself, would have left the medieval reader entirely untouched by the mystery and terror of damnation which is the fable's burden.'

69. Cf. Jordan, p. 229 (on ParsT); Stevens–Falvey, *ChR*, 17, 145-6; Elbow, pp. 133 (beautifully) on the retractions as an 'act of choosing ... between oppositions', and p. 137 on Pard 'trying to climax his ironic dance by producing not just thoughts and feelings but behaviour as well'.

70. T. Halverson, 'Chaucer's Pardoner and the progress of criticism', *ChR*, 4 (1969-70), 199, notes his use of 2 sg. pron. in the speech to the Host as answering the Host in kind; Barney, Faulkner, p. 94, sees a sexual insult in the Pardoner's reference to the Host's 'purse' which invites the latter's reaction.

71. Also noted Barney, Faulkner, p. 94.

72. See further Kolve, p. 267 and n.; Allen–Moritz, p. 53; and cf. VII, 1963-4 (Host–Mk exchange).

73. And, of course, at the expense of those who share the joke against the Pardoner: the Knight (Barney, Faulkner, p. 95), the *gentils* (Howard, p. 375), the pilgrims (Allen–Moritz, p. 52). For a reading which takes their laughter straight, see Burlin, p. 175. Many writers view PardT primarily as unwitting self-revelation, e.g. Stevens–Falvey, *ChR*, 17, 147; and David, pp. 194, 200. Such readings sometimes yield impressive insights. Wetherbee, Economou (1975), p. 89, talks of 'the perversion of what is basically a deeply religious nature'; Elbow, pp. 137, 40, finds the Pardoner 'a man capable of great irony and sophistication ... but incapable of the redeeming ability to shed this irony and become fully human.' For a review of criticism about the Pardoner, see Halverson, *ChR*, 4, 184-202; and G.G. Sedgewick, 'The progress of Chaucer's Pardoner, 1880-1940', *MLQ*, 1 (1940), 431-58; reprinted in Schoeck-Taylor, I, 190-220, Wagenknecht, pp. 126-58. All the same, I do not regard the Pardoner as primarily self-revealing; rather, he is a function for revealing others to themselves, a point well urged by D. Pearsall, 'Chaucer's Pardoner: the death of a salesman', *ChR*, 17 (1982-83), 358-65.

74. For a more positive reading of this moment, see David, p. 203.

75. Payne talks (p. 163) of 'the concentration of plot precision [in PardT] to a point at which it becomes figurative demonstration'.

76. See Howard (p. 183) for comparison of the 'ironic permissiveness' of the narrator with that of the old man in PardT.

77. Cf. Beichner (*PMLA*, 82, 38): 'not every lion encountered in a story represents either Christ, or St Mark the evangelist, or the devil, or a vice; some lions represent only themselves.'

10 THE NUN'S PRIEST'S TALE

The problems posed by the Nun's Priest's tale are at least as great as those of the Pardoner's tale, but can be formulated, initially at least, more simply. If we did not know from the prologue and the cancelled epilogue to the tale that the narrator was a priest, what grounds could we find for calling this work a religious story?[1] This question may seem naive, even otiose. There is, after all, the formal religious ending, which offers 'moralite', 'doctrine' and 'fruyt' as the purpose, or 'mateere', of the story:

> But ye that holden this tale a folye,
> As of a fox, or of a cok and hen,
> Taketh the moralite, goode men.
> For seint Paul seith that all that writen is,
> To oure doctrine it is ywrite, ywis;
> Taketh the fruyt, and lat the chaf be stille.[2]
>
> (VII, 3438-43)

Similarly, the opening description of the 'povre wydwe' reads very like a religious emblem:

> A povre wydwe, somdeel stape in age
> Was whilom dwellyng in a narwe cotage
> Biside a grove, stondynge in a dale.
>
> (2821-3)

The grove is familiar to us from the Pardoner's tale as an emblem of the divine visitation; the dale in which the house stands is likewise a well-established emblem of humility; and we hardly need the emblem of Grisilde's enforced separation from her husband, which she describes as a widowhood (IV, 836), to help us interpret the 'povre wydwe' as an emblem of the soul separated from God and indwelling the 'narwe cotage' of the body. The soot which discolours the walls and ceiling of the cottage (2832) can then be interpreted — and was so read — as sin.[3] And if the widow is the soul, her two daughters (2829) might then be the soul's principal powers, will and sensuality; which is how the two daughters of

271

Laban, in Genesis 29, were traditionally interpreted.[4] Admittedly, this emblematic reading does not cover all points of the description. Ingenuity would be hard pressed to accommodate the inconvenient particularities of the widow's living arrangements — notably, her three pigs, three cows, and sheep called Malle (2830-1) — to any simple iconographic scheme. Ingenuity resolves this difficulty by a simple shift in the focus of the emblem. Instead of representing the Christian soul, the widow then represents holy poverty, or the Christian life, and, in particular, the life of a professed religious: not her widowhood, then, but her poverty becomes the primary sign.[5]

The widow's poverty is not the enforced regime of total material deprivation which the Man of Law presented in his prologue, in contrast to the life of the undeserving rich (II, 99-121). Nor is it the voluntary acceptance of material deprivation rejected by the Pardoner (VI, 441) and preserved, as a legal fiction, by the 'povre freres' (I, 232; cf. III, 1873, 1906-7). Rather, it is the life of the 'povre folk' of the village where Grisilde lives, and which she perfectly embodies (IV, 200-31). Such a life carefully husbands what God sends (2828), and does not want for the basics (2844). Nevertheless, it is determined by the exigencies of its own situation (2836), and best described, in spiritual terms, as the acceptance of constraints — 'in pacience ladde a ful symple lyf' (2826), with 'hertes suffisaunce' (2839). All the same, the widow's poverty takes much of its colour from its implied contrast with the life of the wealthy. Her colours, the 'whit and blak' of her staple foods, milk and bread, are contrasted with the white and red wines as far beyond her means (2842-4) as they were beyond Grisilde's (IV, 215-16). Her 'sklendre meel' is likewise contrasted with the 'poynaunt sauce' and 'deyntee morsel' (2833-5) demanded by the glutton in the Pardoner's sermon (VI, 520, 544-5). The relative poverty of her lifestyle ('repleccioun ne made hire never sik': 2837) is set against that of her wealthy neighbours in respect of the diseases to which the latter are subject (gout and apoplexy: 2840-41; cf. VI, 513-16): she enjoys good health, which is just as well, since she has no 'phisik' but what her own humble circumstances can readily provide (2838-9).

Still, if her widowhood is not in itself the primary emblem of this opening passage, it makes for a ready connection of the tale with others in this study: most of them have focused narrowly on, or at least referred, to the three religious states of virginity (the

Physician's tale), marriage (Clerk's, Second Nun's, Man of Law's, *Melibee*) and widowhood (Prioress's); several, indeed, have gone further and implied the interdependence of those states (the virginal marriage of Cecilie, the 'widowhoods' of Grisilde and Custance, the Monk's portrait of Zenobia as maiden, mother and widow). Whether she is read literally or emblematically, then, the widow appears to provide a clear pointer to the work's overall religious meaning. Unfortunately her witness is neither single nor, once we have left the opening passage behind, particularly important. We see her only once more, near the end of the story, as part of the general mêlée provoked by the fox's seizing of the cock. Then, a very different emblem is in process of being created: that of the general chaos immediately preceding Christ's second coming and the end of the world ('it semed as that hevene sholde falle': 3401).[6] This emblem owes its colour to the preceding sequence, in which the cock, deceived by the fox, has re-enacted the Fall, and possibly, since the drama takes place on a Friday (3341), the passion of Christ.

The emblem of widowed poverty, then, is far from being a fixed quantity like Grisilde's patience, Cecilie's fortitude, and Prudence's wisdom. It is closer in spirit to the double readings of the characters of Custance, Virginia and Zenobia offered by their respective narrators; alternatively, to the shifting perspectives on the ideas of tragedy provided by the Monk's collection (such shifting perspectives often result from the conflation of sources). On the other hand, because the widow is seen so fleetingly in the action, we are not likely to be struck greatly by this shift in the perspective of the emblem.[7] And once we leave her behind, and draw towards the hero of the story, the prize item in her little collection of livestock, we are almost bound — since we reckon to be dealing with a religious narrative — to read her as a norm which the story will temporarily disrupt, but finally reinstate: if not in her own person, then in the person of the protagonist. Had she returned at the end as a simple restatement of the ideal, the story would have evolved a form like that used in *A Midsummer Night's Dream*; since she does not, we look for a form analogous to that used in Shakespeare's *Henry IV*, where an ideal stated at the outset but incapable of realisation by the father will be realised at the end by the son, notwithstanding the latter's initial commitment to misrule. The narrative appears therefore to sanction a reading of the cock as a rake whose progress to a tragic end can be averted only by self-knowledge and repentance. It encourages us to read Chauntecleer as an emblem of all that the widow's lifestyle opposes. If she is humble, he is proud (3191): compared to a royal prince (3176, 3184), and to that common emblem of pride, the lion (3179), he walks about 'deign[ing] nat to sette his foot to grounde' (3181). He further demonstrates his pride when he stands on tiptoe, stretching out his neck, to sing (3331-3), and even, possibly, when he casts up his eye to observe the course of the sun (3193): its ascent into the heavens provides him with the cue to crow, but may also symbolise his own moral state.[8]

Then, too, the widow's life of measured restraint appears to oppose the cock's at all important points. The narrative counter-points its account of Chauntecleer's pride (3176, 3179-81) with a picture of his lovemaking with Pertelot:

> He fethered Pertelote twenty tyme
> And trad hire eke as ofte, er it was pryme.
>
> (3177-8)

In so vigorously making up for time lost at night because of the constraints of his 'narwe' perch (3167-9), Chauntecleer is ironic-ally opposing himself to the widow's acceptance of the constraints of her 'narwe cotage' (2822). He is also making common cause with the Monk, to whom the Host had applied the same image of treading ('thou woldest han been a tredefowel aright': 1945) as a way of playfully exposing the unnecessary constraints imposed by his religious profession on the sexual energies of 'a manly man, to been an abbot able'. According to Harry Bailly, monks are the sturdy seed, and vigorous sowers, of lechery:

> Religioun hath take up al the corn
> Of tredyng ...
> This maketh that oure wyves wole assaye
> Religious folk, for ye mowe bettre paye
> Of Venus paiementz than mowe we;
> God woot, no lussheburghes payen ye!
>
> (1954-5, 1959-62)

This latter passage develops a metaphor not found in the portrayal of Chauntecleer, that of a man skilled in 'Venus paiementz' (this image goes back, in fact, to the Shipman's tale). But, near the end of his story, the Nun's Priest will take up the Host's reference to Venus. As the fox is carrying Chauntecleer off to almost certain death, the narrator calls on the 'goddesse of plesaunce' (3342-6), whom Chauntecleer has served, 'moore for delit than world to multiplye', to protect the servant whom she appears to be deserting, on the very day (Friday, *dies Veneris*) when she might have been expected to give him her special protection.

Nor is that all. When Pertelot puts forward her commonsense understanding of the probable causes of her husband's dream, and proposes remedies for it, she identifies herself with the widow and, by implication, opposes Chauntecleer's lifestyle to the widow's. Dreams, she tells him, are produced by the 'replecciouns' (2923; cf 2957), to which the widow was never subject (2837); the superabundance, or 'superfluytee', of humours (2925-7) from which the widow's 'attempree diete' and 'hertes suffisaunce' protected her; and the 'fume' rising from the stomach to the brain, whose likeliest cause is over-indulgence in food and drink (cf. VI, 567). Like the widow, Pertelot settles, in the absence of professional advice, for that 'phisik' readily to hand, herbs and worms, which will restore health by forcing Chauntecleer to evacuate the offending matter (2948-53, 2961-7). Pertelot also sees the 'sonne in his ascensioun' not as the cue for her husband to strut self-consciously about the barnyard crowing but as the sign of the 'humours hoote' which will kill him if he does not do something about them (2956-7). And while we are looking at Pertelot's emblematic role, we might also note the comic emblem of humility which she opposes to his pride: as he struts up and down, she is having a dust bath (3267-9).

The narrative places its hero in other ways, too. We meet him first, in a comic reworking of the superlatives used by the Monk for his heroes, as a superlative voice (2850-4, 2858) and a riot of colour (2859-64). The former is specifically placed, we may feel, by its comparison to the 'murie orgon/On messe-dayes that in the chirche gon' and the 'clokke or ... abbey orlogge', even as the Monk's jingling bridle, in the General Prologue, irresistibly suggested to the narrator a comparison with the chapel bell. Later the cock crowing will be compared to the singing of the mermaid, on the authority of the Latin bestiary (3269-72): a knowledge of the context — according to the bestiary, the mermaid lures mariners to their death by her song, and is thus a cardinal symbol of deceitful appearances — suggests a judgement on the moral state of the

hero.[9] As for the cock's colouring, a simple emblematic reading
might find in its vivid sheen and polish a striking contrast with the
widow's humble 'whit and blak' — and regardless of any forcing
of the image (for a cock's colouring is natural after all) read the
two figures as symbolising respectively Art and Nature. In any case
the portrait of Chauntecleer contains suggestions of that supreme
expression of rule and artifice, the person who serves Venus
'moore for delit than world to multiplye', the courtly lover. The
Physician's and Pardoner's tales have implied a criticism of Art's
attempts to counterfeit, or refine, Nature. We know even from the
heterodox de Meun, in his continuation of the *Roman*, what we
are to make of the figure of the courtly lover. Whether, therefore
the hero acts as an emblem of a courtly lover or, more simply and
comprehensively, as an emblem of pride and excess, he seems to
be riding for a fall. Hence the appropriateness of the narrator's
dating the story by reference to the Creation — which also implies
the Fall — of Adam (3187-90).

As with the character, so with the narrative structures. For the
most part, as this study has shown, religious narratives follow a
particular emblematic structure, whose linear development takes
the form of a (sometimes repeated) test.[10] The protagonist passes
the test and is rewarded, as in the Clerk's tale, or fails and is
punished, as in the Pardoner's. Punishment does not follow failure
if the individual repents. (By this light, failure is itself a kind of test
of the character's ability to learn from his mistakes.) The agent of
temptation can be identified either with God (so the Clerk's tale)
or the Devil (so the Physician's). The passing of the test dramatises
the triumph of faith over instinct. Instinctively the hero fears the
death, literal or metaphoric, represented by the test (so Virginia
in the Physician's tale and the brothers in the Second Nun's);
embracing the test, he overcomes fear and triumphs.

Elements of this structure are firmly lodged in the Nun's Priest's
narrative, and appear to underline its fundamental religious cast.
We begin with a hero instinctively fearful of death (fear, indeed, is
the undercurrent of the whole work). Waking from his dream in
the grip of fear (2895), Chauntecleer calls upon God to interpret
the dream for him and keep him safe (2896-7).[11] The dream has
presented him the image of an animal he has never seen before,
'lyk an hound', which has stolen into the yard with wicked designs
on him. From it he draws a fearful meaning for himself: of coming
'meschief'; of the possibility of seizure and imprisonment: above

all, of death (2894, 2897, 2900-1). In reply, Pertelot accuses him of cowardice (2911-20), and urges him to make light of his fears since fearful dreams have very prosaic origins and point not forwards but back: to recent physical excess, or an imbalance of the humours. She is imprudent enough to offer 'Catoun' in support of her view. Her response may itself be a test, since her accusation of cowardice leads her to offer a list of the qualities that make men desirable to women (2913-17). Though most of them are consonant with a religious understanding of human nature, they are not in themselves religious; and, what is worse, they have an echo in the opening tale of the group, the Shipman's, when the merchant's sensual wife is making advances to the monk hero (173-7).[12] The cock passes the test — if that is what it is — with flying colours.[13] He has read stories of 'many a man moore of auctorite' than Cato — he will quote chapter and verse (3064-6), and he wishes she had read them too (3120-1) — which support his instinctive sense that it is not cowardly to fear the portents of a dream (3063, 3109): dreams point not back, but forwards. He tells several stories to prove his point; all include a religious element, and use religious language. The most obviously religious concerns a holy child — shades of the 'litel clergeon'[14] — warned in a dream that he would be murdered, but too holy, and too young, to protect himself (3110-19); then there are dreams from Old Testament times (3127-35) and pagan times (3123-6, 3136-48).

The first and longest story, expressing an idea earlier used by the Prioress, that 'mordre wol oute', tells how two pilgrims are forced to separate for the night by the limited accommodation available. One lodges in an ox stall, where he is robbed and murdered; his body is then hidden 'prively' in a dung cart (we may be reminded of the privy where the *clergeon* ended up). Yet if this Biblical setting, the ox stall, symbolises the divine visitation only backhandedly and ironically — contrast its use near the beginning of the Clerk's tale (IV, 206-7) — other features of the narrative clearly express its prevailing religious dimension.[15] The cock uses philosophical terms later appropriated by the Nun's Priest for his own commentary ('necessitee': 2992; reappearing at the heart of the 'greet altercacioun' in the *scole*: 3245, 3250; 'aventure ... or fortune': 2999; invoked as the force that saves the hero, 3403). Chauntecleer also goes much further than his maker is prepared to do. Not only does the Nun's Priest credit Fortune with the happy outcome of the story; he also apostrophises 'destinee' rather than

God at the moment of crisis (3338). By contrast, Chauntecleer
addresses God at the moment when the crime is about to be
discovered, and therefore identifies himself with the production of
a narrative like that of the Prioress. She, we recall, apostrophised
God in very similar terms at the same point in her narrative:

> O blisful God, that art so just and trewe,
> Lo, how that thou biwreyest mordre alway!
> Mordre wol out, that se we day by day.
> Mordre is so wlatsom and abhomynable
> To God, that is so just and resonable
> That he ne wol nat suffre it heled be.

(3050-5)

> O grete God, that parfournest thy laude
> By mouth of innocentz, lo, heere thy myght!

(607-8)[16]

The religious element in the second story is not so clearly
presented. Again we have two friends going on a journey. One is
warned in a dream not to take ship the following day. His friend
refuses to follow his advice and goes down with his ship, which sinks
in full view of others sailing alongside. This time the narrator is not
so certain about the part played by God in the story:

> Noot I nat why, ne what myschaunce it eyled,
> But casuelly the shipes botme rente.

(3100-1)

Nevertheless, he permits us to discover a religious meaning in the
tale when he tells of the effect of fear produced on the dreamer by
his dream (3088). This fear has clear parallels in the first story
(3008) and in Chauntecleer's own situation.

Chauntecleer, then, resists the temptation to dethrone God as
the principal *auctor* of human affairs, and asserts his belief in the
fundamental religious (prophetic) dimension of dreams. Unfortunately, the triumph is inconclusive and temporary. Inconclusive
because, although Chauntecleer is certain that his dream portends
only 'adversitee' (3153), he knows very well that 'dremes been
significaciouns/As wel of joye as of tribulaciouns' (2979-80), and
are not always certain portents: 'dremes be somtyme — I sey nat

alle — / Warnynge of thynges that shul after falle' (3131-2). His *ensample* of St Kenelm is ironic, too, in ways he can hardly appreciate. If for very different reasons, that holy child does exactly what Pertelot is urging her husband to do, and sets little store by his dream. While dreams may avail to convert the sinner and confirm the believer's little faith, they have nothing to say to the holy heart. Chauntecleer's fear of his dream thus places him significantly lower in the religious hierarchy than the saints: as does his dispute with his wife, which disrupts the harmonious relationship of the couple at the beginning of the story, where we see them singing together 'in sweete accord' (2879).

Paradoxically, the clearest sign of the dream's religious dimension comes in the moment when, having proved his point to his own satisfaction, the hero then undercuts his own religious sense with a proposal to 'speke of myrthe, and stynte al this' (3157). I shall have more to say about this speech later. Here we may note the hero's playful appropriation of religious language for secular purposes: 'madame Pertelote, so have I blis/Of o thyng God hath sent me large grace' (3158-9). The hoped-for bliss, the 'large grace': both are in different ways, though not so named, properties of Chauntecleer's dream; both can be applied, without strain, to his dear wife ('blis', for example, at 3166, 3200). Parallel to this change in the language is the displacement of religious sense by sensual instinct. The physical beauty of his wife lays his fear to rest (3161-2) and fills him with such joy and comfort — notwithstanding the constraints of that narrow perch — that he can 'diffye bothe sweven and dreem'. He now resumes the role, given to him at the outset of the narrative, of the great lover with the beautiful voice (3157-3203, 3267-72; cf. 2850-8, 2865-79). When next he speaks, he is calling Pertelot his 'worldes blis' and repeating that his heart is full 'of revel and solas'. It is not too hard to read this passage as a judgement on the backslider who has received a heavenly visitation and turns his back on the offered heavenly grace in favour of the earthly sort.

Like several of the characters in the Monk's tale, this emblem, as he has now become, of *inconsideratio futurorum*, is given a second chance. The dream comes true. The fox makes his appearance among the cabbages, and reduces the great songster to a frightened cluck and a panicky instinct for flight. Denying his own emblematic role of tempter and betrayer (3286-8), the fox seduces the cock into ignoring the heavenly portent once more. He presents himself as a friend of the family and a lover of good music. Whatever men may say about singing, he knows that no human agent can compare with Chauntecleer in singing. Only the angels in heaven could stand the comparison (3291-2); and, of course, Chauntecleer's own father, who was unsurpassed in his own time (3310-11). The comparison with the song of the angels irresistibly, and wickedly, suggests a religious dimension to the cock's crowing which other details in the fox's speech support. Chauntecleer's father, he tells him, sang from the heart (3303), and took great pains 'to make his voys the moore strong' (3304-8). He was as wise as he was musical (3309-11). Not even the cock hero of 'daun Burnel the asse', who comes readily to the speaker's mind as an expression of the former quality, could match Chauntecleer's father (3317-19).[17] Such a paragon of virtue well deserves the speaker's blessing. Were the son willing to 'countrefete' his saintly father, he would be performing a truly charitable act (3320-1). This coolly impudent sales pitch is undercut by the sense that the voice and discretion of Chauntecleer's father availed only to send him, by way of the fox's den (3297), to that heaven whose inhabitants had provided the fox with his initial comparison. The cock does not see through it. His father's son, it seems, in all things, he closes his eyes to the plain truth of the fox's 'traysoun', even as he turned his back on the truth of his dreams. His metaphoric ravishing by the beauty of his wife, a prelude to his literal ravishing of her, is ironically realised when he is ravished by the fox's flattery (3324). This, in turn, preludes his literal ravishing by the fox, as he imitates his father and stretches on tiptoe, closing his eyes to crow.

It is at this next stage in the narrative, with the fox approaching the wood a little ahead of the hue and cry, and the cock helpless on his back like swag, that the story suddenly undercuts the simple religious reading which its carefully presented details have appeared to endorse. Once more in the grip of fear — and the fox obligingly realises that grip for us by his hold on Chauntecleer's throat — the cock rouses himself to outsmart his opponent: invites the fox to turn on his pursuers and warn them off; and, when the fox opens his mouth to agree to the plan, breaks free from his grip and flies into a tree. This development is unexpected and problematical. (We get some sense of the difficulty if we remember that the Nun's Priest invokes not God or human agency to explain it, but Fortune.) Following the lead given by the Monk's tale, the story could have yielded one of two outcomes: either death for the hero as a fit punishment for wilful blindness (so Croesus, ironically used by Chauntecleer as one of his own 'ensamples': 3138-40); or repentance and restoration to grace (so Nebuchadnezzar). Neither scenario is considered here. Nor is the third pattern, which had appeared prominently in the tales of the Clerk, Prioress, Second Nun and Man of Law, of faith tested and vindicated. No precedent exists in religious literature for the sinner to save himself, least of all by the wit that until now has seemed all too easily corrupted.

At this point, then, Chauntecleer stops being an overtly religious symbol.[18] He now symbolises, ironically, only the 'wisedom and discrecioun' with which the fox credited his father for his own devious purposes. The son has passed the test which the father failed, and hence surpassed his father, as the fox predicted he would; for the real test was not how well he could sing but, though neither tempter nor tempted knew it, what powers of survival he could summon up. Survival, though, is not in itself a religious position. The survivor is an emblem only of himself — or, at best, of Nature. By Nature, however, we no longer understand the purposive and personal 'vicaire general' of God presented by the Physician, but simply an aggregation of natural effects, the force that makes things 'wane and waxe': another version of what the Monk calls Fortune. That force is well represented in the story, as we shall see, in the depiction of fear and desire as the conditions of life which men share with the animals. But where, previously, we have felt able to read Chauntecleer's fear as the symbol of a religious emotion (for 'the fear of the Lord is the beginning of wisdom'), we now find ourselves forced to question the possibility of a religious sphere independent of the natural order which incarnates it both literally and symbolically. Such a question the other religious narratives could consider, for the most part, only backhandedly, in critical comments by the narrator (I have in mind particularly the Clerk) or in images whose implications were not developed (I have in mind the zeal of the Sultan to embrace both Christianity and Custance in the Man of Law's tale, and the openness of the ghetto 'at eyther ende' in the Prioress's). Such a question is rooted in the very form of the Nun's Priest's tale: or perhaps I should say, forms.

The principal form is that of the beast fable. In more orthodox hands, as in the Middle English poem *The Thrush and the Nightingale*, and many of the stories about animals in the *Gesta Rome -*

orum, the beast fable serves unambiguously religious purposes, the animal heroes then becoming, almost literally, stalking-horses for religious intent: or, to change the metaphor, human beings, or moral qualities proper to human beings, barely concealed by a fancy dress of fur and feathers, assuming not the identities but only the names of animals. The Nun's Priest's tale does not work like this. It seizes the satiric and comic possibilities of the beast fable with both hands — even more boldly than in Chaucer's earlier example of the genre, *The Parliament of Fowls* — and requires us to see the animals, before ever they are humans, as themselves. If they behave like humans, and are regularly so described:

as man that in his dreem is drecched soore (2887)
as man that was affrayed in his herte (3278)
as a prince is in his halle (3184)

they also remain firmly rooted in an animalness as vividly realised as any of the details of the Pardoner's narrative. Consequently, they force the reader to constant shifts of perspective inimical to the expression of a simple religious view of the material universe:[19] or of any other view, for the beast fable exposes the singleminded attempts of allegorists and materialists alike to force the *matere* of experience into their preconceived *sens*. Nature red in tooth and claw is no more and no less the subject of the beast fable than nature transformable and transformed into the song of the angels. While, that is, the beast fable satirises human aspiration by viewing it in the context of animal instinct — and satire is no very safe tool for the religious artist to use — it also backhandedly endorses it: the glory and the absurdity of the human is its subject.[20] Within the terms of the present work, the beast fable stresses the necessary coexistence of, and tension between, natural and spiritual realms, as the condition of religious, and all other, awareness. Neither can be understood in isolation from the other. Hence, the most exotic humanising item in Chauntecleer's wardrobe, that stage beard with which Pertelot credits him (2920) (she cannot believe that so faint a heart could wear so fine a beard) is as respectable a property of the animal as of the human world. Hence, too, the necessary and ironic connections between the fear of the Lord and the love of a good woman (or hen).

Now, coexistence does not require, and may even be opposed to, the linear narrative development we have identified with religious art. As with all surreal art, the narrative which makes coexistence its theme and irony its perspective realises itself in the moment when it makes us see the intimate and necessary links between what we thought discrete and opposed entities.[21] This moment of seeing — available to the reader, though not the characters of the story or, as we shall see, the narrator — symbolises, and realises, the whole life of which it is so brief a part (even as, in a very different context, the visions of Julian of Norwich do for her). Development, therefore, is less likely to be orderly and linear than spasmodic and circular: or coextensive with plot, than realised in the isolated image. In terms of content such a narrative will not be exclusive but inclusive and comprehensive.

This can be very easily demonstrated by a comparison of the role of speech in more orthodox religious narrative with that in the Nun's Priest's tale, where it furnishes the chief symbol and generates an important secondary form: we might call it, the talking head. This talking head can figure prominently in religious narratives, particularly those of an apologetic cast. Almost half of the Second Nun's tale is taken up with speech-making; in *Melibee* almost nothing else happens. Formally distinct from other actions in the story, and either caused by or the cause of them, speech-making is nevertheless identified with them, and hence with the linear development of the whole story, for a very simple reason: it enacts the same religious awareness. It does this directly, when a character prays to God, or indirectly, when he represents his religious position to himself or others by way of religious imagery and language, drawn most readily from the Bible. The unity of speech and action in the life of the believer thus imitates the unity of word and act in the life of God. Ironies are therefore of a very limited sort, as when a character says one thing and means another (the voice of the tempter) or speaks an irreligious word which he must later retract (for example, Joseph in the cycle plays when confronted by the pregnancy of the Virgin). Competing voices will be so placed as to give prominence to the voice of the believer; any last words will achieve that 'consummation devoutly to be wished' to which the actions themselves have tended.

The contrast with the Nun's Priest's tale is striking. If we except the speech of the fox, acting in his role of tempter, the speeches in the tale either have no clear direction or else seem to vanish into thin air as soon as they are spoken.[22] This is most evident in Chauntecleer's long speech. Far from defining a religious position to which the rest of the narrative can bear direct or indirect witness (direct if the character remains faithful, indirect if he backslides), the cock's acknowledgement of the religious dimension of his experience seems merely to mark time while he is collecting his spirits. The sense of time passing — the terrors of night give way to the common light of day (3149-50) — makes possible a change in the focus of attention.[23] The displacement of the initial, religious, explanation for a disturbed night (divine visitation) by another (enforced abstinence because of that narrow perch) leads from past fears to future pleasures on the barnyard floor. This sense of marking time in the first part of the speech is reinforced by the increasing scantiness of the exempla as the speech draws towards its close. At first fully developed and carefully presented, the stories become increasingly brief, little better than summaries of their respective narratives. Now, a developing religious sense does not necessarily require a corresponding development in the length of the speeches (in this case, 'ensamples'): yet one might reckon, other things being equal, that a firm religious conclusion could be reached more easily by such means than by the opposite course favoured by Chauntecleer (similar reasonings, as earlier noted, explain the long final speeches of Grisilde and Cecilie in their respective stories).[24] In any case, Chauntecleer turns out to have a very prosaic reason for rejecting his wife's advice. Almost as an afterthought — admittedly, he may be taking his cue from the order of her speech, which ended with practical matters — he tells her that he hates her offered alternative, laxatives, 'for they been venymous'.

In two important respects this speech is a perfect mirror-image of the beast fable which generates it. First, its placing relative to the erratic movements of instinct throws in question the vaunted independence of thought from its own material circumstances, and its pretensions to systematise experience on any but an *ad hoc* basis. At best, thought is a rationalisation before or after the event.[25] The importance of this image for Chaucer's whole output hardly needs stressing. His central image is that of the talking head, whose words exist in ambiguous relation to the speaker's, or other character's, actions. As the Reeve observes, those who can do; those who can't, talk about it (I, 3881): exactly the Wife of Bath's view:

The clerk, whan he is oold, and may noght do

Of Venus werkes worth his olde sho,
Thanne sit he doun, and writ in his dotage
That wommen kan nat kepe hir mariage!

(III, 707-10)

Hence, in *The Parliament of Fowls*, we have a narrator who begins
and ends with books; noble birds whose elegant speech-making
fails to produce the desired result; and, contrasted with them,
common birds who, when granted their desires, do not talk about
it but fly off singing. But if the talking head satirises the pretensions of thought 'a greater than itself to know', it also satirises
the opposite error, both graver and sillier, which advocates the
pursuit of instinct at the expense of intellect. For good or ill, we
live in both worlds at once.

For our purposes, though, the speech is making a more important point. The juxtaposition of religious and erotic language
forbids us to see religious language, by itself, as an adequate explanation of the complex and contradictory experiences of nature.
(To this point the simpler religious narratives of the Second Nun
and Chaucer himself bear eloquent, if inadvertent, witness.) At the
same time, it warns against the opposite error, which would make
those who use religious language hypocrites (so the friar in the
Summoner's tale and the monk in the Shipman's) or self-deluding
fools (like the husband in the Miller's). Those who read religious
language, in the terms here used — and most often used by
Chaucer — merely as the expression of repressed or sublimated
sexuality (or of any other given, whether social, historical,
economic or political)[26] are reading as foolishly as religious apolo-
gists who would deny the saints any human instincts. Chauntecleer's speech challenges the reader to find a comprehensive
definition of human nature which will both contain, and reconcile,
colliding and competing systems of belief. Two tales provide a
literary equivalent for this moral position in *The Canterbury Tales*.
One is the Nun's Priest's tale, the other, the Pardoner's tale, whose
narrator requires his hearers to assume a double role in relation to
his offering, and read literature as both *sentence* and *solaas*.

Paradoxically, the Nun's Priest seems unable to sustain the
weight of this awareness. As the moment of crisis approaches, he
seems to lose sight of the comic tone which the Host had requested,
and he had agreed to attempt (2811-17). Far from transforming
the notes struck by his predecessor — and by other narrators of

religious stories, notably the Prioress and Man of Law — he seems rather to be emphasising them. When, in the moment before his fall, Chauntecleer reckons to be 'ful ... of revel and solas', the narrator enters with a scaled-down version of the complaints of the Monk and Man of Law:

> Bot sodeynly hym fil a sorweful cas,
> For evere the latter ende of joye is wo;
> God woot that worldly joye is soone ago.
>
> (3204-6; cf. II, 1132-4; VII, 2061; 2137-8)[27]

Shortly after, he is apostrophising the luckless hero (3230-3) even as the Man of Law and Monk had done, and exclaiming against the villain in terms reminiscent of the Monk, Man of Law and Prioress:[28]

> O false mordrour, lurkynge in thy den,
> O newe Scariot, newe Genylon,
> False dissymulour, o Greek Synon,
> That broghtest Troye all outrely to sorwe!
>
> (3226-9)

This account of the 'false mordrour' probably parallels the Prioress's account of the hired assassin 'that in an aleye hadde a privee place'; the personalising of the enemy as a 'Newe Scariot, newe Genylon' clearly echoes her description of the Jews as the 'cursed folk of Herodes al newe'. Then, the comparison of the fox to Genilon reminds us of the Monk's description of Oliver Mauny, one of those responsible for the death of King Peter of Spain, as 'Genylon-Olyver'. The general denunciation of the villain has parallels in the Prioress's and Man of Law's tales; the comparison with Synon 'that broghtest Troye all outrely to sorwe' reminds us of the Man of Law's use of the Troy story to cast a sense of foreboding over the Sultan's proposed marriage. More significantly, the narrator's apostrophe is also picking up threads from his hero's long speech on dreams. That speech included an exemplum, from the Troy story, of Andromache warned in a dream that her husband would die if he went to battle the following day, but unable to persuade him to stay at home. As noted, it also tells the story of the two pilgrims, which ironically anticipates the narrator's comment on the murderers 'that in await liggen to mordre men ... lurkynge in [her] den'.

The pattern of direct address to the characters revealed by the previous quotation reappears when the fox seizes Chauntecleer and makes off with him to the wood. In rapid succession, the narrator addresses 'destinee' (3338), Venus (3342-6), Geoffrey of Vinsauf, 'maister soverayn' in the art of rhetoric (3347-51), and the 'woful hennes' (3369-73). The final address, comparing the hens to the wives of the senators murdered by Nero when he put Rome to the torch, clearly echoes the Monk's version of the Nero story. It has also been prepared for by a pair of epic similes. The first compares the hens to the Trojan women of the *Aeneid*, when 'Pirrus ... hadde hent Kyng Priam by the berd/And slayn hym' (3355-61); the second compares Pertelot to the wife of the Carthaginian leader, killed during the sack of Carthage by the Romans (3362-8. Pertelot outdoes Hasdrubal's wife, if not in 'stedefast herte' — for the latter burned herself to death — at least in the noise she makes). The reference to the Troy story sends us back to the narrator's earlier apostrophe, and to Chauntecleer's use of it for his final exemplum: that to the Carthaginian wars echoes one in the Man of Law's tale, which similarly joins Troy and the Carthaginian wars to create an atmosphere of doom. Now, direct address identifies the narrator, as in the other tales here studied, with the hero and against the villain; it produces a very definite effect on the moral frame of the work. Where the narrative appeared to present Chauntecleer as an emblem of the prodigal, and unfold a tragedy of character, this pattern of address gives us a victim and — that pattern beloved of the Monk — a tragedy of suffering.

Hence the narrator plays down any sense that Chauntecleer is to blame for his own fall. [29] The likeliest candidate for blame must be the fox, who flatters Chauntecleer into singing with his eyes closed. The fox's actions provide the occasion for a piece of sententious moralising to the nobility:

> Allas! ye lordes, many a fals flatour
> Is in youre courtes, and many a losengeour
> That plesen yow wel moore, by my feith,
> Than he that soothfastnesse unto yow seith.
> Redeth Ecclesiaste of flaterye;
> Beth war, ye lordes, of hir trecherye.
>
> (3225-30)

This address to the nobility has clear parallels in the tales of the

Man of Law, Physician and, especially, Pardoner (VI, 627-8); it probably derives from the *Communiloquium* of John of Wales.[30] Ironically, this comment implicates the cock in the process of his own downfall, for the noble lords with whom he is tacitly compared are seen to prefer lies to the hard truth which a preacher must utter. The deception of the fox, that is, partners, and is made possible by, a wilful self-deception on the part of the cock. This has to be the point of the earlier noted comparison of Chauntecleer's song to that of the mermaid: Chauntecleer lures no one to destruction by his beautiful voice but himself. It is also the point of the concluding *auctoritas*, one not found in John of Wales, with which the address to the nobility concludes (3229-30). Several Biblical texts have been advanced as the likely referents of the phrase 'redeth Ecclesiaste of flaterye'. They all share the sense that flattery, a covert expression of enmity, prepares the way for overtly hostile acts, even as the fox's flattery will do. In this respect 'Ecclesiaste of flaterye' points to Chauntecleer as the victim of another's deception. But one of the Ecclesiasticus texts (27: 25-6) reveals an unexpected similarity with the hero of our story: the hypocritical flatterer, it tells us, winks slyly ('annuens oculo') as he plots mischief. In our story the cock 'wynketh whan he sholde see' (3431) and so puts himself in jeopardy. Hypocrite and fool, then, the fox and the cock jointly bring about the latter's downfall.

In any case, the narrator senses, almost from the beginning, that the two are not really acting as free agents. Both are on the receiving end of heavenly influences and driven by purely natural instincts, neither of which can be gainsaid. Heavenly influences have entered the poem in Chauntecleer's dream. They are seen at work when the fox enters the yard 'by heigh ymaginacioun forncast' (3217) on the very night when Chauntecleer is dreaming about him. Clearly, this 'heigh ymaginacioun' forecasting future action carries a share of the responsibility for such action. But whose is it? The fox's, or Chauntecleer's (via his dream)? Or even God's?[31] After all, the Monk's stories had regularly, though not invariably, invoked God as the heavenly *auctor* of human tragedy. The Man of Law, though formally identifying with his audience's inability rightly to read 'thilke large book/Which that men clepe the hevene' (II, 190-1; cf. 315) had nevertheless allowed for, and tacitly laid claim to, the wisdom which enables *clerkes* to penetrate the mysteries of God's 'prudent purveiance' (480, 483). By contrast, the Nun's Priest is not so much unwilling as unable to relate God directly to the events of his story. His reluctance reveals a proper sense of the difficulties attending the attempt. The 'scole' is far from speaking with a single voice on this question; it witnesses 'greet altercacioun/... and greet disputisoun/And hath been of an hundred thousand men' (3237-9), an altercation with a comic equivalent in the tale itself in the debate between Chauntecleer and Pertelot. This 'disputisoun' the narrator can no more 'bulte ... to the bren' than he can presume to sift the 'fruyt' from the 'chaf' of his own tale (3443). He thus advances the possibility of a larger understanding of the action, only to withdraw from it: 'I wol nat han to do of swich mateere;/My tale is of a cok' (3251-2). His reticence contrasts markedly with the readiness of the Wife of Bath to engage in dispute with the 'scole', and the dependence of the Man of Law and Monk on its pronouncements. (Admittedly, the Man of Law's comments about the hand of God in his story are mostly delivered after the event, with the benefit of hindsight; similarly, the Monk is willing to read God into his narrations only when authority has already decided the question for him.) This reticence has a clear parallel among the more ambitious religious productions of *The Canterbury Tales* only in the reluctance of the Pardoner, once his narration is under way, to invoke any supernatural cause extrinsic to the psychology of the characters themselves. In the event, though Chauntecleer, Pertelot and the fox regularly invoke God (e.g. 2894, 2909, 3408, 3425, 3433-4),[32] the narrator himself ascribes Chauntecleer's unexpectedly lucky escape from the fox not to God but to Fortune (3402-4) — the third in the Monk's triad of tragic causes, and ambiguously placed in relation to the 'heigh ymaginacioun forncast' of God and man alike.

Natural instincts are as important an element in the tragedy as 'Goddes worthy forwityng'. When first Chauntecleer spots the fox hiding among the cabbages, and starts up with a frightened cluck, he is behaving, the narrator assures us, completely instinctively:

> For natureelly a beest desireth flee
> Fro his contrarie, if he may it see,
> Though he never erst hadde seyn it with his ye.
>
> (3279-81)

This picture of animal behaviour contrasts markedly with what the narrative has presented until now. Chauntecleer has seen his 'contrarie', at least in his dream, and the narrative has left us in no doubt about its malign purposes (3223); he also rejects laxatives because they are poisonous and, anyway, he hates them (3154-6). Otherwise, we have seen nature, throughout, as a system of what we might call sympathetic attractions, mediating God and Nature to man, and men to one another. Men may compute the movements of the heavens whether or not they are 'depe ystert in loore' (II, 4; the less 'depe ystert', the more approximate their measurements: X, 3-6): Chauntecleer knows those heavenly movements by instinct (2855, 3196). Likewise, wanting a professional herbalist, Pertelot knows the herbs whose natural properties restore health (2952-3). This view of nature points to a fundamentally comic vision of life, whether on a cosmic or a domestic scale. To it is opposed Chauntecleer's panicky reaction to the fox, clearly focused by the narrator's comment, quoted earlier in this paragraph. The attractions of nature, we see, exist only relative to an equally powerful set of repulsions, of which the greatest, as in the Pardoner's tale, is death (hence the *Roman de la Rose* presents sexual instinct as the chief alternative to death). Nevertheless, Nature as the expression of instinct merits neither praise nor blame; it simply is. Some other cause must be found to bear the responsibility of Chauntecleer's fall.

Pertelot is an obvious candidate. If the narrative made Chauntecleer an emblem of Adam, the narrator can make her his Eve. After all, she advised the hero to ignore his dream; she represents an innocent temptation to concupiscence; his acceptance of her advice, because her beauty turns him on, makes her the accidental cause of his fall:

> Wommennes conseils been ful ofte colde;
> Wommannes conseil broghte us first to wo,
> And made Adam fro Paradys to go,
> Ther as he was ful myrie and wel at ese.
>
> (3256-9)

This reading has the support of other moments in both the narrative and the commentary. There is the anti-feminist 'sententia' given to Chauntecleer, even though he reverses the obvious sense in translation (a comic version, perhaps, of Prudence's quest for the higher understanding in the *Melibee*):[33]

> For al so siker as in principio,

Mulier est hominis confusio —
Madame, the sentence of this Latyn is,
Womman is mannes joye and al his blis.

(3163-6)

Woman the ruin of man would seem to be as certain a fact of life
as the eternal generation of wisdom in the mind of God (the 'in
principio' of John 1:1), or the creation of the material universe
(the 'in principio' of Genesis 1:1) whose beginning saw Eve's
temptation of Adam. The hero's conclusion seems to chime with a
clearly expressed view of his creator. A little later, the Nun's Priest
is inviting 'every wys man' in the audience to take his story
seriously. His recently uttered 'sententia' on the brevity of worldly
joy is a 'soverayn notabilitee' which any 'rethor' might be glad to
use as a theme of his 'cronycle'. (The Monk and Man of Law had
so used it.) The narrator is making a tacit equation between the
truth of his own story and that of a chronicle: as a possible further
sign of that claim, we note how he dates the events of his story
relative to the creation of man. To this equation he tacitly opposes
what passes for truth with women: 'the book of Launcelot de
Lake/That wommen holde in ful greet reverence' (3212-13).[34]
Whatever the ladies say in this story, they cannot win. Their understandings are either earthbound (Pertelot's commonsense view of
the dream) or romantically unrealistic (not reason but 'reverence'
rules). But this anti-feminist reading of the story turns out as
elusive and illusory as the others; the narrator can no more commit
himself to it than to the theological reading which he might have
produced in imitation of the speculations of the 'scole'. Inevitably
the picture of Chauntecleer as an Adam innocently 'myrie and wel
at ese' until 'wommannes conseil' unparadised him is as partial as
the earlier noted picture of Chauntecleer the innocent seduced by
that 'fals flatour' the fox. Nothing so far seen in the story suggests
this prominent role for Pertelot–Eve; she has a much shorter
speech than her husband; she speaks first; and, as earlier noted,
her speech seems to identify her with the widow. In any case,
though the fall has already received attention in the stories of the
Pardoner, Monk and Man of Law, only the last named presents
Eve as the devil's instrument for damnation. In that story, moreover, she appears not so much as the cause of the action but rather
as an obvious element of an iconographic scheme (Eve contrasted
with the Virgin Mary) which the narrative uses to give greater

point to the hostility of actual and prospective mothers-in-law to their new daughters-in-law. Lastly, though Chauntecleer mangles the letter of his text ('mulier est hominis confusio'), and understands it literally, in a way at once earthbound and romantic, as guaranteeing a life of sensuality, there is a higher sense, embodied in the person of the Virgin Mary, which would make woman 'mannes joye and al his blis'.[35] Nor is the book of 'Launcelot de Lake' necessarily the worse for the reverence shown it: reverence is not, in itself, opposed to truth.[36]

The commentary, then, is incoherent and inconclusive.[37] Like the Man of Law and the Monk, the narrator appears to have responded moment by moment to the possibilities of his narrative. He can realise the unified reading which the commentary contains in embryo only by trying now one approach, then its opposite, all the while ignoring or suppressing implications unfavourable to his hero. Yet, even if he were able to produce this unified reading, he could hardly accommodate it to the diverse understandings and expectations of his audience. At the end he seems to fear that his hearers will have taken him literally when he professed a reluctance to engage in speculation, and a readiness to 'be myrie': they will reckon, then, to have heard only the 'tale ... of a cok', and can dismiss it as 'a folye'. He must warn them against such a misreading. So he urges them to find a moral in his offering ('taketh the moralite', 'taketh the fruyt') on the grounds that 'al that writen is/ To oure doctrine it is ywrite'. But he makes no attempt to direct their reading, or explain what moral they should find. He merely takes on board the closing speeches of his chief characters — neither very reliable witnesses, as we have seen — and crafts his own conclusion out of them.[38] Chauntecleer has found a perfectly unambiguous lesson for himself in his story:

> he that wynketh, whan he sholde see
> Al wilfully, God lat him nevere thee.
>
> (3431-2)

The fox finds an equally straightforward lesson for himself:

> ... God yeve hym meschaunce,
> That is so undiscreet of governaunce
> That jangleth whan he sholde holde his pees.
>
> (3433-5)

The narrator does not attempt to arbitrate between the two opposed views, but conflates them, in a way that leaves the apportioning of praise and blame crucially unclear:

> Lo, swich it is for to be recchelees
> And necligent, and truste on flaterye.

(3436-7)

This open admission of limitation becomes, paradoxically, the commentary's greatest strength, for it draws the audience directly into the processes of the tale, and raises fundamental questions about the nature and limits of both religious and literary experience, in the same way as the Pardoner's framing prologue did. Its very inconclusiveness, indeed, proves a perfect equivalent of the thematic open-endedness of the tale itself. It generates a unity between tale and telling which, though foreshadowed in the modest and child-like offering of the Prioress, and realised in the equally modest offerings of the pilgrim translators (the Second Nun and Chaucer) has no parallel in the more ambitious offerings featured in this study except that of the Pardoner.

All this is most clearly seen in the moment when the narrator retreats from his anti-feminist reading of the tale, and denies his own responsibility for the uttered sentiments, even as he tries throughout to absolve his hero from blame. As if fearful of provoking the same hostile response from his hearers ('I noot to whom it myght displese') as the two previous narrators (Chaucer and the Monk) had been forced to endure, the Nun's Priest disarms criticism not by offering something different — as Chaucer himself had done and the Monk had refused to do — but by inviting his hearers to read his offering in a different way: 'passe over, for I seyde it in my game'.[39] Nothing less will probably satisfy the women among his audience, notably the Prioress, with whose style of commentary, as we have seen, he and his hero are both identified. The movement from 'ernest' to 'game', accomplished as speedily as the cock's turning aside from serious matters to speak of mirth, is the symbolic expression of the overarching forms of the tale, the beast fable and the talking head. Like them, it deliberately blurs the line between 'ernest' and 'game', even as the Pardoner did, and compels the same conclusion about the nature of literature as both serious and trivial. Those who would have it otherwise — like the 'goode men' of the narrator's closing words, who ironically need to be urged to read the tale not as a 'folye' but for its 'moralite' — will find the last laugh on them.

But another boundary equally important is being blurred in this moment of the narrator's retreat from his own opinions. If the narrator can successfully persuade us that the offered opinions are not his own, any blame attaching to their expression must be shared by the 'auctours, where they trete of swich mateere'. If anyone disagrees with the offered sentiments — the Wife of Bath, for instance, who holds very definite views about what clerks, in their dotage, have to say about women (III, 707-10) — let her take it up with the 'auctours'. But which 'auctours' must carry the can for this reading of the story? Writers like those who treat of the vexed questions of freewill and predestination — 'the hooly doctour Augustyn/ Or Boece, or the Bisshop Bradwardyn' (3241-2)? Or 'Gaufred, deere maister soverayn' of the arts of rhetoric (3347)? Or the authors of any of the narrator's other named sources (*Phisiologus, Eneydos,* 'Ecclesiaste of flaterye')? Or of any of the obvious anti-feminist tracts known to the Wife of Bath's fifth husband? None of these. Rather, the narrator is sheltering behind his hero, and making Chauntecleer an 'auctour':

> Thise been the cokkes wordes, and nat myne;
> I kan noon harm of no womman divyne

> (3265-6)

Within the fictional scheme of the narrative, the characters, especially the hero, have behaved like their clerkly creator, marshalling authorities to prove points. The narrator's clear regard for his hero has enabled him to incorporate the cock's words in his own commentary. Up to a point, he has seemed to keep a proper distance between himself and his favoured son. On the one hand, he does not share Chauntecleer's certainty of the hand of God in human affairs; on the other, he does not seem to accept the *volte-face* which enables Chauntecleer to reckon the ladies a sufficient ground of grace and bliss (admittedly, the narrator's comment that 'I kan noon harm of no womman divyne' might playfully identify him with this belief of his hero). Yet now he turns authority over not to one of his own kind, but to one of his creatures, on the basis of a scrappy anti-feminist commonplace ('mulier est hominis confusio') whose gross mistranslation must surely have warned him against setting too much store by the speaker's self-proclaimed authority. This moment blurs the dividing line between reality and fiction — and, as earlier noted, between 'ernest and game' — as confusingly as the Host's rejoinder to the Pardoner blended two false relics and a third true one. It has a telling parallel earlier in the tale, when the Nun's Priest placed his own story relative to the truth of chronicle and the reverence accorded to romance, two categories whose potential links the Man of Law's tale has clearly revealed. How radical a moment it is we can see if we compare the only clear parallel outside the tale, in the Merchant's tale: here a fictional character, Justinus, makes an 'auctour' out of a member of the pilgrim audience, the Wife of Bath (IV, 1685-7).

The commentary, then, fails to generate a coherently argued understanding of the tale. Like the tale itself, it is not so much inconclusive — though it is that — as inclusive. It contains several conflicting views of the causes of human action, one of which, 'Goddes worthy forwityng', is itself represented by at least two opposed understandings ('symple necessitee' and 'necessitee condicioneel'). The various potentially conflicting causes of a work of art are allowed for, too, when the commentary locates authority not simply in the teller but now in the tale, now in the audience, and now, by implication, in the whole body of antecedent opinion (the 'scole') in relation to which the individual work is being realised. It transcends the binary opposition of 'folye' to 'moralitee' which, as we saw, characterises the Second Nun's view of literature, and the opposition of fiction to reality which characterises the Parson's. In this latter respect it closely parallels the Pardoner's tale, with this difference of emphasis: where the Pardoner focuses primarily on the moral duties of the artist, the Nun's Priest considers primarily the artist's obligation to truth.[40] We may then see the former as an ironic realisation of the implications of the prologue to the Secnd Nun's tale, the latter as performing a similar function relative to the prologues of the Parson's tale and *Melibee*.

Admittedly, we should not force this distinction. If the Second Nun's prologue stresses the artist's responsibility to morality, her story, which clearly identifies her with her saintly heroine, correspondingly emphasises the Christian's — and hence the Christian artist's — duties to the truth. Nevertheless, to reiterate a point made in the introduction, religion is 'something understood' (the phrase is Herbert's, in 'Prayer I'), before ever it is something performed: a way of seeing which generates a code of conduct. Though each presupposes the other, the former is primary. (That is why, I take it, Julian of Norwich places such stress on seeing God as both the cause and end of prayer and other moral action in her revelations.) I therefore find a symbolic fitness in the diptych shape created by this last pair of tales. Rather as *The Canterbury Tales* reverses elements of its own opening to generate its conclusion (a point noted above, p. 4), so the final section of this book provides an extended mirror image of its own beginning (in particular, of pp. 13-16).

The two tales of this final section also mark a fitting end to this progress of pilgrim narratives. What I have called the inclusiveness of the Nun's Priest's tale — an inclusiveness which it shares only with the Pardoner's tale, though the prologue to the *Melibee* had admitted it as a theoretical possibility — exposes the limitations within which, whether or not they have reacted against them, the religious narratives of the previous sections have, in greater or lesser degree, operated. This can be seen most obviously when the Nun's Priest's tale is compared with the Monk's limited approach to his subject matter: the accidents of the latter's narration, so to say, have become the substance of the former's. It can also be seen if we compare the last tale in the series with the first in terms of their apparent recourse to allegory (a feature observable elsewhere — and then in subtly modified form — only in the *Melibee*). Or we might compare the conjugal relations of Chauntecleer and Pertelot with those of the protagonists of the Clerk's and Man of Law's tales. The former's presentation of a romance heroine who is also a housewife, and a hero in whom lust and love, regard and condescension, jostle for pride of place, must surely strike home to most of us. By contrast, considered simply as stories, and without reference to the jaundiced perspective consistently generated by their narrators' commentaries, the latter only occasionally realise the ambiguities in their emblems, as when the Man of Law invests his heroine, at the outset, and briefly, with some of the attributes of a romance heroine. Again, we might compare the singlemindedness with which certain narratives dictate a tragic outcome (Monk's and Physician's tales) and others, in spite of the appearances, as singlemindedly deny such an outcome (the tales of the first section), with the agile switch from tragedy to comedy, even farce, in a single line of the Pardoner's or Nun's Priest's tale:

And lo, sires, thus I preche

(VI 915)

Lo, how Fortune turneth sodeynly
The hope and pryde eek of hir enemy

(VII 3403-4)

Or we could consider the question of the narrator's relation to *auctoritee* and consequent self-presentation as translator or author of his own story: and contrast the singleminded understanding of the question revealed by the Second Nun's tale and *Melibee* with the more ambiguous relation of the narrator to his sources in the Monk's and Physician's tales. And then we see a cock misuse *auctoritee* to get his own way, and hear the Nun's Priest describe the 'greet altercacioun ... of an hundred thousand men'! Or we hear the Pardoner describe his Latin tags as mere colour in his preaching, and listen to a sermon which expertly interweaves learned material and matter of local interest.

Logically, there can be no end to such comparisons. The 'great middle' from which these tales all come, as earlier noted, has randomness written into its very texture: a randomness which invites a proliferation of shapes and readings, and authorises none (cf. p. 7 above). All the same, such comparisons point to the centrality of the Pardoner's and Nun's Priest's tales in any study of *The Canterbury Tales*. Our study of the more ambitious religious narratives, those of the Clerk, Man of Law, Monk and Physician, has regularly included incidental comparison with the whole work of which they are a part. Such comparisons are most fully justified in the case of the Nun's Priest's and Pardoner's tales: and that for several reasons. First, the distinctive structural features of the overall work are duplicated in these individual tales (the Pardoner uses a framing prologue and epilogue, the Nun's Priest a sequence of framed narratives and the key symbol of the talking heads). Second, the narrators' unwillingness to authorise a single reading of their symbols exactly parallels that of the pilgrim-narrator of the whole work. Third, there is the matter of the specifically narrative values, such as pace and timing, embodied in these two stories. Only the Physician has a comparable instinct for such values; the other narrators either subordinate the specifically narrative values of their stories to the expression of religious positions, or (I have in mind the original of the *Melibee* and the Monk's performances) simply tell their stories badly. This feeling for narrative values further links the Pardoner and Nun's Priest with the narrator of *The Canterbury Tales*: it is a vitally important element both of the framing pilgrimage narrative (see above p. 265 for a single example: the most important must surely be the irruption onto the scene of the sweating Canon, VIII 554-86) and of the cast-list of the General Prologue (see also above pp. 20-1). For all these reasons, the narratives of the Pardoner and Nun's Priest provide a touchstone for the other religious stories of the Canterbury pilgrimage.[41] A future study of those tales which the present work has not been able to consider in any detail might do worse than to remind itself, at the outset, of the narratives of the Pardoner and Nun's Priest.

Notes

1. For a useful summary of critical approaches to NPT, and an interesting contribution in its own right, see D. Brewer, 'NPT as story and poem', *Trames*, 2 (1979), 9-24; reprinted in Brewer (1984), pp. 90-106. See also Fyler, ch. 6; Elbow, ch. 4; and P.W. Travis, 'NPT as a grammar-school primer', *SAC, Proceedings no. 1 1984: reconstructing Chaucer*, ed. P. Strohm and T.W. Heffernan (Knoxville, Tenn., 1985), pp.81-91.

2. For comment on 'seint Paul', see Burlin, pp. 235-6; on 'fruyt . . . chaf', Burnley, p. 85 and n. 6; and Kolve, p. 404, n. 46.

3. So, for instance, the 'house of the soul' described in St Bridget, *Liber* V, rev. 9: 'in domo paupere tria sunt, scilicet parietes maculosi, fumus nociuus et fuligo replens . . . hii parietes maculant, quia opera bona annichilant . . . fumus vero amor est mundi' ['in a poor house are three things, dirty walls, noisome smoke and soot filling everything . . . these foul the walls, because they bring good works to nothing . . . the smoke is the love of the world']. We might also compare ps.-Anselm, *Meditatio*, XIV: *PL* 158, 782; and *Bo*, I, pr. 1, 25-7, on the duskiness of Philosophy's gown.

4. See, for example, *Benjamin Minor*, Hodgson, p. 130.

5. On the 'wydwe' as an ironic inversion of the Prioress of Gen Prol, see Ridley, p. 46, n. 153.

6. For comment on this emblem, see David, p. 228; and cf. Bible texts such as Job 1:16, Matt. 24:29, 2 Pet. 3:10 and Apoc. 6:13.

7. Cf. Kean, II, 139 on the functional separation of animal and human worlds, and Brewer (1984) p. 69 (on *BD*) on the effect of 'spacing' on the 'horizontal context' of a narrative (remarks which bear with equal force on NPT).

8. Elbow (pp.99-100) reads these details very perceptively as exemplary of the intellectual's 'disdain for lowly, common, down-to-earth things'; but the primary reading must surely be the moral one which the narrative seems to invite.

9. For notes on *Physiologus*, see Kolve, pp. 434-5; and on the mermaid, Rowland (1971), pp. 42-4.

10. A pattern regularly noted: so Boitani, pp. 15, 257 (and p. 258 for contrast with the linear patterns of fabliau); E.C. Quinn, 'Religion in Chaucer's *CT*', Economou (1975), pp. 68-9; Mehl, p. 133, on the patterns in *Sir Ysumbras*.

11. On dreams, see Spearing (1976); and R.A. Pratt, 'Some Latin sources of NP on dreams', *Spec.*, 52 (1977), 538-70.

12. This comparison is from Fyler, p. 156.

13. A simpler reading of the moment — that it represents a power struggle

between the sexes — is both possible and illuminating of later developments in the story: Elbow pp. 97 ff., David, pp. 226-7.

14. Also noted by Cooper, p. 185. On St Kenelm, see B. Boyd, *Chaucer and the Liturgy* (Philadelphia, 1967), p. 34.

15. Whittock (pp. 234-5) is more cautious about the offered comparison, but he also notes many 'cross-references to other tales', especially in Chauntecleer's exempla.

16. Ridley (p. 34) sees this echo as an ironic put-down of the Prioress by the Nun's Priest (which, since the words are given by him to Chauntecleer, is likely: it is also true of all the echoes in the tale).

17. For comparison of NPT and the text which includes 'Daun Burnell', see J. Mann, 'The *Speculum stultorum* and NPT', *ChR*, 9 (1974-75), 262-82.

18. Huppé (p. 182) finds, to the contrary, that Chauntecleer symbolises the constant availability of the grace of God, enabling man 'by recourse to reason' to escape from the devil. (Such a reading cuts across both the surface of the narrative and its given meaning: Grace is not Fortune, nor can it be narrowly identified with human reason.) For a beautiful reading of this moment as an emblem of the creative imagination, see Elbow, p. 99; also Rowland (1971), pp. 54-6.

19. This shifting perspective is regularly noted, e.g. David, pp. 225 ff. Elbow (p. 102) notes, as one such shift of perspective, a reduction of human language in the poem to the 'Out! Harrow!' of the chase.

20. Fyler (p. 22), linking Chaucer and Ovid, comments on their common recourse to 'an irony that at once points to the frailty and celebrates the fragile nobility of the human condition'.

21. Visionary literature comes readily to mind as an example of surreal art, and I find it significant that a poet who began his career with a series of dream visions should have given the dream so prominent a place in this, one of his latest works.

22. On the relation of words to deeds in NPT, see Justman, *ChR*, 14, 207.

23. Cf. Elbow (p. 106) on the 'physical matter of Chauntecleer seeing her body in the lightening dawn and simply forgetting about the exegetical dispute'.

24. Cf. Ryding (p. 88) on 'varied repetition': it 'appears to function most effectively as a principle of structure when it is supported by a climactic movement'.

25. Cf. E.T. Donaldson, Bethurum; reprinted in *Speaking of Chaucer* (New York, 1970), p. 149: 'rhetoric is ... the inadequate defence that mankind erects against an inscrutable reality.'

26. For instance, the Host's view of Monk and Nun's Priest as 'tredefowels' (11. 1945, 3451).

27. On NPT relativising MkT, see Fyler, p. 157; Kean II, 136 ff.; David, p. 224; Lawler, pp. 96 ff. Cooper (p. 180) links the moment with *Mel* and MkT (and see Burlin, p. 228, for a further link with *Mel*, the debate on dreams in NPT). On NPT and MLT, see Delasanta, *ChR* 5, 300.

28. On other suggested links of NPT with PrT, see Ridley, p. 35.

29. On this point, see also Donaldson, p. 148.

30. Pratt, *Spec.*, 41, 636; the phrase has a parallel in *RR* (*Rom*, 1050 ff; source Robinson, p. 754). Ecclesiastical 'greats' might be more certain of securing an attentive hearing: see Ross 70/10-23, and comment Owst (1926), p. 21, for a vague parallel with the present passage.

31. Elbow (p. 118) applies the phrase to both God and Chauntecleer. See M.W. Bloomfield, 'The Wisdom of NPT', Vasta–Thundy, p. 78 and n. 21.

32. On their oaths, see Elliott, p. 253.

33. A point implied by Cooper, pp. 180-1, and stated by Burlin, p. 228.

34. Huppé (p. 178) reads as an ironic comment on the courtly tales (WBT and FrankT).

35. For a judicious estimate of these lines, which also recognises their character

of facing both ways, see Brewer (1974), pp. 21-2.

36. On this point, see pertinent remarks by W. Nelson, 'The boundaries of fiction in the Renaissance', *ELH*, 36 (1969), 48, and pp. 38 ff. for the literary context of such asseverations.

37. See also David, p. 227-8; Wetherbee, Economou (1975), p. 89 ('NP seems to have made spiritual peace with the likelihood that certainty about large questions of providence and self-determination is unattainable'); Brewer (1984), pp. 76-7, 102 (and p. 123: 'it is as if the story were a serpentine line and the commentary at any part a straight line at a tangent to the curve').

38. On the relation of the *moralitas* to the tale told, cf. Burlin p. 232 ('the "chaf" becomes the "fruyt"'); Kolve, Brewer (1974), p. 315 ('the real morality of NPT seems to me inseparable from its surfaces, from the letter of its fiction').

39. Those whose cooperation he thus invites are most obviously the readers of the tale; so that this directive identifies NP with the pilgrim-narrator of *CT*, whose need to 'telle a tale after a man' leads him to include morally dubious material which refined sensibilities might also need to 'passe over' (I, 3177).

40. By implication, Gaylord (*PMLA*, 82, 235) sees the primary question of NPT, like that of PardT, as one of the artist's moral status ('all the special pride to which artists ... may succumb'). PardT focuses on the moral status of the artist, and thus creates a link with Prol SecNT, even as, on my reading, the emphasis in NPT on truth links it with Prol ParsT and Prol *Mel.* On PardT, cf. Stevens–Falvey, *ChR*, 17, 146: 'through the Pardoner Chaucer gives us ... his most resounding affirmation of the interdependence of art and morality.'

41. On the centrality of NPT and PardT for any reading of *CT*, see, e.g. Cooper, p. 180; David, pp. 223-4 (on NPT); Josipovici, *CQ*, 7, 195; Zacher, p. 94 (PardT); Muscatine, Brewer (1966), pp. 111-12; Boitani, p. 259 (both); Howard, p. 288 (on retrospective structure of *CT* as a whole and tales of group VII). In only one respect do NPT and PardT fail to match *CT*: that is, their careful avoidance of apocalypse for an ending (Howard, p. 171).

ABBREVIATIONS

Astr.	*A Treatise on the Astrolabe*
BD	*The Book of the Duchess*
Bo	Chaucer's *Boece*
Brewer Intro.	D. Brewer, *An introduction to Chaucer* (full reference, bibliography, Brewer)
CA	Gower's *Confessio Amantis* (full reference, ch. VI, n. 18)
ChR	*The Chaucer Review*
CkT	The Cook's tale
ClT	The Clerk's tale
CQ	*Critical Quarterly*
CT	*The Canterbury Tales* (full reference, bibliography, Robinson; citation by group as in Robinson)
CYT	The Canon's Yeoman's tale
De M	*De Miseria Condicionis Humane* of Pope Innocent III (full reference, bibliography, Lewis)
EETS	Early English Text Society
EHR	*English Historical Review*
ELH	*English Literary History*
ES	Extra Series
Form Age	*The Former Age*
FranklT	The Franklin's tale
FrT	The Friar's tale
Gen Prol	The General Prologue to *The Canterbury Tales*
Guarino	Boccaccio's *Concerning Famous Women* (full reference in bibliography *sub* Boccaccio)
HF	*The House of Fame*
JEGP	*Journal of English and Germanic Philology*
KnT	The Knight's tale
LGW	*The Legend of Good Women*
M AE	Medium Ævum
MancT	The Manciple's tale
McWilliam	Boccaccio's *Decameron* (full reference, bibliography, Boccaccio)
M&H	*Medievalia et Humanistica*
Mel	*The Tale of Melibee*
MerchT	The Merchant's tale
MillT	The Miller's tale
MLN	*Modern Language Notes*
MLQ	*Modern Language Quarterly*
MLT	The Man of Law's tale
MP	*Modern Philology*
MS	*Mediaeval Studies*

NM	Neuphilologische Mitteilungen
OA	*Originals and Analogues of Some Canterbury Tales* (full reference, bibliography, Furnivall)
OS	Original Series
PardT	The Pardoner's tale
ParsT	The Parson's tale
PBA	*Proceedings of the British Academy*
PF	*The Parliament of Fowls*
PhysT	The Physician's tale
PL	*Patrologia Latina*
PLMA	*Publications of the Modern Language Association of America*
PQ	*Philological Quarterly*
Prol	Prologue
PrT	The Prioress's tale
REL	*Review of English Literature*
RES	*Review of English Studies*
Rom	*The Romaunt of the Rose*
RR	*Le Roman de la rose* (full reference, bibliography, Lecoy)
Ryan-Ripperger	See bibliography, *The Golden Legend of Jacobus da Voragine*
SA	*Sources and Analogues of Chaucer's Canterbury Tales* (full reference, bibliography, Bryan)
SAC	*Studies in the Age of Chaucer* (full reference, bibliography, Heffernan)
SecNT	The Second Nun's tale
ShipT	The Shipman's tale
SP	*Studies in Philology*
Spec.	*Speculum*
SqT	The Squire's tale
SumT	The Summoner's tale
Thop	*The Tale of Sir Thopas*
Tr	*Troilus and Criseyde*
Trad	*Traditio*
WBT	The Wife of Bath's tale

BIBLIOGRAPHY

The Bibliography exists only to help the reader identify abbreviated references to works cited more than once in the footnotes; it should be consulted in conjunction with the list of abbreviations which precedes. It does not itemise the contents of anthologies; nor does it list works cited only once in the footnotes

Allen, J.B. *The Friar as Critic: Literary Attitudes in The Later Middle Ages* (Nashville, Tenn., 1971).
—— and Moritz, T.A. *A Distinction of Stories: the medieval unity of Chaucer's fair chain of narratives for Canterbury* (Columbus, Ohio, 1981).
Atwood, E.B. and Hill, A.A. (eds), *Studies in Language, Literature and Culture of the Middle Ages and Later* (Austin, Texas, 1969).
Avril, F. (ed.) *Manuscript Painting at the Court of France, the Fourteenth Century* (London, 1978).
Baldwin, R.F. *The Unity of The Canterbury Tales*. Anglistica 5 (Copenhagen, 1955).
Bartholomew, B. *Fortuna and Natura: a reading of three Chaucer narratives* (The Hague, 1966).
Beichner, P.E. 'The allegorical interpretation of medieval literature', *PMLA*, 82 (1967), 33-8.
—— (ed.) *Aurora Petri Rigae Biblia versificata*, 2 vols, University of Notre Dame Publications in Medieval Studies 19 (Notre Dame, Ind., 1965)
Benson, C.D. '"Their telling difference": Chaucer the pilgrim and his two contrasting tales', *ChR*, 18 (1983-84), 61-76.
Bethurum, D. (ed.) *Critical Approaches to Medieval Literature* (New York, 1960).
Blake, N.F. (ed.) *The Canterbury Tales by Geoffrey Chaucer, edited from the Hengwrt MS* (London, 1980).
Block, K.S. (ed.) *Ludus Coventriae: or the plaie called Corpus Christi* EETS ES 120 (London, 1922).
Bloomfield, M.W. 'Chaucer's sense of history'. *JEGP*, 51 (1952), 301-13.
—— 'Authenticating realism and the realism of Chaucer', *Thought*, 39 (1964), 335-58.
Boccaccio, Giovanni *De casibus virorum illustrium* (Augsburg, 1544).
—— *Concerning Famous Women*, trans. G.A. Guarino (New Brunswick, N.J., 1963).
—— *Decameron*, trans. G.W. McWilliam (Harmondsworth, 1972).
Boitani, P. 'The Monk's tale: Dante and Boccaccio', *MAE*, 45 (1976), 50-69.
—— *English Medieval Narrative in the Thirteenth and Fourteenth Centuries*, trans. J.K. Hall (Cambridge, 1982).
Bornstein, D. 'French influence on fifteenth-century English prose as exemplified by the translation of Christine de Pisan's *Livre du corps de policie*', *MS*, 39 (1977), 369-86.
Brandeis, A. (ed.), *Jacob's Well*, EETS OS 115 (London, 1900).
Brennan, J.P. 'Reflections on a gloss to the Prioress's tale from Jerome's Adversus

Jovinianum', *SP*, 70 (1973), 243-51.

Brewer, D.J. *Chaucer: the poet as storyteller* (London, 1984).

—— *An Introduction to Chaucer* (London, 1984).

—— (ed.) *Chaucer and Chaucerians: critical studies in Middle English literature* (London, 1966)

—— (ed.) *Writers and their Background: Geoffrey Chaucer* (London, 1974).

—— (ed.) *Chaucer: the critical heritage*, 2 vols (London, 1978).

Bridget, St, of Sweden *Revelationes Sanctae Birgittae* (Lübeck, 1492).

Brown, C. *A Study of the Miracle of Our Lady*, Chaucer Society, 2nd Series, 45 (London, 1910).

—— 'The Man of Law's headlink and the prologue of *The Canterbury Tales*', *SP*, 34 (1937), 8-35.

Bryan, W.F. and Dempster, G. (eds), *Sources and Analogues of Chaucer's Canterbury Tales* (Chicago, 1941).

Burlin, R.B. *Chaucerian Fiction* (Princeton, N.J., 1977).

Burnley, J.D. *Chaucer's Language and the Philosophers' Tradition* (Cambridge, 1979).

Carruthers, M.J. 'The lady, the swineherd, and Chaucer's Clerk' *ChR*, 17 (1982-83), 221-34.

Chaucer, Geoffrey *see* Blake, N.F., Manly, J.M. and Robinson, F.N.

Clogan, P.M. 'The figural style and meaning of the Second Nun's prologue and tale', *M&H*, NS 3 (1972), 213-40.

—— 'The narrative style of the Man of Law's Tale', *M&H*, NS 8 (1977), 217-33.

Coleman, J. *English Literature in History 1350-1400: medieval readers and writers* (London, 1981).

Cooper, H. *The Structure of The Canterbury Tales* (London, 1983).

Crosby, R. 'Chaucer and the custom of oral delivery', *Spec.*, 13 (1938), 413-32.

Daiches, D. and Thorlby, A. (eds.), *Literature and Western Civilization: the medieval world* (London, 1973).

David, A. *The Strumpet Muse: art and morals in Chaucer's poetry* (Bloomington, Ind., 1976).

Davis, N. 'Styles in English prose of the late Middle and early modern period', *Les congrès et colloques de l'Université de Liège*, 21, Langue et Littérature, Actes du VIIIe congrès (Liège, 1961), 165-81.

—— and Wrenn, C.L. (eds) *English and Medieval Studies Presented to J.R.R. Tolkien* (London, 1962).

Delasanta, R. 'And of great reverence: Chaucer's Man of Law', *ChR*, 5 (1970-71), 288-310.

Donaldson, E.T. *Speaking of Chaucer* (New York, 1970).

Economou, G.D. *The Goddess Natura in Medieval Literature* (Cambridge, Mass., 1972).

—— (ed.) *Geoffrey Chaucer: a collection of original articles* (New York, 1975).

Elbow, P. *Oppositions in Chaucer* (Middletown, Conn., 1975).

Eliason, N.E. *The Language of Chaucer's Poetry.* Anglistica 17 (Copenhagen, 1972).

Elliott, R.W.V. *Chaucer's English* (London, 1974).

Ellis, R. 'Revelation and the life of faith: the vision of Julian of Norwich', *Christian*, 6 (1980), 61-71.

Faulkner, D.R. (ed.) *Twentieth-century Interpretations of The Pardoner's Tale* (Englewood Cliffs, N.J., 1973).

Friedman, A.B. 'The Prioress's Tale and Chaucer's antisemitism', *ChR*, 9 (1974-75), 118-29.

Furnivall, F.J. (ed.) *Robert of Brunne's Handlyng Synne*, EETS OS 119 (London, 1901).

—— Brock, E. and Clouston, W.A. (eds), *Originals and Analogues of some of*

Chaucer's Canterbury Tales, Chaucer Society 2nd Series, 1, 3 (London, 1872, 1876).

Fyler, J.M. *Chaucer and Ovid* (New Haven and London, 1979).

Gaylord, A.T. 'Sentence and solaas in fragment VII of *The Canterbury Tales*: Harry Bailly as horseback editor', *PMLA*, 82 (1967), 226-35.

Giffin, M. *Studies on Chaucer and his Audience* (Quebec, 1956).

Glasscoe, M. (ed.) *The Medieval Mystical Tradition in England.* Papers read at Dartington Hall, July 1982. (Exeter, 1982).

The Golden Legend of Jacobus da Voragine, trans. and adapted G. Ryan and H. Ripperger (New York, 1941; reprinted 1969).

Grässe, Th. (ed.) *Legenda Aurea* (Leipzig, 1850).

Green, R.F. *Poets and Princepleasers: literature and the English court in the late Middle Ages* (Toronto, 1980).

Halverson, T., 'Chaucer's Pardoner and the progress of criticism', *ChR*, 4 (1969-70), 184-202.

Hanson, T.B. 'Chaucer's Physician as storyteller and moralizer', *ChR* 7 (1972-73), 132-9.

Hatcher, E.R. 'Life without death: the old man in Chaucer's Pardoner's tale', *ChR*, 9 (1974-75), 246-52.

Heffernan, T.J. (ed.) *Studies in the age of Chaucer*, 6, 7, New Chaucer Society (Knoxville, Tenn., 1984-5).

Hirn, Y. *The Sacred Shrine* (London, 1912).

Hodgson, P. (ed.) *The Cloud of Unknowing and Related Treatises*, Analecta Cartusiana 3 (Salzburg, 1982).

Holmstedt, G. (ed.) *Speculum Christiani*, EETS OS 182 (London, 1933).

Howard, D.R. *The Idea of The Canterbury Tales* (Berkeley, Los Angeles and London, 1976).

Hudson, A. and Spencer, H.L. 'Old author, new work: the sermons of MS Longleat 4', *MAE*, 53 (1984), 220-38.

Huppé, B.F. *A Reading of The Canterbury Tales* (New York, 1964, revised 1967).

Jordan, R.M. *Chaucer and the Shape of Creation: the aesthetic possibilities of inorganic structure* (Cambridge, Mass., 1967).

Josipovici, G. 'Fiction and game in *The Canterbury Tales*', *CQ*, 7 (1965), 185-97.

Justman, S. 'Literal and symbolic in *The Canterbury Tales*', *ChR*, 14 (1979-80), 199-214.

Kean, P.M. *Chaucer and the Making of English poetry*, 2 vols (London, 1972).

Kolve, V.A. *Chaucer and the Imagery of Narrative* (London, 1984).

Lancashire, A. 'Chaucer and the sacrifice of Isaac', *ChR*, 9 (1974-75), 321-6.

Lawler, T. *The One and the Many in The Canterbury Tales.* (Hamden, Conn., 1980).

Lecoy, F. (ed.) *Le roman de la rose*, Les classiques français du moyen âge, 92, 95, 98 (Paris, 1966-70).

Leicester, H.M. Jr, 'The art of impersonation: a general prologue to *The Canterbury Tales*', *PMLA*, 95 (1980), 213-24.

Leitch, L.M. 'Sentence and solaas: the function of the Hosts in *The Canterbury Tales*', *ChR*, 17 (1982-83), 5-20.

Lewis. R.E. (ed. and trans.) *Pope Innocent III De Miseria Condicionis Humane*, Chaucer Library (Athens, Georgia, 1978).

Manly, J.M. and Rickert, E. (eds), *The Text of The Canterbury Tales*, 7 vols (Chicago, 1940).

Mann, J. *Chaucer and Medieval Estates Satire* (Cambridge, 1973).

Meech, S.B. and Allen, H.E. (eds) *The Book of Margery Kempe*, EETS OS 212 (London, 1940).

Mehl, D. *The Middle English Romances of the Thirteenth and Fourteenth Centuries* (London, 1968).

Metlitzki, D. *The Matter of Araby in Medieval England* (New Haven and London, 1977).

Middleton, A. 'The Physician's tale and love's martyrs: "ensamples moo than ten"', *ChR*, 8 (1973-74), 9-32.

Miller, R.P. (ed.), *Chaucer: Sources and Backgrounds* (New York, 1977).

Minnis, A.J. 'Late medieval discussions of compilatio and the role of the compilator', *Beiträge zur Geschichte der deutschen Sprache und Literatur*, 101 (1979), 385-421.

—— 'The influence of academic prologues on the prologues and literary attitudes of late medieval English writers', *MS*, 43 (1981), 342-83.

—— *Chaucer and Pagan Antiquity* (Cambridge, 1982).

—— *Medieval Theory of Authorship: scholastic literary attitudes in the later Middle Ages* (London, 1984).

Murphy, J.J. (ed.) *Medieval Eloquence* (Berkeley, Los Angeles and London, 1978).

Norton-Smith, J. *Geoffrey Chaucer* (London, 1974).

Oesterley, H. (ed.), *Gesta Romanorum* (Berlin, 1872).

Owen, C.A., Jr 'The tale of Melibee', *ChR*, 7 (1972-73), 267-80.

—— ' "A certein nombre of conclusiouns": the nature and nurture of children in Chaucer', *ChR*, 16 (1981-82), 60-75.

Owst, G.R. *Preaching in Medieval England* (Cambridge, 1926).

—— *Literature and Pulpit in Medieval England* (Cambridge, 1933; rev. Oxford 1961).

Patterson, L.W. 'The Parson's tale and the quitting of *The Canterbury Tales*', *Trad.*, 34 (1978), 331-80.

Paull, M.R. 'The influence of the saint's legend genre in the Man of Law's tale', *ChR*, 5 (1970-71), 179-94.

Payne, R.O. *The Key of Remembrance: a Study of Chaucer's Poetics* (New Haven and London, 1963).

Pearsall, D.A., 'Chaucer's Pardoner: the death of a salesman', *ChR*, 17 (1982-83), 358-65.

—— and Waldron, R.A. (eds), *Medieval Literature and Civilization: essays in memory of G.N. Garmonsway* (London, 1969).

Pratt, R.A. 'Chaucer and the hand that fed him', *Spec.*, 41 (1966), 619-42.

Ramsey, L.C. ' "The sentence of it sooth is": Chaucer's Physician's tale', *ChR*, 6 (1971-72), 185-97.

Rickert, E. (ed.), *Emaré*, EETS ES 99 (London, 1906).

Ridley, F.H. *The Prioress and the Critics*, University of California English Studies 30 (Berkeley and Los Angeles, 1965).

Robbins, R.H. (ed.) *Chaucer at Albany*, Middle English Texts and Contexts 2 (New York, 1975).

Robinson, F.N. (ed.) *The Works of Geoffrey Chaucer*, 2nd ed (London, 1957).

Rose, D.M. (ed.) *New Perspectives in Chaucer Criticism* (Norman, Oklahoma, 1981).

Ross, W.O. (ed.) *Middle English Sermons edited from the BM MS Royal 18 B xxiii*, EETS OS 209 (London, 1940).

Rowland, B. *Blind Beasts: Chaucer's animal world* (Kent State, 1971).

—— (ed.) *Chaucer and Middle English Studies in Honour of Rossell Hope Robbins* (London, 1974).

Ryding, W.W. *Structure in Medieval Narrative* (The Hague and Paris, 1971).

Salter, E. *The Knight's Tale and the Clerk's Tale* (London, 1962).

—— *Nicholas Love's 'Myrrour of the blessed lyf of Jesu Christ'*, Analecta Cartusiana 10 (Salzburg, 1974).

Schiller, G. *Iconography of Christian Art*, trans. J. Seligman, 2 vols (London, 1971-72).

Schoeck, R.J. and Taylor, J. (eds) *Chaucer Criticism I. The Canterbury Tales* (Notre Dame, Ind., and London, 1960).

Severs, J.B. *The Literary Relationships of Chaucer's Clerkes Tale,* Yale Studies in English 96 (Yale, 1942; reprinted Hamden, Conn., 1972).

Seymour, M.C. (ed.) *Mandeville's Travels* (Oxford, 1967).

Spearing, A.C. *Criticism and Medieval Poetry,* 2nd edn (London, 1972).

—— *Medieval Dream Poetry* (Cambridge, 1976).

Spurgeon, C. (ed.) *500 Years of Chaucer Criticism and Allusion, 1357-1900,* 2nd edn, 3 vols (London, 1925).

Stevens, M. and Falvey, K. 'Substance, accident and transformations: a reading of the Pardoner's tale', *ChR,* 17 (1982-83), 142-58.

Strohm, P., 'The allegory of the tale of Melibee', *ChR,* 2 (1967-68), 32-42.

—— 'Some generic distinctions in *The Canterbury Tales*', *MP,* 68 (1970-71), 321-8.

Utley, F.L. 'Five genres of the Clerk's tale', *ChR,* 6 (1971-72), 198-228.

Vasta, E. and Thundy, Z.P. (eds) *Chaucerian Problems and Perspectives: essays presented to Paul E. Beichner* (Notre Dame, Ind. 1979).

Wagenknecht, E. (ed.), *Chaucer: modern essays in criticism* (New York, 1959).

Wenzel, S. 'Chaucer and the language of contemporary preaching', *SP,* 73 (1976), 138-61.

Whittock, T. *A Reading of The Canterbury Tales* (Cambridge, 1968).

Wood, C. *Chaucer and the Country of the Stars* (Princeton, N.J., 1970).

Woolf, R. *The English Religious Lyric in the Middle Ages* (Oxford, 1968).

Yunck, J.A. 'Religious elements in Chaucer's Man of Law's tale', *ELH,* 27 (1960), 249-61.

Zacher, C.K. *Curiosity and Pilgrimage: the literature of discovery in fourteenth-century England* (Baltimore and London, 1976).

INDEX

Principal entries are given in **bold** type.